Bareither / Beals / Cowan / Dobryden /
Fest / Müller-Richter / Nemec (Hrsg.)

—

Hans Richters *Rhythmus 21*

Hans Richters *Rhythmus 21*

Schlüsselfilm der Moderne

Herausgegeben vom
Forschungsnetzwerk BTWH

Christoph Bareither
Kurt Beals
Michael Cowan
Paul Dobryden
Karin Fest
Klaus Müller-Richter
Birgit Nemec

Königshausen & Neumann

Bibliografische Information der Deutschen Nationalbibliothek

Die Deutsche Nationalbibliothek verzeichnet diese Publikation in der Deutschen Nationalbibliografie; detaillierte bibliografische Daten sind im Internet über http://dnb.d-nb.de abrufbar.

Gedruckt auf säurefreiem, alterungsbeständigem Papier
Umschlag: skh-softics / coverart
Bindung: Zinn – Die Buchbinder GmbH, Kleinlüder

Printed in Germany
ISBN 978-3-8260-4861-6
www.koenigshausen-neumann.de
www.buchhandel.de
www.buchkatalog.de

Inhaltsverzeichnis

Foreword

The present volume is the result of an intense and ongoing collaboration among members of the BTWH (Berkeley-Tübingen-Wien-Harvard) Working Group on the Emergence of German Modernity. Formed in 1998, BTWH is an international research network bringing together scholars of film, media, literature, philosophy, and history for the in-depth research of specific cultural objects. For sixteen years, the group has pursued a mode of scholarship that is collaborative and interdisciplinary at its core.

The idea for this book developed over the course of several years, at a series of workshops in which Richter's seminal journal *G. Zeitschrift für elementare Gestaltung* served as a central 'hub' for multifarious investigations into the links between the avant-garde and everyday life in the early 20th century. The rich network of themes elaborated in *G*—from architecture to automobiles, from fashion to poetry—offers an intriguing pendant to Richter's early filmic practice, and particularly to the apparently 'abstract' character of his classic film *Rhythmus 21*. Consequently, in the spirit of BTWH's historically informed brand of cultural semiotics, the present volume considers this film in a different light, seeing it not as an 'absolute' film, folded in on itself and devoid of content, but rather as a text, like *G*, located at the intersection of numerous cultural discourses. To that end, each article focuses on one theme and probes its relevance to Richter's film, thus revealing a wealth of often surprising perspectives from which the film can be considered.

Fourteen BTWH members are represented in this volume, along with three outside authors who have graciously contributed. It proudly carries the longest list of editors of any BTWH volume thus far, with a total of seven, all of whom have participated actively in the conception and execution of this project. BTWH could not have survived and thrived for so long without the support of the many sponsors of our workshops. We would particularly like to acknowledge the sponsors of our 2010 workshop in Berkeley: the Department of German, the Townsend Center for the Humanities, the Institute for European Studies, the Program in Film Studies, and the Graduate Film Working Group; as well as the sponsors of our 2011 workshop in Tübingen: the Vereinigung der Freunde der Universität Tübingen, and the Forum Scientiarum. We also wish to express our appreciation to the Internationales Forschungszentrum Kulturwissenschaften in Vienna for their support over the years. Finally, we would like to thank all BTWH members, even those who did not contribute directly to the present volume, for their feedback and comments in the course of our discussions. We hope that this book will not only offer a variety of illuminating new angles for considering Richter's *Rhythmus 21*, but also provide a model for more collaborative projects to come.

Einleitung

Die Herausgeber

> L'interdisciplinaire, dont on parle beaucoup, ne consiste pas à confronter des disciplines déjà constituées (dont, en fait, aucune, ne consent à s'abandonner). Pour faire de l'interdisciplinaire, il ne suffit pas de prendre un sujet (un thème) et de convoquer deux ou trois sciences. L'interdisciplinaire consiste à créer un objet nouveau, qui n'appartient à personne.[1]
> —Roland Barthes

Der Titel des vorliegenden Bandes annonciert die kulturwissenschaftliche Untersuchung eines Objekts, für das bereits die Fundamentaldaten festzustellen einige Detektivarbeit erfordert. Und dies, obwohl es von Filmhistorikern als „eines der wichtigsten Werke des Avantgardefilms und der Filmgeschichte überhaupt"[2] bezeichnet und als „der klassische Avantgardefilm schlechthin"[3] apostrophiert wurde. Was genau wann, wo, von wem, unter welchem Titel und in welcher Länge uraufgeführt wurde, nicht zuletzt die Frage, ab wann ein bestimmtes Korpus von (belichtetem) Material tatsächlich ein Film genannt werden kann – niemand weiß es ganz sicher: 1921 oder 1923 oder 1925; uraufgeführt in Paris im Théâtre Michel oder doch anderswo und in anderem Veranstaltungsrahmen, unter dem von uns übernommenen Titel *Rhythmus 21* oder doch unter *Film ist Rhythmus* oder *Filmspiel* oder *Ohne Haupttitel,* von van Doesburg vorgeführt oder während einer großen Dadashow gezeigt, in der Version von nur 1 ½ Minuten Länge oder doch in jener mit zahlreichen ‚Hinzufügungen', die sich mit dem Original dann auf knapp drei Minuten summieren?[4] Roland Barthes' Diktum zur Interdisziplinarität, das dieser Einleitung als Motto voransteht und dem sich dieser Band emphatisch verpflichtet fühlt, wird mit Blick auf *Rhythmus 21* also ganz konkret und auf sehr kuriose Weise

---

1 Roland Barthes: Jeunes chercheurs. In: Ders.: Essais critiques 4. Le bruissement de la langue. Seuil 1984, S. 100.

2 Vgl. Hans Scheugl / Ernst Schmidt jr.: Eine Subgeschichte des Films. Lexikon des Avantgarde-, Experimental- und Undergroundfilms. 2 Bde. Frankfurt a.M. 1974, S. 742-743.

3 O.A.: Hans Richter — Kurzbiographie. In: Patricia Rochard (Hg.): Der Traum von einer neuen Welt. Berlin 1910-1933, Ausstellungskatalog. Mainz 1989, S. 232.

4 Richters Film *Rhythmus 21* ist derzeit in verschiedenen Versionen (u.a. online) erhältlich. Da die verschiedenen Versionen unterschiedliche Vorspannlängen aufweisen, richten sich die in diesem Band angegeben Minuten- und Sekundenangaben nach dem ersten (auf den Vorspann folgenden) Bild.

greifbar, noch bevor die methodologischen Chancen und Herausforderungen des Interdisziplinären überhaupt ins Kalkül gezogen und bedacht werden:

> Die vieldiskutierte Interdisziplinarität basiert nicht so sehr auf einer Konfrontation bereits etablierter Disziplinen (die ihren erprobten Fragehorizont ohnehin niemals überschreiten). Um wirklich interdisziplinär zu arbeiten, genügt es auch nicht, einen Gegenstand oder Thema zu wählen und hierzu zwei oder drei Wissenschaften um ihre Expertise zu bitten. Interdisziplinarität besteht in der Schaffung eines neuen Gegenstandes, der zu keiner Disziplin gehört.[5]

Rhythmus 21 ist – wie jeder Beitrag auf seine Weise dokumentiert – ein in vielerlei Hinsicht kreiertes Objekt unserer Neugier. Was sich aber im Rahmen einer einfachen Titelmeditation zu *Rhythmus 21* vorab sofort festhalten lässt: Die Verstümmelung des tatsächlichen oder fingierten Uraufführungsdatums des Films 1921 auf ‚21' verweist einerseits auf den konstitutiven Hang Hans Richters zur transhistorischen Verallgemeinerung oder Elementarisierung, die sich von vorneherein jeder historischen Vereinnahmung durch eine bestimmte Kunstströmung oder einer Zuordnung zu einer flüchtigen Mode zu verweigern sucht; sie verweist überdies auf den Experimentcharakter des Films, und zwar dadurch, dass die schlichte zweistellige Zahl auch die Idee der Variantennummerierung oder Versuchsfolge konnotieren könnte. Ähnliches trifft auf den zweiten Zeichenkomplex des Titels, das Wort ‚Rhythmus' zu: Kein Thema wird markiert, keine Narration als hermeneutisches Vorurteil gesetzt, Gegenständlichkeit von vorneherein absolviert und abgewiesen. Es zählt vom Titel her allein das Verfahren oder die Struktur oder das Gestaltungsprinzip, abstrakt und sachlich.

Wenn nun die Experimentalfilmemacher der 1920er Jahre nach einem Begriff suchten, um eine rein formalistische Filmkunst zu begründen und gegen andere Phänomene pointiert abzugrenzen, so hätten sie wohl keinen schlechteren finden können als ‚Rhythmus'. Zwar dienten die in ihren Filmen bevorzugten rhythmischen Organisationsprinzipien dazu, eine gewisse Eigenständigkeit für die Filmkunst in Anspruch zu nehmen, indem sie diese von den erzählerischen Künsten – vor allem Drama und Prosa – unterschieden, um sie den weniger auf logischen ‚Inhalt' angewiesenen Kunstformen der Musik [vgl. „Notation"], der Poesie [vgl. „Primitivis-

5 Roland Barthes: Jeunes chercheurs. In: Ders.: Essais critiques 4. Le bruissement de la langue. Seuil 1984, S. 100.

mus"] oder des Tanzes [vgl. „Bewegungskunst"] anzunähern.[6] Andererseits war ‚Rhythmus' in der europäischen Moderne eben alles andere als ein auf den Bereich der Kunst beschränkter Begriff. Er stand darüber hinaus im Zentrum eines dicht verwobenen Netzes von Recherchen und Diskursen über Körper, Wahrnehmung, Technik.[7] So spielte etwa im späten 19. Jahrhundert der Rhythmus eine Schlüsselrolle in den neueren biologischen und psychologischen Forschungen, wurde als das wesentliche Merkmal von Natur und Gemeinschaft verstanden, tauchte als geheimnisvolle Kraft im Okkultismus [vgl. „Spiritualität"] und Parawissenschaft [vgl. „Wirbel"] auf, galt aber auch als regulierendes Prinzip der effizienten Arbeit und wurde sogar bei der Architektur [vgl. „Architektur"] und der Raumgestaltung [vgl. „Bildräume"] beachtet. Zwar wurden dabei verschiedene, sich teilweise gegenseitig ausschließende Begriffe des Rhythmus entworfen. All diesen Bestrebungen gemeinsam aber war die Idee, dass der Rhythmus etwas Grundlegendes – man möchte sagen etwas *Elementares* – darstellte, durch dessen Handhabung das Sozial- und Kulturleben reformiert, Körper und Seele neu trainiert [vgl. „Seelentraining"], die Technik perfektioniert, der Verkehr [vgl. „Verkehr"] reguliert und sogar ein neuer Mensch geschaffen werden könnte.

Es ist vor allem dieser Pathos der Elementarisierung, der von der filmischen Avantgarde bei ihrer Begeisterung für den Rhythmus übernommen wurde – beispielsweise als Germaine Dulac ein neues, auf visuellem Rhythmus basierendes „cinéma pur" forderte: „Das Kino von allen Elementen befreien, die ihm nicht eigen sind, seine wahre Essenz in der Kenntnis der Bewegung und der visuellen Rhythmen suchen, solcher Art ist die neue

---

6 Vgl. Laurent Guido: L'Age du rythme: Cinéma, musicalité et culture du corps dans les théories françaises des années 1910-1930. Lausanne 2007, S. 123-175. Man könnte mit Lev Manovich meinen, diese filmische ‚Spezifizität' sei eigentlich durch eine Rückkehr zur ursprünglichen, vor dem Erzählkino dominanten Form der Schleife identifiziert. Vgl. Lev Manovich: The Language of New Media. Cambridge 2001, S. xxii, 252-253. Interessant aber ist die Tatsache, dass gerade die obengenannten Kunstformen der Musik, des Tanzes und der Poesie auch zu Gegenständen von intensiven Rhythmusforschungen um 1900 (etwa bei Arno Holz, Emil Jaques-Dalcroze) wurden.

7 Seit rund zehn Jahren gibt es eine wachsende Anzahl von interdisziplinären und kulturwissenschaftlichen Recherchen zum Thema. Siehe z.B. Christa Brüstle u.a. (Hg.): Aus dem Takt. Rhythmus in Kunst, Kultur und Natur. Bielefeld 2005; Barbara Naumann (Hg.): Rhythmus. Spuren eines Wechselspiels in Künsten und Wissenschaften. Würzburg 2005; Guido: L'Age du rythme; Michael Cowan: Technology's Pulse. Essays on Rhythm in German Modernism. London 2012. Eine umfangreiche Sammlung von Quellen und Information zur Rhythmus-Forschung findet man auf der von Pascal Michon geführten Internet-Platform *Rhuthmos. Plateforme internationale et transdisciplinaire de recherche sur les rythmes dans les sciences, les philosophies et les arts*. http://rhuthmos.eu/ (8.3.2012).

Ästhetik, die im Lichte eines kommenden Morgens erscheint."[8] Solche Bestrebungen deuten zwar gewiss auf den Wunsch hin, das Medium Film vom Literarischen zu befreien, um eine Art ‚pure' oder ‚absolute' Bewegungskunst daraus zu machen. Gleichzeitig bezog die Avantgarde ihre Ideen über Rhythmus aus anderen Quellen und Wissensgebieten, z.B. als Dulac im selben Aufsatz – an die Rhythmusforschungen der Botanik anknüpfend – den Rhythmus des im Zeitraffer verfilmten Pflanzenwuchses pries[9] oder als Sergei Eisenstein sich auf die deutschen Körperkulturtheoretiker stützte, um den authentischen (dialektischen) Montage-Rhythmus von der einfachen Metrik zu unterscheiden.[10] Das alles verwundert nicht, bedenkt man das generelle Streben der Avantgarde, die Kunst und das künstlerische Experiment wieder für das ‚Leben' relevant zu machen. Denn der Rhythmus galt als die elementare Form von Leben und lebendiger Bewegung überhaupt [vgl. „Körper"]. Und gerade in diesem Elementarhaften diente der Rhythmus solchen Überführungen von Kunst und Leben, auch wenn er dem Film gleichzeitig zu seiner eigenen künstlerischen Essenz verhelfen sollte.

Hans Richters *Rhythmus 21* verkörpert diese Ambivalenz. Als einer der ersten ‚abstrakten' Filme überhaupt und auch als Bestandteil der berühmten Filmmatinee „Der absolute Film" [vgl. „Entstehungsgeschichte"] sollte dieses kleine Animationsexperiment aufzeigen, wozu die Filmkunst fähig ist, wenn sie auf ihre elementaren Bestandteile reduziert wird [vgl. „Elementares Kino"]. Traditionelle filmhistorische Darstellungen tendierten dazu, eben solche formalen Aspekte hervorzuheben, indem sie Richters frühe Filmarbeit vor allem als eine Erweiterung der abstrakten Malerei auf die zeitliche Ebene betrachteten und Richters Biographie [vgl. „Biographie"] im Kontext einer als abgeschlossene Gruppe verstandenen Avantgarde verorteten.[11] Dabei schenkte man seiner Tätigkeit etwa als Werbefilmgestalter [vgl. „Werbe-/Industriefilm"] oder seinem Interesse an der

---

8 Eigene Übersetzung. Im Original: „Dépouiller le cinéma de tous les éléments qui lui sont impersonnels, rechercher sa véritable essence dans la connaissance du mouvement et de rythmes visuels, telle est la nouvelle esthétique qui apparaît dans la lumière d'une aube qui vient." Germaine Dulac: Les esthétiques, les entraves, la cinégraphie intégrale (1927). In: Ders.: Écrits sur le cinéma (1919-1937), hg. von Prosper Hillairet. Paris 1994, S. 98-105, hier: S. 104.

9 Ebd. Zur Rhythmusforschung in der Botanik und ihrer Beziehung zum Wissenschafts- und Experimentalfilm der 20er Jahre vgl. Janelle Blankenship: „Film-Symphonie vom Leben und Sterben der Blumen": Plant Rhythm and Time-Lapse Vision in Das Blumenwunder. In: Intermédialités 16 (Herbst 2010), S. 83-103.

10 Sergei Eisenstein: A Dialectical Approach to Film Form. In: Ders.: Film Form. Essays in Film Theory, hg. Jay Leyda. San Diego 1977, S. 45-64, hier: S. 49.

11 Vgl. z.B. Birgit Hein: Film im Underground. Frankfurt a.M. 1971, S. 24-26; Standish Lawder: The Cubist Cinema. New York 1975, S. 35-64; Jean Mitry: Le cinéma expérimental, histoire et perspectives. Paris 1974, S. 63-98.

Psychologie [vgl. „Einfühlung"] weniger Beachtung. Spätere Forscher haben die Verbindungen Richters zur Politik,[12] sowie seinen Platz innerhalb einer umfangreicheren, auch die Populärkultur umfassenden Geschichte der Animation[13] herausgearbeitet. Gegenwärtig versuchen Filmhistoriker, Richter und die Avantgarde neu zu kontextualisieren, indem sie beispielsweise die Verbindungen Richters zur Filmindustrie hervorheben (bereits in seinen ersten Filmversuchen wurde Richter von der UFA unterstützt[14]), oder die Spuren einer ideengeschichtlichen Tradition von okkultistischen Wissenschaften in seinen Werken aufzeigen.[15]

Voraussetzung des vorliegenden Bandes ist, dass ein Film wie *Rhythmus 21* gerade aufgrund seiner Gegenstandslosigkeit zu multiplen diskursiven Anknüpfungen, historischen Einordnungen und kulturwissenschaftlichen Querverbindungen herausfordert. Den Beiträgen dieses Sammelbandes geht es vor allem darum, das ungeheure Potential, das in diesem kleinen Bildstreifen steckt, nachdrücklich zu betonen, indem man seine Offenheit für kunst-, wissenschafts- und kulturgeschichtliche Lesarten, für produktive intermediale und interdiskursive Interpretationsansätze wahrnimmt. Gewiss kann keine dieser Lesarten den Film erschöpfen, und darin – wie Roland Barthes einmal für die Texte von Kafka hervorgehoben hat – liegt auch die Stärke von *Rhythmus 21*. Als Anstoß des modernen Experimentalfilms lädt dieser Film zu einer Erforschung der dichten kulturellen, philosophischen und wissenschaftlichen Netze ein, in die er selbst eingewoben ist – ohne je darin ganz aufzugehen.

Jede kulturwissenschaftliche Vorgehensweise sieht sich dabei der Gefahr und dem Vorwurf ausgesetzt, die Netze zu weit zu werfen, im Gestus der Dehierarchisierung Querverbindungen zu markieren, die letzten Endes willkürlich oder nebensächlich sind, dies umso mehr, je forcierter versucht wird, Überraschungen und Verstörungen der eingespielten akademischen Frageformen zu erzeugen. Auch bleibt zunächst bei dieser Ethik der Hinterfragung ein theoretisches Problem der Kulturwissenschaften ungelöst, nämlich zu sagen, was es überhaupt bedeutet, dass Texte mit anderen Texten in irgend einer Hinsicht(nahme) gleich oder zumindest ähnlich sind; was daraus zu folgern ist, dass Analogien, Ähnlichkeiten und Kohärenzen über Text- und Diskursgrenzen hinaus feststellbar sind.

Um diesem Problem zu begegnen oder eine Antwort auf diese implizite methodologische Herausforderung gleichsam *in actu* anzudeuten, ver-

---

12 Vgl. Stephen C. Foster (Hg.): Hans Richter. Activism, Modernism and the Avant-Garde. Cambridge, MA 1998.

13 Vgl. Esther Leslie: Hollywood Flatlands. Animation, Critical Theory and the Avant-Garde. London 2004, S. 33-79.

14 Vgl. Malte Hagener: Moving Forward, Looking Back. The European Avant-Garde and the Invention of Film Culture 1919-1939. Amsterdam 2007, S. 46.

15 Vgl. R. Bruce Elder: Harmony and Dissent. Waterloo, ON 2008.

sucht jeder Beitrag nicht nur Verbindungsevidenzen zu erzeugen und diese sodann diskursgeschichtlich zu plausibilisieren, sondern die Evidenz dadurch zu evaluieren, dass sie interpretatorisch an *Rhythmus 21* herangeführt und geprüft wird. Der in Aussicht gestellte interpretatorische Mehrwert für *Rhythmus 21* war das Auswahlkriterium der Herausgeber, welcher der vielen Spuren ins kulturelle Feld im Rahmen dieses Bandes nachzugehen war.

Hinter diesem Sammelband steht demnach die Überzeugung, dass der Gegenstand der Untersuchung in der interdisziplinären Mitte erst während der Arbeit an ihm entsteht und daher auch von jeder Vorentscheidung Abstand zu nehmen ist, was als Vorder- oder Hintergrund dem Objekt näher oder ferner steht, wichtiger oder weniger relevant ist. Dieser Überzeugung haben wir bei der Anordnung der Beiträge und im Inhaltsverzeichnis dadurch entsprochen, dass wir auf eine ausbalancierte Untergliederung in Kapitel ebenso verzichtet haben wie auf Langtitel, die den thematischen Assoziationsraum sofort wieder einschränken. Die glossarähnliche Anordnungslogik mit ihrer alphabetischen Kontingenz soll dabei den anti-hierarchischen Impetus unseres methodologischen Zugangs unterstreichen.

Dem Hauptteil vorangestellt sind zwei Beiträge, die beide auf ihre Weise das historische Koordinatensystem unseres Objekts und seines ‚Autors' entfalten, um es gleichzeitig und sofort, noch bevor es die Interpretationsfreiräume wieder einengt, im Weichzeichner der Ambivalenz verschwimmen zu lassen. Mark Purves' and Rob McFarlands geradlinig angelegte Rekonstruktion des Lebens von Hans Richter (ent)führt uns durch ein letzten Endes verwirrendes Netzwerk von Künstlergruppen, Redaktionsstäben und Seilschaften sowie in eine inkohärente, konträre oder gar kontradiktorische Gemengelage von Strömungen, Ideen und Konzepten, an denen Richter munter und ohne Rücksicht auf ihre Vereinbarkeit partizipierte. Und Holger Wilmesmeiers akribische Rekonstruktion der Entstehungsgeschichte bringt das Objekt noch vor jeglichem analytischen Zugriff in seinen multiplen historischen Facetten und Formen zum Schillern, und zwar umso mehr, je genauer, ja detektivischer er die Historie seiner Vorführung untersucht.

Es leuchtet sofort ein, dass Richters Versuch, Film im dritten Jahrzehnt seiner Existenz als neues und avantgardistisches oder gar revolutionäres Medium mit bislang unerkannt innovativem Potential zu positionieren, ein Projekt sein muss, das sich auch und zunächst, synchron wie diachron, in einem kinematografischen Kontext verorten muss. Christoph Bareithers Beitrag „Seelentraining: *Rhythmus 21* und die Wirkungspotentiale des Films" zeigt, wie Richter seinen elementaren Film als dritte Möglichkeit sowohl gegen die Gebildeten unter den Verächtern des Schundkinos als auch gegen die Naiven unter den Bildungsbürgern des belehrenden Dokumentarfilms zu etablieren sucht. Er tut dies, indem er seinen Film als eine Art Rehabilitationsmaßnahme für das aufgeklärte Subjekt anpreist, das durch die introspektive Einsicht in die eigene Gefühlsstruktur seine Kritik-, Sprach- und Handlungsfähigkeit in der akzelerierten Moderne zurückgewinnt.

Dass solche Introspektion aber durchaus als konkret-mediale Faszination auch im Modus des Dokumentarischen inszeniert werden könnte, belegen Birgit Nemec und Katrin Pilz in ihrem Beitrag „Körper: Pulsierende Quadrate, bewegte Darmentleerung und der Rhythmus des Vitalen“. Denn im Genre des Röntgenfilms findet das gleichsam kantisch-schillersche Modell der ästhetischen Erziehung seine kuriose Fortsetzung als volksgesundheitliches Aufklärungsprojekt zur Funktion des menschlichen Körpers und seiner Organe. Richters kinematografische Kompositionsverfahren – so die These des Beitrags – erlauben eine Rhythmisierung der röntgenvisuell aufbereiteten Körperdarstellungen, die das Organleben des Menschen an das immerschon schützenswerte Vitale vermitteln. Durch den technischen Determinismus und ästhetischen Überschuss der rhythmisch-visuellen Inszenierung wird aber zugleich ein chiastisches Spannungsfeld von Vitalität und Faszination erzeugt, das zu den Aspekten der Kontrolle und der Morbidität seltsam quer steht.

Im Horizont solcher pädagogischen Reflexionen, die um die Wirkungspotentiale der Filmsprache kreisen, ist verständlicherweise auch der Werbe- und Industriefilm zu verorten. Das Kalkül verschiebt sich hierbei auf die affektive Bindung des Konsumenten an das beworbene Produkt, wie Lydia Nsiah in ihrem Beitrag „Werbe-/Industriefilm. Vereinte Empfindungen im Rhythmus von *Philips Radio*“ zeigt. Nsiah fokussiert dabei im Kontext des zeitgenössischen werbepsychologischen Diskurses auf Joris Ivens' Film *Philips Radio*, um darin den bei Richter erprobten semiotischen Holismus eines rhythmischen Verfahrens nachzuweisen, das eine ästhetische Einheit aus der zeitlichen Verknüpfung von Differenz- und Wiederholungsstrukturen zu gewinnen vermag.

Karin Fest erweitert den Blickwinkel des Bandes auf Filme mit durchaus populärästhetischem Anspruch, konkret: auf Pabsts *Die Freudlose Gasse*. Ihr Beitrag „Bildräume: *Die freudlose Gasse* im Rhythmus der Avantgarde“ entwickelt aus einer vergleichenden Analyse der jeweiligen Rhythmisierung des Screen- oder Bildraumes bei Richter und bei Pabst ein Modell gemeinschaftsstiftender Aisthesis, die aus der Avantgarde, deren eigenen Anspruch erfüllend, in die Ebenen des Popularen überspringt.

Soll Film nicht nur irgendeine, sondern eine bestimmte (aufklärerische, volksgesundheitliche, persuasive oder gemeinschaftsstiftende) Wirkung haben, bedarf es freilich Verfahren der semantischen Vereindeutigung – *Rhythmus 21* aber, eventuell sogar gegen die Intention seines Autors, zeigt, dadaistischer als man es bei einem konstruktivistischen Dokument erwarten würde, solcher Eindeutigkeit und Deutungshoheit eine lange Nase. Diesen Verdacht erhärtet Ingo Zechner in seinem Beitrag „Elementares Kino: Fünf Notizen zu Hans Richters *Rhythmus 21*“ durch eine akribische Analyse der phänomenologischen, logischen und ontologischen Mehrdeutigkeiten, deren Erzeugung das eigentliche Telos von Richters Film gewesen sein könnte.

Das transgressive Pathos, das sich schon in Richters Biografie andeutet, gilt insgesamt für eine Avantgarde, die nicht nur die bürgerliche Schwelle zum Alltäglichen überspringen, sondern, als Propädeutikum gleichsam, alle Medien- und Genregrenzen mit überrennen will. Die zwanziger Jahre sind überhaupt ein Jahrzehnt der unerwarteten Medienallianzen, faszinierenden Medienwechsel, intermedialen Formationen und diskursiven Annäherungen zwischen Kunstformen, die zu unerhörten Entscheidungen im neuen Paragonenstreit um die Krone der Künste im neutechnischen Zeitalter führt. In Michael Cowans diskursgenealogischer Untersuchung geht es etwa um die Verbindung von elementarem Film und Bewegungskunst. Er weist nach, dass bedingt durch ähnliche Konzeptinteressen (zum Beispiel Rhythmus) und durch ähnliche ästhetische Verfahren (zum Beispiel Polaritätsstruktur) zunächst vor allem auf der Ebene der intermedialen Notationstechniken sowohl des Tanzes (‚Schrifttanz') als auch des Films (‚Filmpartitur') frappierende Ähnlichkeitsevidenzen entstehen, die auf der primären Ebene der verglichenen ‚Werke' – recht besehen – gar nicht so ohne Weiteres wahrnehmbar werden. Es gehört zu den Kuriositäten der Filmgeschichte, dass in den Neuauflagen der Laokoondebatte über die Grenzen der Mahlerey, des Films, der Poesie und anderer Kunstformen auch fingierte Medienwechsel, etwa zwischen Malerei und Film, oder vorgebliche Gleichsetzungen bzw. Medienanalogien, etwa zwischen Musik und Film, in legitimatorischer Absicht verbreitet werden, dies nicht zuletzt um dem Film das Prädikat künstlerischer Innovativität und sozialer Verantwortung zuzuschreiben. Das ist nur eine der Pointen von Erik Borns Beitrag „Notation: Early Visual Music from Scrolls to Scores".

Lessing hatte den Rangstreit der Künste bekanntlich zugunsten der Literatur entschieden, weil die Literatur anders als das piktoriale Medium der Malerei Handlungen in der Zeit und nicht nur Körper im Raum darstellen könne – angesichts von Lessings aufklärerischem Pathos sprach- und handlungsfähiger Subjektivität ein nachvollziehbares Votum. Auf diesem Hintergrund muss Richters Überzeugung, dass der Film (geometrischen) Körpern in Raum und Zeit elementare Handlungen erlaube, den Film unweigerlich zum Supermedium erklären. Kurt Beals' Beitrag „Primitivismus: The Dada Rhythms of *Rhythmus 21*" entfaltet in genau diesem Zusammenhang die suggestive Poetologie einer Avantgarde, die im Rhythmusbegriff Literatur und Film unter der Ägide des zeitgenössischen Primitivismus zusammenführt und an letzterem ein emanzipatorisches Potential gegen die starre Ordnung des Bürgerlichen und gegen die Eintönigkeit des modernen Maschinentaktes wahrnimmt.

Es versteht sich – wie oben angedeutet – von selbst, dass Medienanalogien und Medientranspositionen immer auch legitimatorische Werkzeuge der Kunstdebatte sind, und dies geschieht trivialerweise nie, ohne dass die Diachronie und Synchronie der Diskurse, die diese Medien reflektorisch begleiten, mit aufgerufen werden. Richters Texte etwa zeigen eine erstaunliche Kenntnis der Überlegungen zur Ästhetik und ihrer Geschichte. Wenn es im 20. Jahrhundert um Poesie, Malerei und Film geht, spielt natürlich nicht nur Lessing und Kant (der bei Richter allerdings bis in die Sprache hinein sehr wörtlich anwesend ist) eine entscheidende Rolle, sondern die virulente Debatte, die an die beiden (und nicht nur die beiden) im 19. und frühen 20. Jahrhundert anschließt. Paul Dobrydens Beitrag „Einfühlung: The Rhythms of Empathy" rekonstruiert den Widerstreit von Abstraktion und Einfühlung in Vorformen und Varianten bei Robert Vischer, Theodor Lipps, Heinrich Wölfflin sowie August Schmarsow und wertet sie hinsichtlich ihrer Relevanz für Richters *Rhythmus 21* und seine ästhetische Schriften aus.

Wohl immer schon, aber besonders im Kontext der Avantgarden erobert der Transgressionsgestus der Kunst auch das Feld der Wissenschaft, die gerne in der Rezeption der Künstler zur Parawissenschaft mutiert und die den zentrifugalen Impuls dieser Paradoxie dazu nutzt, die Kunst über das Etablierte hinaus gleichsam zur Parakunst zu erweitern. Robert Matthias Erdbeers Beitrag „Wirbel" zeichnet diesen Weg über die Physik zur Parawissenschaft und zum Vortizismus nach und führt ihn schließlich bis zu Richters *Rhythmus 21*. Erdbeer sieht in diesen diskursiven Wirbelbewegungen das genuine Projekt einer modernen Esoterik im 20. Jahrhundert ausgebildet.

In seinem Beitrag „Spiritualität: Optische Transmutation in Hans Richters *Rhythmus 21*" verfolgt Benedikt Hjartarson die esoterische Spur von Richter in Kandinskys Kunsttheorie und deren theosophische Grundlagen hinein. Phantasierte Richter seine elementarkinematografische Pädagogik als Unterstützung einer vernünftigen Adaption des modernen Subjekts an veränderte Umweltbedingungen, so führt der Weg von gleicher *Origo* auch in einen sehr anderen Bereich: in die eine kosmische, seelische und geistige Erneuerung verfolgende Abstraktionslehre Kandinskys, die – gegenteilig zu Richter – zur technischen Umwelt eher Ausgleich und Refugium schaffen will.

Ähnliche Ambivalenzen weist auch Klaus Müller-Richters Beitrag „Architektur" nach, und zwar jene zwischen zeitgenössischer Zellbiologie und vitalistischer Philosophie. Müller-Richter zeigt nicht nur, wie mit der Architektur dem Film ein bislang selten gedachter Bruderbund an der Spitze der Künste angeboten wird, sondern auch, wie in *Rhythmus 21* dadurch, dass der Film eine archimedische Arretierung des Zuschauers außerhalb des Filmraumes dezidiert verweigert, eine Elastizität und vitale Vieldeutigkeit des Raumes entsteht, die auch die Architekten bzw. ‚Baukünstler' des Neuen Bauens Mies van der Rohe, Kiesler, Hilberseimer und El Lissitzky in ihren Haus- und Stadtentwürfen umzusetzen versuchen.

Mario Wimmers Analyse schließlich beginnt mit einer veritablen Paradoxie, die darin besteht, dass Richter die „Unwirklichkeit des Filmbildes" umso näher an die Wirklichkeit und ihre Wahrnehmung heranrücken sah, je deutlicher es von ihr abstrahiert. Wimmers Beitrag „Verkehr. *Rhythmus 21* und die elementaren Bewegungsformen der Moderne" startet mit der Intuition einer nur mittelbaren Verbindung von Film und Verkehr, einer nur indirekten Relation zwischen Richters spezifischem Ensemble bildgebender Verfahren (die seinen Film bilden) einerseits und den Innovationen, Mobilitätsformen, Zwangsvorstellungen, Phantasmen, Phantasmagorien und wissenschaftlichen Modellen zu Verkehrströmen andererseits, die den Transportdiskurs des 19. und 20. Jahrhunderts ausmachen. Und er endet mit der unabweislichen Evidenz, dass diese Verbindung im und als Film tatsächlich angelegt ist; und darin als weitere Probe aufs Exempel einer kulturwissenschaftlichen Analyse gelten kann, die den epistemischen Status der Verbindungen letzten Endes offen lassen muss, aber gerade in dieser Offenheit, diesem Mangel – wie der Philosoph Richard Rorty sein Wissenschaftskonzept pointiert – den Anlass eines nie zu Ende kommenden Gesprächs sieht, dessen Anfang stets wir selber sind und das allein auf eine transsubjektive Plausibilität aus sein kann. Diese Plausiblität wäre dann nicht obwohl, sondern gerade weil ein abschließendes Urteil fehlt, erst recht eigentlich Wissenschaft.

Biographie: Hans Richter

Mark Purves and Rob McFarland

Before one can speak of the birth of avant-garde film, the artist and filmmaker Hans Richter once explained, one must have a sense of the "historical impulses" of modern art that made up the "trend and ferment" of the years surrounding the First World War.[1] In this biography, we will outline some of the impulses, individual projects, and collaborative movements that Richter himself connected to his role in the birth of avant-garde film. Johannes Siegfried Richter was born in Berlin in 1888 into a family that cultivated an interest in music and the arts.[2] When referring to his time at school, Richter characterized himself as a mediocre student, but he remembered causing a sensation in his boarding school with his portraits of fellow students and teachers.[3] After briefly studying architecture at the University of Berlin, Richter chose to focus on art by enrolling at the Hochschule für Bildende Kunst in Berlin,[4] taking part in the master class taught by Gary Melchers at the Academy of Art in Weimar (the precursor to the Bauhaus)[5] and attending the Académie Julian in Paris. Richter later described many of his first encounters with modern art in musical terms; an exhibition of Manet's pastel drawings, for instance, evoked "absolutely heavenly music."[6] He initially rejected Cézanne's painting *Les grandes baigneuses* when he encountered it at the Secession exhibit, but it eventually broke through to him with "a kind of musical rhythm."[7] Making sense of his early oeuvre later in life, Richter explained: "Fascinated by music (my first contact with the transcendental) I found rhythmical expression not only in music itself but in the steadily repeated movements of workmen in the streets."[8]

1 Hans Richter: Avant-Garde Film in Germany. In: Roger Manvell (ed.). Experiment in the Film. London 1949, pp. 219-233, here: pp. 219-220.

2 A detailed chronology of Richter's life can be found in Marion von Hofacker: Chronology. In: Stephen C. Foster (ed.): Hans Richter: Activism, Modernism, and the Avant-Garde. Cambridge, MA 1998, pp. 240-278.

3 See Hans Richter: Hans Richter. Introduction by Sir Herbert Read. Autobiographical Text by the Artist. Neuchatel, Switzerland 1965, p. 9.

4 Hans Richter: 40 Jahre Rollenbild und Film. Hannover / Kassel 1960, p. 3.

5 http://www.arsenal-berlin.de/en/arsenal-cinema/pastprograms/single/article/1601/2804//archive/2009/june.html (12.2.2012).

6 Cleve Grey (ed.): Hans Richter by Hans Richter. New York 1971, p. 21.

7 Ibid., p. 22.

8 Hans Richter: Dada: Art and Anti-Art. London 1997, p. 10.

Although Richter is best known for his collaboration with his fellow Dada artists at the Café Voltaire in Zurich during the war years, he had already become acquainted with the luminaries of German modernism while in Berlin. In 1912, Richter became increasingly involved with the literary and artistic circles that gathered at Berlin's Café des Westens, a group that included Emmy Hennings, one of his future Zurich Dada compatriots. Richter was also drawn into the orbit of Herwarth Walden, who was the editor of the avant-garde journal *Der Sturm.* It was in connection with this community of artists—nicknamed "Café Grössenwahn"—that Richter heard F.T. Marinetti present his "Futurist Manifesto" at the *Erster Deutscher Herbstsalon* in the autumn of 1913. Walden sent Richter to pass out copies of Marinetti's manifesto to horse-carriage drivers on Berlin's Potsdamer Platz and Linkstraße. The resulting "grosse Krach"[9] gave Richter a taste for the kind of public escapades he would later undertake with the Dadaists in Zurich. In 1914, Richter began to contribute to *Die Aktion,* an Expressionist journal edited by Franz Pfemfert that combined revolutionary and antiwar ideals with art. He became the main portraitist for *Die Aktion.* Richter also recorded 1914 as the year that he first grappled with the "Haufen von Fragmenten" that he called Cubism.[10] By the time of his first one-man show in 1916, Richter had moved beyond Cubism: "Form and color should from now on definitely be freed from guitars, madonnas, harlequins, nudes and apples. I saw them losing their value."[11]

Upon visiting Zurich in 1916, Richter quickly made the acquaintance of the Dadaists who made up the inner circle of the Café Voltaire.[12] Among the habitués and visitors of the Café Voltaire and the other various flareups of Dada in different cities over the next few years Richter found a rich source of discussion, dispute, collaboration, and creation. He participated in the unique Dada combination of concerts, readings, demonstrations, exhibitions, and brawls. In a speech called "Gegen Ohne Für Dada," which he read publicly at the eighth "Dada Soiree" and distributed in the streets of Zurich, Richter called upon his fellow artists to find the courage to make "einen Sprung in die Form, komponieren wir aus gut verdaulichem Salat Eisenbahnfahrkarten."[13] Tzara called Richter's reading of this speech "malicious, elegant, Dada, Dada, Dada."[14] Participating in Dada's own brand of creative destruction, Richter found a powerful catalyst for his development as an artist:

---

9 Richter: 40 Jahre, p. 3.

10 Ibid.

11 Richter: Hans Richter, p. 16.

12 Richter: Dada, pp. 27-28.

13 Hans Richter: Gegen Ohne Für Dada. In: Dada No. 4/5 (May 1919), n.p.

14 Richter: Dada, p. 78.

> Dada not only had no programme, it was against all programmes [...] at that moment in history, it was just this that gave the movement its explosive power to unfold in all directions, free of aesthetic or social constraints. This absolute freedom from preconceptions was something quite new in the history of art.[15]

In his memoirs, Richter carefully located himself at the geographical, historical, and biographical center of Dada, but he was also careful to separate his own ideological development from that of his collaborators. While he benefited in many ways from his participation in the broad range of discussions, obsessions, performances, and provocations of his fellow Dadaists, his memoirs specifically focus upon the impulses that shaped his own development as an abstract artist. Several of these impulses were particularly relevant to Richter's eventual turn to film: Dada's oscillation between destruction and creation, the Dada fascination with chance, the synesthetic relationship between abstract forms and music, and the political extension of aesthetic ideals.

In between the infamous Dada manifestos and performances that regularly called for the destruction of all art, Richter explored the new possibilities for art that might be brought about by evolving concepts of abstraction. Richter's development in the realm of abstraction was driven by his collaboration with the diverse group of Dadaists and their often conflicting impulses of nihilism and creativity:

> It was not by following the example of other artists—or by reacting against it—that we gradually made our way from representational to abstract art. It was a reaction to the general disintegration of the world around us, the process that Walter Serner followed to its logical conclusion in his pamphlet advocating a *Letzte Lockerung* ('Final Dissolution,' 1918). This dissolution was the ultimate in everything that Dada represented, philosophically and morally; everything must be pulled apart [...] set on its way towards new functions which would only be known after the total negation of everything that had existed before. Until then: riot, destruction, defiance, confusion. The role of chance, not as an extension of the scope of art, but as a principle of dissolution and anarchy. In art, anti-art.[16]

Although, as the title of Richter's memoir suggests, Dada incorporated both destructive and creative artistic impulses, he described Dada as more of an aggregate of individual projects than a unified movement. He counted himself, Hans Arp, and Marcel Janco among the art-positive personalities in the Zurich Dada constellation, for they accepted the "final dissolution" not as a nihilistic worldview but as a "means to an end: a new and brilliant weapon to destroy what was outworn and useless, to ward off the bour-

15 Ibid., pp. 33-34.

16 Ibid., p. 48.

geois and to strengthen the line that separated us from banality."[17] In what he described as a "kurze expressionistische Periode" in 1917, Richter painted a series of hundreds of paintings that he called "visionary portraits," producing 3-4 paintings a day as an exercise in "spontaneous expression."[18] This intense foray into Expressionism allowed him to "meaningfully" grapple with abstraction.[19]

In his memoirs of his Zurich years, Richter connected his development as an abstract artist with his fellow Dadaists' fascination with the phenomenon of chance. Richter explained that members of the Dada group in Zurich came to a mutual conclusion that "chance must be recognized as a new stimulus to artistic creation." He went so far as to call this idea "the central experience of Dada, that which marks it off from all preceding artistic movements." Arp began tearing up his paintings and letting them fall into random patterns; Tzara, Arp, and Huelsenbeck used chance procedures in their poetry; and Richter painted in the dark, in a sort of "auto-hypnotic trance."[20] Aesthetic strategies of chance and association pushed the group into new genres: "from pictorial art to typography, collage, photography, photo-montage, from abstract art to pictures painted on long paper scrolls, from scroll-pictures to the cinema, to the relief, to the *objet trouvé*."[21] Richter described the creative energy that came from the dialectic relationship between the two spheres of chance and order, "zwischen Zufall und Bewußtheit, Improvisation und höherer Ordnung schwankend."[22]

A chance impulse from outside of the visual arts became one of the organizing principles of Richter's art. During an evening spent sitting in front of the Zurich train station and discussing art and music, Richter explained his experiments with positive and negative space to the musician Ferruccio Busoni. Busoni suggested that Richter should study musical counterpoint, specifically various preludes and fugues by Bach.[23] Through musical forms, Richter was able to formulate his artistic vision:

> Trying to translate that idea of polarity (in music and form) from music to painting, I began to orchestrate very simple positive-negative relationships of surfaces, black against white, up against down, etc. [...] Repetitions of the same element, distributed on the surface in various places with smaller or greater variations, led to a kind of

---

17 Ibid., p. 49.

18 Richter: Hans Richter, p.18.

19 Richter: 40 Jahre, p. 3.

20 Ibid., pp. 51-52, 55.

21 Ibid., p. 57.

22 Richter: 40 Jahre, p. 5.

23 Richter: Dada, p. 61.

> musical relationship between form complexes and a clearer composition of the whole.[24]

If an obsession with chance had led the Dadaists into the blurred borderlands between genres, it was a search for order that brought Richter into the place where paintings are "orchestrated." At the same time that Richter was using music to develop a logic of abstraction, Tristan Tzara introduced him to the Swedish painter Viking Eggeling, who had also been struggling to articulate a "complete syntax of form relationships" that he called the "Generalbass der Malerei."[25] After their meeting in the early spring of 1918, the two found themselves united in their search for a fundamental language of abstraction, and often used music as a metaphor for their project. The titles of many works reveal the central role of music in Richter's understanding of his own artistic practice: "Preludium," "Fugue," "Rhythm," "Interval," "Orchestration," etc.

Although Richter downplayed the political context of his various creative projects in several of his autobiographical writings, it is important to place his turbulent interactions with politics beside the other impulses that drove his aesthetic projects in and around the Dada period. In a discussion of Berlin Dada, Richter explained the difference between Dadaism as it was practiced in its earlier phases and the "new," more overtly political nature of Berlin Dada:

> The Berlin Dadaists might well look down upon their Zurich colleagues, who had admittedly insulted the citizenry in all the approved ways, but had no real collapse of the established so-called Order, no revolution to their credit. In Berlin they had a revolution, and they decided to join in [...] This is the light in which we must consider the reckless onslaughts carried out [...] by the political Light Brigade that grew up around Dada.[26]

When Richter compared the Zurich arm of Dada to the revolutionary Berlin group, he downplayed his own revolutionary activity in Zurich and in Munich. Richter and Eggeling did not only see their search for a basic abstract language of form as a purely aesthetic pursuit, but also as a potent political tool. Marcel Janco remembered a point when Richter tired of the "ridiculous and scandalous" side of Dada, which was becoming nothing but "quixotries without sense or belief."[27] After that point, Richter dedicated himself to socialism. Beyond the Dada group, Richter explained, "there

---

24 Richter: Hans Richter, p. 22.

25 Ibid., p. 24.

26 Richter: Dada, p. 101.

27 Justin Hoffmann: Hans Richter, Munich Dada, and the Munich Republic of Workers' Councils. In: Stephen C. Foster (ed.): Hans Richter: Activism, Modernism, and the Avant-Garde. Cambridge, MA 1998, pp. 48-71, here: p. 69.

were other more politically active, more direct approaches to the war, at least as far as I was concerned."[28] Specifically, he befriended Ludwig Rubiner, a German poet and anarchist who was the editor of the magazine called *Zeitecho.* Richter became art editor of *Zeitecho,* and contributed articles and political drawings himself. In one such article from 1917 he claimed that artists have a moral imperative to be politically active:

> Can anyone say that still-lifes nudes or any paintings, titled in some way or untitled, do anything in opposition? Art is well established everywhere, and poor suffering men have the right to expect some artist to be the mouth of their soul, (the soul of those who are less privileged in their ability to use image and word)—their mouth passionately cries out their pain.[29]

Far from merely insulting the citizenry, Richter imagined an art that is active in its sincere political solidarity with the suffering of the poor, not just in mocking, nihilistic Dadaist opposition to the bourgeois notion of beauty. Belying his claim that Zurich Dada had no real revolution to its name, Richter himself became the political agitator behind revolutionary activity in Zurich and beyond. In February 1919, Richter joined socialist groups from all over Europe at a meeting of the Second International in Bern.[30] In April, Richter and Eggeling participated in the organization of the Bund radikaler Künstler in Zurich.[31] According to the group's manifesto, artists are in possession of "the artistic law of motion of our era," a system of abstraction that would bring about "a tremendous expansion of humanity's feeling for freedom." The tools of abstract art can "gather the conscious power of the productive force of all individuals in the performance of their mission into unified achievement," avoiding any "energy-wasting unsystematical activity."[32] The language of the manifesto reveals the influence of Richter and Eggeling's central project of a unified system of abstraction, which moves beyond the world of aesthetics and into the world of politics. Richter recalled Eggeling's insistence that "the abstract form was the real international, the 'universal' language."[33] In early 1919, Richter went to Munich to take a part in the revolutionary activities that led to the founding of the short-lived Münchner Räterepublik. He served on the Art Commissariat of the Central Council's Action Committee, and worked for the

---

28 Grey: Hans Richter by Hans Richter, p. 31.

29 Ibid., p. 32.

30 von Hofacker: Chronology, p. 251.

31 Hoffmann: Munich Dada, pp. 61-62.

32 Quoted in: ibid., p. 61.

33 Hans Richter: Review. Louisa O'Konor: Viking Eggeling, Artist and Film-maker, His Life and Work. In: Journal of Aesthetics and Art Criticism vol. 30 (1972), no. 4, pp. 545-549, here: p. 548.

restructuring of Bavaria's art colleges. He proposed that Marcel Janco and Viking Eggeling be made professors of the Munich Academy of Art.[34] After right-wing militias brutally ousted the various factions of the Räterepublik, Richter was sentenced to prison for his role in the revolution, but was freed through his mother's influence.[35]

After the end of the war and the failed revolution, Zurich Dada dissipated and some members formed the Basel-based group Das neue Leben. Tzara went to Paris, and Berlin became the seat of a new Dada constellation. Although, as Richter explained it, he "held aloof from active participation in Berlin Dada," he still kept in close contact with Raoul Hausmann, George Grosz, Hannah Höch, and other Dada luminaries in Berlin.[36] But whereas many of the Berlin Dada activities continued in the tradition of Zurich Dada's anti-art impulses, Richter and Eggeling were engrossed in an intense artistic exploration of the ideas they had developed in Zurich. The two of them moved to the estate owned by Richter's parents in Klein-Kölzig, roughly 150 kilometers southeast of Berlin.[37] Richter produced thousands of "Exerzitien" with Eggeling around the time of this move. In these experimental drafts, they continued their quest to reduce forms to their basic elements. Eggeling, heavily influenced by the forms of Art Nouveau, was fascinated with lines,[38] while Richter concentrated on "the positive-negative interplay of planes."[39] Before the year was out, Richter had created his first scroll painting, *Prélude*, which he referred to as the "Kontinuität eines Formthemas in einer Reihe von zehn Etappen." Eggeling called his companion scroll painting "Horizontal-Vertikal-Messe."[40] Richter described the breakthrough represented by their move to scroll painting:

> Without aiming for it, we had created in these scrolls a form of dynamic expression which distinguished it from easel painting. This particular sensation [...] lies in the stimulus which the remembering eye receives by carrying its attention from one detail to the other, indefinitely, so that a phase-sequence, a relationship is built. [...] The scroll belongs to the realm of time, but in a special way. It is not physiological movement but rather a psychological one. It is between painting and film. As such it is a movement of the mind.[41]

---

34 Hoffmann: Munich Dada, pp. 63-65.

35 Ibid., p. 66.

36 Richter: Dada, pp. 122-123.

37 von Hofacker: Chronology, pp. 253-254.

38 Richter: Review, p. 548.

39 Richter: Hans Richter, p. 26.

40 Richter: 40 Jahre, p. 5.

41 Richter: Hans Richter, pp. 26-27.

In recounting the development of the first scroll paintings, Richter portrayed the breakthrough as relying on two impulses that he and Eggeling had obsessed about in their Dada days: abstraction and chance. Again slipping into the mythological mode of narration that Richter often used when describing the significant moments of the past, he continued: "We had arrived at a crossroad. The scroll looked at us and it seemed to ask for real motion. That was as much a shock as it was a sensation. Because in order to realize movement we needed film."[42] The implication of real movement was so forceful, Richter recalled, that it "thrust us toward using film instead of canvas."[43]

The result of Richter and Eggeling's experiments was a series of short abstract films, one of which—*Rhythmus 21*—will be the focus of the essays in this volume. First, the pair attempted to create a cinematic version of scroll paintings, which they conceived of as a "score" for the film. They tried to create this filmic version in 1920 with the help of a technician from the UFA film company. Richter was unhappy with the results, as he explained: "Instead of orchestrating form as I had done for 2 years, I had now to orchestrate time."[44] Another experiment included figures painted on thin pieces of rubber that were pulled back and forth like accordions.[45] In the late fall of 1921, Richter conceded that the nature of the filmic medium was different enough from painting that he needed to try a new approach. While Eggeling broke with Richter and continued to work on the incredibly complex task of animating the small lines of his drawings, Richter instead dropped "the well-shaped drawings" of his scrolls and opted to work with more basic shapes, involving the "monstrously imperfect" medium of paper and thumbtacks. He saw the technical simplification as a necessary sacrifice to the idea of a universal language.[46] He described his shift from the space of the painter's canvas to the time of the filmmaker's screen:

> The simple square of the movie screen could easily be divided and orchestrated by using the rectangle of the cinema-canvas as my field of pictorial vision. Parts of the screen could then be moved against each other. Thus it became possible on this cinema-canvas to relate (by both contrast and analogy) the various movements to each other. So I made my paper rectangles and squares grow and disappear, jump and slide in well-articulated time-spaces and planned rhythms.[47]

---

42 Ibid., p. 27.

43 Hans Richter: The Avant-Garde Film Seen from Within. In: Hollywood Quarterly vol. 4 (1949), no. 1, pp. 34-41, here: p. 36.

44 Richter: Hans Richter, p. 29.

45 Richter: 40 Jahre, p. 6.

46 Richter: Avant-Garde, p. 222.

47 Richter: Hans Richter, p. 29.

The resulting film, initially titled *Film ist Rhythmus* and later referred to as *Rhythmus 21,* was the first in a series of "absolute films" in which Richter and Eggeling used the cinematic medium to expand their theories of abstraction, time, surface, and line.[48] Eggeling's own absolute film, *Symphonie Diagonale,* appeared in 1923. Richter followed with several more abstract films, including *Rhythmus 23* and the now-lost *Rhythmus 25,* which was hand-colored frame by frame. Richter and Eggeling acrimoniously parted ways in the spring of 1922, but—according to Richter—the pair rekindled their friendship, and Richter became the executor of Eggeling's body of work after his death in May 1925.[49]

In the post-Dada period, Richter saw the Dadaist dialectic between art and anti-art as finally reaching a productive resolution. Although Malcom Turvey sees Richter's films as an integral part of Dada,[50] Richter's discussion of the films in *Dada: Art and Anti-Art* placed them among the works of art that are "no longer Dada, but quite simply new art, the fruit of Dada. These fruits ripened everywhere." Richter immediately identified his collaboration with Viking Eggeling as "another fruit that was ripening" on the different branches that grew from the former Dada movement.[51] Though Richter ultimately separated his films from Dada, they nevertheless shared one chaotic moment together, a Dada soirée in Paris that Richter calls "Dada's swan song."[52] Along with plays by Tzara, music by Stravinsky, and the typical cardboard costumes and belligerent poetry readings of any good Dada event,[53] the "Soirée du Coeur à barbe" in July 1923 also included a screening of either *Rhythmus 21* or *Rhythmus 23,* as well as films by Man Ray and Charles Sheeler.[54] The evening ended with André Breton breaking a Dada artist's arm with his walking stick, and, in true Dada fashion, an audience riot.[55] In 1925, either *Rhythmus 21* or *Rhythmus 23* was premiered in Berlin along with René Claire's *Entr'acte* und Léger's *Ballet Mécanique* at the UFA theater on Kurfürstendamm.[56] Richter wrote: "Das Publikum, schon ärgerlich gemacht durch diese beiden Filme, von denen es nichts verstand, reagierte auf *Rhythmus 21*, der nur noch Vierecke zeigte, mit explosiver

48 See also the article "Elementares Kino" in this volume.

49 Richter: Review, pp. 545-546.

50 Malcolm Turvey: Dada Between Heaven and Hell: Abstraction and Universal Language in the Rhythm Films of Hans Richter. In: October vol. 105, Dada (2003), pp. 13-36, here: pp. 29-36.

51 Richter: Dada, p. 197.

52 Ibid., p. 190.

53 Ibid.

54 von Hofacker: Chronology, p. 259.

55 Richter: Dada, p. 190.

56 See also the article "Entstehungsgeschichte" in this volume.

Wut."[57] The angry crowd, Richter later recalled, attacked the piano player who was accompanying the film.[58] Parts of *Rhythmus 21* had been incorporated into *Rhythmus 23* for the showing.[59] Regardless of which film was shown, the ensuing riot shows that if his early *Rhythmus* films were, as he claimed, the "fruit" that grew out of Dada, they had not fallen far from the tree.

In Berlin in 1922, Richter had co-founded the Constructivist Group, an extension of the post-Dada group Das neue Leben in Basel and his own Bund Radikaler Künstler.[60] Emerging in Russia, Constructivism aimed to extend the formal language of abstract art into practical design. Its avant-garde tendencies were informed by the ideological concerns of early Soviet thinking, including hostility towards individualism and a preference for impersonal, clear, formal order that would embody the social and economic values of Communism. In 1920, Theo van Doesburg, the Dutch artist and founder of the movement De Stijl, encouraged Eggeling and Richter to publish a magazine. Richter started to gather material from Doesburg, Mies van der Rohe, Hans Arp, Tristan Tzara, Georg Grosz, Kurt Schwitters, and others. After his parting with Eggeling in 1922, Richter raised enough money to move forward with the project. At the suggestion of El Lissitzky, they called the magazine *G*, which stood for *Gestaltung*. An advertisement in van Doesburg's *De Stijl* magazine called *G* "the organ of the Constructivists in Europe," although Richter and other founders and contributors distanced themselves from the increasingly trendy term "constructivism," which had drifted from the meaning they had imagined at the foundation of their group.[61] Proclaiming culture to be the "general problem of existence," the magazine printed articles from artists and thinkers across many disciplines, including art, architecture, city planning, poetry, fashion, philosophy, politics, and many other subjects.[62]

Having dismissed Constructivist art as "passé" in 1924, Richter continued to suffuse his work with Constructivist thinking for the next decade. Richter's use of clocks and other mechanical objects in *Filmstudie* (1925-1926) and *Vormittagsspuk* (1927-1928) reflects the generally positive attitude that Constructivism held towards the machine. The "tyranny of

57 Richter: 40 Jahre, p. 6.

58 Wolfgang Grözinger: Der erste abstrakte Film. Hans Richter in der Lenbachgalerie. In: Süddeutsche Zeitung No. 122. Museum of Modern Art Archives, NY: Hans Richter A. III. 1.

59 Richter: Avant-Garde, p. 223.

60 von Hofacker: Chronology, p. 257.

61 Christina Lodder: El Lissitzky and the Export of Constructivism. In: Nancy Perloff / Brian Reed (eds.): Situating El Lissitzky. Vitebsk, Berlin, Moscow. Los Angeles 2003, pp. 27-46, here: p. 37.

62 Richter: Hans Richter, p. 37.

the individual" that Constructivism claimed to oppose is a defining feature of these films, as inanimate objects—hats, cups, and neckties—act autonomously against their owners, bringing to a close, Richter explained, the master-slave dichotomy governing the conventional world.[63] Scholars interested in the development of Richter's aesthetics often draw on this period, during which the filmmaker's interest in combining mechanical objects into abstract mobile structures began to recede in favor of films that addressed more clearly the social, economic, and cultural issues of his day.[64] Ultimately, the notions underlying the Constructivist movement proved too elastic for Richter, who accused commercial artists of misappropriating its central ideas in order to "march under the banner of Constructivism."[65]

Fortunately for Richter, the admiration he expressed for Russian cinema blossomed during a time that was propitious for experimentation and collaboration between Soviet artists and their Western counterparts. Richter took full advantage of his contact with Soviet filmmakers and graphic artists coming and going between Moscow and Berlin. Kazimir Malevich, the originator of Suprematism in Russia, sought Richter's assistance in dramatizing on-screen the relationship between continuity and motion, the chief tension in Malevich's painting.[66] This interaction also brought Richter together with a man who would arguably become the most important director the Soviet Union ever produced: Sergei Eisenstein. The mutual admiration between Richter and Eisenstein bore little obvious fruit, though one consequence of the 1929 Congress of Independent Cinema, held in La Sarraz, Switzerland, was a project for which both Richter and Eisenstein assumed directorial duties. For sets and costumes, members of the congress pilfered priceless medieval weapons and artifacts from the collections and castle of their hostess, Madame de Mandrot. The film, which focused on the theme "Der Kampf des unabhängigen gegen den kommerziellen Film," was soon lost.[67] Richter rejoined Eisenstein later that year to begin work on *Everyday,* in which he cast Eisenstein as an English police officer going through the banalities, compromises, and confusions of everyday life. Due to a series personal and financial setbacks, the film was shelved until its premiere in 1968, two decades after the heart attack that ultimately claimed Eisenstein's life.

Richter's affinity for early Soviet cinema can be explained in two ways: first, it answered the director's longing to produce socially relevant films;

63 Richter: Dada, p. 198.

64 von Hofacker: Chronology, p. 124.

65 Hans Richter: An den Konstruktivismus. In: G. Zeitschrift für elementare Gestaltung III (1924). Reprint edited by Marion von Hofacker, München 1986, p. 72.

66 Gerry Souter: Malevich. Paris 2008, p. 222.

67 Hans Richter: Köpfe und Hinterköpfe. In: Die Tat (27 May 1967), p. 18.

and second, it refined Richter's technical skills by making him more familiar with the rich resources of cinematography. For Richter, nothing could be further from the manic, nihilistic experiments of his Dada past than the films of Vsevolod Pudovkin (1893-1953) and Aleksandr Dovzhenko (1894-1956), which represented for Richter the ideal mix of social awareness and cinematic innovation.[68] The tendentiousness of their films, in which Russian revolutionaries secure the Communist future by implementing the principles of Leninism-Marxism, is leavened by highly elegant and expressive structures of montage. *Inflation* (1927-28) strongly testifies to the role of Russian filmmaking in Richter's artistic and philosophical evolution. As a partial documentary, it derives its ideological strength from the disastrous losses suffered during Germany's period of hyperinflation from 1921 to 1924, making an unambiguous statement about the social and economic calamities caused by capitalism's failures. The formal elements of *Inflation* reveal a depth that the film's didacticism nearly denies. Richter's employment of dramatic focus and extreme angles indicate his development as an artist; his use of photomontage is evidence of his interest in incorporating and modulating techniques of Russian avant-garde cinema.

Of those figures shaping Richter's approach to film during this period, few are more influential than the documentarian Dziga Vertov (1896-1954). Well known for several Soviet propaganda films commissioned during the Revolution, Vertov made a strong impression on Richter. Following their first meeting in 1929, Richter described the former agitprop director and lifelong Constructivist as a "brilliant master [...] exceptionally fluent in the cinematic language of the camera."[69] Richter was drawn to Vertov for several reasons, not least of which was the Soviet director's insistence on framing the question of the artist's duty to society in the internationalist, collectivist terms that had recently fascinated Richter. The man behind the camera, Vertov explained, must not only capture life, but also reorganize it to show the "new reality" understood as the "proletarian revolution."[70] Richter also shared Vertov's disdain for the mannered "fiction films" produced regularly throughout the West, which relied on a false sense of verisimilitude to confirm the beliefs of its bourgeois audiences. In fact, one of the key motivations for convening the La Sarraz conference later that year was the creation of a unified, international body of filmmakers whose very autonomy would symbolize their rejection of the mercenary, exploitative concerns governing commercial film studios. Evidence of the impact that Vertov had

68 Bernd Finkeldey: Hans Richter and the Constructivist International. In: Stephen C. Foster (ed.): Hans Richter: Activism, Modernism, and the Avant-Garde. Cambridge, MA 1998, pp. 93-121, here: p. 111.

69 Hans Richter: Dziga Vertov Zagranitsei. In: Kino i Kul'tura nos. 7-8 (1929), p. 75.

70 Richard Taylor: The Politics of the Soviet Cinema, 1917-1929. Cambridge, MA 1979, p. 129.

on Richter's work at this time can be found in *Alles dreht sich, alles bewegt sich* (1929), a short film concerning dehumanization in a world preoccupied with wealth. Here, the Russian influence is on full display. As Richter's first sound film, it draws on Vertov's tendency (shared by Pudovkin and Eisenstein) to experiment with image and sound contrapuntally, contrasting the acoustic properties of a film with the visual events unfolding on-screen.

Richter's respect for the Russian cinema was at times excessive. Take, for instance, his response to Eisenstein, whose genius, Richter explained, was the result of living in a country that gave its filmmakers total artistic freedom. This is just one of several misconceptions that Richter maintained about the status that the contemporary artist enjoyed in Soviet Russia (it is speculated that Eisenstein had been placed under surveillance as early as 1925). Elsewhere, Richter contended—on no authority that need be believed—that cinematic experiments in Russia were welcomed by audiences of every conceivable kind. Because film is made not for entertainment but for instruction, he argued, "there does not exist an avant-garde"—an assertion the members belonging to the famous Factory of the Eccentric Actor (FEKS) would find objectionable, if not simply puzzling. Richter's blinkered understanding of the constraints placed on Soviet artists betrayed a naïveté common among Western intellectuals. Similar to the disappointments suffered by luminaries such as André Gide and Arthur Koestler,[71] Richter's rosy image of Socialist society contrasted violently with the reality of the USSR when experienced first-hand. The most trenchant example of this can be found in Richter's failure to bring his film *Metall* to fruition.

Richter's invitation to helm a project that boasted the financial support of both Berlin and Moscow was no doubt the product of the reviews given to *Alles dreht sich, alles bewegt sich* two years before, which accused Richter of "cultural Bolshevism."[72] The sympathy he extended to the Soviet system was scarcely reciprocated, however, a point made clear upon his arrival in the USSR. In a climate of increased hostility for the independent, let alone German artist, Richter struggled to work within the rigid constraints placed upon him—the kind he earlier insisted did not exist. Richter could not work autonomously; "Russian soldiers were even assigned to work for me," he recounted. Despite the fact that upwards of 100,000 feet of film had been shot, *Metall* would remain unfinished due to the debacle following every step of filming in Moscow. In fact, during production one of Richter's crewmembers went missing, which Richter himself attributed to the OGPU, forerunner to the KGB.[73] Richter's experiences in the USSR

71 John V. Fleming: The Anti-Communist Manifestos: Four Books that Shaped the Cold War. New York 2009, pp. 36-37.

72 Grey: Hans Richter by Hans Richter, p. 46.

73 Ibid.

posed the question: how can the artist remain independent in an atmosphere opposed to artistic autonomy?

After emigrating to the United States in 1941, Richter continued his engagement with film in a variety of ways. For nearly fifteen years, he served as director of the Institute of Film Techniques at the City College of New York, during which he directed what would be the signal film of his exile years: *Dreams That Money Can Buy* (1946-1948), a collaboration with Marcel Duchamp, Max Ernst, and Alexander Calder. That same year, Richter was recognized by the Venice Biennale. In 1971, he was honored by the International Film Festival in Berlin. The numerous retrospectives held in Richter's honor since his death in 1971 have done much to recommend him to new audiences, illustrating that for all the depth of his commitment to progressive politics, his films succeed in the triumph they grant ideas over ideology.

Entstehungsgeschichte: Le Film 100 Titres

Holger Wilmesmeier

In Berlin, in der Karl-Liebknecht-Straße, wo sich Retrobeanies und Neobubiköpfe Gute Nacht sagen, mixen sich VJs während der Club Visuals Retrospektive „Screendancing“ (2010) einen avantgardistischen Stammbaum. Dabei greifen sie unter anderem auf jene Filmemacher der 1920er Jahre zurück, die, von den bildenden Künsten herkommmend, sich dem jungen Medium näherten – Künstler wie Fernand Léger, Francis Picabia, Walter Ruttmann, Viking Eggeling und Hans Richter. Ein experimenteller Film von Hans Richter rückt im Zusammenhang dieser Pedigreegenerierung besonders ins Blickfeld: *Rhythmus 21*.

Parallelen zwischen der Arbeitsweise des Dadaisten Hans Richter und derjenigen eines VJs werden benannt: Bildkompositionen werden wie musikalische Arrangements gestaltet, das Material wird ständig neu montiert und bleibt damit im Fluss.

Für diejenigen, die den Avantgardefilmklassiker *Rhythmus 21* nicht als lediglich weiterzuverarbeitendes Material ansehen, sondern ihn als eigenständiges Kunstwerk genauer betrachten und einordnen wollen, stellen sich angesichts solcher kreativen Arbeitsweisen einige Fragen nach der ursprünglichen Erscheinungsform und Identität: Was für ein Film ist eigentlich *Rhythmus 21*? Wie sah er aus, was war auf ihm zu sehen? Wann entstand er und wann wurde er das erste Mal öffentlich vorgeführt?

Ich will versuchen, diese Fragen zu beantworten. Dabei setze ich den Fokus auf ein medienhistorisch bedeutsames Ereignis: die legendäre Avantgardefilm-Schau der Novembergruppe, die unter dem Titel „Der absolute Film“ am 3. und 10. Mai 1925 im UFA-Theater am Kurfürstendamm in Berlin stattfand – wo sich damals die Original-Bubiköpfe Gute Nacht sagten. Dort wurde auch Hans Richters erstes Filmexperiment unter dem Titel *Film ist Rhythmus* auf dem Programmzettel angekündigt.[1]

Wer Sekundärliteratur mag, ist bei der filmischen Avantgarde gut aufgehoben. Hier hat sich mannigfaltiges Material angesammelt. Dies trifft insbesondere auf das Schaffen und Wirken von Hans Richter zu. Allein aus seiner eigenen Feder liegt eine große Anzahl von Veröffentlichungen vor, denn Richter betätigte sich nicht bloß als Künstler sondern auch als Chronist. Vor allem nach dem Zweiten Weltkrieg avancierte Richter zum prominenten Zeitzeugen der deutschen Filmavantgarde der 1910er und

1 Eine ausführliche Beschreibung des gesamten Events findet sich in: Holger Wilmesmeier: Deutsche Avantgarde und Film. Münster 1994.

1920er Jahre und nahm eine Schlüsselstellung bei der Schreibung dieses Kapitels der Filmgeschichte ein. Daraus ergibt sich ein entscheidendes Problem, denn oft fehlen Informationen aus anderen ‚ersten Händen', die einen Vergleich – zur Bestätigung, Korrektur oder Ergänzung – ermöglichen würden. Viking Eggeling starb bereits 1925 im Alter von 45 Jahren, Walter Ruttmann 1941. Hans Richter, dem Praktiker, Theoretiker, Publizisten und Pädagogen war es vergönnt, u.a. auch durch seine lange Lebensdauer, eine Fülle von Informationen verbreiten zu können, die bisweilen allerdings durch Inkonsistenz Fragen aufwerfen, die kaum mehr zu klären sind. Dadaist sein und gleichzeitig eine ernsthafte, wissenschaftliche Chronik zu schreiben, das sind Dinge, die eigentlich konfligieren. Der Versuch der Vermischung scheinbar unvereinbarer Elemente ist jedoch für die Avantgarde der zwanziger Jahre insgesamt kennzeichnend.

Richter war durch seine Affinität zur niederländischen *De Stijl*-Bewegung und deren Elementarismus einerseits Konstruktivist, aber andererseits auch Dadaist mit ausgeprägter surrealistischer Neigung, und er hörte nie auf, besonders letzteres zu sein. Das kündigt sich schon in seiner *Filmstudie* von 1926 an und setzt sich in seinen späteren Filmen *Dreams That Money Can Buy* (1947), *8x8* (1956/57), *Chesscetera* (1956/57) und *Dadascope* (1956-61) fort.

Theo van Doesburg, der in engem Kontakt zu Richter stand und von 1917 bis zu seinem Tod 1931 als Herausgeber der Zeitschrift *De Stijl* fungierte, war gleichfalls geprägt von dieser Doppelnatur der Avantgarde. Dem Surrealismus gegenüber nahm er einerseits eine durchaus skeptische Haltung ein. So erscheint in der Nr. 8 von *De Stijl* 1924 eine von van Doesburg verfasste „Satire op het Surrealisme". Andererseits entfaltet er dann bei seinem abstrakten „surhumanistischen" Fortsetzungsroman *het andere gezicht* – in *De Stijl* erschienen und unter dem Pseudonym I.K. Bonset zwischen 1926-1928 veröffentlicht – selbst ein hohes Maß an surrealer Fantasie.

Die oben angedeuteten Schwierigkeiten wirken sich auch auf die Rekonstruktion der Matinee „Der absolute Film" von 1925 in Berlin aus. Schon allein die Frage, welches Filmmaterial Richter auf der Veranstaltung vorführen wollte, ist nicht einfach zu beantworten. Alle Filmtitel der Matinee lassen sich mehr oder weniger exakt im Zensurkatalog nachweisen. Einen Film mit dem Titel *Film ist Rhythmus* (Programmblatt-Titel) aber sucht man vergeblich. Wann wurde er überhaupt das erste Mal gezeigt?

Anfang der 1960er Jahre machte Richter in einem Interview in der Zeitschrift *Film Culture* folgende Angabe: „Der Originaltitel meines ersten Films war ‚Film ist Rhythmus'" und fügte hinzu: „aber seitdem machte ich andere, 1923 und 1925 und nannte sie alle nur Rhythmus 21, 23, 25."[2] Im selben Interview behauptete er zuvor: „Mein erster Film war ‚Rhythmus

2 Zitiert nach: Birgit Hein / Wulf Herzogenrath (Hg.): Film als Film. Stuttgart 1978, S. 21.

21'."[3] Diese Aussagen legen den Schluss nahe, dass der Titel *Rhythmus 21* und der Matineetitel *Film ist Rhythmus* einunddenselben Film bezeichnen, jenes kinematographische Werk absoluter Filmkunst, das bisweilen als „der klassische Avantgardefilm schlechthin"[4] apostrophiert wurde.

Zur ersten Aufführung von *Rhythmus 21* bemerkt Hans Richter:

> Dieser Film wurde zum erstenmal in einem kleinen Theater in Paris gezeigt. Mein Freund Theo van Doesburg zeigte dieses erste Experiment, das zu dieser Zeit ungefähr 1 1/2 Minuten lang war (ich fügte später 1921 noch etwas hinzu), und stellte mich als Däne vor, denn es gehörte sich nicht, einen Deutschen so kurz nach dem Krieg nach Paris kommen zu lassen. Van Doesburg saß neben einem alten Herrn, der einen Kneifer auf der Nase trug. Dieser sah den Titel und sagte: „Film ist Rhythmus, ach, das ist ja interessant", nahm seinen Kneifer von der Nase, und begann ihn zu reinigen. Als er ihn wieder aufsetzte, war der Film vorüber.[5]

Richter wiederholt diese Version an anderer Stelle. So in seinem Aufsatz „Avant-Garde Film in Germany", den er 1949 in Roger Manvells *Experiment in the Film* publiziert. Dort präzisiert er die Angaben zu Datum und Ort: „He [van Doesburg] showed it at the beginning of 1921 in Paris at the Theatre Michel."[6] Nach Richters Angaben ergibt sich nun folgendes Bild:

1. Richters erster Film *Film ist Rhythmus* ist identisch mit *Rhythmus 21.*
2. Die Betitelung *Rhythmus 21* bezieht sich auf das Herstellungsdatum 1921.
3. Die Uraufführung des Films fand Anfang 1921 in Paris im Théâtre Michel statt und wurde durch Theo van Doesburg realisiert.
4. Bei dieser Uraufführung ereignete sich der Vorfall mit dem älteren Herrn und seinem Kneifer.

Während Marion von Hofacker und andere Biographen diese Angaben Richters übernehmen,[7] gehen Birgit Hein und Wulf Herzogenrath in der

---

3 Ebd.; Vgl. auch Richters Angaben in seiner Kurzhistorie: Hans Richter: Avant-Garde Film in Germany. In: Roger Manvell (Hg.): Experiment in the Film. New York 1949, S. 219-233, hier: S. 223.

4 O.A.: „Hans Richter" — Kurzbiographie. In: Patricia Rochard (Hg.): Der Traum von einer neuen Welt. Berlin 1910-1933, Ausstellungskatalog. Mainz 1989, S. 232. Ähnlich erscheint die Einschätzung von *Rhythmus 21* in Hans Scheugl / Ernst Schmidt jr.: Eine Subgeschichte des Films. Lexikon des Avantgarde-, Experimental- und Undergroundfilms. 2 Bde. Frankfurt a.M. 1974, S. 742.

5 Zitiert nach: Hein / Herzogenrath (Hg.): Film als Film, S. 21.

6 Richter: Avant-Garde Film in Germany, S. 223.

7 Marion von Hofacker: Biografie Hans Richter. In: Hilmar Hoffmann / Walter Schobert (Hg.): Hans Richter, Ausstellungskatalog. Frankfurt a.M. 1989, S. 168.

Dokumentation *Film als Film* vorsichtiger damit um.[8] Ein Film, *Rhythmus 25*, den Richter des öfteren erwähnt, fehlt in ihrer Filmographie ganz. Diese Zurückhaltung erscheint berechtigt, denn, wie bereits bemerkt, lassen sich die Informationen Richters nicht ohne weiteres durch Angaben Dritter bestätigen. Das Nächstliegende wäre, Belege für seine Behauptungen bei Theo van Doesburg, der den Film vorgeführt haben soll, zu suchen.

Tatsächlich findet sich in van Doesburgs Chronologie der *De Stijl*-Bewegung in der Nr. 79/84 (1927) eben dieser Zeitschrift ein Hinweis auf eine Vortragsreise van Doesburgs, die ihn u.a. durch Frankreich führte, und zwar Anfang 1921. Im Text heißt es: „17. Mrt.' 21. Propagandareis door België, Frankrijk, Italië en Duitsland. Vordrachten met medewerking (muziek) van Pétro van Doesburg."[9] Ein Film von Hans Richter wird jedoch nicht erwähnt. Erst 1923 berichtet van Doesburg von einer solchen Aufführung, in der Nr. 2 von Richters Zeitschrift *G*. In einer kurzen Notiz heißt es: „Wenn Richters Film zu Ende ist, meint das Publikum (im Theater Michel), der richtige Film wird noch anfangen."[10] Diese ironische Bemerkung könnte auf die Anekdote vom alten Herrn mit dem Kneifer verweisen. Der Ort, das Théâtre Michel in Paris, stimmt mit Richters Version überein. Doch handelt es sich jetzt um die letzte große Dadaveranstaltung „Soirée du coeur à barbe" vom 6. Juli 1923. Für die Vorführung eines Films von Richter auf dieser Veranstaltung gibt es weitere Belege,[11] so dass, im Unterschied zu der früheren Datierung der Uraufführung auf 1921, die Datierung auf 1923 als wahrscheinlicher angesehen werden muss.

Somit wäre es immerhin chronologisch möglich, dass *Rhythmus 21*, dieser erste Film Richters, auf der Matinee „Der absolute Film" 1925 unter seinem alten Namen *Film ist Rhythmus* lief. Zwar taucht in der Auflistung der durch die Zensurbehörden geprüften Filme, dem sogenannten Zensurkatalog, im Jahr 1925 kein derartiger Film auf, weder mit dem alten noch mit dem neuen Titel. Allerdings könnte er auch schon früher genehmigt worden sein, wenn die Vermutung zuträfe, dass der Film schon vor 1925

---

8 Vgl. Hein / Herzogenrath (Hg.): Film als Film, S. 48f.

9 Theo van Doesburg: Data en Feiten (betreffende de invloedsontwikkeling van ‚DE STIJL' in \`t Buitenland) die voor zich spreken. In: De Stijl 7. Jg. (1927), Nr. 79/84, S. 54.

10 Theo van Doesburg: Pariser Neuheiten. Motiv: Nur. In: G. Material zur elementaren Gestaltung II (September 1923), S. 3; Vgl. auch Doesburgs Erwähnung der Aufführung in: Theo van Doesburg: Licht- en tijdbeelding (film). In: De Stijl 6. Jg. (1923), Nr. 5, S. 58.

11 Z.B. Jane Heap: Comments. In: Margaret Anderson / Ezra Pound (Hg.): Little Review (Exiles' Number) (Spring 1923), S. 27; In einer Aufzählung der Programmpunkte heißt es dort: „three films: ‚The Smoke of New York' by Charles Sheeler and Paul Strand, ‚The Return to Reason' by Man Ray and an abstract film by Hans Richter".

öffentlich gezeigt wurde. Eine Äußerung Richters in seinem Brief an Helga Kliemann vom 25. November 1967, veröffentlicht in ihrem Buch *Die Novembergruppe,* relativiert jedoch:

> Es ist richtig, dass meine Filme gelegentlich bei Veranstaltungen der Novembergruppe gezeigt wurden, auch bei dem Programm „Der absolute Film" 1925, Vorführungen die im kleinen Ufa-Theater am Kurfürstendamm stattfanden. Bei dieser Gelegenheit wurde auch mein Film „Rhythmus 21" oder „Rhythmus 23" gezeigt, nach René Clairs „Entr'Acte" und Légers „Ballet Mécanique".[12]

Filmdatierung ist ohnehin schon problematisch – welchen Zeitpunkt nimmt man als Richtwert: die Fertigstellung der Entwürfe bzw. des Drehbuchs, die Fertigstellung des Films, die inoffizielle oder offizielle Uraufführung? Hier ergibt sich nun noch eine zusätzliche Schwierigkeit durch die ungenauen Angaben Richters. Scheugl und Schmidt vermuten in ihrer *Subgeschichte des Films*, das von Richter angegebene Entstehungsjahr 1921 sei falsch.[13] Damit wird die Möglichkeit einer nachträglich vorgenommenen Vordatierung angedeutet.

Dies ist für die Diskussion um die Frage, „Wer war der erste?" nicht ganz unerheblich.[14] 1960 erscheint in der *Süddeutschen Zeitung* ein Artikel unter dem Titel „Der erste abstrakte Film"[15] (gemeint ist *Rhythmus 21*) zu einem Vortrag, den Hans Richter in der Galerie im Lenbachhaus München gehalten hatte. Kein Wort findet man dort zu Walter Ruttmann, der, im Gegensatz zu Richter, immerhin nachweislich 1921 sein *Lichtspiel opus 1* aufführte.[16] Dafür wird Richters Anekdote kolportiert, nach der „bei der ersten Vorführung des Films im Jahre 1921 das Publikum den Klavierspieler verprügelte, um sich für diese ‚Zumutung' zu rächen!"[17] Dieselbe reißerische Geschichte wiederholt Richter später in seinem bereits erwähnten Brief an Helga Kliemann.[18] Nur,

12 Zitiert nach Helga Kliemann: Die Novembergruppe. Berlin 1969, S. 78, Anm. 61.

13 Scheugl / Schmidt: Subgeschichte des Films, Bd. 2, S. 743. In der dortigen Filmographie auf S. 739 sind alle Filme Richters vor 1925 hinter der angesetzten Datierung mit einem Fragezeichen versehen.

14 Vgl. Wulf Herzogenrath: Wer war der erste? In: Birgit Hein / Wulf Herzogenrath (Hg.): Film als Film. Stuttgart 1978, S. 8ff., Vgl. auch: Jeanpaul Goergen: Walter Ruttmann. Eine Dokumentation. Berlin 1989, S. 46, Anm. 31. Beide, Herzogenrath und Goergen, geben Ruttmann als den ersten an, der öffentlich einen abstrakten Film zeigte.

15 Wolf Grözinger: Der erste abstrakte Film. In: Süddeutsche Zeitung (22.5.1960).

16 Vgl. die Kritik von Bernhard Diebold: Eine neue Kunst — Augenmusik des Films. In: Frankfurter Zeitung (2.4.1921). Wiederabgedruckt in: Hein / Herzogenrath (Hg.): Film als Film, S. 16 f. und in Goergen: Walter Ruttmann, S. 98 f.

17 Grözinger: Der erste abstrakte Film.

18 Vgl. Kliemann: Die Novembergruppe, S. 78, Anm. 61.

dass dieses Mal der bedauernswerte Klavierspieler nicht 1921 in Paris,[19] sondern 1925 in Berlin auf der Filmmatinee der Novembergruppe und der UFA seine Abreibung über sich ergehen lassen musste.

Da – schon zum Wohle der damaligen Kinomusiker – nicht anzunehmen ist, dass es Brauch war, bei jeder Vorführung eines Richter-Films den Pianisten öffentlich zu züchtigen, ist davon auszugehen, dass Richter hier verschiedene Ereignisse vermengt. Damit aber noch nicht genug der Irritationen. Bei der Durchsicht der Kritiken zur Filmmatinee fällt auf, dass in dem überwiegenden Teil der Besprechungen weder der Name Richter, noch einer der anderen oben erwähnten möglichen Filmtitel auftaucht. Die Frage liegt daher nahe, ob der Beitrag Richters überhaupt gezeigt wurde. Jeanpaul Goergen schreibt in seiner Dokumentation *Walter Ruttmann*, dass Richters Film bei der ersten Vorführung der absoluten Filme am 3. Mai nicht gezeigt wurde, da er noch nicht vorführungsbereit gewesen sei. Erst bei der Wiederholung eine Woche später sei er aufgeführt worden.[20]

Dass Richters Film, wie Goergen weiter schreibt, in den Besprechungen dieser Veranstaltung nicht berücksichtigt worden sei, ist nicht ganz zutreffend.[21] Mindestens vier der damaligen Quellen erwähnen Richter.[22] Eine der Quellen scheint sogar Goergens These zu widersprechen. In dem mit „Fi." (Kürzel nicht auflösbar) unterschriebenen Artikel „Der absolute Film", der am 6. Mai 1925 im *Berliner Westen* erschien, also nur die erste Vorführung vom 3. Mai zum Thema haben kann, wird tatsächlich ein Film von Hans Richter mit dem Titel *Film ist Rhythmus* beschrieben. Doch kommen einem bei genauerer Untersuchung des Textes Zweifel an der Exaktheit seiner Wiedergabe des Programmablaufs, denn er enthält nachweisliche Sachfehler. Hierzu ein Beispiel: Der nicht bekannte Autor beginnt seine eigentliche Besprechung der Programmpunkte nach einigen Einleitungsfloskeln mit den Worten:

> Nun zum Film! Die „Dreiteilige Farbensonatine" (Hirschfeld-Mack, Berlin) und „Film ist Rhythmus" (Hans Richter, Berlin) boten neue,

---

19 Vgl. Hein / Herzogenrath (Hg.): Film als Film, S. 21; Richter wiederholt diese Version in seinem Abriss: Avant-Garde Film in Germany, S. 224.

20 Goergen: Walter Ruttmann, S. 108f.

21 Ebd.

22 Vgl. Fi. (das Kürzel konnte nicht entschlüsselt werden): Der absolute Film. In: Berliner Westen (6.5.1925); Balthasar (Pseudonym für Roland Schacht): Vom Absoluten zum ganz Realen. Rubrik Rundschau. In: Das Blaue Heft Nr. 16 (15.5.1925), S. 457 (hier wird nur der Name Richters am Anfang erwähnt); Willi Wolfrad (eigentlich Wolfradt): Der absolute Film. In: Das Kunstblatt 9. Jg. (1925), Nr. 6, S. 187f.; Lisbeth Stern: Film. Rubrik Kunst. In: Sozialistische Monatshefte 32. Jg. (1926), Nr. 63, S. 504. In Auszügen wiederabgedruckt in Louise O'Konor: Viking Eggeling. Stockholm 1971, S. 252, Anm. 47. Sterns Artikel ist aus der Retrospektive geschrieben und sehr summarisch.

> erstaunlich starke, seltene Lichtblicke. Man stand absolut unter dem Bann eines göttlichen überirdischen, wirklich ungegenständlichen Geschehens, eines wunderbaren Farben-Linienspiels![23]

Ähnlich wie in John Willets *Explosion der Mitte*[24] wird hier der irrige Eindruck erweckt, bei der *Farbensonatine* handele es sich um einen Film. Ferner hat man Hirschfeld-Mack, der im Programm als Mitarbeiter des neuen Dessauer Bauhauses ausgewiesen ist, kurzerhand ins schickere Berlin versetzt. Viking Eggelings Film *Symphonie Diagonale*, der nachweislich vorgeführt wurde, erwähnt „Fi." dagegen überhaupt nicht. Von einem „Farben-Linienspiel" kann aber bei Richters Schwarzweiß-Film mit seinen blockhaften, geometrischen Formen keine Rede sein. Unter diesen Voraussetzungen drängt sich der Verdacht auf, dass der Autor dieses Artikels die verschiedenen Beiträge der Matinee durcheinandergebracht hat und/oder zwischenzeitlich abwesend war. Von daher ist diese Quelle zu disqualifizieren.

Glaubwürdiger und zuverlässiger erscheinen dagegen Roland Schachts Artikel „Vom Absoluten zum ganz Realen"[25] und Willi Wolfradts Besprechung in dem von Paul Westheim herausgegebenen *Kunstblatt*.[26] Beide bestätigen Jeanpaul Goergens Vermutung insofern, als dass sie nach dem 10. Mai 1925 erschienen waren und sich somit auf die zweite Matinee, auf der Richters Film gezeigt worden sein soll, beziehen könnten. Was Schachts Artikel im *Blauen Heft* betrifft, ist allerdings eine Einschränkung zu machen: Zwar erscheint Hans Richters Name eingangs in einer wohl dem Programmzettel entnommenen Auflistung der ‚absoluten' Filmkünstler, er taucht aber später nicht mehr auf. Anders in der Besprechung von Willi Wolfradt, einem Kritiker, der sich intensiv mit moderner Kunst auseinandersetzte. Datenverwirrung und Verwechslung der Einzelbeiträge der Matinee erscheinen bei ihm weitgehend ausgeschlossen. In Wolfradts Besprechung aber wird Richters Film in nur einem knappen Satz abgehandelt, ohne dass der zugehörige Titel genannt wird.[27] Damit wäre die Diskussion um Richters Beitrag wieder an den Ausgangspunkt zurückgekehrt: nämlich zu der Frage, welcher Film mit welchem Titel nun eigentlich auf der Matinee gezeigt wurde.

In diesem Zusammenhang ist es instruktiv, die Vorankündigungen zur Matinee zu vergleichen. In der ersten Ankündigung (*Lichtbild-Bühne*,

---

23 Fi.: Der absolute Film.

24 John Willet: Explosion der Mitte. Kunst und Politik 1917-1933. München 1981, S. 146.

25 Balthasar: Vom Absoluten zum ganz Realen, S. 457f.

26 Wolfradt: Der absolute Film, S. 187f.

27 Ebd.: „Vollends Hans Richters eingebungsloses Gestammel ist nur geeignet, die gesamte Bestrebung zu diskreditieren."

23.4.1925) werden nur „Werke von Eggeling – Berlin, Herzfeld [sic] (Bauhaus), Leger – Paris, Richter – Berlin, Ruttmann – Berlin und Piccavia [sic] – Paris“[28] aufgezählt. In einer zweiten Ankündigung in der *Lichtbild-Bühne* werden alle Titel des Programms aufgelistet, mit Ausnahme von Richters Beitrag. Dort heißt es lediglich: „Filmspiel von Hans Richter“.[29]

Die Filme von Eggeling und Ruttmann passierten am 21. April 1925, zwei Wochen vor der Uraufführung im Mai, die Zensur.[30] Am selben Tag ging auch ein Film von 45 Meter Länge durch die Zensur, Titel: *Ohne Haupttitel*, Autor: Hans Richter.[31] Dieses Zusammentreffen lässt den Schluss zu, dass der Film *Ohne Haupttitel* jenen Film bezeichnet, der für die Matinee bestimmt war. Die Existenz von vier verschiedenen Bezeichnungen – *Film ist Rhythmus*, *Rhythmus 21*, *Filmspiel*, *Ohne Haupttitel* – für einen einzigen Film, der obendrein der kürzeste Beitrag von allen auf der Matinee gezeigten war, deutet auf einen eher provisorischen Charakter des Werks hin.

Dafür spricht auch, dass Richter eigenen Angaben zufolge an seinem ‚ersten‘ Film noch Veränderungen vornahm. Legt man eine Projektionsgeschwindigkeit von 18 Bildern pro Sekunde,[32] die damals üblich war, zugrunde, ergibt sich für *Ohne Haupttitel* eine Laufzeit von ca. 2 Minuten und 12 Sekunden. Sicher ist Quantität nicht gleich Qualität. Doch ist der Grundzug des Bruchstückhaften und Vorläufigen in den frühen Filmen Hans Richters kaum zu leugnen. Ob das als bewusste Abgrenzung gegen die herkömmliche Vorstellung von einem in sich geschlossenen Kunstwerk zu werten ist, oder ob es den Problemen von Richter mit dem neuen Medium geschuldet ist, wäre zu klären. Jedenfalls sieht Theo van Doesburg schon 1923 Richters Filmbeitrag zur „Soirée du coeur à barbe“ im Théâtre Michel in Paris nur als einen sehr rudimentären, entwicklungsbedürftigen Versuch an, den er mit Reklametrickfilmen auf eine Stufe stellt.[33]

---

28 O.A.: Der „absolute“ Film. In: Lichtbild-Bühne 18. Jg. (23.4.1925), Nr. 55, S. 5; vgl. auch o.A.: Der absolute Film. In: Berliner Kunstnachrichten Nr. 18 (28.4.1925), S. 9 (fast identischer Text).

29 O.A.: Der absolute Film. In: Lichtbild-Bühne 18. Jg. (Mai 1925), Nr. 63, S. 13; vgl. auch den identischen Text in der Ankündigung o.A.: Der absolute Film. In: Der Film (1925), Nr. 18, S. 39.

30 Vgl.: Karl Wolfsohn (Hg.): Jahrbuch der Filmindustrie 2. Jg. (1923/1925). Berlin 1926, S. 526 (Eggeling) und S. 521 (Ruttmann); vgl. auch: Zensurkatalog. In: Der Film (1925), Nr. 19, S. 36.

31 Genauer Text der Zensurkarte: „ohne Haupttitel. — U. Hans Richter. — A. dito. — Uld. Deutschland — 1 Akt, 45 Meter. — 21.4.25 — B. 10336. — G.“ “In: Wolfsohn (Hg.): Jahrbuch der Filmindustrie 2. Jg. (1923/25), S. 517; vgl. auch: Zensurkatalog. In: Der Film (1925), Nr. 19, S. 36.

32 Zur Laufgeschwindigkeit von Filmen in den zwanziger Jahren vgl. Wilmesmeier: Deutsche Avantgarde und Film, S. 25, Fn. 121.

33 van Doesburg: Licht- en tijdbeelding (film), S. 59.

Bleibt noch die Frage, mit welchem Material der Film gestaltet war. Nach den oben beschriebenen Untersuchungen ist davon auszugehen, dass Richters Film, wie Goergen meint, nur am Wiederholungstermin, dem 10. Mai 1925, gezeigt wurde. Es gibt nur zwei Besprechungen, in denen überhaupt auf diesen Beitrag eingegangen wird: den erwähnten Artikel von Wolfradt und die Rezension von Hans Pander.[34]

Willi Wolfradts knappe Charakterisierung von Richters Film als „eingebungsloses Gestammel" ist für eine Identifizierung des vorgeführten Werks natürlich unbrauchbar.[35] Dagegen ist Panders Behandlung des Filmbeitrags zwar etwas ausführlicher, aber genauso negativ im Urteil. Wichtig für die Bestimmung des vorgeführten Films ist aber vor allem der Satz: „Es waren schwarze und weiße, meistens geradlinig und rechtwinklig begrenzte Flächenstücke, die sich rhythmisch veränderten und bewegten."[36] Von den drei Filmen aus Richters Filmographie, die chronologisch in Frage kommen – *Rhythmus 21*, *Rhythmus 23* und *Rhythmus 25* –, entfällt *Rhythmus 25*, da er in seiner Formensprache komplexer und – noch entscheidender – handkoloriert ist.[37]

Damit ergibt sich als mögliche Schlussfolgerung: Richter zeigte, wie er selbst andeutet, *Rhythmus 21*, der dem Material nach mit dem im Programm der Matinee angekündigten *Film ist Rhythmus* identisch ist. Allerdings bleibt bei dieser Annahme noch zu klären, warum bei der ersten Vorankündigung und der Zusatzvorführung nur provisorische Titel angegeben wurden. Schachts Bemerkung zum Ausbleiben von Richters Beitrag am ersten Matinee-Termin ist hier interessant: „Es folgte, da ein Film Hans Richters noch nicht ganz vorführungsbereit war, eine ‚diagonale Symphonie' Viking Eggelings"[38]. Die Formulierung „noch nicht ganz vorführungsbereit" deutet darauf hin, dass möglicherweise noch an ihm gearbeitet wurde. Dies lässt den Schluss zu, dass Richter der Zensurbehörde ein unfertiges Fragment vorlegte, das auch am Vorführungstermin, dem 3. Mai 1925, noch nicht ganz seinen Vorstellungen entsprach und deshalb nicht gezeigt wurde. Vorausgesetzt, Hans Panders Angaben stimmen, ergeben sich nun zwei Möglichkeiten:

1. Richter arbeitete an etwas vollkommen Neuem.
2. Richter versuchte, aus bereits vorhandenem Material durch Rekombination und/oder durch Hinzufügung Neues zu schaffen.

34 Hans Pander: Vom absoluten Film, Rubrik: Filmschau. In: Der Bildwart (1928), H. 6/7, S. 408ff.

35 Wolfradt: Der absolute Film, S. 187.

36 Pander: Vom absoluten Film, S. 408.

37 Vgl. Scheugl / Schmidt: Subgeschichte des Films, Bd. 2, S. 740.

38 Roland Schacht: Absolute Filme, Rubrik: Kunst, Wissenschaft und Leben. In: Kölnische Zeitung (15.5.1925, Abendausg.).

Schenkt man Richters Angaben in seinem Beitrag „Avant-Garde Film in Germany“ in Manvells *Experiment in the Film* Glauben, so ist letzteres der Fall gewesen:

> My *Rhythm 21*, in its original form, was never shown publicly in Berlin. Parts of it were incorporated in *Rhythm 23* which was shown at the first International avant-garde film show, together with Eggeling's, Ruttmann's and French avant-garde films, at the UFA theatre Kurfürstendamm, Berlin, 1925.[39]

Ähnlich sieht es William E. Moritz. In „Der abstrakte Film seit 1930 – Tendenzen der West Coast“[40] stellt er u.a. Betrachtungen über die von Richters frühem Schaffen erhaltenen Fragmente an. Nachdem er die „Primitivität von Richters ‚Rhythmus‘-Filmen“ und deren „Rohheit der Ausführung“ moniert hat,[41] schreibt er:

> Weiterhin kann man bei sorgfältiger Betrachtung der „Fragmente“ von „Rhythmus“, die Richter bereitstellte, sehen, dass die widersprüchlichen diagonalen Kompositionselemente am Ende des sogenannten „Rhythmus 21“ direkt zu dem Anfang des sogenannten „Rhythmus 23“ gehören. Abgesehen davon, dass sie den vorgetäuschten Formalismus von „Rhythmus 21“ verderben, geben sie sehr wahrscheinlich zu erkennen, dass die Filme, die wir als „Rhythmus 21“ und „Rhythmus 23“ bezeichnet sehen, tatsächlich ein einziger Film, „Rhythmus“, sind, der 1923 oder 1924 hergestellt wurde.[42]

Unter Berücksichtigung all dieser Überlegungen kann mit Vorbehalt konstatiert werden, dass Richter nur am 10. Mai 1925, dem Wiederholungstermin der Matinee, einen Beitrag vorführte, der in irgendeiner Form aus vorhandenem Material zusammengesetzt war, Material, das vor Juni 1925 und nach 1920 entstanden war.

Dass diese Feststellungen so vage ausfallen müssen, liegt nicht zuletzt an dem neuen Selbstverständnis der Künstler und ihrer neuen Einstellung zum ‚Kunstwerk‘ nach dem Ersten Weltkrieg. Helga Kliemann schreibt in ihrem Buch über die Novembergruppe, deren Mitglied Richter laut eigenen Angaben von Anfang bis Ende war: „Auch der Gedanke vom anonymen Kunstwerk wurde diskutiert, die Bilder sollten nur monogrammiert

---

39 Richter: Avant-Garde Film in Germany, S. 223.

40 William E. Moritz: Der abstrakte Film seit 1930 – Tendenzen der West Coast. In: Birgit Hein / Wulf Herzogenrath (Hg.): Film als Film. Stuttgart 1978, S. 128-148, hier: S. 128f.

41 Ebd.; Vgl. auch die kritischen Bemerkungen in Heinz Pramann: Animation – bewegte Bilder. Siegen 1981, S. 77: „Wenden wir uns zunächst dem Rhythmusfilm von Richter zu, obwohl die Wirkung des Films auf den Betrachter nicht hält, was das Thema andeutet.“

42 Moritz: Der abstrakte Film seit 1930 – Tendenzen der West Coast, S. 128 f.

werden."[43] Eggeling, mit dem Richter ca. zwei Jahre zusammenarbeitete, hat keines seiner Werke signiert und nur zwei datiert.

In Anbetracht dieser damals verbreiteten Haltung kann man Richters Zensureintrag *Ohne Haupttitel* auch als revolutionäre Geste deuten. (In völligem Gegensatz dazu stand Ruttmanns Habitus. Seinen Titeln, die er der Zensur unterbreitete, stellte Ruttmann seinen Familiennamen voran; zusätzlich setzte er bei der Autorangabe vor seinen Namen die Bezeichnung „Kunstmaler".) Bei Richter und Eggeling, ähnlich wie bei Hirschfeld-Mack, offenbart sich im Verhalten gegenüber den eigenen Werken ein Widerstreit zwischen romantischem, ‚bürgerlichem' Geniegedanken und sozialistischem Kollektiv-Ideal. Letzteres war Teil der Vorstellungen von einer neuen Kunst, die in der Novembergruppe besonders in der Anfangszeit virulent waren. Die Ambivalenz dieser Haltung äußerte sich in einem Schwanken zwischen einerseits dem demonstrativen Zurücknehmen der eigenen Person im Sinne eines modernen Typus von „Kunstingenieur"[44] und andererseits einem Herausstreichen der individuellen Leistung – Ausdruck der Sorge um Ruhm und Nachruhm. War man einerseits bestrebt, das Kunstwerk seiner ‚Aura' zu berauben – und dies war ja die große Chance, die Walter Benjamin im Film erkannt zu haben glaubte –, so wollte man andererseits doch offenbar nicht auf den Ruhm verzichten, als Avantgardepionier das *erste* Farblichtspiel (Ludwig Hirschfeld-Mack), den *ersten* abstrakten Film oder das erste Fotogramm geschaffen zu haben.

Im Falle Richters bedeutete dieses zwiespältige Verhältnis zum Kunstschaffen, dass er in den zwanziger Jahren seine ersten Filmexperimente wie gewöhnliche Werkstücke behandelte, die jeden Augenblick umgearbeitet werden konnten – mit dem Ergebnis, dass er selbst später kaum noch in der Lage war, vor der Filmgeschichte schlüssig zu belegen, wann und wo genau welche Filme von ihm gezeigt wurden. Dies war umso gravierender, als deren Wirkungsgkraft von vornherein durch ihre Kürze stark eingeschränkt wurde (bis hin zur Gefahr, übersehen zu werden: siehe Richters Anekdote mit dem älteren Herrn und dem Kneifer). Um die Verwirrung späterer Filmhistoriker vollständig zu machen, wird in Textillustrationen zu Richters frühen Filmexperimenten in *De Stijl* und *MA* nicht immer deutlich gemacht, ob es sich lediglich um noch nicht ausgeführte Filmentwürfe oder

43 Vgl. Kliemann: Novembergruppe, S. 11.

44 Bezeichnend ist in diesem Zusammenhang Moholy-Nagys roter „Monteur-Anzug", den er im Bauhaus trug: vgl. die Fotografie von Lucia Moholy-Nagy, abgedruckt in: Magdalena Droste: Bauhaus 1919 – 1933. Köln 1990, S. 61 und Willet: Explosion der Mitte, S. 80; Allgemeine Literatur zum Thema Avantgarde zwischen revolutionärem Pathos und Wirklichkeit: z.B. Karin Hirdina: Pathos der Sachlichkeit. Ost-Berlin 1981; Vgl. auch Josef Franks Vortrag „Was ist modern?" (1930), abgedruckt in: Die Form 5. Jg. (1930), H. 14, S. 399ff.; Die Erwiderung auf Josef Franks kritische Äußerungen veröffentlichte Roger Ginsburger unter dem gleichen Titel in: Die Form 6. Jg. (1931), H. 1, S. 6ff.

um Einzelbilder bzw. Phasenzeichnungen aus bereits realisierten Filmen handelt.[45] Diese Konfusion setzt sich in anderen Publikationen fort. Gleichviel, ob in zeitgenössischen oder in neueren Veröffentlichungen, immer wieder finden sich widersprüchliche oder falsche Angaben zu Standfotos und Zeichnungen von Richter.

‚Dada-Hans' als virtuoser VJ. Richter als souveräner Macher des ersten abstrakten Films. *Rhythmus 21* als der absoluteste der absoluten Avantgardefilme. Wer es hagiographisch mag, lässt es so stehen. „So schwer es uns technisch und ästhetisch damals fiel, sich in diesem neuen Gebiet auszudrücken, so leicht fällt es den Heutigen"[46], schreibt Hans Richter 1968 im Vorwort zu seinem wiederveröffentlichten Buch *Filmgegner von heute – Filmfreunde von morgen* (Erstpublikation 1929) über seine frühen Filmexperimente. Richter und sein damaliger Freund Viking Eggeling hatten große Schwierigkeiten bei der Durchführung ihrer Experimente. Beide waren auf fremde Hilfe angewiesen. Das bedeutete auch finanzielle Investitionen: Unter anderem musste ein Profi-Kameramann stundenweise bezahlt und neue Hardware angeschafft werden. Gerade in der Anfangsphase war die neue Filmtechnik nicht nur eine begeistert aufgenommene, kreative Herausforderung, sondern auch eine große Hürde für die beiden. Die technischen Aspekte wurden dabei von ihnen wohl über weite Strecken eher als notwendiges Übel angesehen und nicht so sehr als Bereicherung der gestalterischen Ausdrucksmittel ausgeschöpft. Hans Richter fühlte sich immer vornehmlich als Maler. Diese Priorität in seinem Schaffen betont er noch 1971, fünf Jahre vor seinem Tod, in *Hans Richter by Hans Richter*: „ich bin Maler, und ich werde ein Maler bleiben, der Filme macht"[47]. Und das bedeutet: eben kein Filmkunstingenieur, der nebenbei auch malt. Nur in diesem vielschichtigen Spannungsfeld von kreativen Ideen einerseits und technischen Anforderungen und Sachzwängen andererseits ist Hans Richters *Rhythmus 21* zu sehen und zu verstehen.

---

45 Vgl. z.B. die Illustrationen zu Theo van Doesburg: Abstracte Filmbeelding. In: De Stijl 4. Jg. (1921), Nr. 5, S. 74. Im Illustrationstext heißt es lediglich: „Hans Richter – Viking Eggeling – Abstrakte Filmbeelding – Middenpartij"; In De Stijl 5. Jg. (1922), Nr. 2, zwischen S. 24 und 25, erscheint eine Abbildung mit dem Beitext: „Hans Richter – Fragment Filmkompositie Zwaar-Licht" (d.h. Filmkomposition Schwer-Leicht). In Richters Beschreibung der Abbildung, in: Hans Richter: Film, die erst in Nr. 6 (1922), S. 91f. erscheint, wird nicht klar, ob es sich um einen Entwurf oder um einen verwirklichten Film handelt. Ähnlich verhält es sich mit den beiden Richter-Illustrationen mit dem Titel „Filmmoment" zu Theo van Doesburg: Licht- en Tijdbeelding (Film). In: De Stijl 6. Jg. (1923), Nr. 5, S. 57 und Hans Richter: Film. In: De Stijl 6. Jg. (1923), S. 65.

46 Hans Richter: Vorwort zur Neuausgabe. In: Filmgegner von heute – Filmfreunde von morgen. Zürich 1968, S. 3.

47 Cleve Gray (Hg.): Hans Richter by Hans Richter. London 1971, S. 152.

Architektur

Klaus Müller-Richter

> Die eigentliche Sphäre des Films ist die des „bewegten" Raumes, der „bewegten" Fläche, der „bewegten" Linie. Bewegt: d.h. Raum, Fläche, Linie vielmals und nacheinander.
> Dieser Raum ist nicht architektonisch oder plastisch, sondern zeitlich, d.h. das Licht bildet durch Wechsel der Qualität und Quantität (Hell, Dunkel, Farbe) Lichträume, die nicht voluminös sind, sondern eben nur durch *Folge* das zum Raum machen, was, wenn man den Zeitverlauf unterbräche, nur Fläche, Linie, Punkt wäre.[1]
> —Hans Richter, 1923

Hans Richters generelle Beschreibung des Mediums Film ist, auf *Rhythmus 21* bezogen, so rätselhaft im Allgemeinen wie phänomenal einleuchtend im Konkreten. Rätselhaft ist zunächst, warum Richter den Film auf eine Dimension reduziert und zugleich erweitert, die der Projektionstechnologie des Kinematografischen mit ihrer zweidimensionalen Filmleinwand eigentlich gar nicht eignet: Räumlichkeit, die eher der Skulptur und vor allem der Architektur zukommt. Der folgende Beitrag zeigt, wie Richters *Rhythmus 21* mit den zeitgenössischen avantgardistischen Bestrebungen in der ‚Baukunst' zusammenhängt. Im ersten Teil markiere ich Aspekte und Verfahren des Films, die ihre interessante Entsprechung in der Architektur und im Architekturdiskurs der 20er Jahre des 20. Jahrhunderts haben. Hierbei konzentriere ich mich zunächst exemplarisch auf Ludwig Hilberseimer und Ludwig Mies van der Rohe (zweiter Teil). Im dritten Teil verweise ich schließlich auf die Nähe von Richters Film zu ausstellungs- sowie bühnentechnischen und städtebaulichen Raum-Utopien Friedrich Kieslers.

I

Natürlich kennen auch die piktorialen Aufzeichnungssysteme in Wissenschaft und Kunst seit langem die Darstellung von Raumrelationen zwischen ihren im Bildraum aufgezeichneten Dingen: den Einzug einer Horizontlinie, die den Bildraum in Vorder- und Hintergrund teilt; Größenverhältnisse, an denen sich die relative Lage der Objekte zueinander im Raum ablesen lassen; Überlappungen der Gegenstände, aus denen die Staffelung der Objekte im Raum hervorgeht; Verblauung der Hintergrundgegenstände; vor allem aber (fluchtpunkt-)perspektivische Ordnungen.

Es ist wohl zunächst Richters Elementarismus geschuldet, also seiner Idee, alle Phänomene auf möglichst wenige Elemente und deren Kombinati-

1 Hans Richter: Film … . In: De Stijl (nach Juni 1923), Nr. 5, S. 65-66, hier: S. 65.

onen zurückzuführen, dass er in *Rhythmus 21* von perspektivischen Verfahren gar keinen Gebrauch macht. Er setzt allein auf Flächenüberschneidungen und Größenunterschiede, um Raumeffekte zu erzeugen. Es scheint, als würde Richter dem neusachlichen Postulat, durch Experimente das Material und seine konstruktiven Möglichkeiten erst analysieren zu wollen, emphatisch nachkommen. Das heißt hier, allein von der materiellen Gegebenheit des Mediums Film, seiner grundsätzlichen Zweidimensionalität nämlich, auszugehen und diese auf seine räumlichen und zeitlichen Möglichkeiten hin zu prüfen. Zugleich aber hat die Abwesenheit perspektivischer Raumordnung einen der Zweidimensionalität zuwiderlaufenden Effekt. Denn sie schafft einen über den Bild- oder Screen-Raum hinausgehenden kontinuierlichen Raum, in dem der Betrachterstandpunkt des Zuschauers undefinierbar bleibt. Er kann seine Position nur noch relativ zu den oft widersprüchlich bewegten Gegenständen wahrnehmen. Ein ‚Sehen in Bewegung' ist die Folge.

Ein weiterer Grund für Richters Verzicht auf das Perspektivische lässt sich aus seinem Versuch erschließen, Räumlichkeit im Film allein aus der temporalen Dimension des Films entstehen zu lassen: Denn in der Perspektive würden Flächen auch im angehaltenen Einzelbild bereits als räumlich oder voluminös erscheinen, als statische Körper in einem (unbewegten) Raum – was Richter in diesem Kontext als Strategie mimetischer Kunsttraditionen denunziert.[2] Die Aspekte der Bewegung und der Konstruktion des Raumes würden wegfallen. In *Rhythmus 21* entsteht, wie Richter einleuchtend ausführt, der sich permanent verändernde Raum allein durch die zeitliche Folge. Dies geschieht beispielsweise dadurch, dass erst im zeitlichen Hintereinander die größer und kleiner werdenden Rechtecke als ein zusammengehöriger Bewegungs-„Vorgang"[3] im Raum wahrgenommen werden können; wodurch auch und gleichzeitig der Raum allererst erzeugt wird.

Das ist wichtig, weil man es in seiner Selbstverständlichkeit gerne übersieht und Richter es offenkundig ausstellt bzw. seinen Zuschauern bewusst machen will: Würden wir die Verschiebungen der polaren Farbgrenzen oder die sich vergrößernden und verkleinernden Rechtecke nicht als identische, sich aber in der Dimension der Zeit verändernde Flächen, Quadrate und Rechtecke verstehen, dann wäre *Rhythmus 21* in der Tat nichts anderes als ein „einfaches Nacheinander von Formen", das „an und für sich sinnlos ist".[4] Richter formuliert es auch genau so. Er setzt dann fort, „dass *Sinn* erst durch die Kunst geschaffen werden kann. Für diese neue Kunst ist es absolut erforderlich, ein*deutige* Elemente zu haben."[5]

---

2 Vgl. ebd.

3 Hans Richter: Prinzipielles zur Bewegungskunst. In: De Stijl 4. Jg. (1921), Nr. 7, S. 9-12, hier: S. 9.

4 Ebd., S. 12.

5 Ebd., Kursivierung von mir. Sie betont Richters Einsicht in die Deutungsnotwendigkeit bzw. die Syntheseleistung des Subjekts.

Der Film verdankt seine postulierte Einheit und Ein*deutig*keit natürlich nicht allein dem apperzeptiven Urteil des Zuschauers, dass Objekte in kontinuierlicher Bewegung auch dann noch dieselben sind, wenn sie sich zu einem späteren Zeitpunkt an einer anderen Raumstelle befinden oder dann eine andere Ausdehnung haben. Richter setzt darüber hinaus eine Vielzahl rhythmischer Verfahren ein, um die Einheit seines Filmes zu erreichen: So sehen wir häufig gegenläufige Bewegungen, etwa wenn sich auf der schwarzen Leinwand von beiden Rändern zur Mitte hin vertikal das Weiß ausbreitet, der Vorgang umgekehrt und als umgekehrter wiederholt wird (0:00-0:05); oder wenn dieses Syntagma nach einem kurzen Zwischenspiel in variierter Form wieder aufgegriffen wird: nämlich als horizontaler Vorgang (0:12-0:17). Solche mikrosyntaktischen Einheiten und variierten Wiederholungen sind schließlich in eine den ganzen Film übergreifende Makroentwicklung eingepasst, die sich in musikalischen Termini durchaus als Exposition, Durchführung und Reprise beschreiben lässt.[6] Ein Beispiel: Gegen Ende des Films steigert sich die Frequenz und Anzahl nach vorne und nach hinten pulsierender geometrischer Formen (2:08-2:10), dann kehrt der Film wieder zu bereits etablierten einfacheren und ruhigeren Syntagmen zurück (Größensprünge des weißen Quadrats [0:47; 2:14-2:18]). Ganz am Ende des Films wird die erste Sequenz im Sinne einer Coda leicht variiert wiederholt (2:52-Ende).

Als Fazit unserer Filmanalyse können wir *Rhythmus 21* als einen Text beschreiben, dessen oberstes Prinzip im Spiel mit polaren Gegensätzen oder scharfen Kontrasten besteht. Diese Kontraste werden gleichzeitig – scheinbar paradox – durch Figuren der Wiederholung, Spiegelung (Wiederholung in kontrastiver Farbigkeit oder Bewegung in Gegenrichtung, Rückkehr zum Ausgangspunkt/-zustand) und Variation zu einer Texteinheit verbunden. Dabei ist der Film elementar und abstrakt zugleich.[7] Elementar, weil das Formvokabular auf Fläche und Linie begrenzt ist. Abstrakt, weil es nicht um „Handlung" im Raum geht, nicht um die Darstellung von „Naturobjekten" im Raum.[8] Es geht hier allein um die Reflexion des Räumlichen selbst. Richters Film hat jeden die Wirklichkeit imitativ wiedergebenden Anspruch abgestreift. Es geht in ihm allein um die Frage und Analyse, wie Raumeindrücke in der Zeit und durch die Zeit entstehen. Es ist kein Zufall, dass Richter an dieser Stelle die kantische Diktion des Transzendentalen aufgreift: Weil es um die Bedingung der Möglichkeit der Raumerfahrung

6 Richters und Eggelings Vorarbeiten zu *Rhythmus 21* tragen stets musikalische Titel: *Komposition*, *Präludium*, *Orchester*; auch in den theoretischen Texten zum elementaren Film ist die musikalische Metaphorik allgegenwärtig.

7 Vgl. hierzu den Beitrag „Elementares Kino" in diesem Band.

8 Mit diesen Begriffen beschreibt Richter nach seiner Ansicht Reste imitativer Kunst noch in den avancierten Bildlogiken Picassos, Dérains und Cézannes. Siehe Richter: Prinzipielles zur Bewegungskunst, S. 9.

geht, nicht um konkrete, empirische oder historische Räume, in denen etwas geschieht.

II

Auch wenn das Zitat, das wir als Motto gewählt haben, eine Verbindung zwischen Film und Architektur herunterzuspielen scheint, ergibt sich eine erste grundsätzliche Verbindung zwischen Richters Film und der Architektur gerade schon aus der ,transzendentalen' Betrachtung des Raumes im Kontext der Filmkunst, wie sie Richter in „Prinzipielles zur Bewegungskunst" theoretisch entwickelt und in *Rhythmus 21* praktisch umsetzt. Der Architekt und Architekturhistoriker Ludwig Hilberseimer, mit Richter durch seine Mitarbeit an dessen Zeitschrift *G. Zeitschrift für elementare Gestaltung* (1923-1926) verbunden, sieht ebenso, und hierin stellvertretend für viele Architekten am Beginn der 20er Jahre, Raum nicht als schlicht Gegebenes, sondern vielmehr als komplexes Produkt kultureller, ästhetischer, wahrnehmungspsychologischer und epistemologischer Praktiken.[9]

Hilberseimer folgert daraus zunächst die Forderung, dass das zu bauende Einzelgebäude stets in seiner Beziehung zum Stadtkontext zu konzipieren ist, als Zelle „in einer umfassenden Organisation wechselseitiger Bedürfnisse und Beziehungen"[10] zur Umwelt. Diese Überzeugung stimmt zusammen mit der grundlegenden Idee einer Vermittlung von Innen (des Gebäudes) und Außen, wie wir sie bei Mies van der Rohes und Siegfried Ebelings Konzept des Raums als durchlässige und flexible Membran antreffen – Ideen wiederum, die sich geistesgeschichtlich verbinden lassen mit der für die 20er Jahre typischen antianthropozentrischen Kritik an emotionaler Innerlichkeit (des Expressionismus), an Individualismus und an dem aufklärerischen Ideal einer bewusstseinsphilosophischen Subjektivität, die dualistisch streng einer Objektwelt entgegengesetzt ist.

Konkrete Verbindungen zwischen *Rhythmus 21* und dem Themenfeld der Architektur sind auch über persönliche Verbindungen Richters plausibilisiert, verweisen auf die Evidenz phänomenaler Ähnlichkeiten zwischen Standbildern aus *Rhythmus 21* und architektonischen Grundrissen oder begründen sich aus manifestantistischen Engführungen der Schwesterkünste

---

9 Diese Einsicht in die Konstruktivität räumlicher Konstellationen verdankt die Kunstdebatte der Raumsoziologie Georg Simmels (1903). Denn schon bei Simmel hieß es, dass die eingezogenen Grenzen zwischen den Einheiten des Raumes keine natürlichen Gegebenheiten seien, sondern symbolisch-soziologische Konstrukte. Vgl. Georg Simmel: Soziologie des Raumes. In: Georg Simmel, Gesamtausgabe, hrsg. v. Ottheim Rammstedt, Bd. 7. Frankfurt a.M. 1995, S. 132-183, hier: S. 133: „Die Grenze ist nicht eine räumliche Tatsache mit soziologischen Wirkungen, sondern eine soziologische Tatsache, die sich räumlich formt."

10 Ludwig Hilberseimer: Der Wille zur Architektur. In: Das Kunstblatt 7. Jg. (1923), Nr. 5, S. 133-140, hier: S. 139.

Film und Architektur. Schließlich beruhen sie auf der Gleichartigkeit der in beiden Bereichen eingesetzten Verfahren und Techniken.

Den Kontakt zwischen Richter und Mies van der Rohe hat der Schriftsteller, Maler, Bildhauer und Architekt Theo van Doesburg hergestellt. Er begründet sein Beharren auf einer Begegnung der beiden mit phänomenalen Ähnlichkeiten zwischen Richters graphischen Vorarbeiten zu *Rhythmus 21* (*Präludium* [1919/20], siehe Abb.1) und Mies' Entwürfen von Häusern aus den Jahren um 1920 (siehe Abb. 2). Diese kommen durch ihre Kombination von schmucklosen, geometrisch angeordneten Baukörpern und ihrem Grundriss aus angrenzenden oder sich überlappenden Rechtecken Richters Arbeiten sehr nahe.[11]

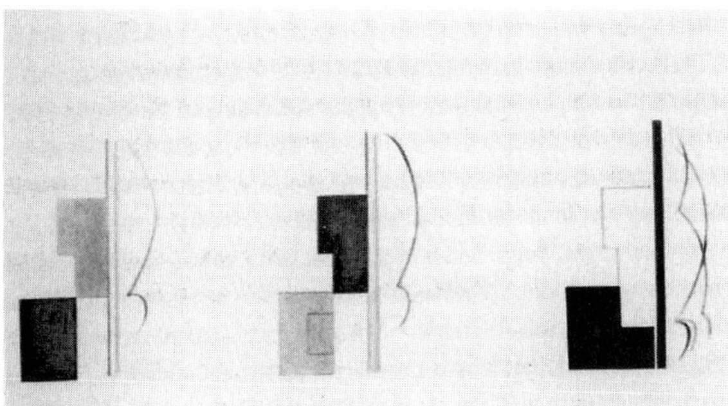

Abb. 1: Hans Richter:
Drei Momente der Komposition *Schwer-Leicht (Präludium)*.

Aus dem Kontakt resultiert eine intensive Zusammenarbeit, die ihren ersten Niederschlag in der Debütausgabe der Zeitschrift *G* (Juli 1923) findet. Auf dem großformatigen Einblattdruck liest man zusammen auf einer Seite: Mies' Bürohausentwurf in Text und Bild, Raoul Hausmanns Essay „Vom sprechenden Film zur Optophonetik" und der zweite Teil von van Doesburgs Manifest „Zur Elementaren Gestaltung", in dem er der Architektur die elementaren Mittel „Raum-Zeit-Linie" und Fläche zuordnet.

Herausgehoben durch seine querformatige Ausrichtung liegt über diesen drei Texten ein Filmstreifen aus einem Elementarfilmprojekt Richters mit dazugehörigen Erläuterungen. Dort heißt es: „Der Film vermittelt in seinem Ablauf (Vorführung) ganz eigentlich die Spannungs- und Kontrastverhältnisse des Lichts. Diese Verhältnisse bestehen zwischen hell und dunkel,

11 Detlef Mertins: Architektur des Werdens: Mies van der Rohe und die Avantgarde. In: Terence Riley / Barry Bergdoll (Hg.): Mies in Berlin. Die Berliner Jahre 1907-1938. München 2002, S. 107-133, hier: S. 115.

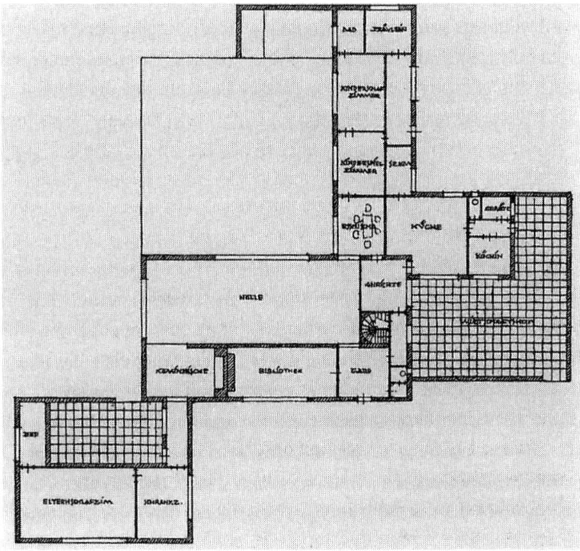

Abb. 2: Ludwig Mies van der Rohe: Haus Lessing,
Potsdam-Neubabelsberg (1923).

groß und klein, schnell und langsam, horizontal und vertikal etc. etc."[12] Die Anordnung der Texte im Seitenlayout und die Themenkonzentration auf Film und Architektur, nicht zuletzt die Verwendung eines identischen Beschreibungsvokabulars belegen die Überzeugung Richters (wenn nicht aller Autoren), dass die Umsetzung einer Programmatik ‚elementarer Gestaltung' zunächst und vor allem von diesen beiden ‚Künsten' zu erhoffen ist.

Auf dem Titelblatt der Septembernummer von *G* stellt Mies van der Rohe – er ist inzwischen im Redaktionsteam von *G* und steuert die Druckkosten bei – seinen Entwurf des *Landhauses in Eisenbeton* vor. Ein Vergleich der zahlreichen Kohle- und Pastellzeichnungen des Landhauses zeigt ebenso wie ein Abgleich der in *G* publizierten Modellfotografie des Landhauses mit erhaltenen Originalen sehr eindringlich, dass und wie Mies mit verschiedenen Fassadenmaterialien und -farben experimentiert, um die von Richter an seinen Filmen hervorgehobene Idee des polaren Kontrastes als Grundelement der Gestaltung auch architektonisch umzusetzen. Auf der Fotografie koloriert Mies etwa den Sichtbeton weiß nach, verdunkelt Fenster und Teile der Außengestaltung, mit dem intendierten Effekt, dass der Kontrast im Modell erhöht wird und die einzelnen Baukörper im Gesamtkomplex artikulierter hervortreten (siehe Abb. 3 und 4).

12 G. Material zur elementaren Gestaltung I (Juli 1923), o.P.

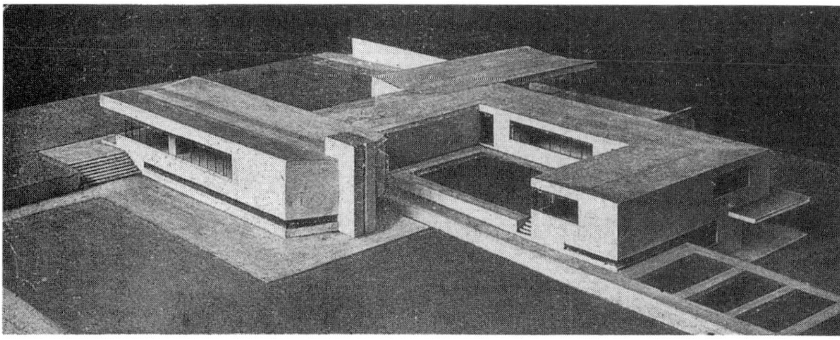

Abb. 3: Bearbeitete Fotografie des Modells *Landhaus in Eisenbeton.*

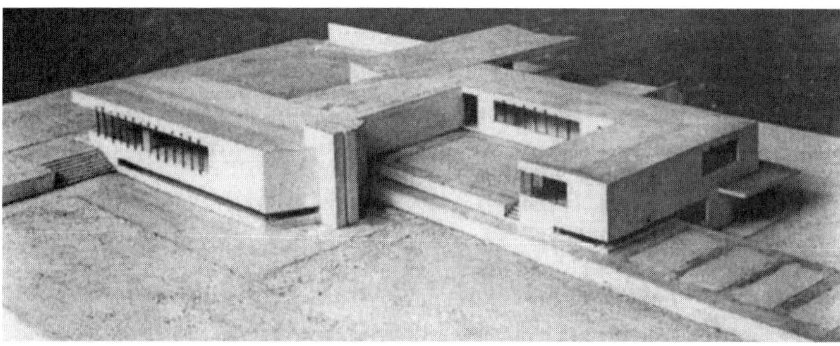

Abb. 4: Originalfotografie.

III

Anders als Mies van der Rohe ist der österreichische Bühnenbauer, Ausstellungsarchitekt und Stadtvisionär Friedrich Kiesler weitestgehend unbekannt geblieben. In Richters *G* publiziert er das kurze Manifest „Stadt in der Luft“[13], das in einer ausführlicheren Version unter dem Titel „Manifest. Vitalbau-Raumstadt-Funktionelle-Architektur“ in der holländischen Avantgardezeitschrift *De Stijl* veröffentlicht wurde, und zwar zusammen mit einem anderen Text Kieslers, in dem er sein innovatives Befestigungssystem für Exponate, das so genannte „Leger-Träger-Ausstellungssystem“

13 G. Zeitschrift für elementare Gestaltung IV (März 1926). Reprint herausgegeben von Marion von Hofacker, München 1986, S. 92.

vorstellt.[14] Kieslers Manifest fordert in drastischen Bildern (Wohnungen als Steinsärge) und in der typischen Oppositions- und Überbietungsrhetorik des Manifestantismus eine „Umwandlung des sphärischen Raums in Städte", eine Raumstadt, die „frei im Raume schwebt", er verlangt, „uns von der Erde los[zu]lösen", „ein System von Spannungen (tension) im freien Raume" zu bilden, eine Architektur, die der „Elastizität der Lebensfunktion adäquat ist".[15]

Das Nebeneinander von Überlegungen zum Stadt- und Museumsraum ist dabei keineswegs Zufall, es folgt einer kuriosen Strategie Kieslers. Denn er flankiert die Präsentation seines Ausstellungssystems auf der Exposition International des Arts Décoratifs et Industriels Modernes in Paris 1925 mit Pressekonferenzen und Flugblättern und lanciert es darin zugleich als Modell zukünftiger Megacities, die – scheinbar absurd – in der Luft schweben und dem Bewohner in diesem endlosen Raum jeden definierten Standpunkt nehmen (siehe Abb. 5).

In *Rhythmus 21* wird die Frage nach Raum im Film zur wahrnehmungstheoretischen Grundfrage abstrahiert. Der Verzicht Richters auf perspektivische Verfahren bzw. Richters Raumerzeugung allein auf der Basis sich ändernder planer geometrischer Formen hat – so hatten wir gesagt – auch den Effekt, dass der Zuschauer seine eigene Position nicht mehr absolut und statisch, in Relation zum filmisch Präsentierten definieren kann. Die Idee des archimedischen Punktes als eines angenommenen ‚absoluten Punktes' außerhalb des Experimentaufbaus wird negiert. Detlef Mertins hat das so formuliert: *Rhythmus 21* suggeriere eine „umfassende fließende und abstrakte Räumlichkeit, in der der Betrachter schwerelos im endlosen, zeitlosen Spiel von Expansion und Kontraktion, Lichtkontrasten und rhythmischer Bewegung schwebt."[16]

Kiesler hat diese Zusammenführung von Dynamisierung und Entgrenzung in einem monistischen Einheitsraum des Lebens – ein Grundgedanke des Vitalismus, dem hier beide folgen – zunächst in den Entwürfen zu seiner so genannten *Raumbühne* zu verwirklichen gesucht. Diese stellt er auf der Internationalen Ausstellung neuer Theatertechnik im Jahre 1924 in Wien als Großmodell vor. Die Gestaltung der Bühne als spiralförmig nach oben laufende Bahn intendiert die Auflösung des dramatischen, an

---

14 Friedrich Kiesler: Ausstellungssystem Leger und Träger. In: De Stijl 8. Jg. (1925), Nr. 10/11, S. 137-141; Friedrich Kiesler: Manifest. Vitalbau-Raumstadt-Funktionelle-Architektur. In: De Stijl 8. Jg. (1925), Nr. 10/11, S. 144-146; In *G* ist die Verbindung zwischen Ausstellungssystemen und Stadt-/Architekturmodellen angedeutet durch drei Fotografien der Ausstellungssysteme, deren Unterschrift das schwebende Traggerüst der Ausstellungsarchitektur als Demonstration der „Möglichkeit einer schwebenden Architektur" lanciert. In: G IV, S. 92.

15 Kiesler: Manifest, S. 142ff.

16 Mertins: Architektur des Werdens, S. 128.

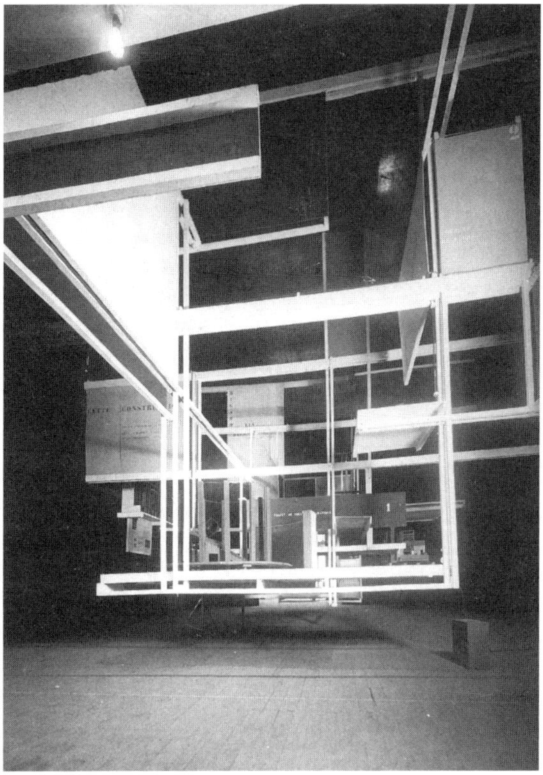

Abb. 5: Kieslers Weiterentwicklung seines Ausstellungssystems.

Charakter und Dialog orientierten Theaters in Richtung auf die Inszenierung reiner Bewegung elementarer Formen; damit geht aber das rezeptionstheoretische Postulat der Aufhebung statischer Wahrnehmungspositionen und -achsen einher. In ihrer visionären Variante sollte sich im Theaterraum schließlich das Publikum um die ebenfalls rotierende Bühne drehen. Privilegierte die Guckkastenbühne eine starre Blicklinie, fordert bei Kiesler die zentrale, von allen Seiten von Zuschauern umgebene Raumbühne zusammen mit der Spiralform der Railway-Bühne eine Dynamisierung der theatralen Gestaltung und Wahrnehmung.

Kieslers Entwurf eines Ausstellungssystems basiert auf einer ähnlichen Idee. Obwohl Kiesler zunächst ökonomische Argumente vorbrachte – Kosten, maschinelle Herstellbarkeit seiner Teile, schneller Auf- und Abbau, seine Wiederverwendbarkeit, nicht zuletzt die Multiplizierung der Ausstellungsfläche im Raum – geht es auch hier vorrangig um den Versuch, die Blickführung des Betrachters und seine Stellung im Raum zu dynamisieren. Die verschieden großen rechteckigen Wände und Auflagen, orthogonal zueinander angeordnet, zwingen den Zuschauer, den Blick zu heben und zu senken, sich zu drehen, sich in komplexen Choreografien durch den Ausstellungsraum zu bewegen (statt nur an der Wand entlang). Es heißt, die Arbeiten können im *Leger-Träger-System* „nur sukzessiv erfasst werden", wodurch ein „optisches Überraschungsmoment" entsteht.[17]

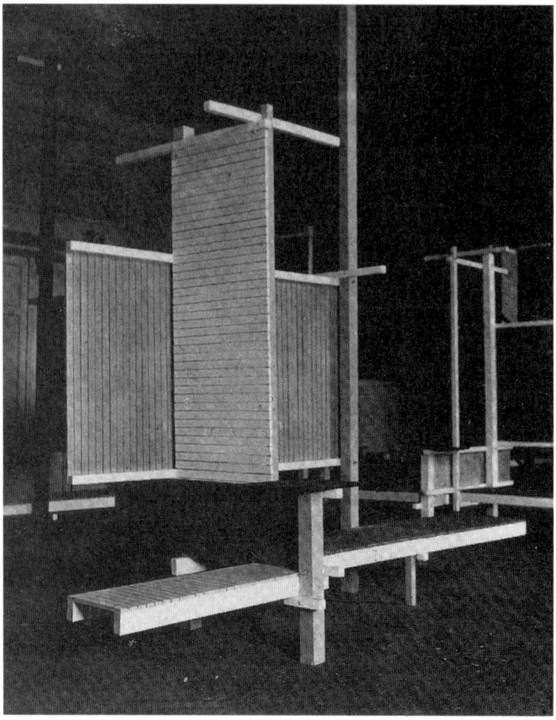

Abb. 6: Kieslers *Leger-Träger-System.*

Die radikalsten und bis ins Absurde reichenden Konsequenzen aus Richters Aufhebung der Trennung zwischen Zuschauer und Medium in einem grenzenlosen, multirelationalen Einheitsraum hat Kiesler in seinem Manifest „Stadt in der Luft" bzw. „Manifest. Vitalbau-Raumstadt-Funktionelle-Architektur" gezogen. Dabei ist deutlich, dass es Kiesler immer zugleich um konkrete bautechnische Aspekte, um das subjektive Raumempfinden der Bewohner und schließlich um symbolische Operationen im Kontext des architektur-manifestantistischen Diskurses geht.

Wenn es in dem Manifest heißt: „Uns von der Erde loslösen, Aufgabe der statischen Achse. [...] Keine Mauern, keine Fundamente"[18], dann ist die

17 Kiesler: Ausstellungssystem Leger und Träger, S. 141.

18 Kiesler: Manifest, S. 144.

Negation der Statik sowohl als ein vitalistischer Angriff auf eine an Monumentalität orientierte Steinarchitektur zu verstehen, als auch als Vision einer Wohnung gedacht, die nach außen transparent ist und eine flexible, sich den Bedürfnissen der Bewohner anpassende Raumform besitzt. In dieser Raumform (Kiesler nennt sie ‚Sphäroid') werden die senkrecht nach unten laufenden statischen Kraftlinien in einen Komplex multidirektionaler Zug- und Druckverhältnisse überführt. So lehnt Kiesler auch Le Corbusiers Wolkenkratzer ab, weil diese, obwohl mit modernen Baumaterialien konstruiert, den Aspekt des flächenorientierten und bodenbezogenen Statischen betonen und die Säulen das freie Bewegen der Bewohner behindern. Um gegen die ‚Erdenschwere' und die Statik eines verkrusteten bürgerlichen Lebens den Aspekt des Schwebens und der vitalen Spannung im Großstadtkontext zu realisieren, entwirft er horizontal gelegte Wolkenkratzer – Ideen, die wie El Lissitzkys „Wolkenbügel"[19] von 1924 nie realisiert wurden.

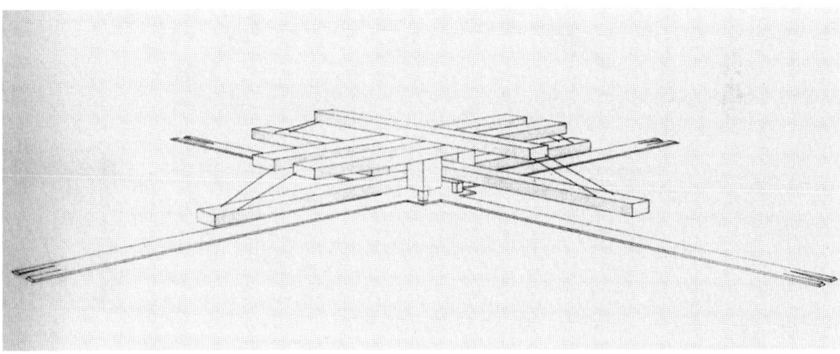

Abb. 7: Kieslers Entwurf eines schwebenden Wolkenkratzers.

Das vermeintliche Schweben des Baukörpers simuliert ein Gleichgewicht zwischen Erdanziehung und Auftrieb, gegenläufige Kräfte, die sich gegenseitig aufzuheben scheinen. Dieser Gedanke Kieslers entspricht strukturell Richters Anspruch, in seinen Filmen extreme „Spannungs- und Kontrastverhältnisse"[20] zu einer organischen Einheit oder einem Gleichgewicht zu führen – relationale und prozessuale Begriffe, die im Avantgardediskurs der 20er Jahre das statische und essentialistische Konzept der Harmonie weitgehend ablösen.

Vor dem Hintergrund einer an Prozess, Energie und Impuls orientierten vitalistischen Philosophie und Biologie verweist das Konzept des „Gleichgewichts" auf die angestrebte Versöhnung der dynamistischen Idee

19 El Lissitzky: 1929. Russland: Architektur für eine Weltrevolution. Berlin 1965, S. 79.

20 G I, o.P.

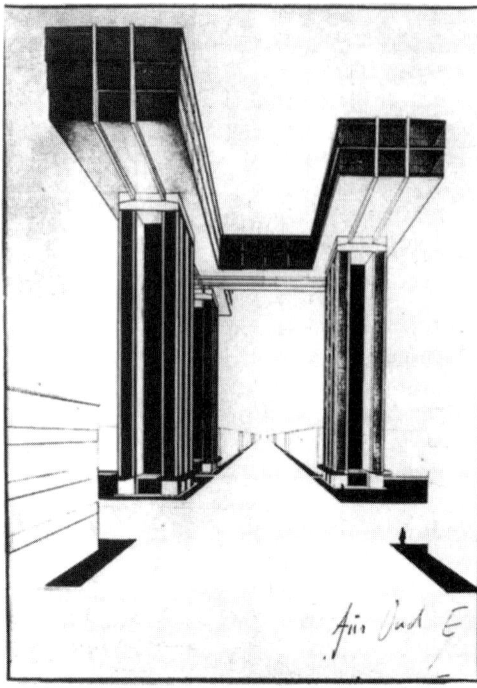

El Lissitzky, Entwurf für einen Wolkenbügel, 1924

Abb. 8: El Lissitzkys Entwurf eines Wolkenbügels.

maximaler Kräfte und potentieller Bewegung einerseits mit der vitalistischen Idee der umfassenden Einheit des Lebens andererseits.[21]

Im konstruktivistischen Horizont der 20er Jahre avancieren so in einem neu aufgelegten Rangstreit der Künste der elementare Film und die elementare Architektur zu Leitmedien *inter pares*. Richter versucht, zwischen beiden Kunstformen eine große Nähe, wenn nicht sogar Identität herzustellen: Indem er die Wahrnehmung des Films durch seine Zeitlichkeit räumlich, das Erleben der Architektur durch ihre Räumlichkeit zeitlich erscheinen lässt.

21 Vgl. hierzu Oliver Botar: Prolegomena to the Study of Biomorphic Modernism: Biocentrism, László Moholy-Nagy's „New Vision" and Ernó Kállai's Bioromantik. Toronto 1998 (Dissertation); vgl. auch nochmals Mertins: Architektur des Werdens.

Abbildungsverzeichnis

Bewegungskunst

Michael Cowan

Hans Richter's filmmaking defies easy labels. Embracing at once the rational pathos of Constructivism (*Rhythmus 21*, *Die neue Wohnung*), the irreverence of Dada (*Zweigroschenzauber*), and the uncanny effects of Surrealism (*Vormittagsspuk*), his work stands out above all for its ability to move between currents. In this, Richter's films could be seen as the heirs to his own formative years in wartime Zurich, where Dadaists, life reformers, Spiritualists, and Constructivists all intermingled in surprising ways. Looking back after WWII on his time in Zurich, Richter recalled in particular the lines of traffic running between the Dadaists of the Cabaret Voltaire and the dancers from the school of Rudolf von Laban:

> [In Labans Tanzschule] trafen wir die jungen Tänzerinnen der Generation: Mary Wigman, Maria Vanselow, Sophie Taeuber, Suzanne Perottet, Maja Kruschek, Käthe Wulff und andere. [...] Durch diesen sehr persönlichen Kontakt [...] wurde schließlich die ganze Labanschule in die Dada-Bewegung verwickelt. Ihre Mitglieder tanzten in den 'Kaufleuten'. Vor den abstrakten Dekorationen von Arp und mir, den Gurkenplantagen, flatterten die Tänzerinnen mit den abstrakten Masken von Janco wie Schmetterlinge von Ensor, wohl diszipliniert und dirigiert nach der Choreographie, die Käthe Wulff und Sophie Taeuber nach dem Laban-System aufgeschrieben hatten.[1]

Richter's recollections raise troubling (and familiar) questions about the unacknowledged role of women in the historical avant-garde; Richter was, after all, married to the dancer Maria Vanselow from 1921 to 1922, and one can only speculate on the role she might have played in his and Viking Eggeling's efforts to introduce movement into visual art through film. But Richter's account of the collaborations between the Laban school and Zurich Dada also suggests a broader set of intellectual connections between the development of experimental film and modern dance, not least of all in their shared interest in abstraction (masks, sets) and movement. While scholars have emphasized the differences between Laban's mysticism and Richter's Dada sensibilities,[2] I want to argue here that Richter and Laban shared a set of fundamental affinities in their understandings of film and dance.

---

1 Hans Richter: Dada—Kunst und Antikunst. Köln 1962, pp. 71-72.

2 Evelyn Doerr: Rudolf Laban. The Dancer of the Crystal. Lanham 2008, p. 66.

As an entryway into the topic, we can recall that Richter and Laban employed the same generic term for the art they sought to forge: "Bewegungskunst." Laban opened his first Schule für Bewegungskunst in Munich in 1910, followed by the Zurich branch in 1915. Similarly, Richter and Eggeling characterized their own turn to film as an effort to create an "art of movement," as Richter explained in his text "Prinzipielles zur Bewegungskunst," published in *De Stijl* in July 1921.[3] One could speculate about the derivations of the term "Bewegungskunst." As the passage from Richter

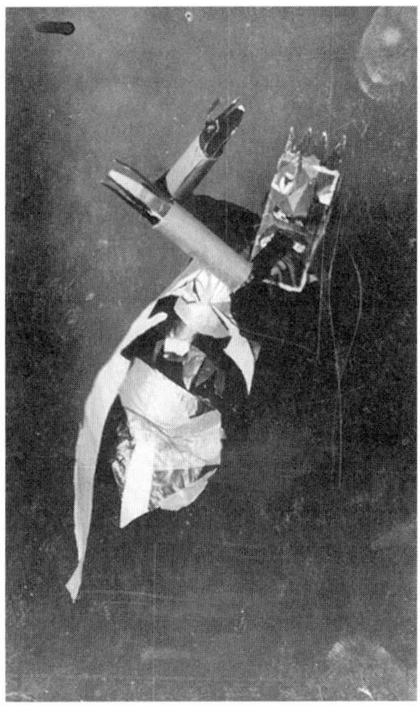

Fig. 1: Sophie Taeuber at the Cabaret Voltaire.

above suggests, Laban's choreographic notation system, which he would later present in published form in *Schrifttanz* (1928), was already in use in the Zurich period, and one might see in Richter and Eggeling's scroll experiments—as well as other similar film 'scores' such as Werner Graeff's *Filmpartitur* (1922)—echoes of Laban's attempts to represent movement in linear form on the printed page via geometric symbols.[4] As Nancy Troy

3 Richter's manifesto, largely a transcription of Eggeling's own ideas, coincided with several other high-profile discussions of their work, including Theo van Doesberg's "Abstracte Filmbeelding," published in *De Stijl* in 1923, and Ludwig Hilberseimer's article "Bewegungskunst," published in the *Sozialistische Monatshefte* in May 1921 and in the Hungarian avant-garde journal *MA* in 1923.

4 See also the article "Notation" in this volume.

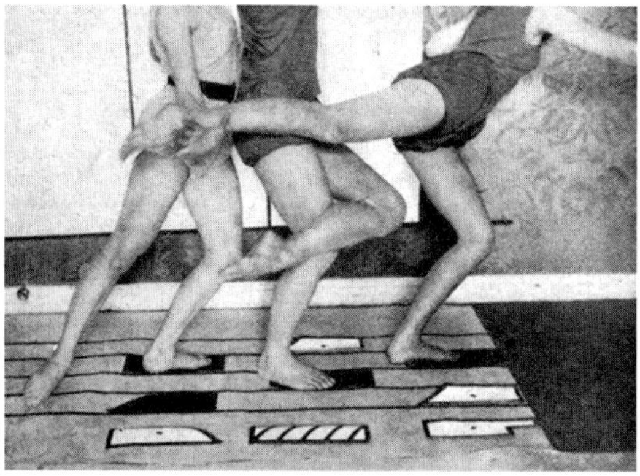

Fig. 2: Rudolf von Laban: page from *Schrifttanz* (1928).

has documented, dance fascinated the artists affiliated with *De Stijl*, who constantly looked for ways to represent the movement of dance through abstract symbols, including some—like Theo van Doesburg's *Rhythm of a Russian Dance* (1918)—that cannot fail to recall Richter's rectangles in movement.[5] Nor was there a dearth of other experiments in abstract movement performance, such as Vilmos Huszar's *Mechanische Dansfigur*, a marionette constructed of rectangular blocks intended for cinematographic and shadow performances. Although these artists tended to cite music as the model for their visual experiments, the frequency of dance as a motif, and the specific connections between Richter and Laban, would suggest another intermedial link.

However, the implications of the term "Bewegungskunst" are broader than any anecdotal accounts could suggest. For the desire to forge a new art of movement was an integral part of modern visual culture across many domains. Tom Gunning has proposed one genealogy of the cinema as an "art of movement" in the light and electricity dances of Loïe Fuller, where—in a visualization of Bergsonian philosophy—"no form remains solid or static, but rather dissolves into a continually changing spectacle of metamorphosis."[6] One could trace a line from Fuller's serpentine dances, with their constant morphing of shape, color and flow, to such signature avant-garde experiments as the synaesthetic color organs of Arnoldo Ginna and Bruno Cora or even the early *Opus* films of Ruttmann, which

---

5 See Nancy J. Troy: Figures of the Dance in *De Stijl*. In: The Art Bulletin vol. 66 (1984), no. 4, pp. 645-656.

6 Tom Gunning: Loïe Fuller and the Art of Motion. Body, Light, Electricity, and the Origins of Cinema. In: Richard Allen / Malcolm Turvey (eds.): Camera Obscura, Camera Lucida. Essays in Honor of Annette Michelson. Amsterdam 2003, pp. 75-90, here: p. 80.

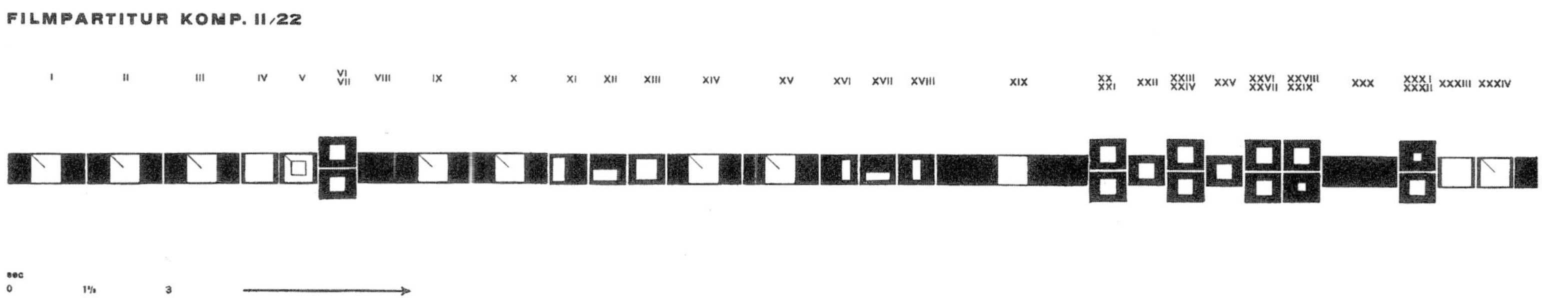

Fig. 3: Werner Graeff: *Filmpartitur* (1922).

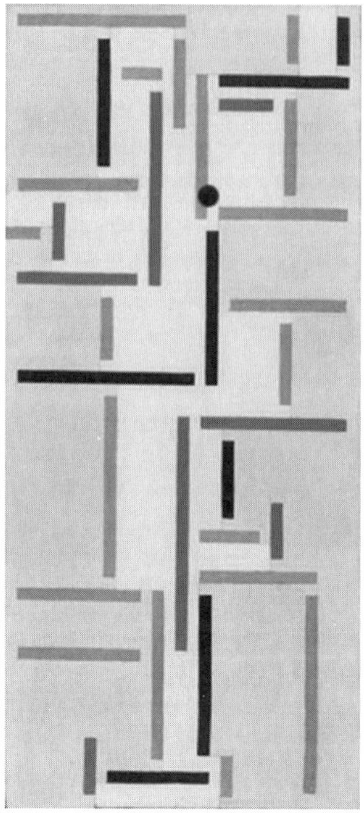

Fig. 4: Theo van Doesburg: *Rhythm of a Russian Dance* (1918).

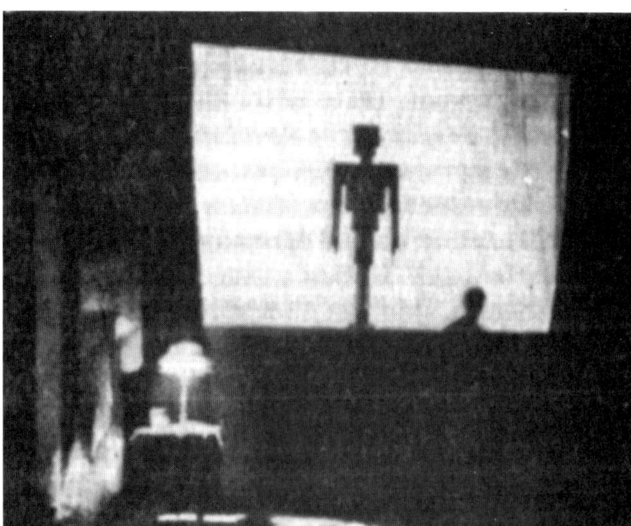

Fig. 5: Vilmos Huszar: mechanical dancing figure.

he described in Bergsonian terms as an effort to capture the "constantly transforming physiognomy of a curve."[7] But Bergson hardly seems an appropriate genealogy for the rectilinear aesthetics of films such as *Rhythmus 21* or Graeff's film score. In what follows, I want to argue that something else was at stake in the efforts both of Richter and Eggeling and of Laban to forge a new "Bewegungskunst" in the period around WWI: namely the desire to imagine a counterpart for visual design in the temporal sphere—a project for a *movement-design* appropriate for the conditions of life in industrial culture. At the center of this affinity, as I will show, lay their shared interest in 'rhythm' and 'polarity,' concepts that had come to define—through a long pedigree of 19th-century science—the fundamental forms of movement in nature and the cosmos.

A key word of early 20th-century modernism, 'rhythm' had already formed the object of intense scientific research in the 19th century, where it came to be associated in particular with notions of life.[8] If early capitalist society discovered 'circulation' as the key concept of vital organization, the industrial age obsessively probed the periodic fluctuations of rhythm, inventing a whole host of apparatuses for inscribing the alternations of heartbeat, breathing, and nervous activity. As a result, rhythm came to be seen as the fundamental principle of life itself. As Wilhelm Fließ would put it: "Durch alles Leben [geht] *ein* Puls, *ein* Rhythmus."[9]

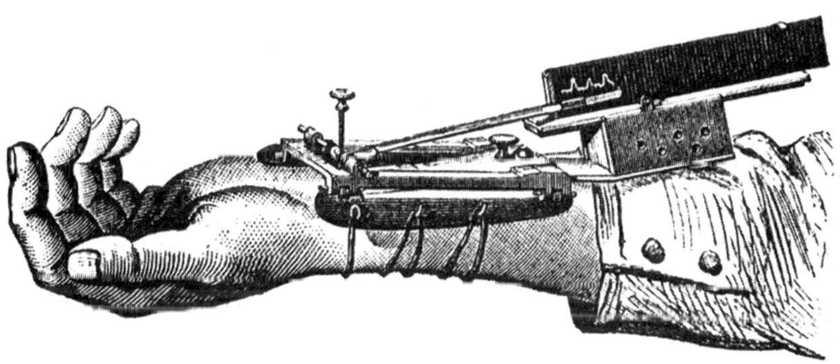

Fig. 6: Étienne Jules-Marey: sphygmograph for transcribing the rhythm of pulse.

7 Walter Ruttmann: Malerei mit Zeit. In: Jeanpaul Goergen (ed.): Walter Ruttmann. Eine Dokumentation. Berlin 1989, pp. 73-74, here: p. 74.

8 For more on rhythm in science and modernism, see Michael Cowan: Technology's Pulse. Essays on Rhythm in German Modernism. London 2012.

9 Wilhelm Fließ: Der Ablauf des Lebens. Grundlegungen zur exakten Biologie. Leipzig 1906, p. 2.

In its association with vital activity, rhythm could easily be understood to stand in opposition to modern processes of technological ordering—a position defended most vehemently in the 1920s by Ludwig Klages and his disciples in gymnastics (Rudolf Bode, Max Mertz).[10] But such reactionary positions hardly exhausted the debate, and rhythm was also seen as a potential principle of industrial organization itself. The most influential publication in this respect was Karl Bücher's 1897 treatise *Arbeit und Rhythmus*, which examined "rhythmical labor"—labor regulated by the rhythms of the body—as an alternative to Taylorist practices. For Bücher, natural rhythm was perfectly compatible with the dictates of industrial efficiency, offering an organic "regulating principle" that guaranteed "most efficient expenditure of energy" in animal and human movement.[11] More importantly, Bücher argued, rhythm could alleviate the modern malaise of alienated labor by reintegrating work with other spheres of human activity. In the endless varieties of premodern rhythmical labor that he analyzed, Bücher saw a common form of collective activity opposed to modern fragmentation, one in which the spheres of work, festival, and art were not yet separated: "Arbeit, Musik und Dichtung, [müssen] auf der primitiven Stufe ihrer Entwicklung in eins verschmolzen gewesen sein. [...] Was sie verbindet, ist das gemeinsame Merkmal des Rhythmus."[12] Reintegrating these spheres through rhythmical labor, Bücher hoped, would restore the "joy in work," a project he later sought to realize when he called for the reintroduction of singing onto the factory floor.

Bücher's understanding of rhythm as the basis for recovering a lost totality would inform many of the key dance reform projects of the 1910s and 1920s. The circle around Jaques-Dalcroze in Hellerau regularly cited Bücher to characterize their pedagogical program—along with the Werkbund experiment in Gesamtkunstwerk-design that was the Hellerau school itself—as an effort to reunite the separated spheres of life in a totalizing aesthetic project based on rhythm.[13] For his part, Laban understood rhythm as a universal principle of both natural and human order. Rhythm, he wrote in *Die Welt des Tänzers*, "spiegelt sich in der ganzen Natur und so auch in

10 See Ludwig Klages: Vom Wesen des Rhythmus. Kampen auf Sylt 1934 (orig. 1923); Rudolf Bode: Rhythmus und Körpererziehung. Jena 1924; Max Merz: Körperbildung und Rhythmus. Vienna 1926.

11 Karl Bücher: Arbeit und Rhythmus. Leipzig 1897, p. 101. Bücher's arguments about rhythm and efficiency would be echoed in numerous subsequent discussions of rhythm, by authors including Richter himself. See Richter: Filmgegner von heute, Filmfreunde von morgen. Berlin 1929, p. 93.

12 Bücher: Arbeit und Rhythmus, p. 78.

13 See Wolf Dohrn: Aufgaben der Bildungsanstalt Jaques-Dalcroze. In: Die Schulfeste der Bildungsanstalt Jaques-Dalcroze. Jena 1912, pp. 7-8.

jeder menschlichen Handlung und Tätigkeit."[14] Like Isadora Duncan and Jaques-Dalcroze, Laban understood his dance as a means of reconnecting with this universal rhythm of nature. As he later described it in *Gymnastik und Tanz*, dance offered an "Abbild [...] der rhythmischen Spannungen in der Natur"[15] and a means of bringing the human body back into resonance with the universe: "Was [...] durch das Mitschwingen mit dem [...] Tanzkunstwerk im Zuschauer geweckt wird, ist [...] die Belebung jener Kraft, die uns instande setzt, mit dem urgesetzlichen Alltanz des Seins dauernd zusammenzuschwingen."[16] In particular, Laban argued that dance had to rediscover the periodic alternation between tension and relaxation that characterized all movement in its natural and harmonious state. In a sentiment that would be repeated by numerous proponents of rhythmical gymnastics, he wrote: "Alle Schönheit beruht auf dem harmonischen Wechsel zwischen An- und Abspannung."[17]

But Laban's "Bewegungskunst" was more than just a means of representing natural rhythm. Like Jaques-Dalcroze, he believed that the shaping of movement in dance also had repercussions for industrial society itself. In Laban's Ascona dance colony (a precursor to the Zurich school), students regularly performed their chores (gardening, food preparation) to rhythmical work songs in the spirit of Bücher, and he clearly saw dance as a means of redesigning everyday movements—"Alltagsformen,"[18] as he put it in *Die Welt des Tänzers*—and particularly the movements of labor in accordance with eurhythmical harmony.[19] Dance could help to inaugurate a new joy in work by infusing it with a sense of festival: "Die rhythmisch ordnende Kraft des Festes schwingt als tänzerischer Sinn in den Alltagsrhythmus hinüber und erweckt dort als Einsicht, Lebens- und Arbeitsfreude die Erfüllung des Kulturideals."[20]

Indeed, regrounding the movements of labor in natural rhythm could infuse the very design (Gestaltung) of products with a new life. Natural forms, Laban argued in a contention drawn from his reading of Ernst Haeckel, were themselves the result of harmonious rhythmical movements, which he described as a "formgestaltende Kraft" whose effects were most clearly visible in the formation of crystals, but also in plants, animal forms,

14 Rudolf von Laban: Die Welt des Tänzers. Stuttgart 1920, p. 125; see also Laban: Gymnastik und Tanz. Oldenburg 1925, pp. 14-15.

15 Ibid., p. 42.

16 Ibid., pp. 162-163.

17 Ibid., p. 52.

18 Laban: Die Welt des Tänzers, p. 151.

19 See ibid., pp. 127-129.

20 Ibid., p. 129; see also Laban: Gymnastik und Tanz, p. 35.

and human anatomy.[21] In analogous fashion, a training in rhythmical movement could affect the "gestaltende Arbeit"[22] of human beings in the design of crafts, architecture, and machines. Laban's famous notion of crystalline dance, in which the dancing body outlined a harmonious "Umraumform"[23] in the shape of an icosahedron, could thus be understood at once as a model for other forms of human design: a crystallization of eurhythmical movement into human production analogous to the crystallization of movement in natural forms.[24]

While Richter hardly shared Laban's mysticism of crystals, he did share an understanding of rhythm as a means for anchoring his "Bewegungskunst" in universal patterns and thereby regaining a sense of unity. "Rhythm," he explained in 1926, "is not definite, regular succession in time or space, but the unity binding all parts into a whole. [...] It [...] is the inner, nature-force [...], through which we are bound up with the elemental nature-forces."[25] In his 1921 text, Richter (following Eggeling) identified such elemental forces more specifically with the term "polarity," citing at turns a "polar concept of construction" ("des polaren Konstruktiongedankens"), a "polar rhythmical principle of intuition" ("polar-rhythmischen Ansschauungsprinzip"), and a "polar synthesis" ("polare Synthese").[26]

Like "rhythm," the concept of "polarity" had a long history in the 19th-century life sciences, stretching back at least to Schelling's philosophy of nature, where it designated an irreducible dualism driving all natural movement from magnetism and electricity to planetary rotation.[27] Goethe would later posit that both nature and thought follow the laws of "Polarität und Steigerung," a dialectical process by which elements separate and reunite on a higher plane.[28] Throughout the 19th century, "polarity"-defined by Schopenhauer as "das Auseinandertreten einer Kraft in zwei qualitativ verschiedene, entgegengesetzte und zur Wiedervereinigung strebende

21 See ibid., p. 75.

22 Ibid., p. 116.

23 Ibid., p. 74.

24 On this point, see Laban's discussion of chair production in: Laban: Die Welt des Tänzers, pp. 146-150.

25 Hans Richter: Rhythm (1926). In: Freunde der deutschen Kinemathek e.V. (ed.): Hans Richter. Film ist Rhythmus. Berlin 2003, p. 38.

26 Hans Richter: Prinzipielles zur Bewegungskunst. In: De Stijl vol. 4 (1921), no. 7, pp. 109-112, here: pp. 109-111. Reprint edited by Ad Petersen.

27 See F. W. J. Schelling: Von der Weltseele. Hamburg 1809, pp. 128-176.

28 Johann Wolfgang Goethe: Erläuterung zu dem aphoristischen Aufsatz "Die Natur." Goethe an den Kanzler von Müller (1828). In: Sämtliche Werke, vol. 4. Paris 1836, p. 320.

Thätigkeiten,"[29] and by Robert Hammerling as "das Princip der Anziehungen und Abstoßungen in der Natur"[30]-would continue to provide a model for understanding the actions of magnetism and electricity, but also such diverse processes as plant growth and language development.[31] Polarity thus designated a kind of universal dance of interacting forces, a pas de deux by which nature sets the world into oscillating movement and creates higher forms of organization. As such, it served, like "rhythm," as a unifying concept. "Daß das Gesetz der Polarität durch die ganze Natur herrsche," wrote one author in 1846, "ist von Philosophen und Naturforschern, alten wie neuern, oft genug gesagt und bewiesen worden."[32] Not surprisingly, the term would be picked up in the early 20th century by numerous neo-romantic philosophers such as Rudolf Steiner and Klages himself in their search for a holistic understanding of man and the world. A host of titles, such as Ernst Eberhardt's *Polarität als Grundlage einer einheitlichen Weltanschauung* (1907) or Walter Hueck's *Die Welt als Polarität und Rhythmus* (1928), attest to the term's status as a vector of desires to reunite the fragmented spheres of modernity.

Clearly, then, Richter could draw on the authority of a long tradition when he wrote in 1921: "Polarität ist ein generelles Lebensprinzip = Kompositionsmethode jeder formalen Äußerung."[33] The move from the identification of a vital principle to a method of composition here is critical. Although Richter (like other abstract artists) rejected the mimetic copying of "natural" forms,[34] he and Eggeling—not unlike Laban—nonetheless understood their "Bewegungskunst" as an effort to model artistic movement on a universal design of movement at work throughout the world. That design consisted precisely in a synthetic interplay of opposing and attracting forces, or what Eggeling and Richter came to refer to as "contrasts" and

29 Arthur Schopenhauer: Die Welt als Wille und Vorstellung, vol. 1. Leipzig 1844, p. 162.

30 Robert Hammerling: Die Atomistik des Willens. Hamburg 1891, p. 101.

31 Titles include Hermann Lövy: Über Polarität. Prag 1831; Christoph Gottlieb Voigtmann: Das Gesetz der Polarität in der Sprache. Göttingen 1854; Henry Forster Baxter: On organic polarity, shewing a connection to exist between organic forces and ordinary polar forces. London 1860; Rudolf Franz: Über die Diamagnetische Polarität. Halle 1878; Theodor Boveri: Über die Polarität des Seeigel Eies. Würzburg 1901; Josef Doposcheg-Uhlar: Studien zur Regeneration und Polarität der Pflanzen. Jena 1911.

32 Voigtmann: Das Gesetz der Polarität in der Sprache, p. 1. Similarly, Hammerling could write: "Polarität [ist] die gesuchte Urkraft selbst." Hammerling: Atomistik des Willens, p. 101.

33 Richter: Prinzipielles zur Bewegungskunst, p. 110.

34 Ibid., pp. 109-10.

"analogies."[35] Like Goethe and romantically-inspired scientists of the 19th century, Eggeling and Richter believed that movement resulted from a basic tension of opposing and attracting elements, which tended to produce a higher order through 'polar synthesis.' As Richter would later describe it: "Synthese der Anziehungs und Abstößungskraft, dem Verhalten von Kontrasten und Analogien, das grundlegende Prinzip der Gestaltung."[36]

Richter and Eggeling had already attempted to represent such a principle of movement-construction in their abstract paintings, several of which accompanied the publication of Richter's "Prinzipielles zur Bewegungskunst" in *De Stijl*. In these paintings, the shapes and lines form relations of contrast and analogy based around several key polarities: vertical-horizontal, rectilinear-curved, level-diagonal, massive-light, sinking-rising, and—not least—black-white.[37] At the beginning of his article, Richter remarked that these illustrations were meant to depict key moments of a process of movement,[38] and it was precisely in an effort to capture this processual character that the two artists turned towards the medium of film, in which they attempted to stage the unfolding interactions of opposing forces in time on the screen. In Richter's *Rhythmus 21*, this includes interactions not only of contrast (black and white), but also of directionality (left, right, up, and down), of size (shrinking, growing), of position on the screen (left, right, top, and bottom), and of proportion (square vs. horizontal rectangle vs. vertical rectangle). Critics have often argued that Richter's film invokes and undermines the conventions of representational art and three-dimensional space by rendering the relations of figure and ground arbitrary, particularly in the famous black and white reversal (2:21). But Richter's growing and shrinking figures are also reminiscent of the many efforts to represent movement abstractly via geometrical symbols—such as Laban's notation system discussed above—and the point of their dance on the screen might be less a Dadaistic undermining of representation than a staging of the polar relation between the geometrical figures and the geometrical space of the screen itself, a relation in constant oscillation as the symbols grow and shrink with respect to the space around them.

Like Laban, Richter saw such representations of polarity on the screen as tapping into universal patterns of movement. But there was also a difference. Where Laban was focused on the body, Richter tends—like Goethe—to associate polarity not only with external nature but also with subjective

---

35 Ibid., pp. 110-111.

36 Hans Richter: Die schlecht trainierte Seele. In: G. Zeitschrift für elementare Gestaltung III (1924). Reprint edited by Marion von Hofacker, München 1986, pp. 44-47, here: p. 44.

37 Cf. Richter's and Eggeling's examples of polar compositions in "Prinzipielles zur Bewegungskunst," in the section "Anhang" of this volume.

38 Richter: Prinzipielles zur Bewegungskunst, p. 109.

faculties: sensation, perception, and intuition. This is precisely the presupposition that allowed Richter and Eggeling to posit the ability of their "Bewegungskunst" to forge a "universal language," whose legibility resided in its ability to tap into the movements at work subjectively within spectators: "Die 'Sprache' (Formsprache), die da 'gesprochen' wird, beruht auf einem 'Alphabet', entstanden aus einem elementaren Prinzip der Anschauung: Polarität."[39] In line with other ideas about "polarity" in the early 20th century, Richter and Eggeling understood this universal language of polar movement as one that could help to reintegrate the fragmented spheres of modern life by reinserting the individual into a universal human community: "Kunst dient der Verwirklichung einer höheren Einheit: der Idee des Menschen in der Menschheit: der Vollendung des Individuums in einer höheren Organisationsform."[40]

Richter would extend his ideas about a universal language of polarity in a subsequent essay from 1924, "Die schlecht trainierte Seele." There, he argued that the reduction of film to elementary processes could liberate movement—here again presented as film's most essential element—from the random and confused collection of psychological associations. The aim was to bring this movement into line with the "elementary laws of our sensory functions,"[41] which resided in rhythmical movement (an "Auf und Ab" with analogies to breathing and heartbeat). More specifically, he argued again that perception and sensation proceeded via fundamental laws of polarity, in which the play of contrasts (necessary in order to perceive anything) and similarities (necessary in order to synthesize individual perceptions into a larger whole)—what Richter calls the "Wechselwirken von Trennen und Verbinden"[42]—drives the synthetic movement of thought. Richter explains that the abstract films that he made with Eggeling sought to project such polarity into the temporal dimension through rhythmical alternation. The article ends with an excerpt from *Rhythmus 21*, presented as an "example of the unified design [einheitliche Gestaltung] of movement" and accompanied by a text explaining that the film's aesthetics resides not in individual forms but rather in the play of polar tensions: "hell:dunkel / horizontal:vertikal / groß:klein / schnell:langsam, etc."[43]

Thus Richter, like Laban and following Eggeling, understood his "Bewegungskunst" as a means for reconnecting with universal and elementary patterns of movement—in this case dialectical patterns—long identified in the

39 Ibid., p. 110.

40 Ibid., p. 111.

41 Richter: Die schlecht trainierte Seele, p. 45.

42 Ibid.

43 Ibid., p. 47. Cf. also Richter's illustration accompanying "Die schlecht trainierte Seele" in the section "Anhang" of this volume.

life sciences. But for both artists, art represented a means not only of reactivating such elemental forces, but also of bringing them under human control. For Laban, dance could both tap into occult powers and render them masterable through performance: "Das Okkulte, Verborgene, im Tanz sind jene zwar in Worten unaussprechlichen, aber dennoch verständlichen Urgesetzte der Bewegtheit des Lebens, die sowohl in der Kunst wie auch im Leben als Macht und Kraftmittel beherrscht und angewandt werden können."[44] Laban's formulation "sowohl [...] wie auch" suggests a particular logic for conceiving the relationship between art and life in the period around WWI. Art, as the design of movement under controlled conditions, would appear as a sort of laboratory for designing movement in everyday life. For his part, Richter understood his filmic "Bewegungskunst" similarly as a means of both tapping into and mastering the principle of rhythmical polarity. In his 1921 text, he explained how his and Eggeling's films could convey "Spannung und Auflösung in einem Sinn, der, weil alle materiellen Vergleiche und Erinnerungen wegfallen, elementar-magisch ist."[45] Recalling Hugo Ball's efforts to strip language of conventional and associative meaning in order to rediscover the primitive "magic of the vocables,"[46] Richter's sentence here suggests a process of abstracting movement to the elementary magic of tension and relaxation. But towards the end of the essay, in a section entitled "Definition der Kunst," Richter subsequently introduces such terms as "Zucht" and "Disziplin" to describe art as a means of mastering the magical power of polar movement.[47] Even more explicitly, in "Die schlecht trainierte Seele," he describes film as an art that might help us to gain conscious control over the powers of polar movement driving human sensation: "Diese lebendige Kraft, die wir in der 'Bewegung' besitzen, an und für sich ein wunderbares Phänomen, kann [...] zum Bestandteil menschlicher Macht werden—aber man müßte im Stande sein, diesen Prozeß zu beherrschen."[48]

One need not look far in Richter's journal *G* to find discussions of the kind of applications Richter suggests here. In an article on amusement parks published in the same issue as Richter's "Die schlecht trainierte Seele," Max Burchartz called for a "unified" (einheitlich) organization of movement in park attractions "according to their elementary possibilities."[49] It is surely not by chance that Burchartz's description of his project for a unified and

44 Laban: Gymnastik und Tanz, p. 164.

45 Richter: Prinzipielles zur Bewegungskunst, p. 109.

46 Hugo Ball: Flight out of Time. A Dada Diary. Berkeley 1996, p. 25.

47 Richter: Prinzipielles zur Bewegungskunst, p. 111.

48 Richter: Die schlecht trainierte Seele, p. 45.

49 Max Buchartz [sic]: Lunapark. In: G. Zeitschrift für elementare Gestaltung III (1924). Reprint edited by Marion von Hofacker, München 1986, pp. 36-38, here: pp. 36-37.

elementary amusement park recalls Richter's notion of polarity governing his and Eggeling's work:

> Gestaltung also der Tempis und der Richtungsmöglichkeiten,
> Von Stillstand und Bewegung
> Des Schnell und Langsam
> Des Plötzlich und Allmählich
> Sowie des Horizontal und Vertikal
> Des Ab und Auf
> Des Vor und Zurück
> Des Rotierens und Pendelns
> Rhythmische Gliederung in Wechsel und Gegensatz ermöglicht durch bestimmte nach Partitur geregelte Bewegungsvorgänge.[50]

With its "score" (Partitur) and its fundamental organization according to elementary oppositions, Burchartz's imaginary amusement park represented nothing short of a demonstration of what the movement-design of absolute film could become when applied to real-life situations.

In extending the findings of absolute "Bewegungskunst" to amusement park design, Burchartz's article enacts the scenario of "art becoming life" that Jacques Rancière has identified as one of the key "emplotments"[51] of the aesthetic regime inaugurated in the 18th century—a scenario particularly associated with the culture of design in the early 1920s that interested the proponents of "life reform" and avant-garde alike. Both Laban and Richter take part in this broader aesthetic project in their conceptualization of "Bewegungskunst" as a laboratory for redesigning movement in the industrial age in line with universal laws. It is this understanding of their art as movement design, moreover, that might help to explain how Richter could so easily move between various currents of modernism and advertising, or how a figure such as Laban could move between the realms of holistic life reform and rational movement study for which he became known in the U.K. after WWII (the results of which were published in his book *Effort* from 1947). It also helps to explain why neither Laban nor Richter understood their respective "movement arts" primarily as a search for "medium specificity." According to Laban: "Es handelt sich [...] in der neuen Tanzkunst [...] nicht nur um den Tanz. [...] Es handelt sich vielmehr um ein für den künstlerischen Ausdruck neu erobertes Mittel, um ein in dieser Form neu entdecktes Gebiet, die Bewegung."[52] Similarly, Richter saw his elementary forms of movement as laws applicable to all arts: "Die ästhetischen Prinzipien des Alphabets zeigen den Weg zum Gesamtkunstwerk, und zwar deswegen, weil diese Prinzipien, deren man sich undogmatisch,

50 Ibid., p. 37.

51 Jacques Rancière: The Aesthetic Revolution and its Outcomes. In: Rancière: Dissensus. New York 2010, pp. 115-134, here: p. 115.

52 Laban: Gymnastik und Tanz, p. 146.

synthetisch bedient, nicht nur für die Malerei maßgebend sind, sondern in gleichem Maß für Musik, Sprache, Tanz, Architektur, Schauspiel."[53] This notion of intermedial transferability stands in marked opposition to any view of modernism or abstract film as a search for artistic specificity. To be sure, Richter, like other avant-garde filmmakers, did seek to "purify" his "Bewegungskunst" of dramatic or representative elements. But we should not conclude that his project was driven by an inherent search for medium specificity or even by any inherent love for film. Rather, Richter saw film as a means of accessing laws of movement more fundamental than any single medium and, ultimately, of rendering those laws available for broader projects of Gestaltung.

Table of Figures

Fig. 1: Anonymous: Sophie Taeuber dancing at the Cabaret Voltaire with mask by Marcel Janco (1916). Clamart: Fondation Arp.
Fig. 2: Anonymous: Dancers using Labanotation signs (1928). Karel Smrž: Problémy dneš ního filmu. In: Rozpravy Aventina vol. 36 (1928-1929) no. 4, p. 358.
Fig. 3: Werner Graeff: Filmpartitur Komp. II/22 (detail). In: De Stijl vol. 6 (1923) no. 5, pp. 378-379.
Fig. 4: Theo van Doesburg: Rhythm of a Russian Dance (1918). New York: The Museum of Modern Art, Lillie P. Bliss Bequest.
Fig. 5: Anonymous: Vilmos Huszar's Simultaneistic-mechanical Dance at Dada-soirée, 19 January 1923, held in Amsterdam. In: Het Leven (27 January 1923). Reprinted in Hubert van den Berg (Hg.): Holland's bankroet door dada. Documenten van een dadaïstische triomftocht door Nederland. Amsterdam 1995, p. 150.
Fig. 6: Anonymous: Sphygmograph for transcribing the Rhythm of the Pulse. In: Étienne-Jules Marey: La méthode graphique dans les sciences expérimentales et principalement en physiologie et en médecine. Paris 1878, p. 281.

53 Richter: Prinzipielles zur Bewegungskunst, p. 110.

Bildräume: *Die freudlose Gasse* im Rhythmus der Avantgarde

Karin Fest

> Man hat Rhythmus gesagt, und man ist zufrieden. Mit einem bisschen guten Willen, könnte man schließlich in jedem Film einen rhythmischen Wert entdecken. Trotzdem ist die filmische Welt an solchem Rhythmus furchtbar arm.[1]
>
> —René Clair, 1926

Die Künstlergruppe rund um die Zeitschrift *G* (1923-1926) – Hans Richter, Viking Eggeling, El Lissitzky u.a. – entwickelt durch verschiedene Konzepte und künstlerische Herangehensweisen eine universelle Formensprache. Die Gestaltung durch elementare Darstellungsformen und die Abwendung von Erzählformen gehen in der Idee der ‚absoluten Kunst' auf. Im Zentrum steht dabei der ‚absolute Film', bei dem alle „Anklänge an individuelle Naturformen abgestreift werden und nur die mathematischen Formen bleiben"[2].

Die Neue Sachlichkeit entwickelt sich als Kunstrichtung in Deutschland fast zeitgleich und erhält mit der Ausstellung „Die neue Sachlichkeit. Deutsche Malerei nach dem Expressionismus" 1925 in der Kunsthalle Mannheim ihre Benennung.[3] Der Stil der Neuen Sachlichkeit konzentriert sich auf eine klare Formensprache und den „Wunsch, die Dinge objektiv zu behandeln, so wie sie sind, ohne in ihnen eine ideelle Bedeutung zu suchen"[4]. Die Neue Sachlichkeit im Film nimmt mit realitätsbezogenen Spielfilmen wie Karl Grunes *Die Straße* (1923) oder Georg Wilhelm Pabsts *Die freudlose Gasse* (1925) ihren Ausgangspunkt.

Die dynamische Montage des Bildraums steht bei beiden, sowohl bei Arbeiten zum absoluten Film als auch bei veristischen Filmen der Neuen Sachlichkeit im Vordergrund. Dabei ist das rhythmische Prinzip der An-

---

1 René Clair: Rhythmus, Rhythmus! In: G. Zeitschrift für elementare Gestaltung IV (April 1926). Reprint herausgegeben von Marion von Hofacker, München 1986, S. 115.

2 Rudolf Kurtz: Expressionismus und Film. Zürich 1965 (erstmals 1926), S. 86.

3 Vgl. Ulrike Lorenz: Kunsthalle Mannheim. Vergangenheit Gegenwart Zukunft. Mannheim 2009, S. 22-25.

4 Georg Friedrich Hartlaub zitiert nach: AFK-Filmstudio: Die Welt im Querschnitt. Walter Ruttmann und sein Montagefilm Berlin – Die Sinfonie der Grosstadt. In: Zwischen den Bildern – Aspekte der Filmmontage. Karlsruhe 1997. http://afk-filmkreis.de/index.php/site/page?view=docs.montage.ruttmann (16.04.2012).

ordnung für die Bewegung der Objekte im Bild genauso wichtig wie für die Montage der Bilder selbst. Die damit einhergehende Dynamisierung der Raumwahrnehmung erhält vor allem durch die filmischen Arbeiten von Hans Richter, die einer bestimmten ‚Bewegungskunst' folgen, Bedeutung.[5]

Das *close reading* von Hans Richters *Rhythmus 21* und G. W. Pabsts *Die freudlose Gasse* soll im Folgenden exemplarisch zu einer Annäherung der beiden Bereiche absoluter Film und Neue Sachlichkeit im Film führen. Rhythmus wird dabei als das strukturierende Element ästhetischer Grundformen der räumlichen Wahrnehmung herausgearbeitet.

I. *Rhythmus 21*

Hans Richters *Rhythmus 21* gilt als einer der frühen abstrakten experimentellen Filme, der innerhalb der Gruppe um *G* entstanden ist. Obwohl oder auch gerade weil in *Rhythmus 21* nur grafisch rechteckige Formen auftreten, aus deren rhythmischer Anordnung heraus Bewegung entsteht, ist die Frage nach dem Bezug zum Alltäglichen von Interesse. Wie kann ein Film, in dem weder Menschen, soziale Räume, Dekors noch Gebrauchsgegenstände auftauchen, als Pionierarbeit für das dahinter liegende Konzept der Überführung von Kunst ins Leben gelten?

Als Herausgeber von *G. Zeitschrift für elementare Gestaltung* beschreibt Hans Richter, an wen sich die dort publizierten Texte wenden: nämlich weder an den Kunstliebhaber noch an innovationsversessene Interessenten einer neuen Kunstrichtung. Vielmehr richtet sich die Zeitschrift an Menschen, „die Grundsätzliches lieben, in der Kunst, wie in allen Zusammenhängen des Lebens"[6]. Richter hofft dabei, „das Problem der Kunst nicht vom ästhetisierenden, sondern vom allgemein kulturellen Standpunkt aus [zu] lösen"[7].

Richters *Rhythmus*-Arbeiten[8], beginnend mit *Rhythmus 21*, versuchen über elementare Formen eine universelle Sprache zu entwickeln. Das rhythmische Anordnungsprinzip der flachen Grundformen führt in *Rhythmus 21* zu einer plastischen Wahrnehmung des filmischen Raums. Die durch Montage und rhythmische Anordnung der elementaren Formen entstehende Raumtiefe soll im Folgenden als ein Grundkonzept von *Rhythmus 21* beschrieben werden.

---

5 Vgl. Helmut Herbst: Mit der Technik denken. Konstruktion einer Augenmusik. In: Herbert Gehr (Hg.): Sound & Vision – Musikvideo und Filmkunst. Katalog zur gleichnamigen Ausstellung im Deutschen Filmmuseum. Frankfurt a.M. 1993, S. 37-41, hier: S. 38; Vgl. auch den Beitrag „Bewegungskunst" in diesem Band.

6 Hans Richter / Werner Graeff: o.T. In: G. Material zur elementaren Gestaltung I (Juli 1923), o.P.

7 Ebd.

8 Vgl. hierzu den Beitrag „Entstehungsgeschichte" in diesem Band.

Der Begriff Rhythmus wird dabei nicht nur für die Ordnung von Bewegung eingesetzt, auch die Raumebenen verschieben sich dadurch: Tiefenbewegungen, Abweichungen ans Bildäußerste, Verkleinerungen und Vergrößerungen der Rechtecke. Ihre Spaltung und Verbindung zu neuen Formen führen zu einem Pulsieren verschiedener bildlicher Raumebenen, die erst durch das rhythmische Anordnungsprinzip eine Bedeutungszuordnung erhalten. Der Prozess der Bewegung wird in Richters *Rhythmus*-Filmen über Lage, Proportion und Hell/Dunkel-Kontraste formalisiert.[9] Über die Funktion von Rhythmus in Filmen schreibt Richter:

> Dieser Film ist auf den Bewegungsvorgang konzentriert. [...] Die Form ist also nicht willkürlich gewählt. – Improvisation ist ausgeschaltet. Sowohl der Bau des Rhytmus [sic] als auch die formalen Verhältnisse im einzelnen sind gebildet innerhalb einer bewussten Ordnung.[10]

Die verschiedenartigen formalen Anordnungen stehen zunächst für sich: das Quadrat, das sich nach vorne bewegt, Rechtecke, die sich seitlich herein schieben, aus dem Bild wieder hinaus führen und sich dabei unterschiedlich schnell abwechseln. Erst die Abfolge äquivalenter Einheiten – das Vor und Zurück der einzelnen Elemente, die prozessuale Wiederholung bestimmter Einheiten – bringt den Vorgang der Bewegung zum Ausdruck. Abstraktion und Formierung zeigen die für sich stehenden Elemente in einer Ordnung, die von eingeübten Wahrnehmungsprozessen losgelöst ist.

In seinem Essay über Rhythmus beschreibt René Clair filmische Momente, die das Publikum aus seiner Passivität herausholen sollen. Durch Montageformen der Abstraktion seien Raum- und Zeitgesetze aufgehoben, werden neue Wahrnehmungseindrücke und Denkbewegungen hervorgebracht. Rhythmus sei dafür das entscheidende Element. Doch, so gibt Clair zu bedenken, sei dieser eben nicht leicht in Filmen ausfindig zu machen. Auch sei der Raum als wichtigste Komponente im Film zu bedenken, um Rhythmus überhaupt erkennen zu können. Daher fordert er für die Einlösung eines „rhythmischen Wertes" im Film die Erfüllung dreier Bedingungen: erstens die kurze Dauer des Bildes, zweitens die Abwechslung der Szenen oder Motive der Handlung und drittens die Bewegung der vom Objektiv fotografierten Gegenstände (Spiel des Darstellers, Bewegung der Dekoration).[11] Bewegung, Abwechslung und Dauer der Aufnahmen werden durch Rhythmus räumlich strukturiert und nach einer strengen Bildlogik geordnet. In *Rhythmus 21* werden elementare Flächen rhythmisiert,

9 Vgl. Hans Richter: Die schlecht trainierte Seele. In: G. Zeitschrift für elementare Gestaltung III (1924). Reprint herausgegeben von Marion von Hofacker, München 1986, S. 44-47.

10 Ebd., S. 47.

11 Vgl. Clair: Rhythmus, Rhythmus!, S. 116.

das heißt, nach einem wiedererkennbaren Modus im Bild sichtbar gemacht. Auf diese Weise entsteht ein dynamischer Bildraum, der als solcher wahrnehmbar ist.

Rhythmus ist somit das Konzept, durch welches sich die neu erfahrbaren Raumebenen entfalten. Elementare Gestaltung bedeutet dann: Ein Ordnungsprinzip zu finden, das die einzelnen Grundformen kennt und daraus Gestaltungsebenen pluralistisch erfahrbar werden lässt. Doch elementare Gestaltung ist nur dann möglich, wenn es ein Inventar von Grundelementen der Gestaltung gibt, die untereinander korrespondieren. „In ihr werden die verschiedenen Künste sich so zu einander verhalten, dass sie imstande sind, ein Maximum von (elementarer) Ausdruckskraft zu entfalten."[12]

Das Arbeiten mit elementaren Grundformen, mit denen eine einheitliche visuelle Sprache entwickelt wird, zeigt sich auch an verschiedenen architektonischen Konzepten. Der Maler und Architekt Theo van Doesburg setzt ans Ende seiner Beschreibungen der elementaren Gestaltung eine Kubus-Skulptur. Als primäre Ausdrucksmittel für die Gestaltung auf elementarer Basis nennt er für die Architektur „Raum-Zeit-Linien, Flächen"[13]. Flächen als raum-zeitliche Gefüge beinhalten automatisch Bewegung. Die Fläche wird zum bewegten Gegenstand, wenn sie sich als Raum-Zeit-Linie zusammensetzt, wie auch der Kubus veranschaulicht. Van Doesburg spricht von einem ausgeweiteten Raum, der entsteht, wenn Formen und Flächen so in ein Verhältnis gesetzt werden, dass sie einen Eindruck von Dynamik bewirken. Dem Künstler bedeutet „Raum eine gewisse Spannung, die im Werke durch Verstraffung von Formen, Flächen oder Linien entsteht. Das Wort Gestaltung bedeutet ihm Sichtbarmachen des Verhältnisses einer Form (oder Farbe) zum Raum und zu anderen Formen oder Farben."[14]

Die Bearbeitung von Flächen ist auch in Richters Filmen zentral. Durch das Verschieben der Flächen im gleichbleibenden Takt entsteht eine Ausweitung des Bildraums: Die regelmäßige, rhythmische Anordnung der geometrischen Formen innerhalb des Bildes verleiht dem wahrgenommenen Raum Tiefe und geben den bewegten flachen Formen den Eindruck von Dreidimensionalität.

---

12 Theo van Doesburg: Zur elementaren Gestaltung. In: G. Material zur elementaren Gestaltung I (Juli 1923), o.P.

13 Ebd.

14 Theo van Doesburg, zitiert nach: Thomas Mank: Die Kunst des absoluten Films. In: Herbert Gehr (Hg.): Sound & Vision – Musikvideo und Filmkunst. Katalog zur gleichnamigen Ausstellung im Deutschen Filmmuseum. Frankfurt a.M. 1993, S. 72-87, hier: S. 84.

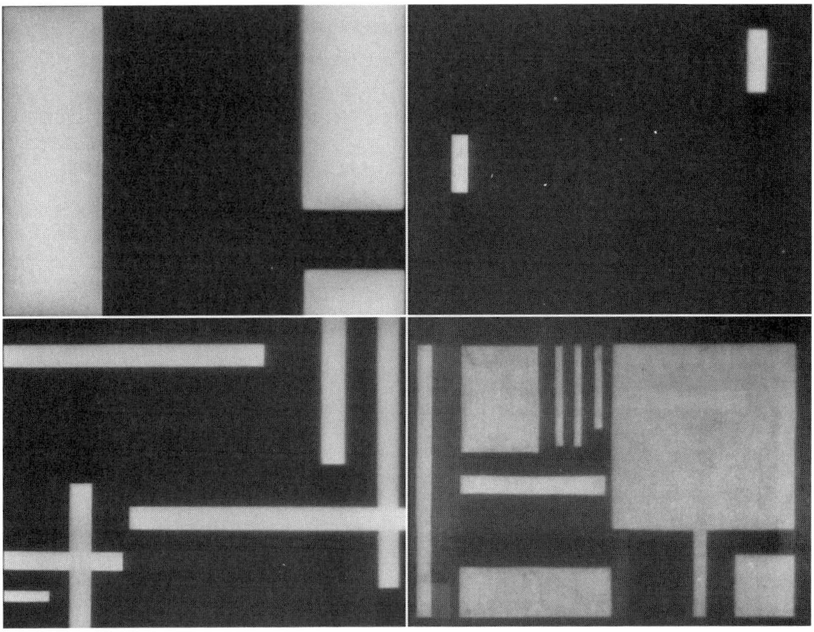

Abb. 1 a-d: Raumeindrücke in *Rhythmus 21.*

Der formale rhythmische Prozess der Gliederung der Objekte im Bild generiert in *Rhythmus 21* parallel ebenso flache wie tiefe, weite wie enge, helle wie dunkle Raumeindrücke, welche – wie Architektur – sinnlich/haptisch wahrgenommen werden. Dieses Konzept der Verschiebung, der wiederholenden Bewegung von Flächen, ist das ausschlaggebende Prinzip in *Rhythmus 21*. Plastizität wird auch dort durch geordnete Bewegungsabläufe von Flächen erreicht.

Das abstrakte Wahrnehmungsregime, das sich in *Rhythmus 21* durch die Dynamik des Bildraums aufbaut, wird in der Neuen Sachlichkeit umgedeutet. Sie greift dieses Konzept filmisch auf und setzt es in der Logik der Raumbildung ein.[15] Pabsts *Die freudlose Gasse* wird in diesem Beitrag als Beispiel für diese Zusammensetzung herangezogen, um zu zeigen, wie eine filmische Erzählung räumlich rhythmisch arrangiert wird.

15 Vgl. Hermann Kappelhoff: Realismus. Das Kino und die Politik des Ästhetischen. Berlin 2008, S. 41.

II. *Die freudlose Gasse*

G. W. Pabsts *Die freudlose Gasse* wird als exemplarisches Werk der Neuen Sachlichkeit im Film wahrgenommen. Der neusachliche Film wendet sich von expressionistischen Darstellungsweisen ab. Es rücken vielmehr Aufnahmen sozial-kritischer Themen mit realistischen Sets und einer klaren, unverzerrten Bildsprache, die sich dem Dokumentarischen annähert, in den Vordergrund. Die Gegenständlichkeit zeigt sich in den detailgetreuen, realistischen Ausstattungen ebenso wie in den Aufnahmen, die so montiert werden, dass möglichst das Gesamtbild einer Situation verständlich wird. Handlungsszenen wechseln sich schnell ab, Parallelmontagen bringen die verschiedenen Erzählstränge miteinander in Verbindung.

Was allen Kunstrichtungen der Neuen Sachlichkeit (Malerei, Fotografie, Film) gemeinsam ist, ist „dass sie die Konstruktion der Bewegung, die Konstruktion des Raums oder die der fotografischen Gegenständlichkeit den expressiven Atmosphären des früheren Weimarer Kinos entgegenstellen."[16] In den Filmen der Neuen Sachlichkeit werden vor allem Details und mikrogeschichtliche Beobachtungsräume sowie persönliche Schicksalslinien der Figuren, die sich an bestimmten Orten verfestigen, aufgebaut. In Pabsts Film *Die freudlose Gasse* werden parallele Handlungen durch die rhythmische Verbindung von Raumebenen im Bild zueinander geführt.

Siegfried Kracauer kritisiert Pabsts Konzentration auf das Gegenständliche, wenn er ihn abwertend als Fotografen ausweist.[17] Die in den Vordergrund gerückte Gegenständlichkeit, welche die neusachliche Kunst auszeichnet, kann hingegen auch als „spezifische Form ästhetischer Abstraktion, die sie dem expressiven Ausdruck entgegenstellt"[18], begriffen werden. Versteht man die „Haltung des Photographen"[19] als ästhetisches Grundprinzip, wird die Montage in ihrer spezifischen Spannung zwischen Diskontinuität und Kontinuität, zwischen Fragmentarisierung des Bildes und Dynamisierung des Raumes, als eigenständige Form kenntlich. Gerade die Konzentration auf das Gegenständliche führt dazu, Szenen so zu verbinden, dass erst im montierten Bildraum die Dynamik des Ganzen ersichtlich wird.

Die freudlose Gasse wurde in der Filmgeschichte zwar vor allem aufgrund des realistischen Stils der Aufnahmen ausgezeichnet, fiel aber gerade deshalb auch Zensur und Kritik zum Opfer. Kracauers Kritik, der Film sei

---

16 Ebd., S. 36f.

17 Vgl. ebd., S. 178.

18 Ebd., S. 37.

19 Hermann Kappelhoff: Der möblierte Mensch. G.W. Pabst und die Utopie der Sachlichkeit. Ein poetologischer Versuch zum Weimarer Autorenkino. Berlin 1994, S. 28.

zu melodramatisch oder die realistischen Szenen seien wahllos eingesetzt und würden bloß innere Geschehnisse symbolisieren, beruht nicht allein auf dem narrativen und ästhetischen Arrangement Pabsts, sondern ist auch der Zensurgeschichte des Films geschuldet.[20]

Die neue Gegenständlichkeit erweist sich in Pabsts Film als ambivalent: Objektgebundener Fotorealismus der Aufnahmen wird gekoppelt mit der melodramatischen Erzählung. Die Gestaltung und der Bezug auf das Gegenständliche entstehen vor allem auf der Ebene der Bildkomposition, ihrem Arrangement.[21]

Die freudlose Gasse zeigt das soziale Elend im Wien der Nachkriegszeit exemplarisch an den gesellschaftlichen Interaktionen innerhalb einer Gasse: Die Melchiorgasse wird als (sozialer) Raum einer ganzen Stadt inszeniert. Einzelne Orte wie das Treppenhaus Frau Greifers werden zu Brennpunkten der Spielhandlung, an denen die Narration rhythmisch strukturiert ist und die verschiedenen Erzählstränge in Verbindung gebracht werden.

Die Figuren und somit die unterschiedlichen sozialen Schichten kreuzen sich in jenem Treppenhaus, das durch ein Hinterzimmer in ein Bordell führt. Finanziell schwache Mädchen arbeiten hier ihre Schulden bei Frau Greifer, der Besitzerin, mit sexuellen Dienstleistungen ab. Neben der Melchiorgasse als Gesamtschauplatz, sind das Treppenhaus und Josef Geiringers Fleischerei als innere Räume der Erzählhandlung strukturiert. Der Keller des Fleischers ist in dunklen Abschnitten dargestellt, die kaum ausgeleuchtet sind. Die innere Raumaufteilung erfolgt vorwiegend aus der Lichtarchitektur, die realistisch eingesetzt wird. Wie die bewegten Flächen in *Rhythmus 21*, die durch ihr abwechselndes Auftreten in unterschiedlich kurzer Dauer eine Bildtiefe erzeugen, kreuzen sich auch in *Die freudlose Gasse* die Handlungsebenen durch Montage an bestimmten Orten, was zu einem ausgeweiteten Bildraum führt.

Ein rhythmischer Wert zeigt sich in *Die freudlose Gasse* zunächst an einem zentralen Ort der Erzählung: Das Treppenhaus ist der Raum, an dem sich die sozialen Topographien (der wohlhabenden Ober- und der armen Unterschicht) verflechten. Hier werden auch die Wege der Figuren gelenkt, die in ein realistisch nachgezeichnetes Setting von Details und Perspektiven hereintreten. Licht und Schatten werden dort eingesetzt, wo es notwendig

20 Vgl. Kappelhoff: Realismus, S. 184; Horak weist auf den Umstand hin, dass Kracauer und andere zeitgenössische Kritiker eine verstümmelte Version, die der Zensur unterlag, gesichtet hätten und so ihre Kritik zu falschen Filmanalysen führte. Eine der Zensurbegründungen lautet etwa, der Film erwecke Abscheu und Mitleid, er sei ein Zeitdokument und verkörpere die schlimmsten Erscheinungen einer schlimmen Zeit. Vgl. Jan-Christopher Horak: Der Fall Die freudlose Gasse. Eine Rekonstruktion im Münchner Filmmuseum. In: Armin Loacker (Hg.): Wien, die Inflation und das Elend. Essays und Materialien zum Stummfilm Die Freudlose Gasse. Wien 2008, S. 185-206.

21 Vgl. Kappelhoff: Der möblierte Mensch, S. 35-46.

ist – etwa um Figuren herauszuheben oder soziale Strukturen wie bürgerliches Wohlbefinden (ausgeleuchtet) und Armut in dunklen Gassen darzustellen. Auch die bürgerliche Welt Gretes bleibt mit den dunklen Topographien Marias unvermittelt. Erst die Montage strukturiert die verschiedenen Räume und sozialen Wirklichkeitsebenen in ein rhythmisches Arrangement der Neuen Sachlichkeit. Die parallele Erzählhandlung an unterschiedlichen Orten verschmilzt räumlich auf zwei Ebenen: dem Treppenhaus Frau Greifers und der Melchiorgasse als Gesamtdarstellung.

Die Montage konstruiert einen abstrakten Bildraum, der im Rahmen eines neusachlichen Realismusmodells dargestellt wird. Die Hell-/Dunkel- bzw. Licht-/Schatten-Kompositionen, welche die Bildräume in *Die freudlose Gasse* bestimmen, setzen das filmästhetische Konzept des dynamisierten Bildraums fort, in dem es zur Auflösung der räumlich-figurativen Strukturen kommt.[22]

Mit der Dynamisierung des Bildraums greift *Die freudlose Gasse* eines der Grundprinzipien elementarer Gestaltung auf und bringt durch rhythmische Anordnung die Narration in eine realistische Darstellungsform bewegter Räume. Der Bildraum „ist selbst Bestandteil einer übergreifenden Rhythmisierung, einer Bewußtseinsbewegung, die das Bild und den Blick auf das Bild einschließt.“[23]

Die Anordnung der Narration in den parallel verlaufenden Erzählsträngen, die nach und nach ineinander geführt werden, bedingt geradezu ein realistisches Setting. Realismus bezieht sich aus der Vielschichtigkeit gleichzeitig verlaufender Episoden, die im Bildraum rhythmisch ineinander geordnet werden.

Wenn Rhythmus, wie für Hans Richter, bedeutet, auf elementare Formen der Gestaltung zurückzugreifen und diese über ein logisches Anordnungsprinzip in Verbindung zu setzen, dann entsteht dadurch ein Bildraum, der sich als solcher in seiner Veränderung durch Tiefe und Weite, Hell und Dunkel, Bewegung und Dauer ausdrückt. Diese Form des Arrangements von Elementen im Bild – bei *Rhythmus 21* sind es die entstehenden, sich bewegenden elementaren Formen – mündet in *Die freudlose Gasse* in Bildräume, die Personen, Objekte und Milieus rhythmisch in eine Bildlogik einbinden. Der Film arrangiert den Mikrokosmos Melchiorgasse als ganze Stadt: In einer (fiktiven) Gasse ist die Heterogenität eines umfassenden Stadtgebildes als Gegensatz von arm und reich, sozialem Auf- und Abstieg, jung und alt, modern und klassisch, realistisch und utopisch abgebildet.[24]

---

22 Vgl. Kappelhoff: Der möblierte Mensch, S. 29.

23 Ebd.

24 Vgl. Gerhard Vana: „Wien..., der Ort ist hier nebensächlich.“ Zur Ausstattung von Die freudlose Gasse. In: Armin Loacker (Hg.): Wien, die Inflation und das Elend. Essays und Materialien zum Stummfilm Die freudlose Gasse. Wien 2008, S. 131-156.

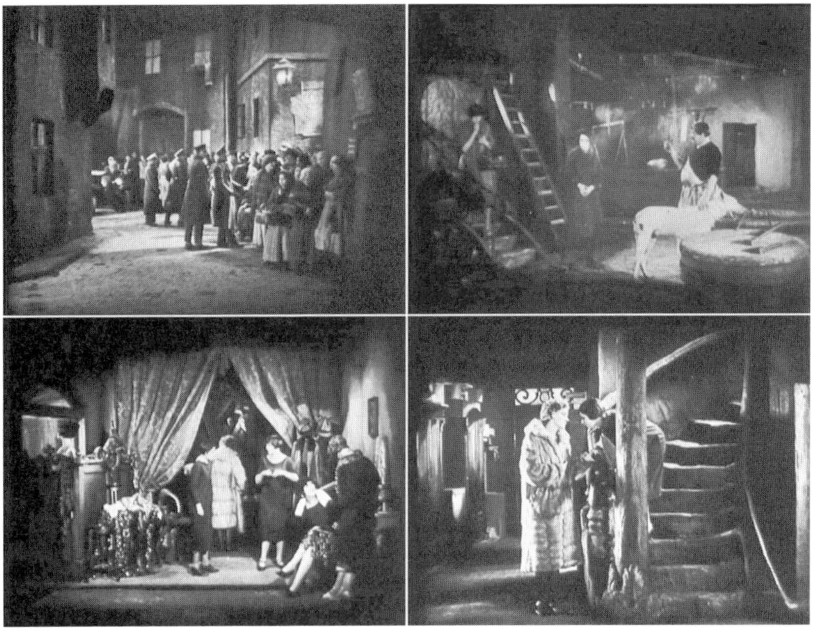

Abb. 2 a-d: Dynamische Bildräume in *Die freudlose Gasse.*

Realismus ist in *Die freudlose Gasse* dem Inhalt der Erzählung, besonders aber der *mise-en-scène* und der räumlichen Ausstattung geschuldet. Die Vermittlung von Realismus auf eine Wahrnehmungsebene, die durch Montage und Lichtführung Tiefe und Dynamik des Bildraums hervorruft, führt auf eine abstrakte Ebene, auf der auch Richters *Rhythmus 21* die Wahrnehmung arrangiert. So entsteht ein zusammenhängender Eindruck von Flächen, die durch Bewegung, Verschiebung und Montage plastisch wahrnehmbar werden. Richters Rechtecke erhalten auf der Ebene der Wahrnehmung des Bildraums ebenso räumliche Tiefe wie die benannten Orte (Melchiorgasse, Fleischerei, Treppenhaus) in *Die freudlose Gasse*.

III. Dynamisierte Bildräume

Der Bildraum erhält dann Tiefe, wenn die verschiedenen Abschnitte miteinander in Verbindung gebracht werden: Rhythmus tritt hierfür als strukturierendes und verbindendes Element auf. Licht/Schatten und Montage geben dem Bildraum in *Die freudlose Gasse* eine innere Struktur. Doch erst der Einsatz sich wiederholender Elemente – etwa das Auftreten von Objekten/Personen an bestimmten Orten/Stellen – gibt dem Bildraum Tiefe und Dynamik. Die Wahrnehmung des Bildraums bleibt so nicht auf der dargestellten Gegenständlichkeit der Ausstattung stehen, sondern wird in eine Gesamtdarstellung überführt. Die Abwechslung der Szenen verschiedener paralleler Erzählstränge tritt durch den rhythmischen Wert der Montage in einen Modus des Wiedererkennens ein. Diese Bewegung führt in einen ausgeweiteten Raum, der die Tiefe und vielschichtigen Ebenen der Erzählung wahrnehmbar macht. *Die freudlose Gasse* bedingt dies vor allem durch die Parallelmontagen und die Gegenüberstellung von Gegensätzen als Stilmittel: die konträren Milieuschichten kreuzen sich im Film bis zu seinem Ende. Auf diese Weise wird vermittels realistischer Settings, trotz des sachlichen Blicks auf soziale Milieus und des parallelen Verlaufs unterschiedlicher Erzählebenen ein abstraktes Konzept in das Alltagsgeschehen eingebracht. Es sind die Sehanordnungen und Denkbewegungen, die durch Montage und Inszenierung wesentlicher Räume der Erzählung im Bildraum rhythmisch geordnet werden.

Die rhythmische Strukturierung des Bildraums führt in *Rhythmus 21* zu beweglichen Flächen: durch eine formale Bildsprache, die plastisch sichtbar wird, entstehen Bewegungsabläufe, die den Bildraum an sich dynamisieren. *Die freudlose Gasse* teilt dieses Konzept in seiner Bildgestaltung und dem rhythmischen Arrangement der Handlungsräume: die Dynamik ergibt sich aus der rhythmischen Anordnung der Erzählhandlung, die sich, da gebunden an eine realistische Darstellung, in topologischen Bildräumen entfaltet.

Rhythmus 21 macht durch die Rhythmisierung von Flächen eine Dynamik des Bildraums wahrnehmbar. Eine Erweiterung des Bildraums durch Tiefe und Plastizität wird in *Die freudlose Gasse* durch die Montage paralleler Erzählhandlungen und die Tiefenstruktur der inneren Bildräume erreicht.

Das Programm eines polydimensionalen Raums[25], wie es van Doesburg vorschwebte, erhält durch Richters filmische *Rhythmus*-Arbeiten Form. Erst Rhythmus setzt die abstrakten Elemente in eine visuelle Formensprache um. Rhythmische Anordnungen strukturieren auch die Flächen in Filmen der Neuen Sachlichkeit zu einem dynamischen Bildraum. Rhythmus ist insofern als strukturelles Element zu verstehen, das zur Bewegung von Flächen und zur Erweiterung von Bildräumen führt.

Abbildungsverzeichnis

Abb. 1 a-d: Hans Richter: Rhythmus 21. DVD. 3 min. London: BFI 2001. (Deutschland 1921).
Abb. 2 a-d: Georg Wilhelm Pabst: Die freudlose Gasse. DVD. 151 min. München: Filmmuseum München/Goethe-Institut München/Deutsche Kinemathek Berlin 2009. (Deutschland 1925).

25 Vgl. Mank: Die Kunst des absoluten Films, S.86.

Einfühlung: The Rhythms of Empathy

Paul Dobryden

> So ist der 'Rhythmus' nicht mehr bloß diese Art der Folge von Taktschlägen, Silben, Tönen, sondern er ist ein Lebenselement, in dem ich lebe. [...] Hiermit ist erst das ästhetische Wesen des Rhythmus eigentlich bezeichnet. Sein Sinn liegt in dieser '*Einfühlung*.'[1]
> —Theodor Lipps, 1903

In his influential 1907 dissertation, art historian Wilhelm Worringer contrasted *Abstraktion* to *Einfühlung*: "Wie der Einfühlungsdrang [...] seine Befriedigung in der Schönheit des Organischen findet, so findet der Abstraktionsdrang seine Schönheit im lebenverneinenden Anorganischen, im Kristallinischen oder allgemein gesprochen in aller abstrakten Gesetzmäßigkeit und Notwendigkeit."[2] Employing a vitalist rhetoric, Worringer links *Einfühlung*—rendered as 'empathy' in the following—to naturalistic representations of living figures and things, while excluding abstraction from the flow of life. To a naïve spectator, Hans Richter's *Rhythmus 21* might seem to embody Worringer's life-denying notion of abstraction. The film's ordered repetition and variation of rectangular shapes transmits little of the warmth, spontaneity, and extremes of affect one associates with the discourse on vitalism around 1900.

As Robin Curtis has argued, however, empathetic viewing need not be restricted to realistic or 'organic' representations.[3] Building on this argument, I will argue that Richter's theory of abstract film—a theory that was never fully developed, but was suggestively formulated in a number of short writings—renews a slightly older discourse on empathy in aesthetics, in which the term by no means excluded non-organic or abstract forms. While Worringer's *Abstraktion und Einfühlung* is now perhaps the best-known discussion of empathy in art from this period, empathy was a key concept for a number of important writers on aesthetics and art history in the late 19th and early 20th century, such as Robert Vischer, Theodor Lipps, Heinrich Wölfflin, and August Schmarsow. Although the major works of

1 Theodor Lipps: Ästhetik: Psychologie des Schönen und der Kunst. Vol. 1. Hamburg 1903, p. 424.

2 Wilhelm Worringer: Abstraktion und Einfühlung: Ein Beitrag zur Stilpsychologie. 9th ed. Munich 1919, p. 4.

3 See Robin Curtis: Immersion und Einfühlung: Zwischen Repräsentationalität und Materialität bewegter Bilder. In: montage AV 17/2/2008, pp. 89-107. Curtis's work on immersion has inspired my approach in this essay.

these figures precede Richter's first foray into abstract film, in some cases by decades, the concept continued to circulate, and not just in aesthetics. By the 1920s one finds empathy discussed in works on philosophy, ethics, pedagogy, and more. In the following I link one of Richter's own theoretical statements to the aesthetic discourse on empathy. August Schmarsow's discussion of architectural rhythm, grounded in the human body's empathetic projection into space, provides a particularly apt framework for approaching *Rhythmus 21*.

Empathy became a crucial term in the psychological aesthetics of the late 19th century, designating not just an aesthetic attitude on the part of the spectator, but an anthropological constant. According to its theorists, aesthetic empathy revealed the human ability to project oneself into other people and things; as Juliet Koss writes, empathy "described a potentially uncomfortable destabilization of identity along the viewer's perceptual borders, a sensation at once physical, psychological, and emotional."[4] Robert Vischer's 1873 book *Über das optische Formgefühl*, the first major work of *Einfühlungsästhetik*, still bears traces of Romanticism. Asking what motivates the empathetic "Verschmelzung von Subjekt und Objekt," Vischer writes that it is nothing less than "der pantheistische Drang zur Vereinigung mit der Welt, welcher sich [...], sei es nun bewußt oder unbewußt, an die Allheit wendet."[5]

Theodor Lipps is perhaps the most representative of the writers of this time who were concerned with empathy. His massive two-volume *Ästhetik* begins with the psychic foundations of empathy, before proceeding to address human identification with natural objects, and finally all forms of art. For Lipps, empathy grounds aesthetic pleasure, constituting a form of "objektivirter Selbstgenuß":

> In jedem Fall ist, was ich einfühle, nicht (oder nicht zunächst) Lust oder Unlust, sondern es ist Leben und Thätigkeit oder eine Weise meiner Selbstbethätigung. Ich fühle etwa kräftiges und gesundes Leben ein in die Form eines menschlichen Körpers; dann nenne ich diesen Körper kraftvoll und gesund. Ich fühle in die weite Halle eine sich aufrichtende und ausweitende Thätigkeit ein. Ich fühle ein anderes Mal in die Geberde oder in die Worte eines Menschen Freude, Trauer, Verzweiflung ein. Auch diese letzten Worte bezeichnen ja Weisen meiner Thätigkeit oder der Bethätigung meiner selbst.[6]

Although the notion of 'objectified pleasure in oneself' brings to mind Nietzsche's will to power, for Lipps the self is profoundly divided, even

4 Juliet Koss: Modernism after Wagner. Minneapolis 2010, p. 67.

5 Robert Vischer: Über das optische Formgefühl. Ein Beitrag zur Ästhetik. Leipzig 1873, p. 28.

6 Theodor Lipps: Einfühlung und ästhetischer Genuß. In: Emil Utitz (ed.): Ästhetik. Berlin 1923, pp. 152-167, here: pp. 152-153.

porous. The process of empathy is not one of mastery or appropriation, but of identification, transfer, and exchange.

The first volume of Lipps' *Ästhetik* also contains a large chapter on rhythm in poetry and music, establishing a relationship between rhythm and empathy that was reflected by other authors of the time as well: Willy Drost's 1919 dissertation *Die Lehre vom Rhythmus in der heutigen Ästhetik der bildenden Künste* contains discussions of Lipps, Worringer, and Schmarsow (Drost was Schmarsow's student), as well as sections on Karl Groos and British writer Violet Paget—both of whom engaged heavily with Lipps' aesthetics.[7] That empathy and rhythm would intersect in these writings is unsurprising. Both concepts played crucial roles in aesthetic and (sometimes pseudo-)scientific attempts during this period to understand how perceptual forms generate and transmit affect. Furthermore, insofar as psychological and physiological processes might explain cultural forms, empathy and rhythm held the promise of reconciling natural and human sciences.

While the notion of rhythm certainly aligns with the much-discussed analogy between absolute film and music, referring exclusively to music underestimates the term's pan-medial appeal. Writing in 1908, the architect Hermann Muthesius went so far as to place rhythm at the root of human culture as a whole: "Der Rhythmus ist jeder menschlichen Tätigkeit eigentümlich, er ist das erste Gesetz aller Äußerungen,"[8] including all forms of ornamentation, agriculture, and religion. For Muthesius, virtually all expressions of culture are rhythmic. The term occurs frequently in the works on the aesthetics of empathy as well. Rhythm appears already in Vischer's 1873 text, in reference to optical-spatial harmony of forms, while Schmarsow uses the term to designate the *Gestaltungsprinzip* of the depth axis in architecture. Along with Heinrich Wölfflin, another major art historian of the day, Schmarsow offered an influential discussion of empathy in architecture in which rhythm played a key role.

As a theory of how we project ourselves beyond our bodies, *Einfühlungsästhetik* gave special attention to the human construction and experience of space. Schmarsow's work in particular offers a concept of rhythm that opens *Rhythmus 21* to an interpretation grounded in a theory of space. In the 1890s, Schmarsow introduced a radically embodied theory of architectural space into art history. According to Schmarsow, most art historians had understood architecture exclusively in visual terms. Moreover, this visual perspective was overwhelmingly static, and could not account for the experience of moving

7 See Willy Drost: Die Lehre vom Rhythmus in der heutigen Ästhetik der bildenden Künste. Leipzig 1919.

8 Hermann Muthesius: Die Einheit der Architektur. Betrachtungen über Baukunst, Ingenieurbau und Kunstgewerbe. Berlin 1908, p. 3.

through space.[9] Schmarsow, who considered architecture the art of *Raumgestaltung*, made the human body the measure of all architectural forms. Drawing on *Einfühlungsästhetik*, Schmarsow conceived of architectural space as a projection of the body. The vertical extension of a building is a projection of human height; its horizontal extension a projection of the width of the shoulders and extended arms; its depth a projection of the body's forward locomotion. Schmarsow thus analyzes architecture according to dimension-specific '*Gestaltungsprinzipien*'—proportion (vertical), symmetry (horizontal, based on the horizontal symmetry of the body), and rhythm (movement in depth):

> im Vollzug der Bewegungsachse des Raumgebildes, d.h. in der Tiefenausdehnung, die erst den freien Spielraum des lebenden Individuums und die Wandelbahn seines Tuns und Treibens von dem engen Gehäuse eines dreidimensionalen Körpers unterscheidet, [waltet] eben dies dritte Gestaltungsprinzip, das ich [...] als 'Rhythmus' angesprochen habe, weil es sich dabei immer um die zeitliche Auffassungsform eines räumlichen oder körperlichen Gebildes handelt, das Symmetrie und Proportion in sich vereinigt, und weil es dabei nicht allein auf die räumlich nebeneinander befindliche, also simultan beharrende, sondern auf die sukzessiv erfolgende oder absehbare, d.h. im Nacheinander erlebbare Wiederkehr solcher Gliederung ankommt.[10]

Humans do not simply have bodies—they have bodies that can move. It is the ability to move, in particular the forward movement of walking, that determines the way we experience and project ourselves into space. It is not just vision, but movement in time, both real and potential, that generates the rhythm of space; the architect is the designer of these spatial rhythms. Schmarsow's notion of spatial rhythm as an empathetic projection of human movement, I argue, offers a more concrete approach to the visual-spatial effects of *Rhythmus 21* than the analogy to music.

In Richter's writings of the early 1920s, one hears echoes of the aesthetic discourse on empathy. "Dieser Film hier," Richter writes in "Die schlecht trainierte Seele," referring to the article's illustrated film strips resembling *Rhythmus 21*, "gibt keine 'Haltepunkte', an denen man in Erinnerungen umkehren konnte, man ist—ausgeliefert—zum 'Fühlen' gezwungen—zum Mitgehen im Rhythmus—Atmen—Herzschlag."[11] It is clear that for Richter,

---

9 Indeed, as Wolfgang Kemp has argued, space was not even a category in architectural theory before Schmarsow. See Kemp: Architektur analysieren. Munich 2009, here: chapter 3.

10 August Schmarsow: Raumgestaltung als Wesen der architektonischen Schöpfung. In: Zeitschrift für Ästhetik und allgemeine Kunstwissenschaft 9 (1914), pp. 84-85.

11 Hans Richter: Die schlecht trainierte Seele. In: G. Zeitschrift für elementare Gestaltung III (1924). Reprint edited by Marion von Hofacker, München 1986, pp. 44-47, here: p. 45.

abstract film does not solicit a purely visual spectatorship; Richter resists, as Schmarsow puts it, the "seltsame Ausschließlichkeit, die das Auge als die einzige Instanz [...] einsetzen möchte und ein Kunstwerk nur insoweit als solches anerkennen will, wie es nach den Forderungen des Auges geordnet sei."[12] The work is meant to engage the spectator's breath and heartbeat, the body's most essential rhythms. Moreover, Richter is also at pains to prevent static contemplation. Like Schmarsow's architectural spectator, the viewer of the film is mobile, even when sitting still. While 'Mitgehen' is clearly meant metaphorically, the choice evokes Schmarsow's earlier image of the human gait as the Urform of architectural depth. Richter thus imagines a spectator strikingly similar to Schmarsow's—embodied, mobile, and empathetic. The film is not meant to be kept at a distance. For Schmarsow, however, the embodied mobile subject is an anthropological reality; it characterizes a universal human experience, but has simply been forgotten by theory. Richter, on the other hand, historicizes this spectator. Employing a rhetoric of decadence, he writes "Die lebendige Kraft die wir im Empfinden besitzen, ist verfettet, der Atmungsprozeß gehemmt."[13] Rhythmic filmmaking is meant as a corrective to this historical degeneration of human receptive capacities.

Given the standard description of absolute film as painting in motion, it would seem appropriate to ask how theorists such as Lipps approached painting. Richter was, after all, a painter before he was a filmmaker.[14] Lipps wrote extensively about geometrical forms, painting, and space in his *Ästhetik*. For Lipps, empathy imparts movement to visual forms. When we attend to a line on canvas, for instance, we see it striving from one point to the next. This is not an imagined movement, but real, "unmittelbar erlebte Bewegung."[15] When we focus on a visual object, separating it from its context, this happens (like all perception) in time; as the object is successively generated in our perception, it moves. In this account, empathy gives life and force to static representations. But what happens when film sets forms themselves into motion? Are these somehow already enlivened, rendering the spectator superfluous? The cinematic spectator is arguably closer to the mobile observer of architecture. Admittedly, the building does not move around an immobile observer, as is the case in the movies; in both cases, however, observer and observed are in motion relative to each other (if only in a virtual sense), regardless of who does the moving.

Proposing what he calls the "Prinzip des malerischen Herausschneidens," Lipps claims that painting "stellt Raum dar und lebende We-

12 Schmarsow: Raumgestaltung, p. 66.

13 Richter: Die schlecht trainierte Seele, p. 46.

14 He was also, at the urging of his father, a student of architecture and a carpenter's apprentice.

15 Theodor Lipps: Ästhetik, vol. 1, p. 236.

sen und Dinge in ihm, sie stellt, genauer gesagt, jedesmal ein *Stück* Raum dar."[16] Lipps' language here seems, rather surprisingly, more appropriate to photography than to painting. Schmarsow's notion of *Raumgestaltung*, by contrast, emphasizes the fully constructed and artificial quality of architectural space; architecture is a projection of human dimensions and movement, not a representation of the natural world. This kind of non-mimetic *Gestaltung* prefigures the term's importance for the German avant-garde of the early 1920s, with Richter himself as one of its chief proponents. It is a short step from the dynamic, constructed space of architecture to the dynamic, fully virtual space of Richter's first abstract film. Unlike Viking Eggeling and Walther Ruttmann, who both prefer the flat canvas, Richter experiments with depth. Films like Eggeling's *Diagonal Symphony* and Ruttmann's *Opus 1* fit more easily between abstract painting and music (as their titles indicate), while *Rhythmus 21*, on the other hand, continually invokes the third dimension. Its canvas invites us to look through it, the face of its images not quite a window, but emphatically not a wall. The viewer peers into an endless space of projection.

The opening frames involve a play of opening and closing. Beginning with a black screen, white spaces enter the frame from left and right, and recede again; after a jump cut the white spaces return, and recede. Our eyes read the white space as front, black behind. The white spaces mimic curtains in a theater, alternately concealing and revealing a black space in the background. The uniformity and speed of their motion, however, as well as their sudden return after the jump cut, tell us that while there is a third dimension in this film, its space is not naturalistic or mimetic, but technologically constructed, virtual, and manipulable. Having set up a contrast between front and back, the film then demonstrates recession into depth. A large white square appears in the center of the frame; then, shrinking on all sides, it appears to move away from us until it is a tiny hole in the distance. Another square jumps into frame and recedes, before giving way to horizontal white 'curtains' that close and open from top and bottom. The various movements in the film can be reduced to three major types: lateral movement, recession and approach, and 'jumping' (forms that suddenly appear or disappear, sometimes reappearing in a different part of the frame). Each type of movement bears upon our perception of the film's space: lateral movements delineate front and back, figure and ground; receding and approaching forms define depth; jumping blocks display the space's virtuality and malleability. This filmic space, in which movement can occur discontinuously, is of a different quality than our own. The film essentially repeats or varies these types of movements in increasingly complex combinations. Differently shaded forms also overlap at times, further complicating our sense of spatial depth. Reading *Rhythmus 21* in terms of Schmarsow's ar-

16 Lipps: Ästhetik, vol. 2, p. 165.

chitectural aesthetics, it is precisely the film's play with movement in depth that constitutes its 'rhythm.' While often discontinuous in its movements, *Rhythmus 21* nonetheless solicits the spectator's sense of depth and constructs a three-dimensional image space. This depth opens the film to the empathetic spectator, who is mobilized by self-projection into the screen's virtual 'space of free play' (*freien Spielraum*).

Schmarsow's theory, however, cannot account for the particularity of the film's rhythms. The rhythms of *Rhythmus 21* are not those of the human gait, in which Schmarsow grounds architectural rhythm. As a virtual space, the film's forms are literally ungrounded—there is no gravity pulling them downward, no sense of weight, none of the downward force that defines the reality of walking. The speed with which the forms approach and recede also changes dramatically. These are, arguably, the modernized rhythms of the factory, of trains and automobiles, of flight, even of ballistics. These technologies greatly expanded the way human bodies could experience space; it is a fallacy to believe, however, that the kinds of movement they enabled are less 'bodily' than walking. They are simply less dependent on legs. Schmarsow's theory is tied to a supposedly universal, authentic, and primal mode of conveyance: the gait. If we do away with Schmarsow's anthropological universalism, however, we can admit that the body is just as implicated by modern forms of movement. Historically, technologically produced motion expands the modes of empathy and spatial rhythm available to human experience. I would thus align *Rhythmus 21* with architectural experiments of the 1920s that responded to new technologies of movement, such as the 'Vorbeifahrarchitektur' of Martin Wagner or Frederick Kiesler's imagined "Stadt in der Luft."[17] Not to mention cinema itself—film was a new mode of virtual mobility that could take viewers across massive distances, while at the same time acclimating audiences to the discontinuous rhythms of editing and montage. In its virtuality, rapidity, and discontinuity, Richter's film goes far beyond the more grounded rhythms described by Schmarsow; it is, however, no less open to spectatorial empathy.

The proponents of empathy rejected the view that the ideal aesthetic perception was intellectual, distanced, and contemplative. Writers such as Vischer, Lipps, and Schmarsow hoped to articulate the ways in which the border between human beings and the things they perceive is, on the contrary, highly porous and fluid. The legacy of this discourse resonated with the historical avant-garde, including Richter, in its attempt to overcome a number of fundamental separations: the separation between mind and body; between spectator and artwork; between individual spectators; between nationalities. Famously, Richter found in film the potential for a 'universal language.' This language might be understood as the language

17 See also the article "Architektur" in this volume.

of empathy, rather than a system of conventional signs—essentially not a language at all. The imagined empathetic spectator inhabits a pre-linguistic state of exchange between self and world—Richter's search for a spectator beyond language and identity thus maintains the problematic universalism found in earlier theories of aesthetic empathy.

Elementares Kino: Fünf Notizen zu Hans Richters *Rhythmus 21*

Ingo Zechner

Der Film beginnt, wo die Malerei endet: mit einem schwarzen Quadrat auf weißem Grund. Das ist das erste Bild von Hans Richters Film *Rhythmus 21*, das erste Bild nach dem Vorspann. *Biographisch* steht es am Anfang des ersten Films eines Künstlers, der sein Medium gewechselt hat: von der Malerei zum Film. *Kunsthistorisch* ist es das erste Bild eines Films, der den Laufbildern den Weg von den Jahrmärkten in die Museen und Galerien gebahnt hat. *Filmhistorisch* gilt dieser Film vielen bis heute als Beginn eines neuen Kinos, das man ‚abstrakten Film', ‚absoluten Film', ‚Cinéma pur' genannt hat, aber besser als ‚elementares Kino' bezeichnen sollte. Mit ihm vollzieht sich *filmtheoretisch* eine kopernikanische Wende, die den Film und das Kino auf ihre elementaren Bestandteile und damit auf die Bedingungen ihrer Möglichkeit zurückgeführt hat. *Ontologisch* ist er – mit Richters Worten – die Einlösung eines Versprechens der Malerei, das sich erst im Film verwirklichen lässt. Seine Bilder haben *logisch* betrachtet jedoch die Form eines Problems. Sie sind *phänomenologisch* mehrdeutig.

Notiz 1: Phänomenologie

Ob das Quadrat für ihn eine metaphysische Bedeutung hatte, sei eine Frage, auf die er keine richtige Antwort geben könne, sagt Richter. Denn selbstverständlich habe das Quadrat für jeden Menschen eine Bedeutung; doch welche Bedeutung es habe, sei hier nicht der Punkt.[1] Und was Richter über die metaphysische Bedeutung sagt, gilt für jegliche Bedeutung. Die geometrischen Formen in seinen *Rhythmus*-Filmen hätten jedenfalls nichts mit der metaphysischen Tragweite zu tun, die Piet Mondrian und Theo van Doesburg dem Quadrat beigemessen hatten.[2]

Richters Selbstbefragung zeugt von Weisheit und Witz: So sehr er selbst sich bemüht haben mag, jegliche Bedeutung der von ihm verwendeten geometrischen Formen zu eliminieren, so entspannt formuliert er die Einsicht, dass ihm das wohl nicht gelungen sein dürfte. Indem er sich selbst in eine Reihe mit allen anderen stellt, gibt er die Deutungshoheit, die den Autoren und Schöpfern bei der Interpretation ihrer eigenen Werke eingeräumt wird, der Lächerlichkeit preis. Ob etwas eine Bedeutung hat oder nicht und was diese

1 Vgl. Cleve Gray (Hg.): Hans Richter by Hans Richter. London 1971, S. 131.

2 Vgl. ebd., S. 82.

Bedeutung ist, hängt nun einmal nicht vom Willen eines Einzelnen ab. Doch jede Bedeutung ist im doppelten Wortsinn gleichgültig, weil es hier nicht nur um keine bestimmte, sondern überhaupt nicht um die Bedeutung geht.

Darin kann man einen Antagonismus zwischen zwei Avantgardebewegungen anklingen hören, denen sich Richter verbunden sah: zwischen *Dadaismus* und *Konstruktivismus*. Richter lässt der Metaphysik den Raum, den *Suprematismus*, *De Stijl* und andere esoterische Spielarten des *Konstruktivismus* ihr gegeben haben. Was wie eine Versöhnung zwischen Dadaismus und Konstruktivismus erscheinen mag, ist jedoch ein kaum verhohlener Triumph des ersteren über letzteren: Die metaphysische Bedeutung muss sich ihren Interpretationsspielraum mit allen anderen Bedeutungen teilen. Das Metaphysische wird auf ein und dieselbe Stufe mit dem Banalen gestellt. Und beide spielen keine Rolle mehr.

Das Bild steht zuallererst für sich selbst, nicht für anderes. Ikonographie, Ikonologie und die mit ihnen verbündete Hermeneutik müssen sich mit einem Nebenschauplatz begnügen. Den Hauptschauplatz besetzen nicht die intelligiblen Eigenschaften des Bildes, sondern die visuellen. Die dadaistische Anarchie bereitet einem radikalen Konstruktivismus den Boden, den sie ihm jedoch gleich wieder entzieht.

Befreit vom Ballast der Bedeutungen erweist sich das Bild erst recht als mehrdeutig – nicht mehr im *symbolischen*, wohl aber im *phänomenologischen* Sinn. Die Mehrdeutigkeit ist Teil seiner *Wahrnehmung*, noch bevor sie Teil seiner *Interpretation* werden kann. Mehrdeutig ist schon seine *Syntax*, nicht erst seine *Semantik*, seine *Form*, nicht erst sein *Inhalt*. Bereits das erste Bild des Films ist ein *Vexierbild*: ein schwarzes Quadrat auf weißem Grund in der Mitte des Bildes und/oder zwei ungleich schmale weiße Rechtecke auf schwarzem Grund an dessen linkem und rechtem Rand.

Notiz 2: Logik

Was gemeinhin als psychologisches Problem gilt, ist tatsächlich ein logisches. In der Wahrnehmung kippen *Figur* und *Grund* des Bildes von Zeit zu Zeit. Der in der Wahrnehmungspsychologie gebräuchliche Begriff einer ‚multistabilen Wahrnehmung' beschreibt dieses Kippen als sukzessiven Wechsel von Zuständen. Das *Kippbild* zeichnet sich jedoch dadurch aus, dass sein Entweder-oder zugleich ein Sowohl-als-auch ist. Anstelle einer exklusiven Disjunktion behauptet sich in ihm eine vermeintlich unmögliche inklusive – in der Form einer *Und/Oder-Verknüpfung* der einander ausschließenden Möglichkeiten.

Wenn sie sich auf die logische Unentscheidbarkeit des Bildes einlässt, droht die Wahrnehmung jeden Halt zu verlieren. Und diese Unentscheidbarkeit beschränkt sich nicht auf die Beziehung von Figur und Grund.

Die schwarze Fläche reicht oben und unten bis an den Bildrand *und/oder* darüber hinaus, die zwei weißen Flächen tun dasselbe oben und unten

Abb. 1: Sequenz 1, Einstellung 1, Kader 5.

sowie rechts und links. Und wenn sie über den Bildrand hinausreichen: Wer kann entscheiden, welche Form diese Flächen tatsächlich haben? Ob nicht ein hohes schwarzes Rechteck, von dem nur ein quadratischer Ausschnitt zu sehen ist, eine weiße Fläche unbestimmter Form abdeckt? Ob nicht zwei weiße Quadrate, von denen nur rechteckige Ausschnitte zu sehen sind, eine schwarze Fläche unbestimmter Form teilweise abdecken? Ob die unsichtbaren Teile der sichtbaren Flächen nicht unregelmäßige Ränder haben? Ob sie einander überhaupt abdecken oder nicht vielmehr alle selbst Figuren sind, die auf einem nicht sichtbaren Grund aneinander stoßen?

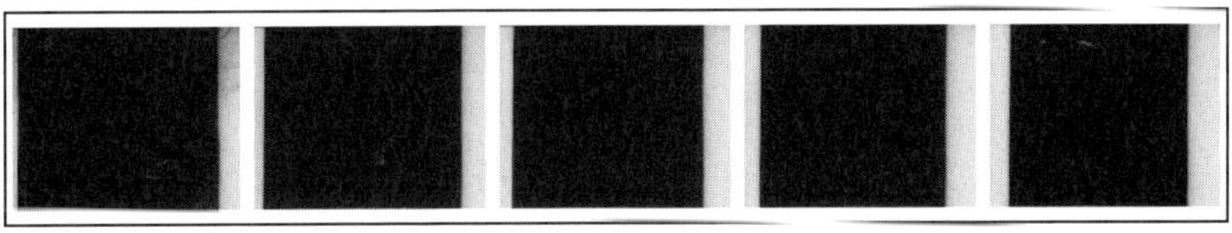

Abb. 2 a-e: Sequenz 1, Einstellung 1, Kader 1-5.

Notiz 3: Ontologie

Ob es sich beim ersten Bild überhaupt um ein schwarzes Quadrat auf weißem Grund handelt, hängt von Entscheidungen ab, die in der Wahrnehmung getroffen werden, aber auch von der Frage, was man im Film als Bild bezeichnet. Nimmt man den Filmstreifen zur Hand und hält ihn gegen das Licht oder legt ihn auf einen Leuchttisch, ist es in jedem Fall falsch, beim ersten Bild von einem schwarzen Quadrat zu sprechen. Die Proportionen lassen selbst für das freie Auge wenig Zweifel, dass es sich allenfalls um ein schwarzes Rechteck handeln kann. Erst das fünfte Bild zeigt ein Quadrat. Spannt man den Filmstreifen hingegen in den Projektor, sind die ersten fünf Bilder und noch zahlreiche folgende in der Projektion Teile ein und desselben Bildes.

Technisch gesprochen: Alles hängt davon ab, ob man sich auf den *Frame* oder auf den *Shot* bezieht, wenn man vom ersten Bild spricht, auf den *Kader* oder die *Einstellung*. Zeigen die Kader verschiedene *Formen*, dann zeigt die Einstellung eine *Transformation* und/oder eine *Translation*.

In der ersten Einstellung des Films erscheint das schwarze Quadrat nicht als Form, sondern *Bestandteil* eines Prozesses, als *Moment* einer Bewegung, als *Stadium* einer Veränderung: ein dickes schwarzes Rechteck auf weißem Grund in der Mitte des Bildes verschmälert sich links und rechts gleichmäßig zu einem schwarzen Quadrat und weiter zu einem dünnen Rechteck *und/oder* zwei ungleich dünne weiße Rechtecke auf schwarzem Grund am linken und rechten Rand des Bildes verbreitern sich gleichmäßig zu zwei dicken weißen Rechtecken *und/oder* zwei weiße Balken unbestimmter Form schieben sich von links und rechts gleichmäßig über einen schwarzen Grund. Das sind nur drei von mehreren Möglichkeiten, diese Einstellung zu *lesen*.

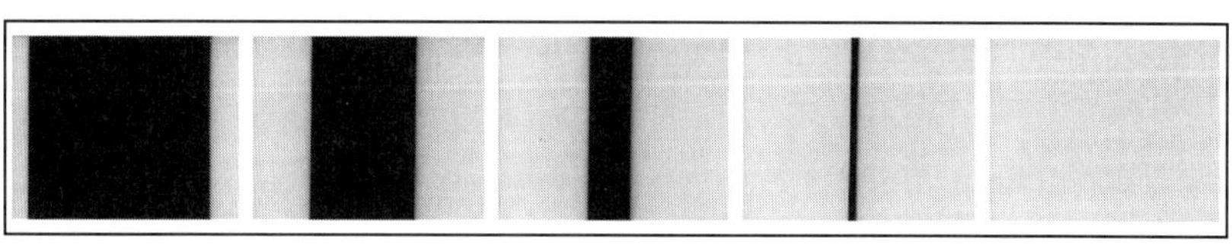

Abb. 3 a-e: Sequenz 1, Einstellung 1 (a-d) + 2 (e), Keyframes.

Auch diesseits der Hermeneutik muss das Bild gelesen werden. Doch seine *Lesbarkeit* kommt in demselben Sinn ohne Text aus wie seine Mehrdeutigkeit ohne Bedeutung. Sie impliziert allerdings eine *Pädagogik* des Bildes, die zu einer Verbalisierung einlädt, obwohl sie keiner Worte bedarf.

Die erste Lektion dieser Pädagogik ist eine über *Differenz* und *Identität*: Was in den Kadern different sein mag, kann in der Einstellung identisch sein. Es sind vielleicht verschiedene schwarze Rechtecke am Filmstreifen zu sehen, aber auf der Leinwand ist es ein und dasselbe Rechteck, das sich verändert. Identität schließt Differenz nicht aus, sondern ein.

Die zweite Lektion ist eine über *Bewegung*: Bewegung ist immer Veränderung – Veränderung der Positionen von Formen im Raum (Translation) oder Veränderung von Formen (Transformation) oder beides zugleich, jedenfalls aber Veränderung der jeweiligen Verhältnisse von Identität und Differenz.

Die dritte Lektion ist eine über das *Bild* selbst: Im Film ist das Bild ein *Möglichkeits-Bild*, noch bevor man – mit dem französischen Philosophen Gilles Deleuze – zwischen einem *Bewegungs-Bild* und einem *Zeit-Bild* unterscheiden kann.

Das Möglichkeits-Bild definiert sich durch seine Beziehung zwischen einem manifesten Bild und einem oder mehreren latenten Bildern. Auf der Ebene der Technik sind die Kader die latenten Bilder der manifesten Einstellung. Auf der Ebene der Wahrnehmung sind es die latenten und manifesten Lesarten des Vexierbildes. Hinsichtlich der Veränderung ist es die Beziehung zwischen den jetzigen, den zukünftigen und den vergangenen Verhältnissen.

Es sind die Verhältnisse und ihre Veränderung, nicht die Formen, die Richter interessieren. Die Definition von Form beziehe sich auf die Wahrnehmung einer formalen Qualität eines einzelnen Objekts oder mehrerer Objekte, sagt Richter. Wenn man aber dieselbe Form wiederhole, immer wieder und in verschiedenen Positionen, dann seien es die Beziehungen zwischen den Positionen, die wahrgenommen würden, nicht die einzelne oder individuelle Form. Man sehe nicht mehr die Form oder das Objekt, sondern eher die Beziehung. Auf diese Weise sehe man eine Art ‚Rhythmus'.[3] Um die Neuartigkeit und Besonderheit des Films als Medium zu akzentuieren, stellt Richter der Orchestrierung von *Form* in der Malerei die Orchestrierung von *Zeit* im Film gegenüber. Durch den Ausdruck ‚Orchestrierung' sollte man sich jedoch nicht zu einer oberflächlichen Analogie zwischen Film und Musik verleiten lassen, umso weniger als Richter ihn sowohl für die Malerei als auch für den Film benutzt. Die Gemeinsamkeit von Film und Musik ist eine strukturelle: Sie besteht im ‚Rhythmus'.

Rhythmus ist für Richter keine Metapher. Als Filmtitel nennt *Rhythmus* den Gegenstand des Films präzise beim Namen. Zugleich formuliert er ein Programm. Rhythmus ist, was Richter mit einem allgemeineren Ausdruck als ‚Artikulation' bezeichnet. Die Abwandlungen und Veränderungen eines Quadrats, wie in der ersten Einstellung von *Rhythmus 21*, nennt Richter nicht länger *Form*, sondern *Artikulation*, genauer: die Artikulation von Zeit – nicht Form. Das ist das Versprechen der Malerei, das sich erst im Film verwirklichen lässt: die Rhythmisierung des Bildes im buchstäblichen, nicht im übertragenen Sinn, die Artikulation seiner Veränderung in der Zeit. Rhythmus ist artikulierte Zeit, sagt Richter. Es sei dasselbe wie Musik. Aber im Film artikuliere man die Zeit visuell, in der Musik auditiv.

3 Vgl. ebd., S. 132.

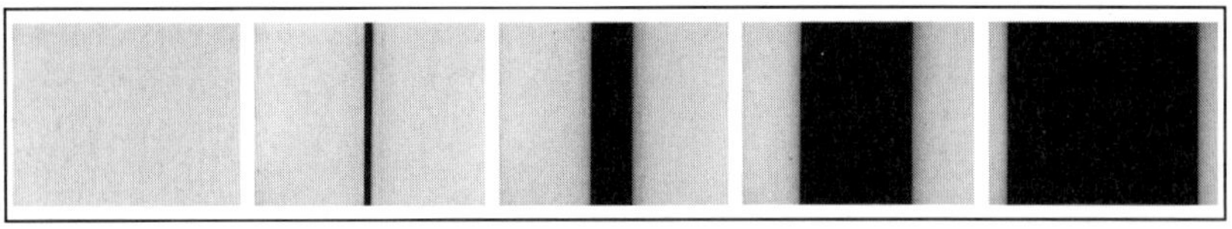

Abb. 4 a-e: Sequenz 1, Einstellung 2 (a) +3 (b-e), Keyframes.

Notiz 4: Filmtheorie

„Wenn sich am Anfang von der Bildmitte aus ein schwarzer Strich verbreitert, bis die schwarze Fläche beidseitig den Rand der Projektionsfläche erreicht", so wirke das „gleichsam wie die Schaffung des Projektionsfeldes, wenn ein Vorhang sich öffnet", schreiben Hans Scheugl und Ernst Schmidt jr. in ihrer *Subgeschichte des Films.*[4] In ihrer assoziativen Beschreibung des Anfangs von *Rhythmus 21* wird dreierlei deutlich: erstens, wie schwierig es ist, die Wahrnehmung von jeglicher symbolischen Interpretation freizuhalten, zweitens dass sich die Wahrnehmung in der Regel für eine der möglichen Lesarten eines Vexierbildes entscheidet und drittens, dass man darüber streiten kann, womit der Film tatsächlich anfängt. Hier gilt nicht mehr die erste Einstellung als Anfang des Films, sondern die dritte, in der die erste noch einmal, diesmal aber in umgekehrter Bewegungsrichtung abläuft. Bleibt man beim Gleichnis vom Vorhang, kann man es dahin erweitern, dass der Vorhang in der ersten Einstellung erst zugehen muss, bevor er in der dritten aufgehen kann.

Doch wer kann schon sagen, ob die Projektionsfläche schwarz oder weiß ist? Wäre es nicht naheliegender, an das Weiß der Leinwand zu denken und die weiße Fläche mit der Projektionsfläche zu identifizieren, nicht die schwarze? Die leere weiße Fläche, wie sie in jener zweiten Einstellung zu sehen ist, die die erste und dritte gleichermaßen trennt und verbindet, nimmt jedoch die Mehrdeutigkeit der vorangehenden und der folgenden Einstellung in sich auf: Ist sie ein weißer Grund ohne Figur oder eine weiße Figur auf unsichtbarem schwarzen Grund? Das hängt von der Lesart ab, für die man sich bei der ersten und bei der dritten Einstellung entscheidet.

Zusammen bilden die ersten drei Einstellungen eine *Sequenz*, zu der auch die folgenden drei gezählt werden können: eine leere schwarze Fläche in der vierten Einstellung als Umkehrung der zweiten, eine Wiederholung der dritten Einstellung in der fünften und noch eine leere schwarze Fläche in der sechsten, bei der allerdings nicht zu entscheiden ist, ob sie als Ab-

4 Hans Scheugl / Ernst Schmidt jr.: Eine Subgeschichte des Films. Lexikon des Avantgarde-, Experimental- und Undergroundfilms. 2 Bde. Frankfurt a.M. 1974, S. 743.

schluss zur ersten Sequenz oder als Anfang zur zweiten zählt, ob sie zu jeder der beiden gehört oder überhaupt selbständig zwischen ihnen steht.

Richters Verfahren, das sich diesseits der gängigen Unterscheidung von Abstraktion und Konkretion bewegt, ist eines der *Elementaranalyse*. Es ist ein transmediales Verfahren, das Richter in der Malerei erprobt hat, im Film neu erfinden musste und im Titel der von ihm 1923-1926 herausgegebenen Zeitschrift *G* zum Programm erhoben hat: *Material zur elementaren Gestaltung*. Er habe Form auf das einfachste Element reduziert, an das er denken konnte, sagt Richter: das Rechteck oder Quadrat, das mit der Form der Leinwand korrespondiert.[5] Die Rede von Elementen und vom Elementaren ist dabei ebenso buchstäblich zu verstehen wie jene vom Rhythmus. Ein Element ist zunächst einmal ein Teil eines größeren Ganzen. In diesem Sinne kann so gut wie alles ein Element sein. Unter den Elementen im engeren Sinn verstand man im späten 19. und frühen 20. Jahrhundert jedoch „die Ur- und Grundstoffe, aus denen die zusammengesetzten Körper bestehen, und in die sie zerlegt werden können, die aber selbst einer weitern Zerlegung nicht mehr fähig sind“[6] oder bisher nicht fähig waren. Weder das eine noch das andere trifft allerdings auf das Rechteck und das Quadrat zu, wie man aus den theoretischen und praktischen Elementaranalysen weiß, die Maler wie Paul Klee, Wassily Kandinsky und Ludwig Hirschfeld-Mack am Bauhaus in Weimar und Dessau parallel zu Richters Arbeiten durchgeführt haben: Beide geometrischen Formen lassen sich jedenfalls in jene Elemente zerlegen, die Kandinsky im Titel seines 1926 publizierten Grundlagentextes der modernen Malerei nennt: Punkt, Linie, Fläche.[7]

Für die Bedeutung von Rechteck und Quadrat mag es entscheidend sein, ob es sich um einfache oder zusammengesetzte Elemente handelt, für ihre Funktion in Richters Elementaranalyse des Kinos ist es ebenso nebensächlich wie die Bedeutung selbst. Was Richter durch sie und ihr Verhältnis zur Leinwand entdeckt und schon in der ersten Sequenz von *Rhythmus 21* vor Augen führt, das sind zwar nicht die Elemente im engeren Sinn, wohl aber die elementaren Verhältnisse des Kinos und ihre Artikulation in der Zeit, die Richtung und Geschwindigkeit ihrer Bewegung, der Rhythmus ihrer Veränderung: das Verhältnis von *Figur und Grund*, von *Schwarz und Weiß*, von *Innen und Außen*, von *Höhe und Breite*, von *oben und unten*, von *rechts und links*. Die Reduktion der Formen und die Eliminierung ihrer Bedeutung öffnen den Blick für das Elementare.

---

5 Vgl. Gray (Hg.): Hans Richter by Hans Richter, S. 82.

6 Elemente (Art.). In: Meyers Großes Konversations-Lexikon. Ein Nachschlagewerk des allgemeinen Wissens. Sechste, gänzlich neubearbeitete und vermehrte Auflage, Bd. 5. Leipzig und Wien 1906, S. 698-700, hier: S. 698.

7 Vgl. Wassily Kandinsky: Punkt und Linie zu Fläche. Beitrag zur Analyse der malerischen Elemente. Bern 1973.

So ist die Abwesenheit anderer Farben nicht einem Mangel der Filmtechnik geschuldet (seinen dritten, nicht erhaltenen Film *Rhythmus 25* hat Richter handkoloriert), sondern ein bewusster Verzicht: Das Schwarzweiß von *Rhythmus 21* zeigt das Verhältnis von *Hell und Dunkel*, von *Licht und Schatten* als das eines maximalen Kontrasts, bevor es mit der Einführung von verschiedenen Grauwerten die Abstufungen zwischen den Extremen sichtbar werden lässt.

Das Verhältnis von *Innen und Außen* ist mehrdeutig wie das von Figur und Grund. Was auf den ersten Blick wie ein in sich geschlossenes Bildfeld aussehen mag, durch dessen Ränder Innen und Außen nicht nur getrennt, sondern vollständig voneinander losgelöst sind, erlaubt auf den zweiten Blick fließende Übergänge zwischen beiden, ein Eindringen ins Bild aus dem Off und ein Verlassen des Bildes ins Off.

Durch ein weiteres mehrdeutiges Phänomen kommen in der zweiten Sequenz zusätzliche Verhältnisse hinzu: das Verhältnis von *groß und klein* und das Verhältnis von *Nähe und Ferne*. Ein großes weißes Quadrat auf schwarzem Grund in der horizontalen Mitte des Bildfeldes schrumpft zu einem kleinen *und/oder* entfernt sich in die Tiefe. Der Bildraum hat plötzlich nicht mehr zwei, sondern drei Dimensionen.

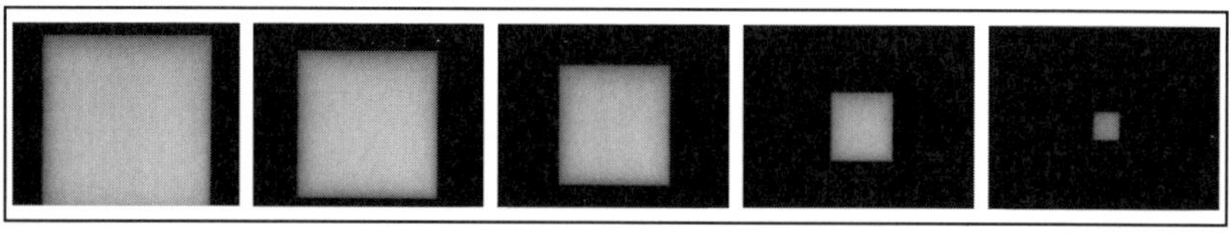

Abb. 5 a-e: Sequenz 2, Einstellung 1, Keyframes.

Wenn Richter diese Bewegung in der zweiten Sequenz zweimal ablaufen lässt, dann tut er das nicht, ohne sie zu variieren. Zwar wiederholt die zweite Einstellung die erste, doch unterscheiden sich ihr Anfang und ihr Ende durch die Größe der Quadrate von der ersten.

Schon die erste Sequenz hat demonstriert, woraus jeder Rhythmus zusammengesetzt ist: aus *Differenz und Wiederholung*. Sie enthält bereits beide Optionen des Prinzips der Variation: die große und die kleine Differenz in der Wiederholung. Die Wiederholung operiert mit Symmetrien, scheinbaren Symmetrien und Asymmetrien.

Die dritte Sequenz scheint in ihren ersten fünf Einstellungen jene der ersten Sequenz zu wiederholen, indem sie das Bild um 90 Grad kippt. Anstelle der Verschmälerung ist eine Schrumpfung getreten, anstelle der horizontalen Bewegung eine vertikale. Tatsächlich handelt es sich aber um völlig verschiedene Einstellungen, deren Unterschiede umso stärker hervortreten, als sie bestimmte Aspekte des Bewegungsverlaufs miteinander teilen. Hier taucht das Quadrat nicht einmal als Durchgangsstadium auf. Wie sollte es auch? Die Leinwand ist schließlich breiter als hoch.

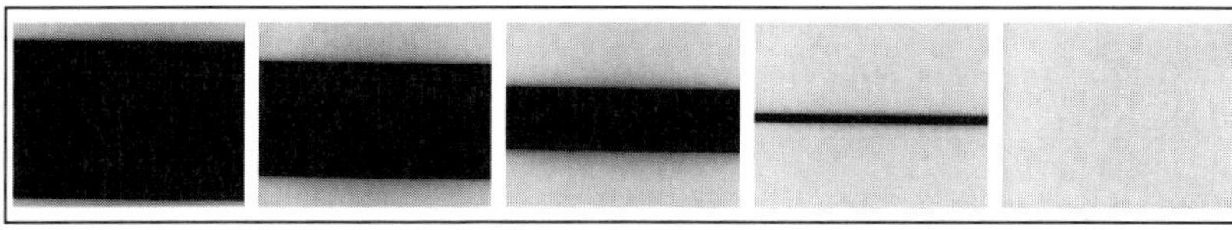

Abb. 6 a-e: Sequenz 3, Einstellung 1 (a-d) + 2 (e), Keyframes.

Rhythmus 21 unternimmt eine systematische Bestandsaufnahme der filmischen Möglichkeiten und ihrer Bedingungen. Paradoxerweise ist es die Reduktion auf das Einfachste, die bereits in den ersten drei Sequenzen die Mannigfaltigkeit der Möglichkeiten hervortreten lässt. Die in den drei Anfangssequenzen erfassten Verhältnisse und ihre Veränderung werden in den folgenden Sequenzen miteinander kombiniert, sukzessive erweitert, mit großen und kleinen Differenzen wiederholt.

Bereits in der verbalen Beschreibung der Mehrdeutigkeit eines statischen Vexierbildes stößt die Sprache an ihre Grenzen, umso mehr wenn das Vexierbild in Bewegung ist. „Unser optisches Begriffsvermögen beruht allgemein ganz eigentlich auf der statischen Raumform der bildenden Künste", sagt Richter. „Der Begriff einer *kinetischen Form* ist bisher kaum vorhanden." Die „Fähigkeit, in *optischen Reihen* zu denken", sei noch „ganz unterentwickelt".[8] Es sind jedoch genau diese Reihen, aus denen *Rhythmus 21* besteht. Statt eines weißen Quadrats, das sich verkleinert *und/oder* in die Tiefe entfernt, sind es schon in der vierten Sequenz zwei, dann drei weiße Rechtecke, von denen sich zwei verkleinern *und/oder* entfernen und das dritte zu schrumpfen *und/oder* sich ins Off des Bildes zurückzuziehen scheint.

Bald kommen gegenläufige Bewegungen einer wechselnden Zahl von Rechtecken und Quadraten in ein und derselben Einstellung hinzu: gleichzeitiges Wachsen und Schrumpfen *und/oder* gleichzeitig ins Bild treten und aus ihm heraustreten, von oben und unten, von rechts und links; gleichzeitiges Wachsen und Schrumpfen *und/oder* sich gleichzeitig entfernen und annähern. Aus dem Verhältnis von Nähe und Ferne wird dadurch eines von *Vordergrund und Hintergrund*, in dem die Rechtecke und Quadrate einander verdecken und hintereinander hervortreten können. Die gegenläufigen Bewegungen bringen pulsierende Rhythmen hervor.

Da die Herstellungstechnik des Bildes im Film wie in der Malerei selbst Teil seiner Form und seines Inhaltes ist, fügt sie seiner Mehrdeutigkeit in bestimmten Sequenzen eine weitere Ebene hinzu: Ist es das weiße Quadrat, das sich in der zweiten Sequenz verkleinert *und/oder* entfernt

8 Hans Richter: Dimension t. In: G. Zeitschrift für elementare Gestaltung V-VI (April 1926). Reprint herausgegeben von Marion von Hofacker, München 1986, S. 114.

und/oder ist es nicht vielmehr die Kamera, die sich von ihm entfernt? Ist es in der fünften Sequenz eine weiße Fläche, die von rechts nach links über eine schwarze Fläche wandert und eine schwarze Fläche, die ihr folgt (mit all den weiteren Deutungsmöglichkeiten dieses Vexierbildes) *und/oder* ist es die Kamera, die sich exakt in die andere Richtung seitwärts bewegt?

In einem späten Interview hat Richter die Techniken offengelegt, mit denen er in *Rhythmus 21* gearbeitet hat:[9] Tatsächlich war die Kamera im ganzen Film statisch über einem Tisch positioniert, der von zwei Seiten beleuchtet wurde. Richter hat dünne Kartons verwendet, die er zu rund 40 oder 50 Quadraten und Rechtecken unterschiedlicher Größe und Helligkeitswerte zugeschnitten hat: von sehr klein bis groß, von weiß über hellgrau zu dunkelgrau. Statt schwarzer Kartons hat er das Negativmaterial des Films verwendet. Damit ist nicht nur die Frage nach den Kamerabewegungen, sondern auch die Frage nach dem Verhältnis von Figur und Grund technisch geklärt: Es ist nicht die Kamera, die sich bewegt, es sind die weißen und grauen Quadrate und Rechtecke, die Richter Kader für Kader aufgenommen und zwischen den Kadern neu platziert oder durch größere oder kleinere ersetzt hat. Im Bild und in seiner Wahrnehmung bleiben sämtliche Mehrdeutigkeiten jedoch erhalten, obwohl Richter sie für den Verstand ausgeräumt hat.

Bleibt die Frage, inwiefern es sinnvoll ist, bei der von Richter angewandten *Stop-Motion-Technik* zwischen Kader und Einstellung zu unterscheiden: Entspricht nicht jeder Kader exakt einer Einstellung, wenn die Kamera nach Aufnahme eines Kaders gestoppt und erst wieder in Bewegung gesetzt wurde, nachdem die Bildvorlage verändert wurde? Nirgendwo zeigt sich klarer, dass die Filmtechnik zwar Teil des Bildes ist, sich das Bild aber nicht in der Technik erschöpft. Der Schnitt und die Montage sind im Animationsfilm zwar zwischen die einzelnen Kader gewandert, allerdings nur in der Herstellung, nicht in der Darstellung des Films, nicht in seiner Projektion.

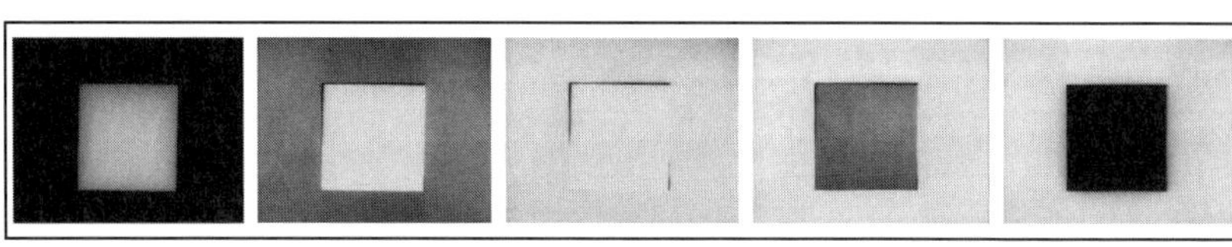

Abb. 7 a-e: Graustufen-Sequenz, Keyframes.

9 Vgl. Richter on Film (with Cecile Starr). DVD. 14 min. Bonus zu Hans Richter – Early Works. Paris: Re:Voir Video 2008. (1972). 2:46 - 3:38 min.

Notiz 5: Filmgeschichte, Kunstgeschichte und Biographie

Roland Barthes hat von einem Nullpunkt der Literatur gesprochen. *Rhythmus 21* ist ein Nullpunkt des Kinos. In dem von Peter Kubelka für das Österreichische Filmmuseum kuratierten permanenten Filmzyklus *Was ist Film* gibt es nur drei Filme, die mehr als einmal gezeigt werden. Einer davon ist *Rhythmus 21.*[10] „In seiner Reduzierung auf Grundelemente des Filmischen" haben ihn Hans Scheugl und Ernst Schmidt jr. als „eines der wichtigsten Werke des Avantgardefilms und der Filmgeschichte überhaupt" bezeichnet.[11] Seine Datierung sei jedoch fragwürdig.

Dass *Rhythmus 21* seinen Entstehungszeitpunkt im Titel nennt, verdankt er dem Umstand, dass Richter seinen ursprünglichen Titel *Film ist Rhythmus* nachträglich ersetzt hat. Richter selbst hat ihn in seiner Autobiographie auf das Jahr 1921 datiert und berichtet, dass van Doesburg ihn noch im selben Jahr in Paris gezeigt habe, er in Berlin aber erst 1924 im UFA-Theater Ku'damm aufgeführt worden sei, zusammen mit René Clairs *Entr'acte* und Fernand Légers *Ballet mécanique.*[12] Tatsächlich fand diese Veranstaltung mit dem Titel *Der absolute Film* aber erst am 3. Mai 1925 statt, wo *Film ist Rhythmus* gemeinsam mit den genannten Filmen, mit Viking Eggelings *Symphonie Diagonale* und Walter Ruttmanns *Opus II*, *III* und *IV* auf dem Programm stand und wo auch Ludwig Hirschfeld-Macks *Reflektorische Farbenspiele* gezeigt wurden.

Wie dem auch sei. Der Status des ersten abstrakten Films lässt sich für *Rhythmus 21* auch dann nicht beanspruchen, wenn Richter sein Entstehungsdatum korrekt angegeben hat. Ruttmanns Film *Opus I* wurde nachweislich schon im April 1921 offiziell aufgeführt und soll im kleinen Kreis bereits 1919 gezeigt worden sein. Erst Mitte 1921 hat van Doesburg in der Zeitschrift *De Stijl* von den vielversprechenden, aber noch erfolglosen Versuchen Richters und Eggelings berichtet, einen abstrakten Film herzustellen, die beide – mit Unterstützung der UFA – seit über einem Jahr unternommen hätten.[13]

Doch Ruttmanns Film und die noch älteren, in den frühen 1910er Jahren entstandenen, aber nicht erhaltenen gegenstandslosen Filme italienischer Futuristen unterscheiden sich von Richters Film nicht nur im Her-

10 Vgl. Stefan Grissemann / Alexander Horwath / Regina Schlagnitweit (Hg.): Was ist Film. Peter Kubelkas Zyklisches Programm im Österreichischen Filmmuseum. Wien 2010.

11 Vgl. Scheugl / Schmidt jr.: Subgeschichte des Films, S. 742-743.

12 Vgl. Hans Richter: Autobiographie. In: Hans Richter – Ein Leben für Bild und Film. Ausstellungskatalog. Berlin: Hochschule für bildende Künste, 17. Oktober bis 16. November 1958. (Vgl. hierzu auch den Beitrag „Entstehungsgeschichte" in diesem Band.)

13 Vgl. Theo van Doesburg: Abstracte Filmbeelding. In: De Stijl 4. Jg. (1921), Nr. 5, S. 71 ff.

stellungsverfahren, sondern auch im Ergebnis. Als handkolorierte Filme waren und sind sie mehr eine Fortsetzung der Malerei mit anderen Mitteln als ein radikaler Bruch, wie ihn Richter nach der gescheiterten Übertragung seiner ab 1919 entstandenen Rollenbilder in das Medium Film vollzogen hat. Mit seinen bunten Bildern und ihren symbolisch assoziationsreichen Formen entbehrt Ruttmanns Film nicht nur der formalen Strenge, sondern jeglicher Systematik. Wenn Bilder überhaupt jemals abstrakt sein können, mag *Opus I* der erste erhaltene abstrakte Film der Filmgeschichte sein. *Rhythmus 21* ist der erste elementare Film. Seine Erstaufführung war die Inauguration eines elementaren Kinos, zu dem man neben Richters *Rhythmus*-Filmen und Teilen seiner späteren Filme auch Ruttmanns *Opus IV* (1925) und zahlreiche wesentlich spätere Filme zählen kann: darunter so unterschiedliche wie *Adebar* (1957), *Schwechater* (1958) und *Arnulf Rainer* (1960) von Peter Kubelka, *Wavelength* (1967), *Standard Time* (1967), *Back and Forth* (1969), *La région centrale* (1971) und *So Is This* (1982) von Michael Snow oder *Film ist.* (2000) von Gustav Deutsch.

Nicht dass er ein Film eines Malers ist, macht *Rhythmus 21* für die Kunstgeschichte interessant, sondern dass die Analyse der Elemente bildlicher Darstellung zu einem bestimmten historischen Zeitpunkt einen Medienwechsel zwischen Malerei und Film erzwingt. Richter wurde später immer wieder gefragt, warum er nach *Rhythmus 23* und *Rhythmus 25* den abstrakten Film aufgegeben habe und zum sogenannten Realfilm zurückgekehrt sei. Wo sich Augen von Gesichtern ablösen und in weiße, tanzende Kreise verwandeln wie in Richters *Filmstudie* (1926) und wo Menschen hinter dünnen Laternenmasten verschwinden wie in Richters *Vormittagsspuk* (1927-1928), kann man jedoch statt einer Rückkehr eine konsequente Fortsetzung, Ausdehnung und Weiterentwicklung der Verfahren entdecken, die Richter vom Nullpunkt des Kinos aus erschlossen hat.

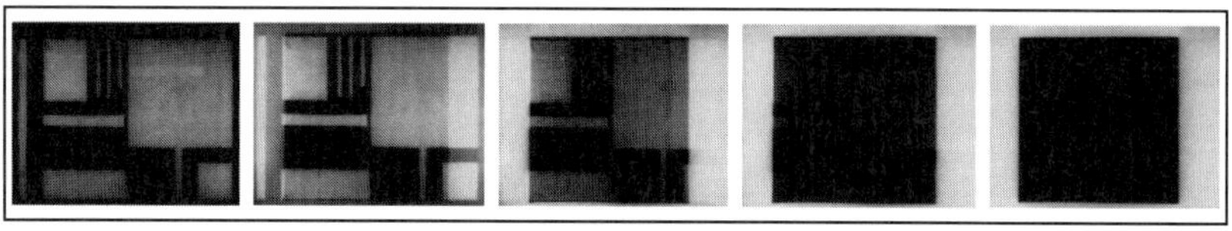

Abb. 8 a-e: Überblendungs-Sequenz, Keyframes.

Abbildungsverzeichnis

Abb. 1-8: Hans Richter: Rhythmus 21. Deutschland.[14]

14 Die Analyse stützt sich auf die 35mm Kopie im Archiv des Österreichischen Filmmuseums.

Körper: Pulsierende Quadrate, bewegte Darmentleerung und der Rhythmus des Vitalen

Birgit Nemec / Katrin Pilz

Hans Richter bezeichnet Rhythmus als „articulation of time and movement“[1]; in seinem häufig als ersten ‚abstrakten‘ Film bezeichneten *Rhythmus 21* setzt er dies durch die Montage rechteckiger Elemente um, die als Akteure gegeneinander verschoben werden, in den Vordergrund treten und wieder verschwinden. Rhythmus, „ein unwiderstehliches Naturprinzip“[2], „the inner, nature-force [...], through which we are bound up with he elemental nature-forces“[3], soll in dieser neuen Form der filmisch-rhythmischen Komposition durch ein Wechselspiel von Hell und Dunkel, Fragment und Ganzem erzeugt und vermittelt werden. Nur auf diesem Weg, so Richter, gelingt es, die Kunst wieder für das Alltagsleben relevant zu machen. Nur auf diesem Weg, über den Rhythmus, gelingt es, den Betrachter direkt anzusprechen, Rhythmus, Atmung, Herzschlag körperlich erleb- und erfahrbar zu machen. Nur über diese ‚universelle Sprache‘ kann das Publikum im Innersten erreicht, können die ‚Seelen‘ orchestriert werden.

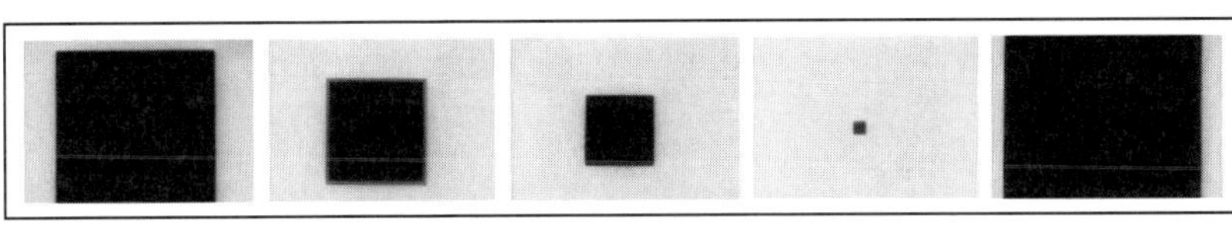

Abb. 1: Im Rhythmus des Herzschlags: *Rhythmus 21* (2:49 - 2:56 min.).

Etwa zeitgleich mit Hans Richters filmisch-experimenteller Rhythmus-Serie[4] liefen röntgenkinematographische Filmproduktionen europaweit auf Hochtouren. Körperliche Abläufe, Bewegungen, der Rhythmus des Körpers und der inneren Organe konnten neuerdings in Bewegung – in schwarz und weiß – dargestellt werden. Zunächst aus Faszination am tech-

1 Cleve Gray (Hg.): Hans Richter by Hans Richter. New York 1971, S. 131.

2 Hans Richter: Film von Morgen (1929). In: Freunde der deutschen Kinemathek e.V. (Hg.): Hans Richter – Film ist Rhythmus. Berlin 2003, S. 56-62, hier: S. 57.

3 Hans Richter: Rhythm (1926). In: Freunde der deutschen Kinemathek e.V. (Hg.): Hans Richter – Film ist Rhythmus. Berlin 2003, S. 38.

4 Vgl. hierzu den Beitrag „Entstehungsgeschichte“ in diesem Band.

nisch Möglichen, als Experiment, später zu Lehrzwecken entstanden bis in die 1930er Jahre hinein Filme wie *Verdauungssystem*[5] oder *Trinken*[6]. In Letzterem zeigt der bekannte Bonner Radiologe und passionierte Röntgenkinematograph Robert Janker den Vorgang des Trinkens, in schnellen rhythmischen Bewegungen, vom Griff zum Trinkgefäß bis zum Weg der Flüssigkeit durch den Körper:

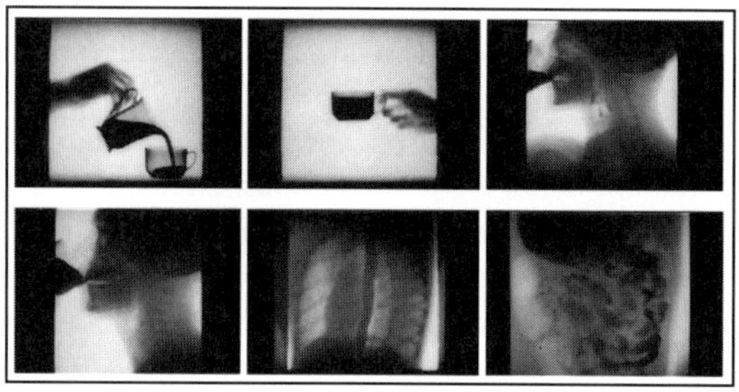

Abb. 2: Robert Janker: *Trinken*.

Eine mit Röntgenstrahlen ‚durchleuchtete' Hand schenkt eine dunkle Flüssigkeit aus dem linken Bildrand in eine transparente Tasse ein. Fast gleichzeitig tritt von rechts die zweite Versuchsperson auf, die Kontrastflüssigkeit wird zum Mund geführt, geschluckt, sie rinnt die Speiseröhre in schnellen rhythmischen Bewegungen hinunter, der Vorgang wird wiederholt.

Janker nützt das neue Medium offenkundig dazu, den inneren Rhythmus des Körpers zu registrieren; im nächsten Schritt wird der gewonnene Einblick für die medizinische Praxis, aber auch für ein breiteres gesellschaftliches Publikum, instrumentalisiert.

Ausgangspunkt des vorliegenden Beitrags sind vorerst stilistische Anschlüsse der Dramaturgie früher Röntgenfilme an Hans Richters abstrakte Filme, zu denen *Rhythmus 21* den Auftakt bildet. Schnittflächen medizinischer Körperbilder und -diskurse mit jenen der Avantgarden der 1920er Jahre erzwingen geradezu eine Erforschung des dichten kulturellen Netzes, des zeitgenössischen Umfelds der Filme. Es scheint, als haben sich

5 Robert Janker: Röntgenfilm I. Das Verdauungssystem, Kauen und Schlucken beim Menschen. Digitale Kopie aus dem Archiv des Deutschen Röntgen-Museums. 11 min. Bonn: Institut für Film und Bild in Wissenschaft und Unterricht. (Deutschland ca. 1936). http://www.roentgenmuseum.de/(14.05.2012).

6 Robert Janker: Trinken. Digitale Kopie aus dem Archiv des Deutschen Röntgen-Museums. 1 min. (Deutschland ca.1935). http://www.roentgenmuseum.de/ (10.5.2012).

medizinische sowie künstlerisch-gestalterische Diskurse gegenseitig wichtige Impulse gegeben, denen anhand zentraler Begriffe (*Bewegung*, *Type*, *Rhythmus als Chiffre*, *Kontrolle*) nachgespürt werden kann.

Ermöglicht durch die neue Technik des Films (*Bewegung*) wurden spezifische Konzepte von Rhythmus neu verhandelt; Auffassungen von Körperlichkeit und Subjektivität (*Type*), Leben, Vitalität und deren Steuerung (*Rhythmus als Chiffre*) gerieten ins Wanken. Aushandlungen des Verhältnisses von Individuum und Gesellschaft (*Kontrolle*) lassen nicht zuletzt auf unterschiedliche Visionen der Moderne schließen.

Bewegung

Hans Richter kam ursprünglich aus der Malerei zum Film. Seine Experimente mit abstrakten Formen in seiner Dada-Periode beschreibt er nachträglich nicht nur als Versuch, der Kunst ihre soziale Funktion zurückzugeben, sondern auch als Entwurf einer neuen Methode der visuellen Kommunikation.[7] Sein Bestreben, das Publikum direkt zu erreichen, wahre Bedeutungen und Gefühle – unverfälscht von sozialen, kulturellen oder nationalen Realitäten – zu erzeugen, setzt er konsequent im Film fort.[8] *Rhythmus 21* und die folgenden frühen Filme Richters gehen vom formalen Element der Leinwand, vom Rechteck aus. Vom Potential bewegter Bilder verzaubert[9], wollte Richter nicht mehr Form, sondern Zeit und Bewegung sowie ‚Rhythmus' artikulieren und vor allem den Betrachter ‚bewegen'.[10]

Richters Rhythmuskonzeption entstand parallel zu tiefgreifenden Veränderungen in medizinisch-gestalterischen Kulturen. Neue Erkenntnisse von Funktionen und Strukturen des Körpers hatten bereits im 19. und frühen 20. Jahrhundert zu einem Wandel des Organismus-Begriffs geführt: In Wissenschaft und Kunst lösten abstrahierende Bilder und systemische, funktionale, an Strukturen interessierte Körperdarstellungen die von Perspektive und anatomischer Bildtradition geprägten Visualisierungsformen ab. Im medizinischen Bereich hatten die laufende Bewegung und der Rhythmus im Film einen ebenso wichtigen Stellenwert wie im abstrakten Film. Die rhythmischen Bewegungen des Herzens als eines der wenigen Organe, die auch ein Laie ohne technische Hilfsmittel sowohl hören als

7 Vgl. Gray (Hg.): Hans Richter by Hans Richter, S. 110.

8 Vgl. ebd., S. 130.

9 Vgl. ebd., S. 128.

10 Vgl. ebd., S. 130-131. Richter kritisiert an Eggelings *Symphonie Diagonale* (1921), dass der Film zwar Bewegung thematisiert, sie für den Betrachter jedoch nicht spürbar macht. Erst das herzschlagartige Pulsieren der graphischen Elemente in *Rhythmus 21* ging von der Malerei ausgehend einen Schritt weiter in den dreidimensionalen Raum und damit auch in die ‚gefühlte' Bewegung, so Richter.

auch fühlen kann, wurden durch die Entdeckung der Röntgenstrahlen und die Entwicklung des Kinematographen ab etwa 1900 sichtbar und darstellbar. Nach ersten Jahren der Anwendung und des Experimentierens mit diesen zwei neuen Techniken etablierte sich die Röntgenkinematographie um 1909.[11]

Zeitgleich mit dem Entstehen von Richters *Rhythmus 21,* Anfang der 1920er Jahre, wurden Abläufe, Bewegungen und der Rhythmus im Inneren des Körpers bereits im institutionellen Rahmen modern ausgestatteter Röntgeneinrichtungen medizinischer Institute filmisch festgehalten. Die fast ausschließlich aus dem medizinischen Bereich stammenden Röntgenkinematographen inszenierten in ihren Lehrfilmen eine Dramaturgie, die stilistisch den avantgardistischen Kunstfilmen aus den 1920er Jahren sehr ähnlich ist. Häufig als Montagefilme umgesetzt, waren ‚Magenbewegungen' und rhythmische Visualisierungen des Herzschlags und des ‚Schluckaktes' bereits in den Produktionen der 1910er Jahre wichtige Sujets[12] und sie blieben es auch weit nach 1920 in medizinischen Lehrinstituten.[13]

Robert Janker kam wie Hans Richter von einem unbewegten Medium zum Film. Der deutsche Radiologe erlebte während seiner Ausbildung Anfang der 1920er Jahre den Aufschwung der neuen Technik und erkannte deren Potential. Unter seiner Leitung entstand zwischen 1928 und 1937 am Röntgeninstitut der chirurgischen Klinik der Universität Bonn eine umfangreiche Sammlung röntgenkinematographischer Aufnahmen[14]; ab 1937 drehte Janker schließlich in seinem neu errichteten unabhängigen Röntgeninstitut. Aus Jankers Bonner Phase stammt der Großteil der heute zugänglichen Filmdokumente.[15]

Doch Jankers filmisches Wirken war vielseitig: Er produzierte Lehrfilme für das Institut für Film und Bild in Wissenschaft und Unterricht (FWU)[16] sowie experimentell- künstlerische Filme im privaten Rahmen. Mit dem Einbezug von einigen von Jankers Filmen, darunter *Trinken,*

---

11 Vgl. Martin Weiser: Medizinische Kinematographie. Dresden / Leipzig 1919, S. 68.

12 Vgl. ebd., S. 69.

13 Vgl. Oskar Kalbus: Der Deutsche Lehrfilm in der Wissenschaft und im Unterricht. Berlin 1922.

14 Hauptthemen waren abermals der Schluckakt, Bewegungen des Magens und stereoskopische Röntgenaufnahmen des Herzens.

15 Die Röntgenfilme Robert Jankers stellen ein bislang wenig erforschtes Gebiet dar. Im vorliegenden Artikel greifen wir daher, was Jankers frühes Filmschaffen betrifft, teils auf schriftliche Quellen und teils auf undatierte Filmdokumente zurück. Besser dokumentiert und bereits digital für die Forschung zugänglich gemacht sind Jankers spätere Filme aus den 1930er Jahren, weshalb wir vorrangig Filmbeispiele aus dieser Periode wählen mussten.

16 Ab 1934 „Reichsstelle für den Unterrichtsfilm".

in den UFA Kulturfilm *Röntgenstrahlen*[17], zusammengestellt durch den Schweizer Physiker Martin Rikli, gelang Janker nicht nur der Anschluss an internationale Kollegen sondern auch die Teilnahme an der Filmbiennale 1937. Eine interessante Querverbindung: Trickfilmelemente und animierte Montagebilder aus *Rhythmus 21* wurden wie die seit 1919 zahlreich hergestellten medizinischen Lehrfilme ebenfalls im Hintergrund der UFA, an der sogenannten Abteilung für Kulturfilm produziert.[18]

Robert Janker experimentierte, wie auch Hans Richter, bereits in seiner Frühphase mit dem neuen Medium Film. Er trug so zu dessen Popularisierung und später zu dessen Institutionalisierung und Genrebildung im medizinischen Bereich bei. Als kinematographisch interessierter Mediziner hatte er freilich wichtige Vorläufer: Die wissenschaftliche und im Besonderen die medizinische Kinematographie spielten in der Geschichte des frühen Kinos eine wichtige Rolle; das „Kino der Attraktionen"[19] von Lumière und Méliès prägte seit dem ausgehenden 19. Jahrhundert die ersten Jahrzehnte der Film- und Kinokultur. Parallelen zwischen frühem Kino, Avantgardefilm und medizinischem Film können daher anhand gemeinsamer Stilmerkmale, wie etwa dem experimentellen, dokumentarischen und gestalterischen Charakter der Filmdokumente ausgemacht werden. Der medizinische Film entzieht sich – gerade in seinen Anfängen – einer klaren medienhistorischen Zuordnung; eine Phase der ‚Anarchie' späterer Genres wird durch die Kombination dokumentarischer, fiktionaler und animierter Elemente sichtbar. Neben der aufklärenden Funktion als Lehrfilme ermöglichten sie experimentelle Versuchsanordnungen zur Sichtbarmachung von bislang unsichtbaren Prozessen, die Generierung neuen Wissens über den Körper und ein Experimentieren mit neuen Technologien.

Anhand von Röntgenfilmen wie jenen Robert Jankers wird klar, dass es in den frühen radiologischen Filmen nicht nur um Wissenserzeugung, sondern auch um die Faszination am technisch Möglichen geht; um ein Spiel mit den neuen Seh- und Zugriffspotentialen, deren ästhetischer Überschuss teils Faszination, teils Verstörung auslöst. Der Blick in das lebende Individuum und dessen Reduktion auf elementare Abläufe hat seinen Mehrwert gerade in der filmischen Inszenierung; im Gefallen daran, Rhythmus über bewegte Bilder zu kreieren und erfahrbar zu machen.

17 Martin Rikli / Robert Janker: Röntgenstrahlen. 18 Min. (Deutschland 1937).

18 Vgl. Gray (Hg.): Hans Richter by Hans Richter, S. 131. Sowie: Peter Zimmermann / Kay Hoffmann (Hg.): Triumph der Bilder. Kultur- und Dokumentarfilme vor 1945 im internationalen Vergleich. Konstanz 2003, S. 41.

19 Tom Gunning: The Cinema of Attractions. Early Film, Its Spectator and the Avant-Garde. In: Thomas Elsaesser (Hg.): Early Cinema: Space – Frame – Narrative. London 1990, S. 56-62.

Type

Hans Richter und sein Kollege Viking Eggeling teilten mit den Pionieren des frühen Röntgenfilms das Interesse für die Reduktion auf das Elementare, das ‚Verschwindenlassen' des Individuums und die Kontrolle des Lebenden. „I gradually lost interest in the subject and focused instead on the positive-negative (white-black) oppositions"[20], beschreibt Richter seinen Weg in den Film. „Repetition of the same element with minor or major variations permitted a certain control".[21]

Im Hintergrund der Entstehung des absoluten und des radiologischen Films stand, wie schon angedeutet, eine Neuordnung des Körperverständnisses. Durch die Industrialisierung am Ende des 19. Jahrhunderts wurde der menschliche Organismus zunehmend entlang technologischer Metaphern strukturiert. Wie die Forschungsliteratur überzeugend gezeigt hat, standen der Orientierung an Kategorien der Effizienz, Technologie und Leistungsfähigkeit Natürlichkeitsdiskurse, ‚maschinistischen' Körpermodellen und Normalitätsmodelle gegenüber, die sich aus Bezügen auf das Organische und auf den Bereich des Belebten speisten.[22] Die Ablösung von individualisierten, stark durch die Bildersprache der Renaissance und der Romantik geprägten Körperdarstellungen durch abstrakte Körperbilder in Kunst und Massenmedien der 1920er und 1930er Jahre zeichnet ein Verlust von Subjektivität zugunsten eines Aufgehens des Individuums in der (urbanen) Massengesellschaft aus. Hans Richter war bereits als Maler aktiv an der Entwicklung dieser neuen visuellen Formensprache beteiligt. Alltagserfahrungen, die zunehmend durch Typisierung, Normierung, Durchschnitt und technologische Leistungsfähigkeit geprägt waren[23], bilden jedoch auch den Referenzrahmen für Jankers fragmentierte, dynamisch-bewegte Körperdarstellungen. Die ent-subjektivierte Type des Röntgenfilms liest sich unter den medizinischen Filmen als Inbegriff der Moderne.

---

20 Gray (Hg.): Hans Richter by Hans Richter, S. 112.

21 Ebd.

22 Vgl. hier vor allem Michael Cowan / Kai Marcel Sicks (Hg.): Leibhaftige Moderne. Körper in Kunst und Massenmedien 1918 bis 1933. Bielefeld 2005.

23 Michael K. Hays: Modernism and the Posthumanist Subject. The Architecture of Hannes Meyer and Ludwig Hilberseimer. Cambridge 1992.

Rhythmus

Für Hans Richter ist Film Rhythmus, das Gegenspiel von Zeit und Bewegung.[24] Rhythmus ist aber auch die elementarste Form von Bewegung und damit des Lebens, er ist stark über Emotion und Empfindungen definiert und daher die ‚Essenz emotionalen Ausdrucks'.[25] Daher war Richter überzeugt, mit Hilfe der Kunst, des neuen Mediums Film und vor allem des filmisch vermittelten optischen Rhythmus zeigen zu können, was es bedeutet, richtig zu fühlen. Auf diesem Weg wollte er zum einen die Kunst mit individuellen Lebenswelten (Alltag) versöhnen, zum anderen aber durch dessen gezielte Instrumentalisierung die Wahrnehmungen steuern, zum Fühlen zwingen, die Seele trainieren.[26] Wie Michael Cowan bereits gezeigt hat, ist Richters Anspruch hier nicht mit einem Vitalismus von Rudolf Bode oder Ludwig Klage zu verwechseln, sondern vielmehr als Balanceakt zwischen Ordnung und Unordnung, Intentionalität und Zufall, Intellekt und Gefühl zu verstehen.[27]

Ganz anders liegen in dieser Hinsicht die Dinge im Röntgenfilm Robert Jankers, der im Rhythmisieren, Durchleuchten und Archivieren des (‚entindividualisierten') Körpers die Bühne des modernen wissenschaftlichen Labors öffnet und die totale Plan- und Steuerbarkeit des Menschen, die Quantifizierbarkeit, die Kontrollierbarkeit, die Visualisierung eines Durchschnittsmenschen von der Nahrungsaufnahme bis zur Ausscheidung zelebriert.

> Noch interessanter sind die inneren Organe des Menschen, ein durchleuchteter Brustkorb: das flaschenförmige pulsierende Gebilde in der Mitte ist das Herz, es schlägt im normalen Rhythmus; anders bei körperlicher Anstrengung; stellen wir diese Hürdenläufer vor den Rontgenschirm, so zeigt das Herz in Folge der Anstrengung rascheren Schlag.[28]

Dass Janker und Richter bereits in ihren experimentellen Frühphasen sehr unterschiedliche Konzeptionen von Rhythmus entwerfen, wird vielleicht besonders in Jankers späteren Beispielen seiner filmischen Entwicklung,

24 Vgl. Gray (Hg.): Hans Richter by Hans Richter, S. 110.

25 Vgl. Richter: Rhythm.

26 Vgl. Hans Richter: Die schlecht trainierte Seele. In: G. Zeitschrift für elementare Gestaltung III (Juni 1924). Reprint herausgegeben von Marion von Hofacker, München 1986, S. 44-47. (Vgl. hierzu auch den Beitrag „Seelentraining" in diesem Band.)

27 Michael Cowan: The Heart Machine. Rhythm and Body in Weimar Film and Fritz Lang's Metropolis. In: Modernism/modernity 14. Jg. (2007), Nr. 2, S. 225-248.

28 Martin Rikli / Robert Janker: Röntgenstrahlen. (Deutschland 1937), hier: Herz, 11:05-11:35.

wie dem hier zitierten Teil aus *Röntgenstrahlen*, deutlich. Die durch die visuelle Kultur der 1920er Jahre geprägten rhythmischen Bewegungsdarstellungen in schnellen und langsamen Montageschnitten wichen zunehmend einer sichtbaren Nähe zur durch Totalitarismus geprägten medizinischen Mainstream-Ästhetik der 1930er Jahre.[29]

Kontrolle

Bereits 1917 suchte Hans Richter nach einem „strukturierenden Prinzip", um die grenzenlose Freiheit der neu gewonnenen, unbeschränkten „Form und Farbwelt"[30] vor der Anarchie zu bewahren. Er fand es schließlich im Gegenspiel (‚counterpoint') – rückblickend als natürliche Folge des Umstandes, dass er sich in seinen Arbeiten nur über Kontraste und Analogien ausdrücken konnte. Das ‚Gegenspiel' wurde für Richter mehr als nur eine künstlerische Technik, „it became a philosophy which was important for my general outlook in life"[31].

Parallel zu Hans Richters *Rhythmus 21* ist für den radiologischen Film die Darstellung eines visuell-kinematographischen Rhythmus konstitutiv. Die Bewegung und rhythmische Abstraktion des Lebens mit Hilfe von Bergsons ‚Kinematographischem Mechanismus'[32] betonend, etablierte Richter eine neue Art der Formentypologie und des Formenvokabulars hin zu bewegten, rhythmischen und abstrakten Bildern. Frühe Adaptionen dieser neuen Visualität findet man als Montagesequenzen in bekannten filmischen Schauplätzen der Verhandlung von Körperbildern, wie etwa Wilhelm Pragers und Nicholas Kaufmanns Körperkultur-Klassiker *Wege zu Kraft und Schönheit*.[33] Ähnlich Hans Richters Experimenten für seine *Rhythmus*-Filme wurden offensichtlich Pappausschnitte von Röntgenbildern gegeneinander montiert, um den Blick in den durch die Atmung bewegten Brustkorb zu simulieren.

---

29 Das überrascht wenig, weiß man, dass Janker 1933 als Parteimitglied der NSDAP beitrat, im Rahmen des Bonner Röntgeninstituts eine durchaus einflussreiche Stellung inne hatte und an Zwangssterilisationen durch Röntgenbestrahlung beteiligt gewesen sein soll, was bei den Entnazifizierungsprozessen 1946 jedoch unerwähnt blieb. Vgl. UA Bonn, PA 3618 Janker, Gutachten des universitätsinternen Untersuchungsausschusses von Weber / von Redwitz / Ceelen, Sitzung vom 03.11.1945.

30 Gray (Hg.): Hans Richter by Hans Richter, S. 86.

31 Ebd.

32 Vgl. Henri Bergson in Gilles Deleuze: Das Bewegungsbild. Kino 1. Frankfurt a.M. 1989.

33 Wilhelm Prager / Nicholas Kaufmann: Wege zu Kraft und Schönheit: Ein Film über moderne Körperkultur. 104 min. (Deutschland 1925), hier: 16:30ff.

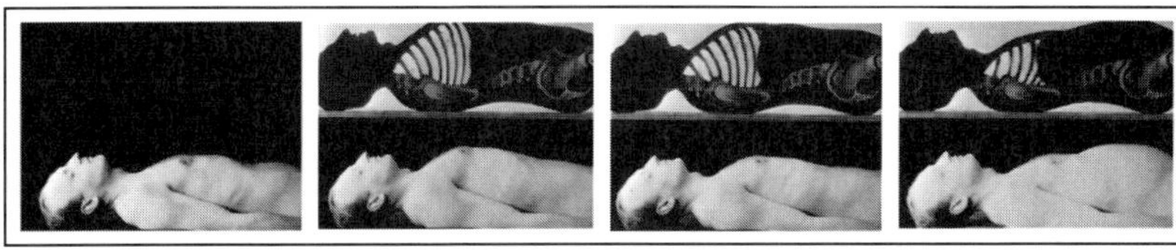

Abb. 3: Montagesequenzen in *Wege zu Kraft und Schönheit.*

Das strukturierende Prinzip des Röntgenbildes, das Gegenspiel von Hell und Dunkel, von Licht und Schatten, wurde übernommen; körperliche Bewegung vorerst durch Montagen simuliert. Der sich zeitgleich entwickelnde Röntgenfilm geht allerdings einen Schritt weiter: Denn den Röntgenfilm strukturiert der radiologisch wahrnehmbare Rhythmus des Lebenden, der Herzschlag, die Bewegungen der Organe. Ein üblicher Kommentar der Off-Stimme wirkt kontrollierend; er weist den Bildern Bedeutung, dem Film ein Genre zu.

In Robert Jankers Film *Verdauungssystem*[34] wird diese Entwicklung deutlich. Er zeigt dem Zuschauer den Weg einer durch Kontrastmittel sichtbar gemachten Speise, die den Darm durchwandert und schließlich ausgeschieden wird. Entgegen dem Untertitel „Kauen und Schlucken beim Menschen“, wird der Verdauungsvorgang jedoch Großteils an Versuchstieren dargestellt.[35] Das Medium Röntgenfilm wird hier genutzt, um Lebendes im vermeintlich natürlichen Rhythmus darzustellen. Die bei der rhythmischen Darmentleerung mitschwingende Ambivalenz aus Technikeuphorie und Horror erinnert nicht zufällig an Walther Ruttmanns Vision urbaner Moderne in *Berlin, Die Sinfonie der Großstadt*[36]: Rhythmus, Beschleunigung, Modernisierung finden sich als Leitthemen auch hier wieder; in abstrakten Montagen bedient auch Ruttmann sich Tieren (schreienden Affen und Hunden), um die Unmöglichkeit der Selbstkontrolle ‚nervöser‘ Stadtbewohner auszudrücken.[37] Und dennoch entwerfen die drei Filmemacher unterschiedliche Ausblicke: Ruttmann scheint eine großstädtische

34 Janker: Röntgenfilm I.

35 Der Text des Beiheftes informiert: „Die weitere Darstellung des Verdauungskanals ist nun wegen der beim Menschen notwendigen hohen Röntgenintensitäten unterlassen worden. Sie wurde, weil es sich im Prinzip um gleiche Dinge handelt, am Tier und zwar an der Katze und am Kaninchen aufgenommen.“ Robert Janker: Beiheft Röntgenfilm I. Das Verdauungssystem, Kauen und Schlucken beim Menschen. Institut für Film und Bild in Wissenschaft und Unterricht. München ca. 1936, S. 1-11, hier: S. 6.

36 Walther Ruttmann: Berlin. Die Sinfonie der Großstadt. 62 min. Edition Filmmuseum 2008. (Deutschland 1927).

37 Cowan: The Heart Machine, S. 229.

Moderne zu skizzieren, Richter eine visuelle und Janker eine medizinische Moderne filmisch zu propagieren.

Jankers röntgenkinematographische *Darmentleerung* treibt Ruttmanns ambivalente Rezeption moderner Lebenswelten implizit auf die Spitze (wenngleich der Film sie explizit negiert und stattdessen den wissenschaftlichen Fortschritt feiert): Das regelmäßige Nachspritzen von Kontrastmitteln, die eigentlich aus der Bearbeitung von Leichen und Leichenteilen kommen, und die intensive Bestrahlung am Tier führen langfristig zum Tod. Angewandt auf den lebenden Körper – um Vitalität darzustellen – wirkt diese Verbindung paradox und verstörend: Das Individuum im Mittelpunkt der Aufzeichnung scheint im Dienst der Wissenschaft seines persönlichen Rhythmus enthoben; der Film wird zur Ouvertüre des Sterbens.

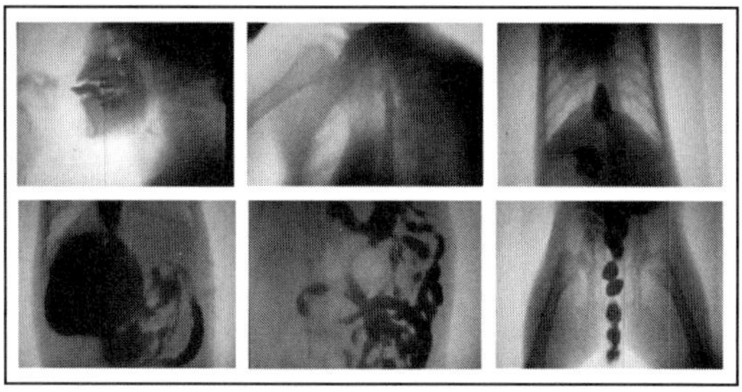

Abb. 4: Robert Janker:
Das Verdauungssystem, Kauen und Schlucken beim Menschen.

Moderne

Durch das Ziehen von Linien, das Verteilen von Flächen und das Anordnen von Worten, so Jacques Rancière, findet eine Aufteilung des gemeinsamen Raumes statt. Konfigurationen des Sicht- und Denkbaren beeinflussen symbolische und materielle Konfigurationen sowie die Formen für das Bewohnen der sinnlichen Welt.[38]

Das Schaffen von neuen Praktiken der Inszenierung des Körpers und dadurch produzierten Sinnpotentialen und Darstellungskonventionen leisten die hier untersuchten Medien in unterschiedlicher Weise: Hans Richters *Rhythmus 21* oder Robert Jankers Röntgenfilm, dynamisch angesiedelt zwischen avantgardistisch-künstlerischen, alltäglichen und wissenschaftlichen Feldern, verleihen sich gegenseitig neue Dynamik, Bedeutungen und Relevanz. Ganz im Sinne der *G*- und *MA*-Avantgardisten scheinen die Grenzen zwischen Alltagsobjekten, Gestaltung, Kunst und Körper zumin-

38 Jacques Rancière: Politik der Bilder. Zürich 2005.

dest zeitweise aufgehoben; das Verschmelzen mit Sinneswahrnehmungen und Dingen als Kennzeichen von Körperkonzepten der ausgehenden Moderne manifestiert sich, wie die Beispiele gezeigt haben, in verschiedenen Formen. Die vorerst paradoxe Vereinbarkeit von Technikeuphorie, Technoutopie und esoterischen Strömungen, von mechanischen und organischen Prinzipien, wird erst durch den Befund eines Außerkraftsetzens des stabilen Verhältnisses von Kunst und Leben bzw. von Kunst, Alltag und Wissenschaft verständlich.

Rhythmus, eines der wesentlichen Schlüsselwörter der europäischen Moderne, wird in den ersten Jahrzehnten des 20. Jahrhunderts zu einer Chiffre für das Vitale und das Intakte. Zugleich erleben programmatische Arbeiten am Menschen und das Generieren von Menschenbildern durch Experimente und Versuchsanordnungen eine Hochkonjunktur.

Richter suchte die ‚Melodie der Bewegung' in Menschen, Tieren, Landschaften; für ihn war alles vom „Flow of Rhythm"[39], einem artikulierten Zeit-Element unterlegt. *Rhythmus 21* ist das Ergebnis einer konsequenten Suche nach einer neuen Formensprache. Die den ersten röntgenkinematographischen Experimenten inhärente stilistische Offenheit und Polysemie sowie die Faszination am Blick in den Körper münden am Ende der 1930er Jahre in die Darstellung der totalen Kontrolle und Archivierbarkeit des Individuums. Der Zugriff auf intime Vorgänge erhält nicht zuletzt durch die rhythmische Wiederholung der lebenswichtigen Vorgänge, die überwachende Off-Stimme des Mediziners und der Kombination von Mensch und Versuchstier seine speziell verstörende Wirkung. In diesem Kontext liest sich die *Zweite präsentistische Deklaration* Viking Eggelings und Raoul Hausmanns von 1923 umso eindringlicher:

> Unsere Aufgabe ist es, im Sinne einer universalen Verbindlichkeit an den physikalischen und physiologischen Problemen der Natur und des Menschen zu arbeiten und wir werden unsere Arbeit dort beginnen müssen, wo die modernen Wissenschaft aufhört, weil sie inobjektiv ist, weil sie nur das System der Ausbeutungsfähigkeit verfolgt und fortwährend Standpunkte einnimmt, die einer erledigten Zivilisationsform angehören. Wir haben voraussetzungslos und unvoreingenommen die ersten Schritte einer Naturbetrachtung zu unternehmen, die die Physik und Physiologie auf ihre eigentliche Wirkungsebene bringt, im Sinne einer kommenden klassenlosen Gesellschaft [...][40]

Hans Richter und die Avantgardefilmemacher der frühen 1920er Jahre entwickelten eine neue visuelle Sprache, die röntgenkinematographische Arbeiten grundlegend beeinflusste. Und auch umgekehrt wäre *Rhythmus 21*

39 Gray (Hg.): Hans Richter by Hans Richter, S. 131.

40 Viking Eggeling / Raoul Hausmann: Zweite präsentistische Deklaration. Gerichtet an die internationalen Konstruktivisten. In: MA. Deutsches Sonderheft (1923).

ohne die Entdeckung der ‚Strahlen' vielleicht nicht möglich gewesen. Das dichte Netz gegenseitiger Bezugspunkte sowie deren Vielfalt an Funktionen und Bedeutungshorizonten legen es nahe, die radiologischen Filme Robert Jankers neben Hans Richters *Rhythmus 21* als Medien des Austauschs verschiedener kultureller Sphären – mehr noch als Schlüsselmedien der Moderne – zu lesen.

Abbildungsverzeichnis

Abb. 1: Hans Richter: Rhythmus 21. DVD. 3 min. London: BFI 2001. (Deutschland 1921). 2:49 - 2:56 min.
Abb. 2: Robert Janker: Trinken. Digitale Kopie aus dem Archiv des Deutschen Röntgen-Museums. 1 min. (Deutschland ca. 1935). http://www.roentgenmuseum.de/ (10.5.2012).
Abb. 3: Wilhelm Prager / Nicholas Kaufmann: Wege zu Kraft und Schönheit. Ein Film über moderne Körperkultur. VHS. 104 min. Deutschland 1925.
Abb. 4: Robert Janker: Röntgenfilm I. Das Verdauungssystem, Kauen und Schlucken beim Menschen. Digitale Kopie aus dem Archiv des Deutschen Röntgen-Museums. 11 min. Bonn: Institut für Film und Bild in Wissenschaft und Unterricht. (Deutschland ca. 1936). http://www.roentgenmuseum.de/ (14.5.2012).

Notation: Early Visual Music from Scrolls to Scores

Erik Born

The search for a solution to the problem of movement in the graphic arts motivated diverse experiments in early visual music. The problem, seminally articulated by Ernst Brücke and Carus Sterne in the 1880s, was most clearly spelled out in Ludwig Volkmann's popular history of movement from painting to photography, *Das Bewegungsproblem in der bildenden Kunst*.[1] How is it possible, asks Volkmann, for the graphic arts to represent movement, even though graphic artworks are spatially fixed and motionless, and even though our experience of them is temporally momentary, rather than procedural?[2] Significantly, the problem was not formulated as that of representing or reproducing the natural movements of people, animals, or things themselves. It was more a matter of creating a shared perception of the experience of movement between the artist and the viewer: "Wie der Künstler die Bewegung erlebt hat, so muß sie der Beschauer mit ihm erleben können, dann wirkt das Werk auf ihn als ein von innen heraus bewegtes und bleibt lebendig für alle Zeiten."[3] The clear formulation of the problem of movement in terms of a discrepancy between mediated and unmediated experience may have contributed to experimentation in diverse media, but its very formulation in these terms made the problem insoluble.

"Die Bewegung in der bildenden Kunst zum Ausdruck zu bringen ist ein Problem, dessen Lösung schon viele schöpferische Geister beschäftigt hat," observed Ludwig Hilberseimer in the *Sozialistische Monatshefte* of May 23, 1921, and enthusiastically reported, "Viking Eggeling und Hans Richter haben unter Benutzung eines neuen Mittels, des Films, das Bewegungsproblem auf die radikalste Weise gelöst."[4] Their purported solution to the problem of movement involved the synthesis of a new medium, the film, and an old medium, the scroll. Whereas the earliest reproductions of Eggeling's scrolls do bear some visual, though little conceptual, resem-

1 See Ludwig Volkmann: Das Bewegungsproblem in der bildenden Kunst. Esslingen 1908.

2 Ibid., pp. 2-3.

3 Ibid., p. 60.

4 Ludwig Hilberseimer: Bewegungskunst. In: Sozialistische Monatshefte vol. 27 (23 May 1921), pp. 467-468; see also Hans Richter: Prinzipielles zur Bewegungskunst. In: De Stijl vol. 4 (July 1921), no. 7, pp. 109-112. Reprint edited by Ad Petersen; Viking Eggeling: Theoretical Presentations of the Art of Movement. In: MA vol. 6 (1 August 1921), no. 8, pp. 109-112.

blance to his film *Symphonie Diagonale*, Richter's scrolls are fundamentally different from his *Rhythmus* films (see fig. 1). Given this discrepancy, their premature claim of a solution to the problem of movement raises questions about what potential Richter and Eggeling saw in the two media, what solution was actually required for the realization of their artistic visions in film, and why, above all, the problem of movement was even considered to be a problem.

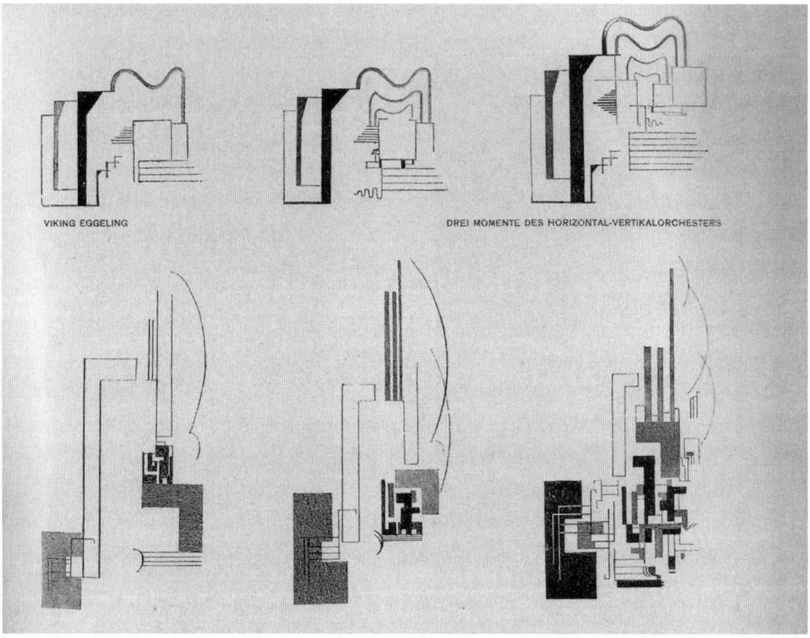

Fig. 1: Viking Eggeling: *Drei Momente des Horizontal-Vertikalorchesters* (top); Hans Richter: *Drei Momente der Komposition "Schwer-Leicht" (Präludium)* (bottom).

The transition from the graphic arts to film engendered reflection on the nature of media, for as Richter revealed in 1929, "Selbst die kleinsten Teile dieser Entwürfe zu verwirklichen, kostete enorme Mühe. Der Film war hier nur vom Künstlerisch-Ästhetischen aus begriffen, seine natürlichen Mittel noch nicht erkannt."[5] An awareness of film as a *time-based*, rather than an *image-based*, medium increasingly informs Richter and Eggeling's publications over the course of the decade, but the shift was neither ex-

5 Hans Richter: Leitsätze einer Vorhutarbeit. In: Filmtechnik 11 (25 May 1929), p. 219.

clusively, nor primarily, conceptual. Their collaborator Werner Graeff provides a good indication of their scrolls' inadequacy as templates for films: "vor allem gaben sie über den gedachten Ablauf der Bewegungen, über Tempo und Rhythmus keinerlei Auskunft. In diesem Sinne waren es keine 'Partituren.'"[6] The fundamental shift required for the realization of their films, as Graeff's statement indicates, is not to be found in a sudden change of representational technology, as Richter and Eggeling claimed, but rather in their gradual abandonment of an imagistic system of notation in favor of a symbolic system—not in the transition from painting to film, but from scrolls to scores.

"Easel—Scroll—Film" was long a dominant genealogy of abstract cinema, perpetuating a selective lineage solidified, in retrospect, by Hans Richter himself.[7] But the emergence of abstract film, though pioneered by visual artists, was not simply the logical conclusion of experiments in the visual arts, nor did the screen become a substitute for the canvas.[8] The multiple origins of abstract film, as revisionist film historians have shown, can be located in a wide range of experiments across media, including light sculptures, color organs, and kinetic devices for the stage.[9] Even the original description of Richter and Eggeling's new art of movement, at least in Hilberseimer's account, is hardly medium-specific, with their "Bewegungskunst" being considered to have larger social, economic, didactic, and technological implications.[10] Nevertheless, the common denominator for these diverse experiments continues to be the idea of "visual music," a category that includes almost any artwork made of images or light that bears some relation to musicality. For some, the idea of visual music still contains the imaginative power of an intermedial art form[11]; for others, it remains a possible art form with no real historical or philosophical potential.[12] The common touchstone of these debates, the desirability of ex-

6 Werner Graeff: Zu meinen Filmkompositionen von 1922. http://www.werner-graeff.de/film/filmkassette.html (4 May 2012).

7 See Hans Richter: Easel—Scroll—Film. In: Magazine of Art (Feb. 1952), pp. 78-86.

8 See Standish D. Lawder: The Cubist Cinema. New York 1975, pp. 35-64.

9 See R. Bruce Elder: Harmony and Dissent: Film and Avant-garde Art Movements in the Early Twentieth-Century. Waterloo, ON 2008, p. 39ff.; Karin von Maur: Vom Klang der Bilder. Die Musik in der Kunst des 20. Jahrhunderts. München 1985.

10 See Hilberseimer: Bewegungskunst, p. 468; see also the article "Bewegungskunst" in this volume.

11 See Wendy Everett: Image, Music, Film. In: Studies in European Cinema vol. 5 (2008), no. 1, pp. 7-16.

12 See Jerrold Levinson: Non-existent Artforms and the Case of Visual Music. In: Contemplating Art: Essays in Aesthetics. Oxford 2006, pp. 129-142.

periencing movement through media, still needs to be interrogated more forcefully.

Analogies to music were used frequently for paintings in the 1910s and subsequently for films in the 1920s.[13] What Theo van Doesburg called "sichtbare Musik" and Bernhard Diebold "Augenmusik" would come to be codified, for Richter, as "visuelle Musik, von der wir sprachen, über die wir diskutierten, an der wir arbeiteten und die wir im Film realisierten."[14] The locus criticus for Richter and Eggeling's understanding of visual music is an analogy between film and music in the reports on their new art of movement. Implicitly, the analogy maps the musical ear onto the filmic eye and, explicitly, music's perceived abstraction and temporality onto the visual arts:

> Der Vorgang selbst ist eine dramatische Evolution und Revolution in der Sphäre des Reinkünstlerischen vermittelst abstrakter Formen; analog der uns für das Ohr geläufigen Geschehnisse der Musik. Die abstrakten Formen vermeiden gleich denen der Musik Analogien oder Erinnerungen an Naturobjekte, finden Spannung und Auflösung in sich, und sind, da alle materiellen Vergleiche und Erinnerungen wegfallen, elementar magisch.[15]

The description of their working procedure, despite its apodictic style, may primarily serve an explanatory function, mapping the known qualities of music onto the unknown qualities of film; and the emphasis on autonomy may serve a legitimizing function, drawing on the prestige of absolute music to establish the fledgling genre of art film in the Weimar hierarchy of the arts.[16] In the context of Hilberseimer's article, however, the immediate purpose of the analogy is to support a narrative of artistic innovation and social progress, a narrative that decisively fails to square with a history of failed experiments.

In the years leading up to the completion of their films, Richter and Eggeling did produce many exquisite scrolls, partly in search of a universal language[17] and partly for the purposes of soliciting funding to support their

---

13 See Malcolm Cook: Visual Music in Film, 1921–1924: Richter, Eggeling, Ruttman. In: Charlotte de Mille (ed.): Music and Modernism, c. 1849–1950. Newcastle, UK 2011, pp. 206-228.

14 Hans Richter: Köpfe und Hinterköpfe. Zurich 1967, p. 70.

15 Hilberseimer: Bewegungskunst, p. 467.

16 See Joel Westerdale: The Musical Promise of Abstract Film. In: Christian Rogowski (ed.): The Many Faces of Weimar Cinema: Rediscovering Germany's Filmic Legacy. Rochester, NY 2010, pp. 153-166.

17 For a reconstruction of their pamphlet on Universelle Sprache, see Stephen C. Foster (ed.): Hans Richter: Activism, Modernism, and the Avant-garde. Cambridge, MA 1998, pp. 184-239.

costly time at the UFA studios.[18] While the avowed inspiration for their scrolls lay in ancient Chinese and Egyptian models,[19] their unacknowledged influence may also have included Torah scrolls, a clear point of reference for some of El Lissitsky's contemporary work. In this respect, the ancient and sacred otherness often ascribed to the models for their scrolls may encode the perception of Jewishness among the assimilated avant-garde.[20] The epistemological traditions of Richter and Eggeling's scrolls resonate further with Goethe's *Generalbaß der Malerei*[21] and Leibniz's *ars combinatoria*.[22] But they were intended primarily as a system of notation for another medium: "Entwurfszeichnungen für die Ausführung im Film, in dem sie bereits, zum Teil wenigstens, schon ausgeführt sind."[23]

Having created an illusion of continuous movement across the extended surface of a scroll, Richter and Eggeling thought they had created templates for filming. But had the studio technicians they were working with at UFA[24] photographed each image and assembled the footage, the resulting film would have created an unintended effect: the discontinuous flicker of non-sequential images. A document of this failed attempt can be found in the earliest reproduction of still frames from one of Richter's *Rhythmus* films, and it may even survive as the frenetic middle section of *Rhythmus 23*.[25] The images of a filmstrip might create the perception of continuous movement for the viewer whose eyes travel over them, but they would not produce those same movements when passed through a projector. Scrolls are ultimately inadequate, if not impossible, templates for films, because they represent images, rather than providing the information necessary to produce those images in film.

The main difficulty of realizing scroll paintings in film, immediately transparent from our privileged critical vantage point and evident to Rich-

---

18 See ibid., pp. 7-8, 15; Malte Hagener: Moving Forward, Looking Back: The European Avant-Garde and the Invention of Film Culture, 1919–1939. Amsterdam 2007, p. 31.

19 Hans Richter: Easel—Scroll—Film, p. 81.

20 See Albert Boime: Dada's Dark Secret. In: Rose-Carol Washton Long (ed.): Jewish Dimensions in Modern Visual Culture: Antisemitism, Assimilation, Affirmation. Lebanon, NH 2010, pp. 90-115.

21 See R. Bruce Elder: Harmony and Dissent, pp. 137-148.

22 See Pasi Väliaho: Mapping the Moving Image: Gesture, Thought and Cinema Circa 1900. Amsterdam 2010, pp. 175-176.

23 Hilbeseimer: Bewegungskunst, p. 467.

24 The role of UFA's studio technicians, Svend Noldan and Otto Schmalhausen, remains completely unknown and unresearched.

25 See R. Bruce Elder: Harmony and Dissent, p. 194, n. 208.

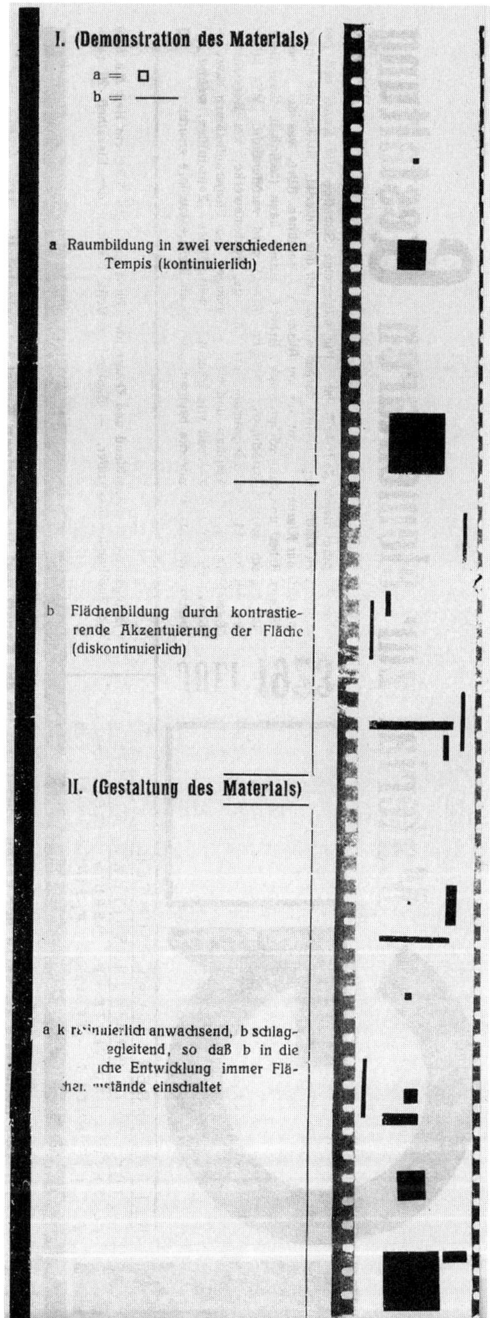

Fig. 2: In the earliest reproduction of celluloid from the *Rhythmus* films, the individual images are still conceived of on analogy with individual images drawn on a scroll.

ter only late in his career,[26] is that painting and film, though often grouped together as visual media, bear radically different relations to time. Moving images and non-moving images, as Stefan Beyst brilliantly observes, differ in *kind* rather than *degree*.[27] With non-moving images, the viewer must read each mark separately and somewhat arbitrarily; and the artist, working with a flat surface, always runs up against the problem of its edges. A provisional workaround is to extend the surface itself, as is the case with a scroll, but eventually the movement must begin and end when the viewer's eyes or hands reach the boundaries of the medium. Any attempt to create movement on the same terms for both moving and non-moving images will necessarily fail, an observation that may seem self-evident but that only gradually occurred to Richter and Eggeling due to their equation of painting and film.

After their initial failures to realize their films in 1921, the two artists broke off their friendship, partly for personal reasons, and the 33-year-old Richter more quickly abandoned his scrolls as a template for filming than did the 41-year-old Eggeling.[28] One reviewer still perceived their common concerns for movement and music, which became linked through the myth of an immediate experience of time: "Das Moment der Zeit, unmittelbar erlebt durch den räumlich-optischen Ablauf der Bewegung, setzt Verwandtschaft mit der Musik."[29] Another contemporary differentiated between Eggeling's "poliphone Instrumentation der Form *mit Hilfe* des Lichtes" and Richter's "poliphone Instrumentation des Lichtes."[30] The description resonates strongly with Richter's frequent contrast between Eggeling's "Orchestration der Form" and his own "Orchestration der Zeit," indicating his increasing advocacy of rhythm and temporality in cinematic reform (see fig. 3).

A gradual realization of film's temporality increasingly informs Hans Richter's writings throughout the 1920s, and becomes most evident in the April 1926 issue of his periodical *G. Zeitschrift für elementare Gestaltung*. This issue, devoted to the creation of film art and the reform of industrial cinema, features a lengthy excursus on "dimension t," or time, which appears as the

---

26 See Hans Richter: My Experience with Movement in Painting and in Film. In: Gyorgy Kepes (ed.): The Nature and Art of Motion. New York 1965, pp. 142-157.

27 See Stefan Beyst: Visual Music: An Inquiry into the Musical Potential of the Image (Nov. 2001). http://d-sites.net/english/visual%20music.htm (15 April 2012).

28 See Hans Richter: My Experience with Movement in Painting and in Film, p. 150; Louise O'Konor: Viking Eggeling 1880–1925: Artist and Film-Maker, Life and Work. Stockholm 1971, pp. 69-71.

29 Ernö (Ernst) Kállai: Konstruktivismus. Jahrbuch der jungen Kunst 5 (1924), p. 380.

30 B.G. Kawan: Abstrakte Filmkunst. In: Film-Kurier (22 Nov. 1924), n.p.; my emphasis.

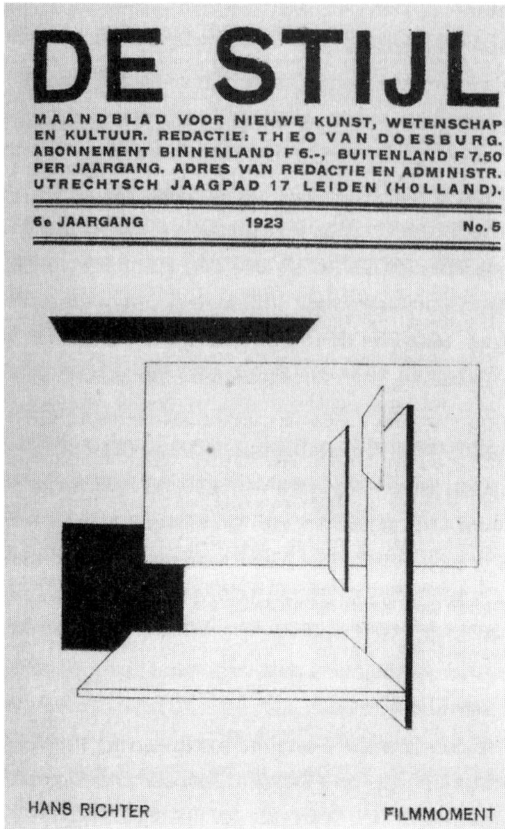

Fig. 3: Hans Richter: *Filmmoment.* The film is now conceived of in three (or four) dimensions.

running footer for eight pages and the supraheading for Richter's seminal article, "Bei 25 Meter pro Sekunde geht es nicht mehr um das schöne Bild!"[31] In the article, Richter dismisses imagistic descriptions of film, thereby emphasizing its temporality, which he claims has been neglected due to the popularity of English categories such as "the Pictures" or "Moving Pictures":

> Gewiß hat der Film einzelne Bilder, aber solange man das nicht vergißt, kommt man nicht dazu, zu begreifen, was im Film wesentlich wirkt, denn Bewegung kann nicht als eine Summe von Einzelbildern, von statischen Teilen, gedacht werden, Bewegung bleibt auch im kleinsten Teil Bewegung.

31 Hans Richter: Bei 25 Meter pro Sekunde geht es nicht mehr um das schöne Bild! In: G. Zeitschrift für elementare Gestaltung V-VI (April 1926). Reprint edited by Marion von Hofacker, München 1986, p. 114.

Je deutlicher auf eine mittlere Stundengeschwindigkeit von hunderttausend Bildern eingegangen wird, und je verständiger die *Zeit* (in ihren Teilen und als Einheit) gehandhabt und gedacht wird, um so fühlbarer erhält der Film seine Gestalt. Die Orientierung im Film geschieht bisher ganz allgemein, mehr nach Bildform, als nach Zeitform.[32]

This assessment of the filmic medium, like the *Rhythmus* films themselves, resonates strongly with the Bergsonian concepts of duration and continuity, as Pasi Väliaho argues, and Richter's later recollection of how, in film, "the single image disappeared into a flow of images" calls to mind Bergson's description of how, in pure duration, multiple images merge together like the notes of a melody.[33] Nevertheless, these ideals of rhythm and flow remain fundamentally in tension with Richter's aspirations for meter, counting, and measured time—the ideals not only of avant-garde film, but also of contemporary science film.[34]

Throughout the 1920s, Richter and Eggeling were searching for a means not only of aligning corporeal, aesthetic, and natural rhythms, but also of articulating and communicating the content of their artistic visions to their collaborators. The transition to scores, a practice adopted earlier by Werner Graeff and Ludwig Hirschfeld-Mack among others,[35] documented only partially for the *Rhythmus* films (see fig. 4).

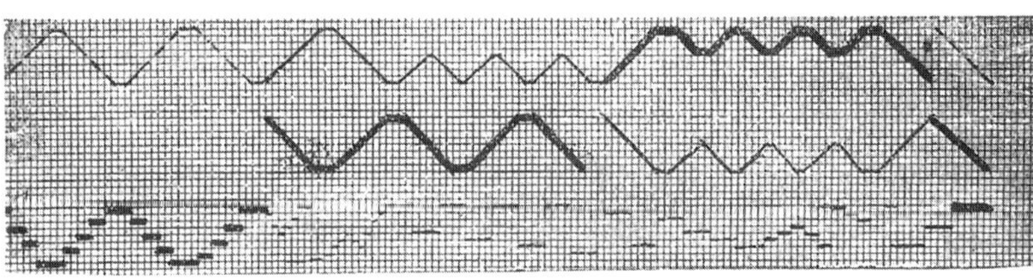

Fig. 4: Hans Richter: Teil einer Partitur zu dem Film *Rhythmus 25*. An indication of the shift from scrolls to scores.

A sort of score or sheet music, as Richter explains, provides information for the performance of the film in the studio: "Die Partitur ist für die Aufnahme bestimmt. Die Bewegungsarten sind durch Steigen und Fallen

32 Ibid.

33 Pasi Väliaho: Mapping the Moving Image, pp. 175-176.

34 See Malin Wahlberg: Documentary Time: Film and Phenomenology. Minneapolis 2008.

35 See Werner Graeff: Über den Ursprung des abstrakten Films. In: Film als Film. 1910 bis heute. Köln 1977.

(Größer- und Kleinerwerden) der Figur anschaulich gemacht."[36] In other words, the score communicates to its performers, i.e., studio technicians, how to play three instruments, i.e., the proportional figures a, b, and c, through precise modulations of light and darkness over space and time.

Apart from fulfilling these communicative functions, the score also indicates Richter's shift from a graphic system of notation to a musical system, manifest in his abandonment of representational graphics in favor of non-representational graphs. In this respect, the score verges on becoming an autonomous object, not even in need of filming: "von der Partitur ist *ohne weiteres* das Größer- und Kleiner-, das Heller- und Dunkler-, das Schneller- und Langsamerwerden der Figuren abzulesen."[37] The fact that the score accounts for three main variables of change (spatial extension, the intensity of light, temporal duration), without indicating a form's position, may further indicate that the lateral movements in the *Rhythmus* films were a matter of improvisation, in contrast to the more deliberate planning of changes to forms remaining at fixed points. Despite this interplay of planned and improvised movements, the *Rhythmus* films notoriously appear to lack visual rhythms, meters, and tempos, a function of our embodied experience of them in time.[38] The disjuncture is that between our experience of mediated and unmediated movements, precisely the problem of movement in early visual music.

Solutions to the problem of movement in early visual music had primarily sought to make representational technologies express, record, store, or translate an embodied experience of movement. A turning point, for Hans Richter and Viking Eggeling, came not in their early adoption of the filmic medium for the creation of an autonomous artform, but rather in their gradual recognition of the shared qualities among media—namely, in the ability of both films and scores to store time. "Texte und Partituren – andere Zeitspeicher hatte Europa nicht," argues Friedrich Kittler for the period before the invention of phonographs and cinematographs.[39] Even after the invention of these technologies, diverse systems of notation continued to compete for the storage of time in symbolic form. Although scores may serve as better templates for films than scrolls, the eventual articulation of a cinematic language among the avant-garde never fully subsumed such paracinematic resources. The desire to experience movement through

36 Hans Richter: Teil einer Partitur zu dem Film Rhythmus 25. In: G. Zeitschrift für elementare Gestaltung V-VI (April 1926). Reprint edited by Marion von Hofacker, München 1986, p. 117.

37 Ibid.; my emphasis.

38 See Hans Emons: Das mißverstandene Modell – Zur rolle der Musik im abstrakten Film der Zwanziger Jahre. In: Klaus-Ernst Behne (ed.): film–music–video oder Die Konkurrenz von Auge und Ohr. Regensburg 1987, pp. 51-63.

39 Friedrich Kittler: Grammophon, Film, Typewriter. Berlin 1986, p. 11.

media, made possible by a system of notation, still preserves a desire to transcend time.

Table of Figures

Fig. 1: Viking Eggeling: Drei Momente des Horizontal-Vertikalorchesters. In: De Stijl vol. 4 (1921) no. 7, p. 112. Reprint edited by Ad Petersen, Amsterdam 1968, p. 85.
Fig. 2: Hans Richter: Filmstreifen. In: G. Material zur elementaren Gestaltung I (Juli 1923). Reprint edited by Marion von Hofacker, München 1986, p. 3.
Fig. 3: Hans Richter: Filmmoment. In: De Stijl vol. 6 (1923) no. 5, title page. Reprint edited by Ad Petersen, Amsterdam 1968, p. 373.
Fig. 4: Hans Richter: Teil einer Partitur zu dem Film *Rhythmus 25*. In: G. Zeitschrift für elementare Gestaltung V-VI (April 1926). Reprint edited by Marion von Hofacker, München 1986, p. 117.

Primitivismus: The Dada Rhythms of *Rhythmus 21*

Kurt Beals

Hans Richter's *Rhythmus 21* is most frequently seen as an exercise in order. Norbert M. Schmitz emphasizes the film's "geometrisch strenge Formen," writing, "Die an die abstrakten Kompositionen der russischen Konstruktivisten erinnernden Rechtecke thematisieren so die Relation von Raum, Tiefe und Geschwindigkeit als Funktionsweisen menschlicher Wahrnehmung."[1] Michael Cowan likewise focuses on the Constructivist aspects of the film, noting that Richter "maintained a view of film as a means of controlling rhythm throughout his career [...]. And he saw his abstract films [...] as experiments in placing this vital force under the rational control of the will."[2] However, as Cowan notes, other scholars have highlighted the film's irregular moments. While *Rhythmus 21* begins with smooth, unified movements—a single square or rectangle slowly receding, or two white planes concealing or revealing a black background—the movements soon become more complex. Multiple rectangles grow and recede more and more quickly, sometimes independently, sometimes in opposition to one another. Towards the end of the film, two rectangles even appear briefly at a diagonal, disrupting the horizontal and vertical lines that have dominated up to that point (2:31). Malcolm Turvey explores the significance of these "unpredictable variations," but ultimately concludes that "an impression of order is maintained in spite of the moment-by-moment disorder,"[3] citing this balance of order and chaos as one key characteristic linking Richter's abstract films to the Dada movement.

Even if it is true, though, that order wins out in the end—a conclusion that is reinforced by the film's closing shot, in which a single square once again recedes into the background (albeit now a black square against white background)—the disorderly aspects of Richter's film deserve more thorough consideration. Building on research into the discourses of rhythm in the early twentieth century, Cowan's work suggests that these disruptions could be understood in terms of the organic or vital rhythms associated

1 Norbert M. Schmitz: Der Film der klassischen Avantgarde, oder Die Gescheiterte Autonomie des Kinos. In: Heinz Arnold (ed.): Aufbruch ins 20. Jahrhundert: über Avantgarden. Munich 2001, pp. 138-154, here: p. 142.

2 Michael Cowan: Advertising, Rhythm, and the Filmic Avant-Garde in Weimar: Guido Seeber and Julius Pinschewer's Kipho Film. In: October 131 (2010), pp. 23-50, here: pp. 33-34.

3 Malcolm Turvey: Dada Between Heaven and Hell: Abstraction and Universal Language in the Rhythm Films of Hans Richter. In: October 105 (2003), pp. 13-36, here: p. 30.

with German body culture, with the qualification that Richter did not share the goals of body culture advocates, but rather sought "to harness the affective power of 'rhythm' in the service of the (constructivist) intellect."[4] However, while acknowledging the importance of this opposition between vital rhythms and rational intellect, the present essay will suggest that the film's rhythms can also be understood in the context of primitivism, an aesthetic tendency that took root in Europe in the first decades of the twentieth century.

Particularly in the visual arts, but also in poetry and music, primitivism was characterized above all by the adoption of so-called 'primitive' techniques and forms from Africa and Oceania. In the Dada movement, with which Richter was closely associated, primitivism particularly took the form of rhythmic chants and dances, frequently accompanied by the beating of a drum. When Richter's film is viewed in the context of the Dadaists' primitivist poetry and performances, it appears not merely as an abstract experiment in order and disorder, or an opposition of vital rhythms to mechanical regimentation, but also as a part of the primitivist turn to non-European cultures in search of elemental forms and artistic renewal.

Vital Rhythms and Primitivism

In discussions of rhythm in the early twentieth century, 'Rhythmus' was frequently associated with natural, organic, vital impulses, and contrasted to 'Takt,' which stood for the regular, metrical repetition characteristic of modern industry.[5] As Christine Lubkoll writes, "In einer kulturkritischen Perspektive wird so der 'Rhythmus des Lebens', der in allen natürlichen Erscheinungen waltet, subversiv gegen die 'eintönige Raserei' des Maschinenzeitalters ausgespielt."[6] Similarly, Gabriele Brandstetter writes that thinkers including Ludwig Klages, Rudolf von Laban, and Rudolf Bode saw

> Rhythmus als [einen] naturgegebene[n] Zustand, der in der gegenwärtigen Epoche durch die Herrschaft der Technik (die Entwicklung

4 Michael Cowan: The Heart Machine: "Rhythm" and Body in Weimar Film and Fritz Lang's Metropolis. In: Modernism/modernity 14, no. 2 (2007), pp. 225-248, here: p. 246, n. 44.

5 For detailed discussions of the rhythm discourse of the early twentieth century, see e.g. Cowan: The Heart Machine; Christine Lubkoll: Rhythmus: Zum Konnex von Lebensphilosophie und ästhetischer Moderne um 1900. In: Christine Lubkoll (ed.): Das Imaginäre des Fin de siècle. Freiburg im Breisgau 2001, pp. 83-110; Gabriele Brandstetter: Rhythmus als Lebensanschauung. Zum Bewegungsdiskurs um 1900. In: Christa Brüstle et al. (eds.): Aus dem Takt: Rhythmus in Kunst, Kultur und Natur. Bielefeld 2005, pp. 33-44.

6 Lubkoll: Rhythmus, p. 84.

> des Maschinellen, des Automatisierten) in einen Status der Arrhythmie des Menschen verkehrt sei; und dieser Effekt der Zivilisation müsse durch einen therapeutischen Prozess der Re-Rhythmisierung des arbeitenden Menschen ausgeglichen und geheilt werden.[7]

Rather than strict regularity and order, rhythm here is associated with natural life processes free of any standardized constraints imposed from without. As both Lubkoll and Brandstetter note, this opposition of natural 'Rhythmus' to mechanical 'Takt' leads to contradictions: Lubkoll points out that the 'natural' rhythms of life are only observable within the regular framework provided by 'Takt,'[8] while Brandstetter remarks that "Re-Rhythmisierung" is, paradoxically, a cultural process aimed at counteracting the effects of culture. But as Brandstetter further argues, "Gerade diese Aporie aber treibt einen Essentialismus hervor, der Rhythmus als Prinzip von Ursprünglichkeit mit Rasse, Nationalgefühl ('Volkskraft') und mit entsprechend hierarchisierten Topoi der Geschlechterdifferenz koppelt."[9] In some cases, the valorization of rhythm provided the basis for doctrines of German racial superiority.[10]

But the "Logik des 'Ursprünglichen'"[11] that informed these theories of rhythm also led some artists to look outside of European culture for models of life, and of artistic production, that seemed untouched by the 'Ent-Rhythmisierung' of modern society. Here the rhythm discourse intersects with the current of so-called 'primitivism' that had a powerful impact on European art in the first decades of the twentieth century.[12] Although sculptures, masks, and other artworks and artifacts from Africa and Oceania had been in circulation in Europe in the nineteenth century, the 'discovery' of African art by European artists is generally dated to around 1906. Picasso's 1907 painting *Les Demoiselles d'Avignon*, which was influenced by his viewing of African masks, put these newfound influences to work, initiating

---

7 Brandstetter: Rhythmus als Lebensanschauung, pp. 35–36.

8 Lubkoll: Rhythmus, p. 84.

9 Brandstetter: Rhythmus als Lebensanschauung, p. 42.

10 For discussions of Bode's racial ideology, see Brandstetter: Rhythmus als Lebensanschauung; Cowan: The Heart Machine.

11 Brandstetter: Rhythmus als Lebensanschauung, p. 37.

12 For a discussion of the term "primitivism," see William Rubin: Modernist Primitivism: An Introduction. In: William Rubin (ed.): "Primitivism" in 20th Century Art: Affinity of the Tribal and the Modern, vol. 1. New York 1984, p. 5. While I do not wholly agree with Rubin's defense of primitivism, I do find his distinction between the term "primitive" (a frequently pejorative term applied to groups of people) and the term "primitivism" (a word denoting a development in Western art, and not the non-Western works that inspired it) to be useful, and I use the latter term in Rubin's sense. For a strong critique of primitivism, see Hal Foster: The "Primitive" Unconscious of Modern Art. In: October 34 (1985), pp. 45-70.

the trend of primitivism in Western art that would grow in the following decades. For many artists, works from Africa, Oceania, and elsewhere "seemed to evoke a deeper and more universal sense of humanity."[13] Like the rhythm discourse discussed by Brandstetter and Lubkoll, this turn to primivitism reflects a belief that natural ways of life and forms of artistic production had been drowned out by the more rigid forms imposed by modern European culture, and a desire to recover 'originary' or 'elemental' impulses and forms.

Of course, this search for a "universal sense of humanity" in the works of non-Western cultures entails its own set of essentializing biases: these cultures are frequently conflated with one another (the term 'l'art nègre' was often applied indiscriminately to African and Oceanic works) and depicted as vestiges of earlier stages in cultural development that Europe has long since left behind.[14] The desire to see in these cultures certain universal characteristics originally shared by all humanity entails the denial that these cultures possess any distinctive character and history of their own.[15] A particularly egregious version of this view was articulated in 1916 by Marius de Zayas, a Mexican artist, writer, and gallerist who became acquainted with African art in Paris, and arranged an exhibition of African art in 1914 at Alfred Stieglitz's gallery 291 in New York. While praising African art itself, de Zayas held that "although there is a difference of culture between the Negro of the forest and the Negro of the plains, at bottom their mentality is identical," and that "the African Negro savage has the most rudimentary cerebral condition. His brain can be considered as being in the first state of the evolution of the brain of man. To him, therefore, must belong the first state of the evolution of the conception of form."[16] If champions of vital rhythms such as Rudolf Bode used their views to justify a doctrine of German racial superiority, the image of African art promoted by de Zayas was likewise shot through with racial prejudice. Nevertheless, while the risks of these ideological positions should be borne in mind, the importance of primitivism in the history of European art is undeniable. Whereas the proponents of vital rhythms focused on the body as the source of natural, organic rhythms that resisted the mechanization of modern culture,

13 Jack Flam: Introduction. In: Jack Flam / Miriam Deutch (eds.): Primitivism and Twentieth-Century Art: A Documentary History. Berkeley 2003, pp. 1-22, here: p. 3.

14 See Evan Maurer: Dada and Surrealism. In: William Rubin (ed.): "Primitivism" in 20th Century Art: Affinity of the Tribal and the Modern, vol. 2. New York 1984, p. 538.

15 See Foster: The "Primitive" Unconscious of Modern Art.

16 Marius de Zayas: African Negro Art and Modern Art. In: Jack Flam / Miriam Deutch (eds.): Primitivism and Twentieth-Century Art: A Documentary History. Berkeley 2003, pp. 92-99, here: p. 94, 98.

artists influenced by primitivism, particularly the Dadaists, turned to non-European cultures as sources for rhythms that would disrupt or counteract Europe's metrical malaise.

Dada Rhythms

Primitivism first took root in France, but the trend quickly spread to other parts of Europe. An important theoretical foundation for this development was provided by Wilhelm Worringer's 1907 dissertation *Abstraktion und Einfühlung*, in which Worringer defended the importance of abstraction and stylized representation, arguing that abstraction represented a distinct, more primitive artistic drive than the naturalistic representation that had dominated in Europe since the Renaissance: "der in seiner Gesetzmässigkeit vollkommenste Stil, der Stil der höchsten Abstraktion, der strengsten Lebensausschliessung ist den Völkern auf ihrer primitivsten Kulturstufe zu eigen."[17] Worringer did not go so far as to endorse African or Oceanic art—in fact, he argued that many of the creations of *Naturvölker* did not qualify as art at all.[18] Nevertheless, his praise of the abstraction that he identified in many non-European traditions, particularly in Egyptian and East Asian art, was soon applied by other critics to African art. Also crucial was Worringer's assertion that this 'primitive' drive to abstraction played an important role for modern artists as well, a point that he made particularly clearly in his 1911 essay "Entwicklungsgeschichtliches zur modernsten Kunst."[19]

Carl Einstein's 1915 book *Negerplastik* also attracted attention in the German-speaking world, examining African art from a perspective more aesthetic than anthropological, and, like Worringer, noting its importance for modern European artists.[20] In the same year, Richard Huelsenbeck, who would play a significant role in both Zurich and Berlin Dada, first performed his *Negergedichte* at an *Expressionistenabend* in Berlin.[21] Thus, by the time the Dada movement as such took shape in Zurich in 1916, its

---

17 Wilhelm Worringer: Abstraktion und Einfühlung: Ein Beitrag zur Stilpsychologie. Munich 1921, p. 22.

18 Ibid., p. 70.

19 Wilhelm Worringer: Entwicklungsgeschichtliches zur modernsten Kunst: In: Im Kampf um die Kunst: die Antwort auf den "Protest deutscher Künstler": mit Beiträgen deutscher Künstler, Galerieleiter, Sammler und Schriftsteller. Munich 1911, pp. 92–99.

20 Carl Einstein: Negerplastik. Munich 1920.

21 Hans Bolliger / Guido Magnaguagno / Raimund Meyer (eds.): Dada in Zürich. Zurich 1985, p. 83.

members' affinity for primitivism had already been established.[22] At times, this affinity was displayed in the visual arts: Marcel Janco, for instance, designed an advertising poster for one Dada event that depicted African figures in a style inspired by African visual art, and for other occasions he created 'Negro masks' that were worn during the performance of dances or poems.[23] Hans Richter later recalled the impact of these "abstract Negro masks of Janco, which carried the audience from the primeval language of the new poems into the primeval forests of the artistic imagination."[24] The visual impact of these masks is attested to by many accounts of the Dadaists' performances at the Cabaret Voltaire in Zurich.

But primitivism did not only influence the Dadaists' visual art; its importance is also strongly felt in their poetry, which was often performed together with dancing and the beating of Huelsenbeck's notorious drum. Hugo Ball emphasized the dominance of rhythm in his introduction to the Dadaist anthology *Cabaret Voltaire*: "Am 26. Februar kam Richard Huelsenbeck aus Berlin und am 30. März führten wir eine wundervolle Negermusik auf (toujours avec la grosse caisse: boum boum boum boum – drabatja mo gere drabatja mo bonooooooooooo –)."[25] The connection of these rhythms to African sources is made clear in several Dadaist poems. Ball composed a number of *Lautgedichte* that drew on the sound patterns of Bantu and Swahili, though largely dispensing with any semantic dimension.[26] Huelsenbeck similarly paired repetitive rhythms with arbitrary borrowings from African languages. The first poem in his 1916 book *Phantastische Gebete*, for instance, includes apparently meaningless repetitions such as "da umba da umba da umba hihi," but also incorporates words most likely drawn from African sources, such as "Mfunga," "kamo," "kara," "Mpala," and "sokobauno."[27] Another poem in the same collection, entitled simply "Die Primitiven," is reproduced here in its entirety:

22 On this topic, see e.g. Hanne Bergius: Das Lachen Dadas: Die Berliner Dadaisten und ihre Aktionen. Giessen 1989, pp. 326–327; Maurer: Dada and Surrealism; Richard Sheppard: Modernism–Dada–Postmodernism. Evanston, IL 2000.

23 Bolliger / Magnaguagno / Meyer (eds.): Dada in Zürich, p. 87 (citing Hugo Ball), pp. 128-129. The poster that Janco designed for the event entitled "le Chant nègre" was never actually printed.

24 Hans Richter: Dada: Art and Anti-Art. New York 1965, p. 20.

25 Hugo Ball: Introduction. In: Cabaret Voltaire. Zurich 1916, p. 5.

26 See J. C. Middleton: The Rise of Primitivism and Its Relevance to the Poetry of Expressionism and Dada. In: Peter F. Ganz (ed.): The Discontinuous Tradition: Studies in German Literature in Honour of Ernest Ludwig Stahl. Oxford 1971, pp. 183-203, here: pp. 198-199.

27 The words "mfunga," "kamo," and "kara" all occur in Swahili. "Mpala" is the stem of the Zulu word "impala," while "sokobauno" suggests the Zulu "sakubona" (or "sawubona"), meaning "good day."

« indigo indigo
« Trambahn Schlafsack
« Wanz und Floh
« indigo indigai
« umbaliska
« bumm DADAI

Like many of Huelsenbeck's primitivist poems, "Die Primitiven" is driven by a repetitive rhythm, suggestive of a chant. This emphasis is consistent with Ball's recollection, "Huelsenbeck [...] plädiert dafür, daß man den Rhythmus verstärkt (den Negerrhythmus). Er möchte am liebsten die Literatur in Grund und Boden trommeln."[28] In poems such as Ball's and Huelsenbeck's, these 'primitive' rhythms offer an alternative to the mechanical rhythms of the *Trambahn*.

Particularly in the context of the Dadaists' performances, accompanied by drums and improvised dances, the rhythmic pulse of these primitivist poems suggested a spontaneity on the verge of breaking into chaos. Of course, there are exceptions to this general rule: Tristan Tzara, for instance, took an interest in 'poésie nègre' and published his French versions of Australian aboriginal poetry in the first two issues of *Dada* magazine, taking inspiration from the sound of the original poems but largely neglecting their meaning; however, Tzara's versions generally observed conventional French syntax, and did not employ the same sorts of rhythmic repetition as Ball's or Huelsenbeck's poetry.[29] Nevertheless, the connection is consistent enough to deserve serious attention: for Ball, Huelsenbeck, and many other Dadaists, rhythm was closely linked to primitivism, and these 'primitive' rhythms were perceived as disruptive, posing a challenge to the reigning order of industrialized society, and to the aesthetic traditions of Western culture.

Richter's Rhythms

Insofar as Richter's *Rhythmus 21* is an abstract composition of planes and rectangles, it does not make the sort of direct reference to the art forms, languages, or cultures of so-called 'primitive' peoples that Janco's masks and Ball's and Huelsenbeck's poems do. Nevertheless, the film can be usefully considered in the context of the primitivist trend in Western art in general, and in the Dada movement in particular. Richter actively participated in Zurich Dada, and took part in a Dada exhibition at the Galerie Corray in January-February 1917 that also featured African sculpture. The previous year, Richter had written an introduction to the catalog of an ex-

28 Hugo Ball: Die Flucht aus der Zeit. Zurich 1992, p. 80.

29 See Peter Nicholls: Modernisms: A Literary Guide. Basingstoke 1995, p. 230.

hibit in Munich in which his works were included, attacking the "bourgeois cowardice, which is so attached to the conventions it has come to take for granted that an attraction toward African sculpture and cubism appears as a precious artistic trick, on which they may elaborate intellectual judgments of their never adventuresome thinking."[30] Richter was thus clearly not only acquainted with the currents of primitivism, but also prepared to defend them against reductive or trivializing interpretations.

The rhythms of Richter's film also strongly suggest a primitivist influence. As argued above, the irregular variations that interrupt the film's smooth movements can be seen as a sort of Dionysian disruption of Apollinian order. These apparently impulsive bursts of motion function, much like the rhythmic refrains in Ball's and Huelsenbeck's poems, not to establish order and uniformity, but rather to introduce disorder and spontaneity. If these rhythmic irregularities are considered in the context of primitivism, rather than only as manifestations of the vital rhythms discussed above, then these intrusions appear not merely as the self-assertion of a biological or organic force against the imposition of mechanical order, but also as a search for a new creative force outside the formal constraints of Western art. This possibility is also suggested in an interview that Richter gave in 1968: "Bach passt nicht zu meinen Filmen – ich bevorzuge Boogie-Woogie. Ich möchte den Rhythmus von *Rhythmus 21* betonen."[31] Although spoken with more than 40 years' hindsight, this comment suggests that the rhythms of the film, in Richter's view, might be better suited to African-influenced dance rhythms, such as those that inspired Huelsenbeck's drumming, than to Bach's orderly orchestrations.

Richter's abstract film can be linked to primitivism in other ways, as well. One of the key aspects of African art that interested many European artists, particularly the Cubists, was the unfamiliar mode of representing three-dimensional space that they found in many African works. For many painters, African art offered a clear alternative to traditional forms of perspective, and provided new techniques for representing movement. Worringer saw the reduction of three-dimensional space to two-dimensional geometrical forms as a fundamental characteristic of abstraction, which he considered to be motivated in large part by *Raumscheu*, the "primitive Angst" experienced in the face of a world that cannot be fully known or mastered.[32] Einstein discussed this issue in more formal terms in *Neger-*

30 Cited in Marion von Hofacker: Chronology. In: Stephen C. Foster (ed.): Hans Richter: Activism, Modernism, and the Avant-Garde. Cambridge, MA 1998, pp. 240-278, here: p. 245.

31 Quoted in Jonas Mekas: Movie Journal. In: Freunde der deutschen Kinemathek e.V. (ed.): Hans Richter: Film ist Rhythmus. Berlin 2003, pp. 130-131, here: p. 131. (Originally published in English in: The Village Voice. New York [20 June 1968].)

32 Worringer: Abstraktion und Einfühlung, pp. 20-21.

plastik, writing, "Die dreidimensional situierten Teile müssen gleichzeitig dargestellt werden, das heißt, der zerstreute Raum muß in ein Blickfeld integriert werden."[33] De Zayas likewise addressed these forms as the solution to a formal problem, writing that the "flat representations of the African Negro," with their "geometrical drawings" "represent movement and therefore have an abstract expression."[34] The view that African art offered European artists new means of depicting both depth and movement is summed up by Christopher Middleton, who writes that "primitivism has to do with plane surfaces, in painting and in poetry. [...] Depth is reduced, and forms come to occupy a frontal plane."[35]

For Richter, too, representing both depth and motion in two dimensions, and without recourse to traditional techniques of perspective, was a fundamental goal. As Standish Lawder writes, "Richter was interested in the interplay of surfaces, of areas." After exploring the possibilities of representing motion in the form of a scroll, both Richter and his collaborator Viking Eggeling found that "The next step was inevitable—film, the logical medium to extend this dynamic potential into actual kinetic movement." But whereas "normally, the movie screen is perceived as a kind of window, more or less arbitrarily circumscribed, and behind which an illusion of space appears; in *Rhythm 21*, by contrast, it is a planar surface activated by the forms upon it. Thus, its forms, like those of an abstract painting, seem to have no physical extension except on the screen."[36] Although a sense of depth is created in Richter's film as the rectangles grow and shrink, appearing to move towards and away from the viewer, it is crucial to note that Richter makes no use of standard visual perspective, and that the shapes on the screen are all flat surfaces, with no depth of their own. Like many artists who drew on African influences, Richter here seeks a means of depicting space and motion that does not depend on perspective to create an illusion of three-dimensional space.

A final intersection of Richter's film with the currents of primitivism that surrounded him might be seen in the programmatic text that he and Eggeling composed in 1920, arguing for a "Universelle Sprache." Although this pamphlet is lost, Richter later recalled that it expressed "our thesis that abstract form offers the possibility of a language above and beyond all national language frontiers. The basis for such language would lie in the identical form perception in all human beings and would offer the promise

33 Einstein: Negerplastik, p. xviii.

34 Zayas: African Negro Art and Modern Art, p. 98.

35 Middleton: The Rise of Primitivism, p. 196.

36 Standish D. Lawder: The Cubist Cinema. New York 1975, pp. 42, 46, 49.

of a universal art as it had never existed before."[37] On the one hand, this vision of universality is clearly projected into the future; this "universal art," as Richter says, "had never existed before." On the other hand, though, the appeal to "the identical form perception in all human beings" relies, like primitivism, on the assumption of certain fundamental aesthetic categories common to all humanity. In the case of primitivism, these categories are frequently assumed to be both conceptually and chronologically prior to the more 'advanced' forms of European art, such that the cultures in which such forms still dominate are associated with an earlier stage in human development. In the case of *Rhythmus 21*, in contrast, experiments with rhythm and with the two-dimensional representation of three-dimensional space and movement are presented as something new and forward-looking. Nevertheless, the elements of this 'universal language,' its rhythms and planar surfaces, closely resemble those employed in the primitivist works of the Dadaists and their contemporaries, and the search for elemental, universal artistic forms that challenge the status quo of Western art is one that Richter shared with his primitivist contemporaries.

Conclusions

To say this is not to suggest that *Rhythmus 21* should be recast as a 'primitivist film.' The overall impression created by the film is one of order and unity, and this impression is echoed not only in the majority of critical literature on the film, but also in numerous statements by Richter himself. Writing of himself and Eggeling, Richter recalled "our belief that a precise polar interrelationship of opposites was the key to an order, and once we understood this order we knew we could control this new freedom."[38] This balance between order and freedom—or to put it another way, this orderly employment of freedom—is fundamental to Richter's film, and if order gives way at times to disorder, that disorder is soon brought back under control. Nevertheless, even, or especially, if order dominates in Richter's film, it is important to give disorder its due, and to consider what role this disorder plays in the film, and what form it takes.

Given that Richter characterized his *Rhythmus* films as Dada films, it is reasonable to seek affinities between these films and the works of the other Dadaists. While Turvey cites the balance of order and disorder itself as a characteristic linking Richter's films to the Dada movement,[39] primi-

37 Cited in Justin Hoffmann: Hans Richter: Constructivist Filmmaker. In: Stephen C. Foster (ed.): Hans Richter: Activism, Modernism, and the Avant-Garde. Cambridge, MA 1998, pp. 72-91, here: p. 76.

38 Cited in Turvey: Dada Between Heaven and Hell, p. 32.

39 Ibid., pp. 30–31.

tivism provides another illuminating connection. Dadaists such as Marcel Janco, who created visual art inspired by African masks and sculptures, and Ball and Huelsenbeck, who performed their poems inspired by African chants to the accompaniment of drums and dancing, drew on these traditions in part to disrupt the repetitive rhythms of European art and society, and in part to seek a universal element in artistic creation. These disruptive rhythms and aspirations to artistic universality are fundamental to Richter's *Rhythmus 21*, as well.

While the rhythm discourse of the early twentieth century, with its contrast between vital, organic 'Rhythmus' and modern, mechanized 'Takt,' can contribute to our understanding of Richter's film, primitivism, particularly in its Dadaist form, adds an important supplement. A recognition of the centrality of rhythm to Dadaist primitivism sheds additional light on Richter's *Rhythmus 21*, suggesting that the film cannot be seen merely as an abstract study in the representation of motion and form. Rather, to the extent that Richter's film incorporates the 'primitive' rhythms that the Dadaists employed in their poems and dances, and the planar surfaces associated with African art, the film can be seen as part of a movement in the first decades of the twentieth century in which many European artists looked to other continents for new forms or sources of inspiration. Although this primitivist trend was plagued by misunderstandings, misrepresentations, and at times outright claims of racial inferiority, it left an indelible mark on Western art history, informing even seemingly abstract works such as Richter's *Rhythmus 21*.

Seelentraining: *Rhythmus 21* und die Wirkungspotentiale des Films

Christoph Bareither

Durch sein filmisches Erstlingswerk *Rhythmus 21* – so das Argument dieses Beitrags – artikulierte Hans Richter die Hoffnung, dass man dem modernen Menschen durch das Medium Film die verkümmerte Fähigkeit zu wirklichem Fühlen und Empfinden wieder ‚antrainieren' könne. Dass Richter der Filmkunst ein entsprechendes Wirkungspotential zutraute, verdeutlichte er in seinem 1924 erschienenen Essay „Die schlecht trainierte Seele", den er seinem 1925 erstmals in Deutschland aufgeführten *Rhythmus 21* als theoretischen Kommentar mit auf den Weg gab.[1]

Aus dieser Perspektive lässt sich Richters Film im Kontext zeitgenössischer Debatten um die Wirkungspotentiale des Films verorten. Diese Wirkungspotentiale wurden in der Öffentlichkeit des späten Deutschen Kaiserreichs und der Weimarer Republik kontrovers diskutiert. Vor allem die sogenannte Kinoreformbewegung thematisierte in zahlreichen Publikationen die eigentümliche Macht, die der Film über die Emotionen und das Gefühlsleben der Zuschauer zu haben schien.[2] Während ein Teil der bildungsbürgerlichen Reformbewegung – die sich aus Pädagogen, Psychiatern, Juristen, Journalisten und Professoren zusammensetzte – in dieser Macht vor allem eine Gefahr sah, wollten andere Pädagogen die Wirkungen des Films in positivem Sinne nutzbar machen. Mein Artikel zeichnet die Entwicklung dieser Debatte um die Wirkungspotentiale des Films nach,

1 Vgl. Hans Richter: Die schlecht trainierte Seele. In: G. Zeitschrift für elementare Gestaltung III (1924). Reprint herausgegeben von Marion von Hofacker, München 1986, S. 44-47.

2 Einführungen in die Geschichte der frühen deutschen Kinoreformbewegung mit unterschiedlichen Schwerpunkten finden sich u.a. bei Helmut H. Diederichs: Frühgeschichte deutscher Filmtheorie. Ihre Entstehung und Entwicklung bis zum Ersten Weltkrieg. Frankfurt a.M. 2001 (erstmals 1996). Online-Publikation; Thomas Hausmanninger: Kritik der medienethischen Vernunft. Die ethische Diskussion über den Film in Deutschland im 20. Jahrhundert. München 1993, S. 79-201; Kaspar Maase: Die Kinder der Massenkultur. Kontroversen um Schmutz und Schund seit dem Kaiserreich. Frankfurt a.M. 2012, S. 122-149; Kaspar Maase: Massenkunst und Volkserziehung. Die Regulierung von Film und Kino im deutschen Kaiserreich. In: Archiv für Sozialgeschichte 41 (2001), S. 39-77; Corinna Müller: Der frühe Film, das frühe Kino und seine Gegner und Befürworter. In: Kaspar Maase / Wolfgang Kaschuba (Hg.): Schund und Schönheit. Populäre Kultur um 1900. Köln / Weimar / Wien 2001, S. 62-91; Alice Schmerling: Kind, Kino und Kinderliteratur. Eine Untersuchung zum Medienumbruch in der Kinderkultur der Kaiserzeit und der Weimarer Republik. Köln 2007, S. 44-153.

um Richters Filmwirkungskonzept, das er mit *Rhythmus 21* praktisch umzusetzen versuchte, darin verorten zu können.

Gefährliche Gefühle – Wirkungspotentiale des ‚Schundfilms'

Ausgangspunkt der schon 1906 begonnenen Debatte um die Wirkungspotentiale des Films war die Kritik gegen die sogenannten „Schundfilme“[3], die in den großstädtischen Lichtspieltheatern und Kintopps zum Standardprogramm gehörten. Als Kritiker waren vor allem Lehrer und Pädagogen aktiv, insbesondere jene, die sich bereits im Kampf gegen ‚Schmutz und Schund' in der Literatur hervorgetan hatten und diesen Kampf nun gegen das Kino fortsetzten. Unterstützt wurden sie von Geistlichen, Psychiatern und Professoren.

Diesen Reformern zufolge konnten vor allem Unterhaltungsfilme „namentlich bei jugendlichen und empfindsamen Menschen das Nervensystem bis zur Qual“[4] erschüttern, die „Verrohung des Geschmacks“[5] befördern oder eine „sozialgefährliche Überreizung der Phantasie“[6] bzw. eine „phantastische Trübung des Wirklichkeitssinns“[7] auslösen. Dadurch trieb das Kino angeblich „die sittliche Zersetzung des deutschen Volkes“[8] voran und bewirkte eine „Verschlechterung des sittlichen Denkens und Fühlens, die notwendigerweise auch zu einer Verschlechterung des sittlichen Handelns führen muß“[9].

Dem Film wurde also das Potential zugesprochen, auch über die Zeit des Kinobesuchs hinaus auf das Denken, Fühlen und aktive Handeln des Publikums – das dadurch „gewissermaßen vergewaltigt“[10] wurde – einzuwirken. Verschiedene Kinoreformer beschrieben beispielsweise Fälle wie den eines Dienstknechts, der nach dem Genuss entsprechender Filme Handtaschen zu stehlen begann[11], den eines Hausmädchens, das nach Vorbild eines Sensationsdramas ihre Arbeitgeber zu vergiften versuchte[12], den eines unbe-

---

3 Vgl. Maase: Die Kinder der Massenkultur, S. 132ff.

4 Robert Gaupp / Konrad Lange: Der Kinematograph als Volksunterhaltungsmittel. München 1912, S. 9.

5 Albert Hellwig: Schundfilms. Ihr Wesen, ihre Gefahren und ihre Bekämpfung. Halle a.d.S. 1911, S. 42.

6 Ebd., S. 43.

7 Ebd., S. 47.

8 Walther Conradt: Kirche und Kinematograph. Eine Frage. Berlin 1910, S. 14.

9 Karl Brunner: Der Kinematograph von heute – eine Volksgefahr. Berlin 1913, S. 20.

10 Gaupp / Lange: Der Kinematograph als Volksunterhaltungsmittel, S. 9.

11 Adolf Sellmann: Der Kinematograph als Volkserzieher? Langensalza 1912, S. 25.

12 Ebd., S. 24f.

scholtenen Jungen, der aufgrund einer im Kino gesehenen Szene seine Mitschüler mit einem Messer attackierte[13] oder gar den einer Gruppe Kinder, die nach einem Film über Kannibalen einen Gleichaltrigen braten und essen wollten[14].

Den Ausführungen des Tübinger Psychiaters und Kinoreformers Robert Gaupp zufolge konnte der Film diese besondere Macht über sein Publikum erlangen, indem er auf ungeahnt intensive Weise das Gefühlsleben der Zuschauer ansprach. Durch die Erzeugung intensiver Empfindungen setzte das Medium Gaupp zufolge die Fähigkeit zu rationalem Vernunftdenken – die vor allem bei Frauen, Jugendlichen, Ungebildeten und Kindern ohnehin ‚mangelhaft' ausgebildet war – gänzlich außer Kraft und wurde zur Gefahr:

> Der verdunkelte Raum, das eintönige Geräusch, die Aufdringlichkeit der Schlag auf Schlag einander folgenden aufregenden Szenen schläfern in der empfänglichen Seele jede Kritik ein und so wird gar nicht selten der Inhalt des Dramas zur verhängnisvollen Suggestion für die willenlos hingegebene jugendliche Seele. Wir wissen, daß alle Suggestionen tiefer haften, wenn die Kritik schläft. Starke Gefühlserregung schläfert sie ein. Daß aber die Dramen des Kinematographen Gefühle und Leidenschaften der Kinder und der Ungebildeten in ihren Grundtiefen aufrütteln, dafür sorgt eine geschäftskundige Industrie mit schlauer Berechnung und großer Findigkeit.[15]

Das Aufrütteln von Gefühlen und Leidenschaften war für Gaupp der erste Schritt auf dem Weg zur nachahmenden, verbrecherischen Zwangshandlung. Gefühl und Verstand stehen sich in diesem Modell geradezu feindlich gegenüber. Ähnlich argumentierte der Reformer Albert Hellwig:

> Während dieser [der Psychologe oder Pädagoge, C.B.] kalt und objektiv abwägt, welche Szenen auf dem Film ethisch und welche verrohend zum Verbrechen anreizend wirken könnten, sind diejenigen Zuschauer, denen kriminelle Schundfilms überhaupt gefährlich werden können, nicht mit ihrem Verstand, sondern mit ihrem Herzen bei der Sache; voll leidenschaftlicher Anteilnahme verfolgen sie die Phasen des verbrecherischen Tuns oder der Verfolgung des Verbrechers [...][16]

Mit dem Herzen dabei zu sein – in den Augen vieler bildungsbürgerlicher Reformer bedeutete das bereits Gefahr. Diese bestand darin, dass rohe, instinktive, triebhafte Gefühle gegen das zivilisierte Über-Ich aufgehetzt und so die Vernunft außer Kraft gesetzt werden könnte. Über diese im Kino-

13 Ernst Schultze: Der Kinematograph als Bildungsmittel. Halle 1911, S. 122.

14 Gaupp / Lange: Der Kinematograph als Volksunterhaltungsmittel, S. 11.

15 Ebd., S. 9.

16 Hellwig: Schundfilms, S. 74.

reformdiskurs präsente Angst schreibt der Kulturwissenschaftler Kaspar Maase:

> Der Film wird zur sozialen Gefahr, wo die neue Massenkunst verführerisch zu den Sinnen spricht und auf ein Publikum trifft, das disponiert ist, im Flug der Einbildungskraft das Realitätsprinzip eine Zeit lang hinter sich zu lassen. [...] Am Spielfilm aktualisierte sich die bürgerliche Angst davor, die Kunst vermöchte die Beherrschung der Einbildungskraft durch die Vernunft schwächen.[17]

Entscheidend für den vorliegenden Beitrag ist, dass die Bedrohung der bürgerlichen Wert- und Weltordnung für viele Reformer nicht in erster Linie von den dargestellten Inhalten ausging, sondern von der Fähigkeit des Films, die Barrieren der Vernunft zu unterwandern und als Medium des ungezügelten Empfindens die unbewussten wie unerwünschten Gefühle und Emotionen des Volkes wachzurütteln. Aus dieser Beobachtung ergibt sich auch der Bezug zu Hans Richters filmischem Erstlingswerk. Doch zuerst soll hier noch eine weitere Strömung innerhalb der Kinoreformbewegung berücksichtigt werden, die in der eigentümlichen Macht des Films weniger eine Gefahr als vielmehr eine Chance erkannte.

Gute Gefühle – Die Wirkungspotentiale des belehrenden Films

Für viele der frühen Kinoreformer war der Film nicht nur „Volksverderber“, sondern vor allem „Volkserzieher“.[18] Als anschauliches Unterrichtsmaterial für Schüler und ‚Ungebildete‘ sollte er vor allem geistig belehren und informieren. Er sollte die Vernunft stärken, anstatt sie – wie der Unterhaltungsfilm – zu unterwandern.

Weil die Wirkungen des Films auf das Gefühlsleben als gefährlich galten, wurden sie bei diesen progressiven Reformbemühungen vorerst ausgeblendet. 1912 bemängelte ein Reformer, dass man bei den konstruktiven Reformbemühungen „das Herz, die Empfindung, die Seele [...] doch häufig recht stiefmütterlich behandelt“[19] habe.

Eine deutliche Wende in dieser Einstellung setzte gegen Ende des Ersten Weltkriegs ein, als Erwin Ackerknecht die „psychologische Vertiefung“[20] der Kinoreform in seiner Schrift *Das Lichtspiel im Dienste der Bildungspfle-*

17 Maase: Massenkunst und Volkserziehung, S. 65.

18 Sellmann: Der Kinematograph als Volkserzieher?, S. 3.

19 Alois Wurm: Ein Vorschlag für volksbildnerische Verwertung von Lichtbildern. In: Bild & Film. Zeitschrift für Lichtbilderei und Kinematographie 2. Jg. (1912/13), S. 73-74, hier: S. 73.

20 Erwin Ackerknecht: Das Lichtspiel im Dienste der Bildungspflege. Handbuch für Lichtspielreformer. Berlin 1918, S. 3.

ge ausarbeitete. Ackerknechts „Lichtspielpsychologie“[21] zielte darauf ab, das Kinopublikum durch die „Gefühlswirkungen“[22] des Films positiv zu beeinflussen.

Zentral waren dabei Filme, in denen das Alltagsleben (Arbeitsprozesse u.ä.), vor allem aber die Natur dokumentarisch portraitiert wurde.[23] Der belehrende Film erzeugte Gefühle nicht durch die Zurschaustellung menschlicher Emotionen oder durch die Inszenierung dramatischer Szenen, sondern durch die Darstellung natürlicher Bewegung und der in ihr verborgenen Kraft und Schönheit. Dadurch sollten die belehrenden Filme erstens eine durch Empfindungen angereicherte Vermittlung belehrender Inhalte erreichen. Zweitens sollten die Gefühlswirkungen des Films ein emotionales Verständnis des Menschen für seine Umwelt fördern. Durch seine Gefühlswirkungen war der belehrende Film in der Lage, „geradezu die natürlichen Grenzen unseres gefühlsmäßigen Verhältnisses zur Welt der Wirklichkeit zu erweitern.“[24]

Dass der hier vollzogene Perspektivenwechsel hin zu einer Nutzbarmachung der Gefühlswirkungen des Films einflussreich war, dokumentieren einige Artikel unterschiedlicher Pädagogen in der seit 1923 erschienenen kinoreformerischen Zeitschrift *Der Bildwart*. Das Leben, hieß es schon in der ersten Ausgabe, „kann nicht erkannt, es kann nur erlebt werden. Somit wendet sich das Wesentliche des Films nicht in erster Linie an den Intellekt, sondern an das Lebensgefühl.“[25]

Zwar waren die konservativen Stimmen, die in den Gefühlswirkungen des Films vor allem eine Gefahr sahen, noch längst nicht verstummt. Doch durch die Fortführung von Ackerknechts Modell etablierte sich in den 1920er-Jahren eine Variante der Kinoreformbewegung, die eine positive Nutzbarmachung dieser Wirkungen anstrebte.

---

21 Ebd., S. 35.

22 Ebd., S. 37.

23 Allerdings lehnte er auch Unterhaltungsfilme nicht mehr gänzlich ab, wenn sie „das Gemütserregungsbedürfnis“ der einfachen Menschen auf akzeptable Weise befriedigten. Vgl. ebd., S. 62.

24 Ebd., S. 46.

25 Franz Brunner: Inwieweit läßt sich der Unterrichtsfilm in den Volksschul-Unterricht einbauen? In: Der Bildwart. Blätter für Volksbildung (Januar/Februar 1923), H. 1, S. 25-28, hier: S. 26; Vgl. hierzu auch insbesondere die Monographie von Friederich Lampe: Der Film in Schule und Leben. Berlin 1924.

Rhythmus 21 – Die Wirkungspotentiale des elementaren Films

Inmitten dieser öffentlich präsenten Diskurse entstand der ‚elementare Film'[26] *Rhythmus 21*, dem sein Macher Hans Richter in seinem Text „Die schlecht trainierte Seele" ein sehr spezifisches Wirkungspotential zuschrieb. Zwar nannte er seinen Film im Text nicht beim Namen, doch durch die Beschreibungen des entsprechenden Filmkunstwerks und die beigefügten Abbildungen verwies er deutlich auf sein filmisches Erstlingswerk.[27]

Den Bezug zur Debatte um die Wirkungspotentiale des Films stellte Richter bereits im Titel durch den Begriff der „schlecht trainierte[n] Seele" her. Die ‚Seele' hatte bereits den frühen Reformern als zentrales Schlagwort gedient. Auf Seiten der konservativen Kinoreformer war häufig von einer Gefährdung der Seele die Rede, von „Störungen des seelischen Gleichgewichts" oder „gewaltigen Seelenerschütterungen".[28] Im Kino wurde den Pädagogen zufolge eine „seelenlose, phantasieabtötende Kost"[29] serviert und man erschrak selbst vor dem eigenen „süßschauerlichem Empfinden, das die mit den stärksten Mitteln arbeitende Sensationsmache in der grausam-wollüstigen Seele hervorruft."[30]

Aber auch Ackerknecht und die progressiven Kinoreformer hatten bei der Nutzbarmachung der positiven Wirkungen des Films „jene Grundkraft des Irrationalen, des Seelischen im engeren Sinne"[31] im Blick. Aus den belehrenden Filmen sollte sich ein „reicher Segen in abertausend Seelen ergießen."[32]

Die Sprachformel der Seele, die Hans Richter für seinen Text wählte, war also von Beginn an im Diskurs präsent. Pastoren, Lehrer, Pädagogen, Professoren und Psychiater setzten das Schlagwort dabei sehr unterschiedlich, aus ihrem je eigenen Horizont heraus ein, was es zu einer genauso schwammigen wie wirkungsvollen kulturellen Chiffre innerhalb ihrer Debatten werden ließ. Über den Begriff artikulierte sich die Vorstellung einer unbewussten ‚Innerlichkeit' des Menschen, eines Zentrums des Fühlens und Empfindens, über das der Film Macht erlangen konnte, indem er starke Emotionen erzeugte und so die Vernunft unterwanderte.

---

26 Vgl. hierzu den Beitrag „Elementares Kino" in diesem Band.

27 Vgl. Richter: Die schlecht trainierte Seele.

28 Hellwig: Schundfilms, S. 56.

29 Franz Pfemfert: Kino als Erzieher (1911). In: Anton Kaes (Hg.): Kino-Debatte. Texte zum Verhältnis von Literatur und Film 1909-1929. Tübingen 1978, S. 59-61, hier: S. 61.

30 Brunner: Der Kinematograph von heute – eine Volksgefahr, S. 16.

31 Ackerknecht: Das Lichtspiel im Dienste der Bildungspflege, S. 32.

32 Roland Abramczyk: Der Film im Unterricht. In: Der Bildwart. Blätter für Volksbildung (September 1924), S. 98-99, hier: S.99.

Richter setzte genau hier an. Er griff dabei sowohl Gedanken der konservativen wie der progressiven Strömungen innerhalb der Kinoreformbewegung auf. Ähnlich wie die konservativen Kinoreformer attestierte er dem modernen Menschen eine verkümmerte, schwächliche Seele und benannte den Unterhaltungsfilm als Mitverursacher dieser ‚Krankheit'. Richter schrieb:

> Was heute als ‚Empfinden' blüht, ist ein passives Ausgeliefertsein an Unkontrollierbares ..... (von Helden, keuscher Jungfrau und smarten [sic] Geschäftsmann, s. oben) von konfektionierten Gefühlen vergangener und nie dagewesener Jahrhunderte, aus denen sich unsere Seele als ein tolles Wesen zusammensetzt, das uns tyrannisiert und das Weltbild hin und herzerrt.
> Die lebendige Kraft die wir im Empfinden besitzen, ist verfettet, der Atmungsprozeß gehemmt, die Seele ohne eine Kultur ihrer Mittel, weniger eine Macht als eine Schwäche.[33]

Mit der Hervorhebung jener konfektionierten Gefühle spielte Richter auf die Produkte der Unterhaltungsindustrie und auch der Filmindustrie an, denen er die aktive Macht zuschrieb, falsche Weltbilder zu erzeugen, die Wirklichkeit zu verzerren und dadurch die menschliche Seele zu gefährden – Thesen, die in weiten Teilen denen der konservativ orientierten Kinoreformer entsprachen.

Doch wo diesen Reformern filmische Gefühlswirkungen als solche bereits bedrohlich erschienen, differenzierte Richter in verschiedene Qualitäten des Fühlens: die konfektionierten Gefühle einerseits und eine Art ‚eigentliches' oder ‚wirkliches' Fühlen andererseits. Das Medium Film war in der Lage, beide Arten des Fühlens hervorzubringen – der Verfettungsprozess der Seele konnte unterstützt, doch genauso konnte er durch den Film aufgehalten und in sein Gegenteil verkehrt werden.

Den Glauben an eine positive Wirkkraft des Films teilte Richter mit der neueren Strömung innerhalb der Kinoreformbewegung. Doch im Gegensatz zu dieser setzte er den Filmen des konfektionierten Fühlens nicht den belehrenden dokumentarischen Film, sondern den elementaren Film entgegen. Richters *Rhythmus 21* war eine Art Prototyp dieser Filmkunst, die eine Überwindung der konfektionierten Gefühle zugunsten eines wirklichen Empfindens erreichen sollte:

> Dieser Film hier gibt keine ‚Haltepunkte', an denen man in Erinnerungen umkehren könnte, man ist – ausgeliefert – zum ‚Fühlen' gezwungen – zum Mitgehen im Rhytmus [sic] – Atmen – Herzschlag; – ... der durch das Auf und Ab des Vorgangs, das deutlich machen kann, was Fühlen und Empfinden eigentlich ist ... ein Prozeß – Bewegung.[34]

33 Richter: Die schlecht trainierte Seele, S. 46.

34 Ebd., S. 45.

Rhythmus und Bewegung waren zentrale Elemente dieser Filmkunst, die das Publikum zu wirklichem Fühlen zwingen sollte. Dass diese Elemente zentraler Bestandteil der Gefühlswirkungen des Films waren, darauf hatte bereits Ackerknecht[35] hingewiesen: „Kurzum, die Bewegung, diese geheimnisvolle sinnliche Urtatsache, bleibt ihrer unmittelbaren Wirkung auf unser Gefühlsleben sicher, mag unser Verstand seinen Segen dazu spenden oder nicht. Es leuchtet nun wohl ohne weiteres ein, daß das Besondere aller Wirkung des Lichtspiels, als des Trägers optischer Bewegungsreize, im Gefühlsmäßigen liegt."[36]

Auch Richter wollte die Macht der Bewegung und des Rhythmus für den Film nutzbar machen, jedoch nicht durch das Aufzeigen des Rhythmus der natürlichen Umwelt, sondern durch eine abstrakte Filmsprache. Die filmische Bewegung sollte in der Wahrnehmung der Zuschauer zu einem „optischen Rhytmus [sic]" werden, indem sie den zwei tragenden Gesetzen „Äußerster Gegensatz" (Kontrast) und „Innere Verwandschaft"[37] (Analogie) der Formen folgte. Beide Prinzipien leitete Richter aus den Arbeiten seines langjährigen Freundes Viking Eggeling ab. Im optischen Rhythmus des Films konnten sie zur Synthese geführt werden – „Durch das zusammenhängende Funktionieren beider, durch das Wechselwirken von Trennen und Verbinden entsteht Empfinden."[38]

Durch die rhythmisierte Bewegung von Kontrasten und Analogien sollte der Film den Prozess des Empfindens in seiner elementarsten Weise vermitteln. Mit diesem Programm einer ‚Elementarisierung' des Empfindens – der Herausarbeitung seiner grundlegendsten Formen – fügt sich Richters Modell in das breitere Projekt der ihn umgebenden avantgardistischen Bewegung ein. Davon zeugen verschiedene Beiträge in der von Richter herausgegebenen *Zeitschrift für elementare Gestaltung*. Auch in Bezug auf die Architektur, die Mode, die Fotografie, den Maschinenbau oder die Theatertechnik bestand dieses Programm erstens in der Reduktion

35 Noch vor Ackerknecht betonte Hermann Häfker die Bedeutung des Rhythmus der Naturbewegungen für die filmische Gestaltung. Vgl. u.a. Hermann Häfker: Kinematographie und echte Kunst. In: Bild & Film. Zeitschrift für Lichtbilderei und Kinematographie 1. Jg. (1912), S. 5-8; Hermann Häfker: Kino und Kunst. M. Gladbach 1913, S. 32ff.

36 Ackerknecht: Das Lichtspiel im Dienste der Bildungspflege, S. 37-38.

37 Richter: Die schlecht trainierte Seele, S. 45.

38 Ebd. In einem 1926 auf Englisch erschienenen Text bringt Hans Richter den essentiellen Zusammenhang von Rhythmus und Empfinden bzw. Emotionalität auf eine prägnante Formel: „Just as the path of the intellectual formulating-power leads to thought, as a justifying moment of intellectual activity, so the emotional formulating-power leads to rhythm as the essence of emotional expression." Hans Richter: Rhythm (1926). In: Freunde der deutschen Kinemathek e.V. (Hg.): Hans Richter. Film ist Rhythmus. Berlin 2003, S. 38.

aller Dinge auf ihre elementarsten Formen, zweitens in der Rekombination dieser grundlegenden Elemente.

Die ‚Elementarisierung' des Empfindens hatte für Richter nicht einfach eine demonstrative, sondern eine pädagogische Funktion. In einem autobiographischen Text berichtet er von einem Mädchen, das bei einer Aufführung von *Rhythmus 21* in Paris plötzlich lachen musste. „Gefragt, warum sie denn lache, wollte sie erst nicht mit der Sprache heraus und flüsterte schließlich ihrem Begleiter zu: ‚C'est comme faire l'amour'..."[39] Das Mädchen hatte freilich ganz im Sinne des Künstlers gelacht. Sie hatte den Zusammenhang der bewegten Bilder mit den Prinzipien menschlichen Fühlens erkannt, oder besser: empfunden.

In Richters „Die schlecht trainierte Seele" wird die Hoffnung sichtbar, dass ein solches Nach- oder Mitempfinden der lebendigen Bewegung auch den Zugang zum eigenen Fühlen filmisch vergegenwärtigen und somit gewissermaßen auf das Publikum übertragen könne. Der Film sollte die Zuschauer zu wirklichem Fühlen zwingen und dadurch – wie es der Titel des Textes bereits besagte – ihre Seele trainieren, d.h. ihrer Seele eine „Kultur ihrer Mittel"[40] an die Hand geben und sie dadurch wieder zu wirklichem Empfinden befähigen. Ziel war jedoch nicht eine Empfindungsfähigkeit um des Genusses willen. Der Film sollte vielmehr das Empfinden, das für Richter „ein ebenso präzise organisierter und mechanisch exakter Prozeß wie Denken"[41] war, „zum Bestandteil menschlicher Macht werden"[42] lassen und so ein aktives und kritisches menschliches Dasein ermöglichen.

Damit ergänzte Richter die Debatte um die Wirkungspotentiale des Films um eine wesentliche Wendung. Zwar folgte er den konservativ orientierten Kinoreformern in ihrer Ablehnung eines ‚wirklichkeitsverzerrenden' Unterhaltungskinos und beschrieb wie Ackerknecht und die ihm folgenden Reformer Bewegung und Rhythmus als zentrale Elemente positiver Gefühlswirkungen des Films. Doch im Gegensatz zu diesen beiden bildungsbürgerlich geprägten Strömungen strebte der Avantgardist Richter nicht den Schutz der Seele und auch nicht ihre harmonisierende Vereinigung mit der Natur an. Seine Filmkunst zielte vielmehr auf die Ausbildung eines Denkens, das die Gesetzmäßigkeiten menschlichen Fühlens verstehend beherrscht und sich dadurch selbst zur Kritik befähigt:

> Die Kultur solcher ‚Gesetzmäßigkeiten' gehört zu den elementaren Erziehungsfragen unserer Psyche, die auf diese Weise mit einer gewissen ‚Denkfähigkeit' ausgestattet wird – einer solchen die zwar in

39 Hans Richter: Autobiographischer Text des Künstlers. Einführung von Herbert Read. Neuchâtel, Schweiz 1965, S. 114.

40 Richter: Die schlecht trainierte Seele, S. 46.

41 Ebd., S. 44.

42 Ebd.

> ihrem Bau vorgesehen ist aber brach liegt. Diese Denkfähigkeit gibt der Seele Machtmittel: Urteilskraft und Aktivität, d.h. Eigenschaften, die dem ganzen Menschen in seinem Handeln zu gute kommen und für seine allgemeine Orientierung unentbehrlich sind.[43]

Zwar gab Richter seine rein aus abstrahierten Formen geschaffene elementare Filmkunst schon wenige Jahre nach diesen Worten auf und entwickelte sich mit seinen folgenden Arbeiten stilistisch in eine andere Richtung.[44] Aber auch seine ab Mitte der Zwanziger Jahre folgenden Filme, die gegenständliche Aufnahmen zu teils surrealistischen Bildkollagen verdichteten, waren Kompositionen aus Kontrasten und Analogien, und auch in ihnen nahmen Bewegung und Rhythmus eine zentrale Funktion ein.

Ebenso ging auch seine in „Die schlecht trainierte Seele" formulierte Hoffnung auf das Wirkungspotential des Films nicht gänzlich verloren. Vielleicht aus Einsicht in die Unzugänglichkeit seiner rein abstrakten Filmkunst für die Massen näherte sich Richter bald auch filmtheoretisch und kulturpolitisch dem Unterhaltungskino an. Seine erste Monographie *Filmgegner von heute – Filmfreunde von Morgen*[45] von 1929 dokumentiert jedoch sein Bestreben, jene elementaren Gesetze der Bewegung, des Rhythmus und des Empfindens auch für das ‚große Kino' fruchtbar zu machen. Die dort entwickelte Formästhetik suchte noch immer einen Weg, um die bereits 1924 beschriebenen Wirkungspotentiale des Films zu realisieren:

> wir können den Menschen neue Lebensinhalte geben. sie aktivisieren [sic]. sie sehen lehren, ihre Sinne verfeinern. sie erfrischen. sie unterhaltend stärken, ihren Menschenverstand und ihr Wissen schärfen. ihren Horizont erweitern. sie zu Weltbürgern machen. Es gibt keine Kunst, die in nur annähernd ähnlichem Maß zur Erfüllung solcher Aufgaben befähigt wäre, wie der Film.[46]

Im Sinne dieser Überzeugung lässt sich Richter als ein ungewöhnlicher Filmreformer verstehen, der sowohl Elemente einer konservativ als auch einer progressiv orientierten Kinoreformbewegung aufgreift. Sein eigenwilliger Ansatz will durch das neue Medium Film eine Kultivierung des Empfindens und damit die Erziehung zur selbstständigen Kritik-, Urteils- und Handlungsfähigkeit des gesellschaftlichen Individuums erreichen. Diese Grundintention seines filmischen Schaffens ist in *Rhythmus 21* bereits vorgezeichnet.

---

43 Ebd., S. 46.

44 Vgl. zu Richters Filmen ab 1927 u.a. Marion von Hofacker: Richter's Films and the Role of the Radical Artist, 1927-1941. In: Stephen C. Foster (Hg.): Hans Richter. Activism, Modernism and the Avantgarde. Cambridge, MA 1998, S. 122-159.

45 Hans Richter: Filmgegner von heute – Filmfreunde von morgen (unter Mitarbeit von Werner Graeff). Frankfurt a.M. 1981 (erstmals Berlin 1929).

46 Ebd., S. 97.

Spiritualität: Optische Transmutation in Hans Richters *Rhythmus 21*

Benedikt Hjartarson

Die Eröffnungsszene von Hans Richters *Rhythmus 21* präsentiert eine schwarze Bildfläche, die langsam von zwei vertikalen, von den Außenrändern ausgehenden weißen Flächen eingeengt wird. In einem regelmäßigen Rhythmus nähern sich die zwei viereckigen weißen Flächen, bis sie in der Mitte aufeinandertreffen und die Leinwand damit ganz überdecken. Nach dem Zusammenstoß bewegen sich die beiden weißen Vierecke im selben Rhythmus zurück an den Bildrand und auch dieser zweite Vorgang wird wiederholt. Die Szene ist etwas erstaunlich in einem ‚absoluten Film', welcher – den Grundsätzen der geometrischen Abstraktion folgend – mit jeder Vorstellung von Gegenständlichkeit bzw. Abbildung der Wirklichkeit programmatisch brechen will. Die Eröffnungsszene enthält deutliche Anspielungen auf eine Theatervorstellung: Der Vorhang geht auf und die Bühne ist frei für das darauffolgende Spiel der abstrakten geometrischen Formen. Die erste Szene nach diesem Auftakt präsentiert ein weißes Quadrat, das sich in die Tiefe einer schwarzen Bildfläche hinein bewegt. Das weiße Quadrat wird stets kleiner bis es endgültig in die Tiefe der Dunkelheit verschwindet.

Das filmische Werk ist ein Produkt jener Ästhetik der ‚Kontrast-Analogie', die Richter zusammen mit dem schwedischen Künstler Viking Eggeling entwickelte. Es geht um die systematische Erforschung der Wechselwirkung kontrastierender und analoger Elemente in der Bildfläche, wobei *Rhythmus 21* mit dem Farbenkontrast schwarz-weiß und dem Zusammenspiel von analogen, in Bewegung gesetzten geometrischen Formen experimentiert. Die „Wechselwirkung von Kontrast und Analogie" folgt den „Prinzipien einer neuen Optik" und präsentiert die „praktische und theoretische Formulierung eines allgemeinen Gestaltungsgesetzes",[1] wie Richter in einem Text über die Filmkunst von Eggeling erklärt, der 1926 in der von Richter herausgegebenen Zeitschrift *G* veröffentlicht wurde. Somit ließe sich der Film als geregeltes Spiel mit reinen geometrischen Formen, der Materialität der Zeichen, Kontrasten und Analogien beschreiben, das integraler Bestandteil der konstruktivistischen Suche nach elementaren Regeln und rationalen Gestaltungsprinzipien ist. Dabei stellt sich jedoch die folgende Frage: Was ist mit dem sich in die Tiefe der Bildfläche bewe-

1 Hans Richter: Viking Eggeling †. In: G. Zeitschrift für elementare Gestaltung IV (März 1926). Reprint herausgegeben von Marion von Hofacker, München 1986, S. 96-98, hier: S. 97.

genden Symbol des weißen Quadrats, das die eigentliche ‚Handlung' des Films einleitet?

Der weiße Strahl

Durch die optische Illusion führt das weiße Quadrat am Anfang von *Rhythmus 21* den Zuschauer hinein in einen unsichtbaren, unter der Oberfläche der zweidimensionalen Leinwand liegenden Raum. Der Akt markiert die Einweihung des Zuschauers in eine fremde Bildwelt, in der er sodann mit dem Spiel geometrischer Formen konfrontiert wird. Das Quadrat wird in eine Art Lichtsäule transformiert, die den Zuschauer in eine Dimension der reinen abstrakten Formen hineinführt. Diese Einweihungspraktik lässt sich durch einen Blick auf Wassily Kandinskys theoretische Schriften zur abstrakten Kunst näher bestimmen. Im Aufsatz „Über die Formfrage", der 1912 in *Der Blaue Reiter* erschien, beschreibt Kandinsky, wie der Mensch „an dem in geistiger Form in ihm lebenden neuen Wert eine materielle Form zu finden" sucht und diskutiert dieses „Suchen des geistigen Wertes nach Materialisation".[2] Es heißt:

> Die Materie ist hier eine Vorratskammer, aus welcher der Geist das ihm in diesem Falle *Nötige* wählt, wie es der Koch tut.
> Das ist das Positive, das Schaffende. Das ist das Gute. *Der weiße befruchtende Strahl.*
> Dieser weiße Strahl führt zur Evolution, zur Erhöhung. So ist hinter der Materie, in der Materie der schaffende Geist verborgen.
> Das Verhüllen des Geistes in der Materie ist oft so dicht, daß es im allgemeinen wenig Menschen gibt, die den Geist hindurchsehen können. Es gibt sogar viele Menschen, die in einer geistigen Form den Geist nicht sehen können.[3]

In Kandinskys Kunsttheorie ist der hier angedeutete Weg der spirituellen Evolution unmittelbar mit der Abstraktion verbunden: „Die Kraft, die auf der freien Bahn den menschlichen Geist nach vor- und aufwärts bewegt, ist der abstrakte Geist."[4] Auffallend an dieser Stelle ist nicht nur die Gleichsetzung von Fortschritt und spiritueller Erhöhung bzw. Transmutation, sondern auch die Kodierung des ‚weißen Strahls' als eine in die unsichtbare Dimension des Geistigen hinter der Materie hineinführende Kraft, wo-

2 Wassily Kandinsky: Über die Formfrage. In: Ders. / Franz Marc (Hg.): Der Blaue Reiter. Dokumentarische Neuausgabe von Klaus Lankheit. München 1965, S. 132-182, hier: S. 132.

3 Ebd.

4 Ebd., S. 136.

durch die Evolution des Menschen als „Verschieben der Schranken"[5] des Bewusstseins dargestellt wird. Die geistige Dimension bedeutet in Kandinskys Schriften, und hierin an Madame Blavatskys theosophische Lehre anknüpfend, einen Raum von spirituellen Schwingungen und Vibrationen, die dem körperlichen Auge entgehen. Im Hinblick auf die Funktion des weißen Strahls in Kandinskys Schriften lässt sich das weiße Quadrat, mit dem Richter seinen *Rhythmus 21* einleitet, als Initiation des Zuschauers in eine okkulte Dimension des reinen Rhythmus bezeichnen. Die spirituellen Konnotationen des weißen Strahls werden noch deutlicher, wenn man berücksichtigt, dass Kandinsky dieses Symbol einem Text von Madame Blavatsky entnommen hat. Im Buch *The Key to Theosophy*, das Kandinsky 1911 in *Über das Geistige in der Kunst* in deutscher Übersetzung zitierte,[6] vergleicht Blavatsky die Theosophie mit einem weißen Strahl, der die Offenbarung der ewigen Wahrheit bringt:

> Theosophy, on earth, is like the white ray of the spectrum, and every religion only one of the seven prismatic colours. Ignoring all the others, and cursing them as false, every special coloured ray claims not only priority, but to be that *white ray itself*, and anathematizes even its own tints from light to dark, as heresies. Yet, as the sun of truth rises higher and higher on the horizon of man's perception, and each coloured ray gradually fades out until it is finally reabsorbed in its turn, humanity will at last be cursed no longer with artificial polarizations, but will find itself bathing in the pure colourless sunlight of eternal truth.[7]

In Bezug auf *Rhythmus 21* ist dabei weniger Blavatskys Gegenüberstellung von Theosophie und (anderen) religiösen Denksystemen wichtig als die mit dem Symbol des weißen Strahls verbundene Vorstellung der spirituellen Evolution und der Erschließung ‚okkulter' Gesetzmäßigkeiten bzw. einer höheren ‚Wahrheit'.

Der Wille zur reinen Anschauung

Von Kandinskys theosophisch inspirierter Abstraktionslehre und der ihr inhärenten Idee eines geistigen Wertes zu Richters streng geregelten geometrischen Werken, die die sinnliche Wahrnehmung in den Vordergrund

5 Ebd., S. 137.

6 Wassily Kandinsky: Über das Geistige in der Kunst, insbesondere in der Malerei. Bern 2004, S. 47.

7 H.P. Blavatsky: The Key to Theosophy. Being a Clear Exposition, in the Form of Question and Answer, of the Ethics, Science, and Philosophy for the Study of Which the Theosophical Society Has Been Founded. Los Angeles 1962 (erstmals 1889), S. 58.

stellen, scheint ein langer Weg. In diesem Sinne ließe sich, einer kunsthistorischen Tradition folgend, grundsätzlich zwischen zwei Strömungen der modernen Abstraktion trennen, wobei die eine sich mit „dem Geistigen in der Kunst“ und die andere sich mit „dem Technischen in der Kunst“ auseinandersetzt.[8] *Rhythmus 21* zeigt jedoch, dass Denkmuster und diskursive Versatzstücke aus dem Feld spiritueller Evolutionslehren auch in Werken der wissenschaftlichen fundierten Ästhetik der geometrischen Abstraktion zirkulierten. Am Film Richters lassen sich die diskursiven Überschneidungen von modernem Okkultismus und der wissenschaftlich fundierten Ästhetik des abstrakten Konstruktivismus exemplarisch zeigen. Zu diesem Zweck erweist sich ein näherer Blick auf die okkultistische Symbolik als ertragreich, die in der ästhetischen Rhetorik des Konstruktivismus zirkuliert. In seinem Aufsatz „Bewegungskunst“, der 1923 in der mit *G* verbundenen ungarischen Kunstzeitschrift *MA* erschien, proklamiert Ludwig Hilberseimer: „Der Mythus starb aus. Der gläubige Gehalt ging verloren.“[9] Die Formulierung des Architekten und Stadtplaners scheint zunächst auf eine im Zeichen der Rationalisierung stehende Entwicklung hinzudeuten – doch gleich im nächsten Satz heißt es:

> An Stelle religion-kultischer Gebundenheit ist nach einer Zeit hypertrophierten Individualismus eine solche kosmischen Bewußtseins angebrochen. [...] Sogenannte Wirklichkeit, die doch nur konventionelle Natürlichkeit ist, wird um des Geistigen willen, das eine neue Wirklichkeit schafft, verlassen.[10]

Die neue Bewegungskunst hat, aus Hilberseimers Sicht, „[m]it neuer Schwungkraft alte kosmische Gleichnisse belebt, denn ahnungsweise existiert dieses Problem seit jeher: als Sprache der Psyche.“[11] Der Verlust des ‚gläubigen Gehalts‘ führt somit weniger zur Epoche des Rationalen als zur Öffnung kosmischer Dimensionen, die auf einer tradierten okkultistischen Auffassung von Übereinstimmungen beruht.

Von Hilberseimers kosmischer Fantasie zu Überlegungen aus dem Nachlass von Eggeling, die 1926 in *G* erschienen, ist es nur ein kurzer Schritt: „Abstraktion ist neues Bewußtsein. Abschüttlung des Respekts vor Betrug. Abscheu vor Aberglauben. [...] Abstraktion ist die ungeheu-

---

8 Sixten Ringbom: Kunst in der ‚ZEIT DES GROSSEN GEISTIGEN‘. Okkulte Elemente in der frühen Theorie der Abstrakten Malerei. In: Beat Wyss (Hg.): Jahresring 40. Jahrbuch für moderne Kunst. Mythologie der Aufklärung. Geheimlehren der Moderne. München 1993, S. 26-72, hier: S. 56. Der Text erschien zuerst auf Englisch: Art in the ‚Epoch of the Great Spiritual‘. Occult Elements in the Early Theory of Abstract Painting. In: Journal of the Warburg and Courtauld Institutes 29. Jg. (1966), S. 386-418.

9 Ludwig Hilberseimer: Bewegungskunst. In: MA 8. Jg (1923), H. 5-6, o.P.

10 Ebd.

11 Ebd.

erlichste Manifestation des Willens der Menschheit zur reinen Anschauung, ist mehr als nur individueller Wille."[12] Der von Eggeling proklamierte Bruch mit dem Reich des Aberglaubens zugunsten einer Kunst der „reinen Anschauung", der zunächst den Schritt hin zu einer rein sinnlichen ästhetischen Praxis anzudeuten scheint, deutet vielmehr auf eine Praxis hin, die den Bereich des Sinnlichen überschreitet – gesucht wird der Weg „zum Absoluten, zur reinsten Kunst".[13] Die neue künstlerische Praxis ist, so Eggeling, „die Manifestation des *Glaubens an einen großen Sinn im Lebendigen*"[14] – die Verwandtschaft mit Kandinskys spirituell fundierter Abstraktionslehre und der darin sich manifestierenden „Neigung zum ‚Versteckten', zum Verborgenen" ist unübersehbar.[15] Eggeling strebt eine neue künstlerische Praxis an, die mit der „begriffliche[n] Kultur" bricht und unter die „Oberfläche der Dinge" taucht – eine Praxis, in der „mit der *Erscheinung* gebrochen wird und die Tiefe als Maßstab aufgestellt wird", um „das Terrain ungetrübter Erkenntnis" zu entdecken.[16] Eggeling erklärt, dass die hier entworfene Ästhetik die Grenzen des rationalen Verstandes zu überschreiten hat: „Der Armseligkeit rationalistisch sinnlichen Erkennens stets bewußt bleiben. Jenseits- und Diesseits-Mensch sein."[17]

Die Seele des Auges

In Richters Schriften lassen sich ähnliche Anspielungen an die Bindung der neuen künstlerischen Praxis an geistige Werte finden. Am Anfang seiner Überlegungen zu einem der späteren *Rhythmus*-Filme erklärt er: „In der Rapidität der Bewegung erhält das Auge eine neue Seele und erlebt Dinge, die ihr bis dahin nur verstreut und in keiner Kunstform ins Bewußtsein gerückt wurden. Was man erlebt, ist Bewegung."[18] Im Film geht es nicht um sinnliche Wahrnehmung von materiellen Bildern, sondern vielmehr um einen auf einer tieferen Bewusstseinsebene liegenden Wahrnehmungsprozess. Ziel dieser künstlerischen Praxis ist die ‚Gestaltung' eines neuen Den-

12 Aus dem Nachlass Viking Eggelings. In: G. Zeitschrift für elementare Gestaltung V-VI (April 1926). Reprint herausgegeben von Marion von Hofacker, München 1986, S. 125.

13 Ebd., S. 112.

14 Hans Richter: Viking Eggeling †, S. 96

15 Zitiert nach Ringbom: Kunst in der ‚ZEIT DES GROßEN GEISTIGEN', S. 27.

16 Aus dem Nachlass Viking Eggelings, S. 84.

17 Ebd.

18 Hans Richter: Dimension t. In: G. Zeitschrift für elementare Gestaltung V-VI (April 1926). Reprint herausgegeben von Marion von Hofacker, München 1986, S. 114.

kens in kinetischen Formen, die sich von „der statischen Raumform der bildenden Künste" absetzen und dem Menschen die Fähigkeit geben, „in *optischen Reihen* zu denken".[19]

Angestrebt wird hier weniger die Erforschung optischer Vorgänge als die Überwindung des Sehens, und zwar im Sinne einer spirituellen Transmutation. Wie Richter in einem späteren Text behauptet, kann das filmische Medium den Menschen nicht nur „neue Lebensinhalte geben, sie aktivisieren [sic], sie sehen lehren, ihre Sinne verfeinern, sie erfrischen", darüber hinausgehend kann dieses Medium, dank seiner besonderen ‚Sprache', „ihren Menschenverstand und ihr Wissen schärfen, ihren Horizont erweitern".[20] Die besonderen Möglichkeiten des Films liegen in dessen „magic, poetic, irrational qualities".[21] Der Verweis auf die magischen Eigenschaften des Filmmediums hebt dessen entscheidende Rolle im Prozess der spirituellen Transmutation des Zuschauers hervor.

Im Aufsatz „Die schlecht trainierte Seele" von 1924 beschreibt Richter die in seinen abstrakten Filmen entwickelten Verfahren eines „optischen Rhythmus", wobei es ihm darum geht, „nur Bewegung zu sehen, organisierte Bewegung".[22] *Rhythmus 21* steht somit ganz im Zeichen der später von Richter als „avantgarde" bezeichneten Filmpraxis der 20er Jahre, die einen „conscious attempt to overcome reproduction" darstellt und „the free use of the means of cinematographic expression" anstrebt.[23] Das filmische Werk markiert in diesem Sinne die Befreiung des Subjekts aus der gegenständlichen Wirklichkeit und dessen Einführung in eine Dimension des rein Rhythmischen, in der eine in der Moderne verloren gegangene Eigenschaft des Menschen zum präzisen und mechanisch geregelten Empfinden wiederentdeckt wird: „Empfinden ist ein ebenso präzise organsierter und mechanisch exakter Prozeß wie Denken; aber das Bewußtsein dieses Prozesses oder noch mehr die IDENTITÄT mit ihm ging verloren, fehlt".[24] Wie Richter am Ende von „Die schlecht trainierte Seele" erklärt, strebt die Praxis des absoluten Films die Verwirklichung eines radikalen ästhetischen Projekts seelischer Regeneration und kultureller Revitalisierung an: „Die lebendige Kraft die wir im Empfinden besitzen, ist verfettet, der Atmungsprozeß gehemmt, die Seele ohne eine Kultur ihrer Mittel, weni-

---

19 Ebd.

20 Hans Richter: Filmgegner von heute – Filmfreunde von morgen. Berlin 1929, S. 97.

21 Hans Richter: The Film as an Original Art Form. In: College Art Journal 10. Jg. (1951), H. 2, S. 157-161, hier: S. 159.

22 Hans Richter: Die schlecht trainierte Seele. In: G. Zeitschrift für elementare Gestaltung III (Juni 1924). Reprint herausgegeben von Marion von Hofacker, München 1986, S. 44-46, hier: S. 44.

23 Richter: The Film as an Original Art Form, S. 159.

24 Richter: Die schlecht trainierte Seele, S. 44; Vgl. hierzu auch den Beitrag „Seelentraining" in diesem Band.

ger eine *Macht* als eine *Schwäche*."[25] Im mechanisch geordneten Spiel der geometrischen Formen in *Rhythmus 21* geht es somit nicht um „,formale' Spezialfragen", sondern um eine der „elementaren Erziehungsfragen unserer Psyche".[26]

Richters Verweise auf Fragen des Seelischen und des Psychischen in der Schlusspassage des Aufsatzes unterstreichen, dass es ihm nicht nur um die Demonstration bzw. Entdeckung mechanischer oder rationaler Vorgänge, sondern darüber hinausgehend um die Gestaltung einer neuen Synthese des Rationalen und des rein Intuitiven geht. Schließlich bezieht sich seine Programmatik nicht auf die Arbeit mit dem ,schlecht trainierten Auge', sondern mit der ,schlecht trainierten Seele' – insoweit Richters Metaphorik eine solche Trennung überhaupt zulässt.

Rhythmische Vibrationen

Der weiße Strahl, der die ,Handlung' von *Rhythmus 21* einleitet, führt den Zuschauer in eine Dimension rein rhythmischer Bewegungen, die nicht vom ,physischen', sondern von einem ,inneren Auge' wahrgenommen werden. In einem Text, der vermutlich aus dem Jahr 1922 stammt, hat Gert Caden die Prinzipien der hier zum Ausdruck gebrachten konstruktivistischen Ästhetik diskutiert. Es geht um die Arbeit mit geometrischen Formen im Sinne von „objektiven Elementen", die „in Funktion gesetzt werden". Somit „entsteht im Raum ein dynamisch-konstruktives Kraftsystem von innerster Gesetzmäßigkeit und höchster Spannung".[27] Diese „innerste Gesetzmäßigkeit" beschreibt Caden nachfolgend als „eine klare, innerlich notwendige Lebensgestaltung, in der eine genaue Ausbalancierung der Kräfte stattfindet."[28]

In dieser Formulierung lässt sich eine enge Verbindung erkennen zwischen der Auffassung der geometrischen Abstraktion in der Rhetorik jener Gruppe von radikalen Konstruktivisten einerseits, zu der Richter und Eggeling gehörten, und Kandinskys spirituell fundierter Abstraktionslehre andererseits. Die ,innere Notwendigkeit' dient als Schlüsselbegriff in Kandinskys kunsttheoretischen Schriften, in denen er den inneren Drang des Menschen zur Schöpfung künstlerischer Formen bezeichnet, wobei „das Wichtigste in der Formfrage ist [...], ob die Form aus der inneren Not-

25 Ebd., S. 46.

26 Ebd.

27 Aus einem undatierten Brief Cadens an Alfred Hirschbroek. Hier zitiert nach Bernd Finkeldey: Im Zeichen des Quadrates. Konstruktivisten in Berlin. In: Irina Antonowa / Jörn Merket (Hg.): Berlin – Moskau 1900-1950. München / New York 1995, S. 157-161, hier: S. 159.

28 Ebd.

wendigkeit gewachsen ist oder nicht".[29] Der Begriff, der bei Kandinsky an die Idee der Materialisierung einer inneren „Seelenvibration"[30] des Schaffenden in künstlerischen Formen gebunden ist, erweist sich weiterhin als eng verbunden mit der Vorstellung eines „inneren Klanges" der Materie, den Kandinsky in „Über die Formfrage" näher erklärt: „Die Welt klingt. Sie ist ein Kosmos der geistig wirkenden Wesen. So ist die tote Materie lebender Geist."[31] Die Passage beschreibt eine innere Dimension von Klängen und Vibrationen, die nur für die seelisch Bereiten wahrnehmbar ist. Sie wirft weiterhin ein unerwartetes Licht auf die grundlegenden synästhetischen Verfahren und das klanglich kodierte Bewegungsspiel geometrischer Formen in *Rhythmus 21*.

Die grundlegenden synästhetischen Verfahren in *Rhythmus 21* lassen sich nicht ausschließlich auf die ästhetische Erbschaft des Symbolismus und deren Weiterführung in den transästhetischen Experimenten der historischen Avantgarde mit der Zusammenführung unterschiedlicher Kunstmedien zurückführen. Synästhetische Konzepte spielten auch eine wichtige Rolle im Diskurs des modernen Okkultismus, nicht zuletzt in den Schriften der Theosophie, die in Kandinskys Kunsttheorie eine konstitutive Funktion innehatten. In einer Publikation von 1901, die sieben Jahre später in deutscher Übersetzung erschien,[32] entwarfen Charles W. Leadbeater und Annie Besant eine Theorie von sogenannten „thought-forms", die auf der Vorstellung beruhte, „that the entire cosmos is made up of a single, subtle substance that vibrates".[33] Die Vorstellung ist symptomatischer Ausdruck einer im modernen Okkultismus vorherrschenden, monistischen Weltauffassung, die davon ausgeht – wie R. Bruce Elder bemerkt – „that the material world, apparently so solid, is really only the outward appearance of an inner spiritual reality".[34] Diese innere Substanz erschien im okkultistischen Diskurs der Moderne zunehmend „more like energy than like matter or mind"[35] und die Aufgabe der Theosophie (sowie des modernen Okkultismus im weiteren Sinne) bestand darin, „to coach seekers on the ways to study those hidden forces, those hidden realities".[36] Wie Rudolf Steiners *Wie*

29 Kandinsky: Über die Formfrage, S. 142.

30 Wassily Kandinsky: Über Bühnenkomposition. In: Ders. / Franz Marc (Hg.): Der Blaue Reiter. Dokumentarische Neuausgabe von Klaus Lankheit. München 1965, S. 189-208, hier: S. 192.

31 Kandinsky: Über die Formfrage, S. 168.

32 Vgl. Ringbom: Kunst in der ‚ZEIT DES GROSSEN GEISTIGEN', S. 39.

33 R. Bruce Elder: Harmony and Dissent. Film and Avant-garde Art Movements in the Early Twentieth Century. Waterloo, ON 2008, S. 24.

34 Ebd., S. 17.

35 Ebd.

36 Ebd.

erlangt man Erkenntnisse der höheren Welten? von 1905 zeigt, kam der ästhetischen Einbildungskraft teilweise eine besondere Rolle in diesem Prozess der spirituellen Transmutation zu, insofern das „*künstlerische* Empfinden [...] die beste Vorbedingung für die Entwicklung der geistigen Fähigkeiten ist." Steiner erklärt: „Dieses Empfinden dringt ja durch die Oberfläche der Dinge hindurch und gelangt dadurch zu deren Geheimnissen."[37]

Im Rahmen der theosophischen Lehre bestand die Entdeckung dieser verborgenen Substanz nicht nur in der Entdeckung okkulter Vibrationen. Leadbeaters und Besants *Thought-Forms* zeigt, dass diese Lehre weiterhin auf der Vorstellung einer Möglichkeit zur Visualisierung der inneren Vibrationen der Materie beruhte. Das Buch enthielt eine Serie von Demonstrationen jener abstrakten Formen, die nur mit dem ‚inneren Auge' wahrzunehmen sind, jenen aber unbekannt bleiben, „who are confined to the physical senses as their means of obtaining information".[38] Im Schlusskapitel des Buches präsentieren die Autoren eine Reihe von „Forms Built by Music", die musikalische Werke von Mendelssohn, Gounod und Wagner in abstrakte Bilder übersetzen.[39] Interessant sind diese sachlich konzipierten Bilder nicht nur als Vorläufer der abstrakten Malerei im Feld der bildenden Kunst, sondern auch als synästhetische Versuche zur bildnerischen Darstellung klanglicher Phänomene und als Illustrationen „übersinnlicher Vibrationen" bzw. einer „vermeintlichen Wirklichkeit hinter den physischen Erscheinungen".[40] Kandinskys Schriften unterstreichen ihrerseits, dass die in den ‚Gedankenformen' der Theosophen zu erkennenden Vibrationen ihre Entsprechung in inneren Vibrationen des Rezipienten finden – so ist das „Ziel eines Werkes" ein „bestimmter Komplex der Vibrationen" und der „undefinierbare und doch bestimmte Seelenvorgang (Vibration) ist das Ziel der einzelnen Kunstmittel".[41]

An die hier beschriebene Tradition eines modernen „Form Mystizismus"[42] anknüpfend lässt sich *Rhythmus 21* als Illustration von Vibrationen beschreiben, die hinter der Materie verborgen sind. Der Titel enthält mehr als eine Anspielung an ein musikalisches Konzept, das als Grundlage für Experimente in einem anderen Kunstmedium aufgenommen wird. Der ‚Rhythmus' verkörpert vielmehr die Idee innerer Vibrationen der Materie, die im filmischen Medium offenbart werden und dadurch eine direkte Wirkung auf die geistige Verfassung der Zuschauer gewinnen. Das

37 Rudolf Steiner: Wie erlangt man Erkenntnisse der höheren Welten? (1. Teil). Rudolf Steiner Gesamtausgabe, Band 10. Dornach 1992, S. 47.

38 Annie Besant / C.W. Leadbeater: Thought-Forms. London 1901, S. 75.

39 Ebd., S. 82-84.

40 Ringbom: Kunst in der ‚ZEIT DES GROSSEN GEISTIGEN', S. 41, 44.

41 Kandinsky: Über Bühnenkomposition, S. 191.

42 Ringbom: Kunst in der ‚ZEIT DES GROSSEN GEISTIGEN', S. 40.

optische Spiel mit rein geometrischen Formen entpuppt sich am Ende als eine okkultistische Einweihungspraktik, der Film dient als Medium der spirituellen Transmutation der Zuschauer.

Vielschichtigkeit der Materie

In einem Aufsatz, der im ersten Heft von *G* erschien, beschreibt Werner Graeff die Figur des „neuen Ingenieurs", der als Verkörperung des neuen Ideals des Künstlers im Konstruktivismus gelten kann.[43] In seinem Plädoyer für die neue ‚elementare Gestaltung' erklärt Graeff jedoch etwas unerwartet, dass dieser neue Künstlertypus „unbeeinflußt von den Methoden der mechanistischen Technik" bleibt und seine Kräfte vielmehr der „neuen großartigeren Technik der Spannungen, der unsichtbaren Bewegungen, der Fernbeeinflussungen und solcher Geschwindigkeiten, die im Jahre 1922 noch nicht einmal vorstellbar sind", widmet.[44] Graeffs Text zeigt auf exemplarische Weise, dass selbst die Figur des ‚neuen Ingenieurs', die eine zentrale Funktion im ästhetischen Diskurs des Konstruktivismus einnahm, nicht gänzlich im Zeichen des ‚Mechanischen', ‚Technischen' oder ‚Rationalen' stand, sondern seinerseits an okkultistische Denktraditionen gebunden war. Seine Bestimmung der Grundsätze der ‚elementaren Gestaltung' richtet den Fokus somit auf die vielfachen diskursiven Überschneidungen, die die ästhetische Praxis des Konstruktivismus im frühen 20. Jahrhundert geprägt haben.

Eine Analyse von *Rhythmus 21*, die den Fokus auf das Feld des modernen Okkultismus und dessen Bedeutung für die frühe künstlerische Abstraktion richtet, liefert einen wichtigen Beitrag zur Beschreibung der semantischen Komplexität von Richters Film. Anders als die traditionelle Historiographie der ästhetischen ‚Moderne' es haben möchte, lässt sich dieses Werk nicht auf ein „totally self-contained kinetic composition of pure plastic forms"[45] reduzieren. Der Film lässt sich nur schwerlich in eine lineare Erzählung von der Entwicklung der modernen Kunst hin zur Entdeckung der ihr eigenen, reinen Formen und Materialität integrieren. In seiner Tendenz setzt sich Richters Film eindeutig von der okkultistisch inspirierten Formenlehre von Kandinsky und seinen Gesinnungsgenossen ab, doch der Film ist zugleich ein signifikantes Produkt jener „Epoche des Grossen Geistigen", die Kandinsky und Franz Marc im Jahr 1912 ausge-

43 Werner Graeff: Es kommt der neue Ingenier [sic]. In: G. Material zur elementaren Gestaltung I (Juli 1923), o.P.

44 Ebd.

45 Standish D. Lawder: The Cubist Cinema. New York 1975, S. 161.

rufen haben.[46] Der Film lässt sich jener Praxis des frühen abstrakten Films zuordnen, die Elder mit einer in der Moderne weit verbreiteten Tradition der „pneumatic epistemology“ verbunden hat.[47] Dem ‚absoluten Film‘ ging es weniger um die Erforschung der Materialität der Zeichen als darum, „to emphasize film's immateriality, its gaseousness, and in doing so release cinematic form from representation“[48]. Im Fall des optischen Illusionsmediums Film mag dies selbstverständlich scheinen, doch die frühen abstrakten Filme lassen sich in dieser Hinsicht als symptomatisch für eine wichtige, aber häufig übersehene semantische Dimension der konstruktivistischen Ästhetik bezeichnen: die Tendenz zur Abstraktion ging mit Versuchen einher, die äußere Hülle der Materie zu durchdringen und zu einer anderen, rein spirituellen Wahrnehmung zu gelangen. Am Ende war auch dieses Suchen nach dem rein Geistigen integraler Bestandteil der konstruktivistischen Erforschung der Materialität – doch nicht der physischen, sondern einer ‚pneumatischen‘.[49] Es ist gut bekannt, dass okkultistische Strömungen, die wichtiger Bestandteil der kulturellen Moderne im Europa des frühen 20. Jahrhunderts waren, eine zielgerichtete Polemik gegen den Kult des Materialismus und der Oberflächlichkeit geführt haben – und es ist auch bekannt, dass diese Skepsis gegenüber der Materie in vielen Kreisen europäischer Künstler und Dichter geteilt wurde. Ein Text des Chemikers Wilhelm Ostwald, der im frühen 20. Jahrhundert von vielen Künstlern und Kulturkritikern eifrig gelesen wurde, zeigt jedoch, dass die Skepsis gegenüber der Materie auch im wissenschaftlichen Diskurs zunehmend ihren radikalen Ausdruck gefunden hat: „Die Materie ist ein Gedankending, das wir uns, ziemlich unvollkommen, konstruiert haben, um das Dauernde im Wechsel der Erscheinungen darzustellen.“[50] Wenn selbst die moderne Chemie den Begriff der Materie über Bord wirft, wen nimmt es da wunder, dass auch ein konstruktivistischer Künstler vom Schlage Hans Richters die äußere Hülle des Materiellen durchdringen will, um in diesem verborgenen Raum die elementaren Werte zu entdecken?

46 Wassily Kandinsky / Franz Marc: Almanach ‚Der Blaue Reiter‘. In: Dies. (Hg.): Der Blaue Reiter. Dokumentarische Neuausgabe von Klaus Lankheit. München 1965, S. 315-317, hier: S. 315.

47 Elder: Harmony and Dissent, S. xi.

48 Ebd., S. 7.

49 Vgl. ebd., S. xii-xiii.

50 Wilhelm Ostwald: Die Überwindung des wissenschaftlichen Materialismus. In: Abhandlungen und Vorträge allgemeinen Inhaltes (1887-1903). Leipzig 1904, S. 220-240, hier S. 234.

Verkehr: *Rhythmus 21* und die elementaren Bewegungsformen der Moderne

Mario Wimmer

> In einem Buche etwas aus Filmen zu zeigen ist schwierig, da die Bewegung fehlt.[1]
> —Hans Richter, 1929

Sieht man in den Bildfolgen von Hans Richters *Rhythmus 21* etwas vom Verkehr moderner Großstädte?[2] Ließ sich das „pulsende Leben" der „Verkehrswelt" von Berlin in den Rhythmus von Lichtbildern übersetzen?[3] Freilich nicht unmittelbar, doch in den Lichtbildern werden Bewegungsformen der Moderne sichtbar, die mit der Expansion des Verkehrswesens zu Beginn des 20. Jahrhunderts in Beziehung stehen. Aus der „dokumentarischen Phase"[4] der frühen Filmästhetik sind viele Filmrollen mit abgefilmten Straßenszenen, Eisenbahnfahrten und dem Treiben der modernen Großstädte überliefert. Durch die Abstraktionsleistung der Formexperimente Richters werden grundlegende Bewegungsformen modernen Großstadt- und Verkehrslebens in die künstlerische Filmsprache übersetzt. Dabei nutzte Richter die „Unwirklichkeit des Filmbildes"[5], seine Materialität und technische Darstellung, um die Wahrnehmung der modernen Welt jenseits der mechanischen Reproduktion der Alltagsrealität vorzuführen. Der Verkehr wurde dadurch, wie ich zeigen möchte, zu einem Residuum kultureller Energie, aus dem sich die Dynamik moderner Bewegungsformen speiste, mit denen Richter als engagierter Beobachter ästhetisch experimentierte. Er wollte die Wahrnehmung der Welt nicht nur künstlerisch beschreiben, es ging ihm

---

1 Hans Richter: Filmgegner von heute – Filmfreunde von morgen. Berlin 1929, S. 6.

2 Die Arbeit an diesem Essay wurde durch ein ETH Postdoctoral Fellowship ermöglicht. Ich danke Christoph Bareither und Klaus Müller-Richter für ihre Kommentare sowie meinen Zürcher Kolleginnen Margarete Pratschke, Max Stadler und Vera Wolff für Diskussionen und Hinweise.

3 Hans A. Martens: Psychologie und Verkehrswesen. In: Zeitschrift für angewandte Psychologie Bd. 15 (1919), S. 374–385, hier: S. 374f.

4 Helmut H. Diedrichs: Zur Entwicklung der formästhetischen Theorie des Films. In: Ders. (Hg.): Geschichte der Filmtheorie. Kunsttheoretische Texte von Méliès bis Arnheim. Frankfurt a.M. 2004, S. 9-28, hier: S. 9. Etwas überraschend wurden keine Texte von Hans Richter in diese wichtige Anthologie zur frühen Filmtheorie aufgenommen.

5 Rudolf Arnheim: Film als Kunst. Frankfurt a.M. 2002, v.a. das Kapitel „Parallelismus und Kontrapunkte", hier: S. 242.

darum, den Film als Mittel für die „Umbildung der modernen Psyche“[6] zu verwenden, das sich nicht dem Geschmack der Massen fügte.

Seit dem ausgehenden 19. Jahrhundert nahm man die deutsche Gesellschaft „unter dem Zeichen des Verkehrs“[7] wahr. Die Städte waren Knotenpunkte im internationalen Netzwerk des Weltverkehrs, das gleichermaßen Transport- und Kommunikationsmittel einschloss. Das Wort ‚Verkehr‘ ist eine Übertragung des lateinischen *commercium* ins Deutsche, das erst mit der Industrialisierung und Technisierung der modernen Welt und dem zunehmenden Verkehrsaufkommen in den Metropolen neue Bedeutungen annahm. Nicht nur die Semantik von ‚Verkehr‘ um 1900 bezog ihr Vokabular aus der Zeit der Reiter- und Pferdewagen, auch die Technologie des Verkehrs datierte in ihren einzelnen Elementen aus verschiedenen Zeiten; wirklich neu war erst ihre Assemblage. Nimmt man das weitere semantische Feld der Weimarer Republik in den Blick, so waren auch ältere Bedeutungen noch wirksam und aktuell, weshalb ‚Verkehr‘ selbstverständlich auch Geld- und Schriftverkehr, sozialen und gesellschaftlichen, geistigen und intimen Verkehr meinte. Der Austausch von Gütern und Nachrichten mittels Schiffen, Eisenbahnen, Flugzeugen, Post, Telegraphie und Telefon wirkten in „früher ungeahntem Maße“[8] auf die internationale Vernetzung der modernen Welt. Das chaotische Treiben der Fernverkehrsbahnhöfe war zwar durch die neuen Kursbücher international koordiniert[9], vor Ort erschienen manchem Beobachter die Menschenströme aber als ein unzureichend geleitetes Durcheinander[10].

Es entstanden neue Formen organisierter Bewegung und Kommunikation[11], die in ganz verschiedenen Bereichen eine Rationalisierung und Standardisierung des Austauschs von Gütern, Personen und Informatio-

6 Hans Richter: Film von morgen (1929). In: Freunde der deutschen Kinemathek e.V. (Hg.): Hans Richter. Film ist Rhythmus. Berlin 2003, S. 56-62, hier: S. 62.

7 Handschriftliche Widmung Wilhelm II. An den Staatssekretär des Reichspostamtes Heinrich von Stephan vom 7.1.1891. Hier zitiert nach Cornelius Neutsch: Personalpolitik und Arbeitsbedingungen bei den deutschen Postverwaltungen. In: Thomas Stahl (Hg.): Historische Streiflichter. Untersuchungen zu ausgewählten außen-, wirtschafts- und gesellschaftspolitischen Themen deutscher Geschichte im 19. und 20. Jahrhundert. Münster 2004, S. 149-164, hier: S. 149.

8 Weltverkehr (Art.). In: Brockhaus Kleines Konversationslexikon, Bd. 2. Leipzig 1911, S. 970.

9 Vgl. Markus Krajewski: Restlosigkeit. Weltprojekte um 1900. Frankfurt a.M. 2006.

10 Vgl. den Prolog „Zerstreuung“ in Mario Wimmer: Archivkörper. Eine Geschichte historischer Einbildungskraft. Konstanz 2012.

11 Vgl. James R. Beniger: Control Revolution. Technological and Economic Origins of the Information Society. Cambridge, MA 1986.

nen vorantrieben.[12] Die Industrialisierung und Mechanisierung[13] der modernen Welt führte zu einer „gesellschaftlichen Evolution“[14], in der technische Neuerungen nicht zuletzt auch die sinnliche Wahrnehmung transformierten[15]. Der industrialisierte Weltverkehr wuchs in ungeahnten Ausmaßen, er verdichtete und beschleunigte sich.[16] Parallel dazu entwickelte sich ein modernes Subjekt, das sich im globalen Verkehr dank seiner Menschen- und Bürgerrechte über nationale Grenzen hinweg fortbewegen konnte, dessen Wahrnehmen und Empfinden wurden dadurch einem neuen Regime der Rationalisierung, der Effizienz und der Äußerlichkeit unterworfen. Seine Arbeitskraft wurde untersucht, rationalisiert, und rhythmisch getaktet[17], ähnliches galt für die unscheinbaren Bewegungen im Büro[18] oder auf der Bühne[19].

Die Weimarer Republik erscheint nicht nur im Nachhinein als eine kurze Epoche, in der sich „in kurzer Zeit und in rasantem Tempo die faszinierenden und fatalen Möglichkeiten unserer modernen Welt“[20] verdichteten. Der frühe Film reflektierte die Herausforderungen der neuen Verkehrstechnologien und dokumentiere etwa zahllose Szenen der „destruktiven Kraft“[21] der Automobile, er zeigte die neuen Formen der Mobilität in bewegten Bildern. In den ersten Jahrzehnten bis in die Zeit des Ersten Weltkriegs lebten diese Bilder von ihrer Abbildungskraft, die ästhetische Innovation bestand zunächst darin, Mittel des Theaters in die Filmkunst

12 Vgl. Jakob Tanner: Multiplikationsprozesse in der Moderne – Plädoyer für ein Analysekonzept. In: Historische Anthropologie 16. Jg. (2008), H. 1, S. 2–7.

13 Vgl. Sigfried Giedion: Die Herrschaft der Mechanisierung. Ein Beitrag zur anonymen Geschichte. Frankfurt a.M. 1987.

14 Hans Ulrich Wehler: Deutsche Gesellschaftsgeschichte, Bd. 3, Von der „deutschen Doppelrevolution“ bis zum Beginn des Ersten Weltkrieges. München 1995, S. 14.

15 Vgl. Frederick J. Schwartz: The Eye of the Expert. Walter Benjamin and the Avant-Garde. In: Art History 24. Jg. (2001), H. 3, S. 401-444.

16 Vgl. Wolfgang Zorn: Verdichtung und Beschleunigung des Verkehrs als Beitrag zur Entwicklung der ‚modernen Welt‘. In: Reinhart Koselleck (Hg.): Studien zum Beginn der modernen Welt. Stuttgart 1997, S. 115-134.

17 Vgl. etwa Karl Bücher: Arbeit und Rhythmus. Leipzig 1897; Vgl. auch Anson Rabinbach: Motor Mensch. Energie, Ermüdung und die Ursprünge der Moderne. Wien 2001.

18 Vgl. etwa Wilhelm Heinitz: Vorstudien über die psychologischen Arbeitsbedingungen des Maschinenschreibens. Leipzig 1922.

19 Vgl. Fritz Giese: Girlkultur. Vergleiche zwischen amerikanischem und europäischem Rhythmus und Lebensgefühl. München 1926.

20 Detlev Peukert: Die Weimarer Republik. Krisenjahre der Klassischen Moderne. Frankfurt a.M. 1987, S. 10-11.

21 Dorit Müller: Transfer between Media and Mobility. Automobilism, Early Cinema, and Literature, 1900-1920. In: Transfers 1. Jg. (2011), Nr. 1, S. 50–72.

einzuführen.[22] Noch erinnerte man sich der Schwindelanfälle der ersten Eisenbahnreisenden, diese Form der gleichförmig bewegten Wahrnehmung wurde durch Straßenbahnen und Rolltreppen in die Stadtwahrnehmung verlängert.[23] Als 1896 erstmals ein Zug in einem Kinosaal zum Stehen kam, reagierten die Zuschauer ähnlich irritiert auf die ungewohnte Bewegung der Bilder.[24] Die neuen Verkehrstechnologien haben nicht nur zu einer Industrialisierung der Wahrnehmung geführt, sie haben die „Phantasie der ganzen Welt angeregt“[25].

In Deutschland, schrieb Kurt Tucholsky nicht ohne Ironie, sei der Verkehr „zu einer nationalen Zwangsvorstellung geworden.“[26] In Berlin wäre man sogar „stolz“ auf den „Krach auf den Straßen“, auf den Staub und die vielen Autos in einer sich ständig wandelnden Stadt, die „mit den neuen Formen nicht fertig“ wurde.[27] Die Konsequenz war ein „Gefuchtel, Geblink, Geklingel und Gewink“[28], die Stadtverwaltung reagierte nur verzögert und ohne Plan auf die Neuerungen und wehrte sich mit einem Wust von Verboten und Regelungen. Auch Theodor Lessing hasste das „Geschrei“ und „Getöse“, den „sinnlosen Lärm“ und die „benzinstinkenden Autoungeheuer“, die eine „beständige Gefahr“ darstellten.[29] Die Tageszeitungen und Illustrierten waren voll von Berichten über Verkehrsunfälle[30] und Begegnungen von Mensch und Maschine im städtischen Alltag.

Dieser Blick wurde auf die gesamte Landschaft einer neuen Welt übertragen. So führte etwa der spätere Direktor des Bauhauses, Hannes Meyer, die Spuren, die durch die technische Transformation entstanden waren, in einem Tableau zusammen:

> Das optische Bild der heutigen Landschaft ist vielgestaltiger denn je: Hangars und Dynamohallen sind darin die Dome des Zeitgeis-

---

22 Vgl. Georges Sadoul: Geschichte der Filmkunst. Wien 1957, S. 36.

23 Vgl. Andrea Mihm: Die Rolltreppe. Kulturwissenschaftliche Studien zu einem mechanisch erschlossenen Zwischenraum. Marburg 2005 (Dissertation); zur Geschichte der Förderbänder vgl. Giedion: Herrschaft der Mechanisierung, S. 101-107.

24 Vgl. Auguste und Louis Lumière (Regie): L'arrivée d'un train à La Ciotat. Paris 1895.

25 Giedion: Herrschaft der Mechanisierung, S. 102.

26 Kurt Tucholsky: Der Verkehr. In: Ders.: Gesammelte Werke in zehn Bänden, Bd. 7. Reinbek bei Hamburg 1975, S. 305-308, hier: S. 305.

27 Ebd.

28 Ebd.

29 Theodor Lessing: Ich warf eine Flaschenpost ins Eismeer der Geschichte. Essays und Feuilletons, 1923-1933. Neuwied 1986, S. 400-401.

30 Hans Ulrich Gumbrecht: 1926. Ein Jahr am Rande der Zeit. Frankfurt a.M. 2001, S. 43.

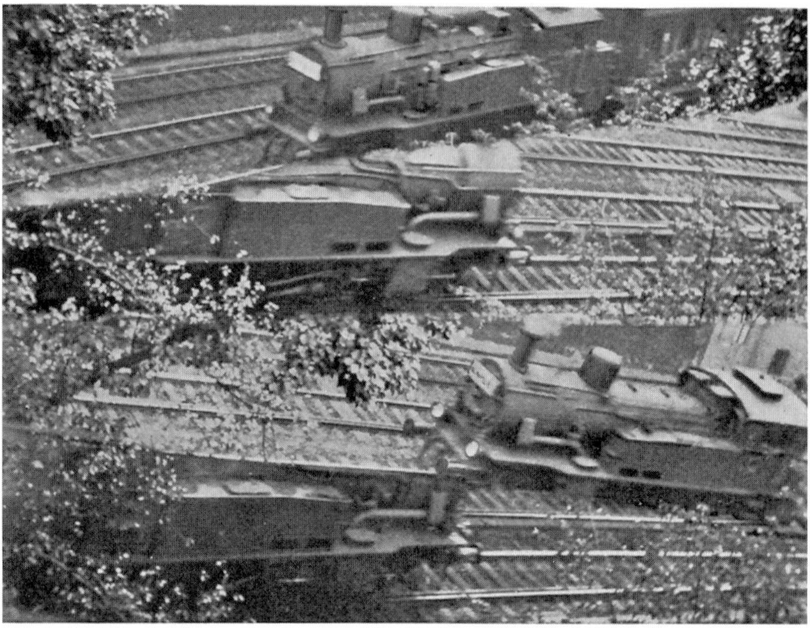

Abb. 1: Verkehrsszenen in Hans Richter:
Filmgegner von heute – Filmfreunde von morgen.

> tes. Bestimmend wird ihre Eindrücklichkeit durch die bestimmten Formen, Lichter und Farben ihrer neuzeitlichen Elemente: der Radioantennen, der Talsperren, der Gitterträger; durch die Parabel des Luftschiffs, das Dreieck der Autowarntafel, den Kreis des Eisenbahnsignals, das Rechteck der Plakatwand; durch das Linienelement der Kraftlinien: Telephondrähte, Fahrdrahtgestelle, Starkstromleitungen; durch Funkturm, Betonmast, Blinklicht und Benzin-Tankstelle.[31]

Der Verkehr bildete ein Netzwerk moderner Technologie und Vorstellungen, durch das der Alltag und das Leben insgesamt nachdrücklich umgestaltet wurden.

Verkehrssinn

Die Wirkungen des neuen Verkehrslebens wurden wissenschaftlich untersucht, sie gaben Anlass zu philosophischer und ästhetischer Verarbeitung

31 Hannes Meyer: Bauen und Gesellschaft. Schriften, Briefe, Projekte. Dresden 1978, S. 28f.

und Reflexion.[32] In diesem neuen „Zeitalter des Verkehrs“[33] war die Wahrnehmung in Bewegung geraten. Die Eindrücke des städtischen Betriebs ließen die Großstädter „eine unerlässliche Fähigkeit [...] entwickeln“[34], um mit den Maschinen Schritt zu halten und die in Bewegung geratene Wahrnehmung des Straßenverkehrs zu bewältigen. Die Bewohner der Großstädte entwickelten etwas, das von Zeitgenossen als ‚Verkehrssinn‘ bezeichnet wurde. Der Verkehrssinn entstand in gesellschaftlicher Koevolution mit den verbreiteten Ängsten vor Geschwindigkeit, Beschleunigung und dem Getöse der neuen Bewegungsformen. Nachdem sich die Automobilfront im Weltkrieg aus den Städten hinaus verlagert hatte, war man an den urbanen Automobilverkehr noch nicht wieder gewöhnt. Das Verschwinden der Automobile aus dem Straßenverkehr während der Kriegsjahre wurde nach deren Rückkehr ins Stadtbild als massiv und bedrohlich wahrgenommen. Die angespannten Nerven der Kriegsjahre kommunizierten nicht einwandfrei mit den alltäglichen Ereignissen des Großstadtbetriebs. Die „technisch hergestellten Reize“ wurden zu „Agenten bei der Zivilisation des Seelenlebens“.[35]

Die Straßen waren voller ‚Lichtspiele‘, die eine Erneuerung und Anpassung der menschlichen Wahrnehmung nötig machten. Jeder stand in einem mittelbaren Verhältnis zum Verkehr: Man stand ihm

> so nahe, dass auch für jeden, sei es der Grossstädter im Gewühl des Strassenverkehrs oder den Reisenden in den Eisenbahnen oder Strassenbahnen oder den Landmann im weltentlegenen Dorfe, der staunend – und fluchend dem vorbeirasenden Auto nachsieht, verkehrstechnische Kenntnisse von Nutzen sind, als deren Grundlage sich die Geisteskräfte in bestimmter Richtung zu entwickeln sind.[36]

Die Verkehrspsychologen nahmen Ergebnisse der Arbeitswissenschaft und Reklameforschung auf, um mit „Verständnis für die Seele des Volkes“[37] angemessene Formen bei der Regulierung des Verkehrs zu finden. Es bedurfte einiger „Nervenarbeit“[38], um die unfallfreie und routinierte Bewegung durch die Stadt zu bewältigen. Ähnlich wie der Verkehr führten auch die Lichtbilder zu einer „Umbildung der heutigen Psyche der Menschheit“[39].

---

32 Martens: Psychologie und Verkehrswesen.

33 Ebd., S. 374.

34 Ebd.

35 Wolfgang Schivelbusch: Geschichte der Eisenbahnreise. Zur Industrialisierung von Raum und Zeit im 19. Jahrhundert. Frankfurt a.M. 1977, S. 150.

36 Martens: Psychologie und Verkehrswesen, S. 374-375.

37 Ebd., S. 382.

38 Ebd.

39 Richter: Film von morgen, S. 62.

Ein Landmann in einem weltentlegenen Dorf widmete in seinem Hauptwerk *Sein und Zeit* den Alltagsszenen des Großstadtverkehrs einige Bemerkungen. Martin Heidegger analysierte das Zusammenspiel von „Verkehrsmitteln und Verkehrsregelungen“[40] als ein neues Zeichensystem. Die neuen Verkehrsformen des modernen Lebens hatten für ihn universellen, semiotischen Charakter: „In der Benutzung öffentlicher Verkehrsmittel, in der Verwendung des Nachrichtenwesens (Zeitung) ist jeder Andere wie der Andere.“[41] In diesen anonymen Strukturen des Weltverkehrs entfaltete „das Man seine eigentliche Diktatur“.[42] Die Beobachtung des anonymen Verkehrsalltags erlaubte einen Abstraktionsprozess, der Aufschluss über den Zeichencharakter der Gegenwart gab. So war, schrieb Heidegger, an den Kraftwagen „neuerdings ein roter, drehbarer Pfeil angebracht, dessen Stellung jeweils, zum Beispiel an einer Wegkreuzung, zeigt, welchen Weg der Wagen nehmen wird.“[43] Die Position des Pfeils wurde zwar durch den Lenker geregelt, aber auch von allen anderen verstanden, in Heideggers Worten waren die Zeichen damit „innerweltlich zuhanden“ und unterhielten zugleich eine Beziehung zum Alltag des Verkehrs, der sich „durch Verweisung“ konstituierte.[44] Die „symbolische Funktion [...] erklärt, warum Heidegger trotz seiner technikfeindlichen Vorurteile“ im Blick auf den Alltag der modernen Welt das Automobil als „ein neues strukturelles Element“ im Großstadtverkehr beschrieb.[45] Während Heidegger philosophisch die Fähigkeit analysierte, die Zeichen im Alltag in einem Verweisungszusammenhang zu deuten, entwickelte man in angewandter Forschung eine Psychologie des Signals, die sich der „Feststellung der besten Signalform“[46] widmete und in neuen Forschungslabors empirisch prüfen ließ. Dieses abstrakte System von Zeichen setzte sich aus elementaren Formen in Bewegung zusammen, die von der empirisch orientierten Wahrnehmungspsychologie und Reklameforschung[47] beschrieben und von Typographen und Architekten[48] neu gestaltet wurden. Soweit zum „Er-

40 Martin Heidegger: Sein und Zeit. Tübingen 1927, S. 78.

41 Ebd., S. 126.

42 Ebd.

43 Ebd., S. 81.

44 Ebd.

45 Gumbrecht: 1926, S. 47.

46 Martens: Psychologie des Verkehrswesens, S. 9.

47 Vgl. etwa Fritz Pauli: Rhythmus und Resonanz als ökonomisches Prinzip in der Reklame. Berlin 1926.

48 Vgl. Janet Ward: Weimar Surfaces. Urban Visual Culture in 1920s Germany. Berkeley, CA, 2001.

kenntnisniveau der Zeit"[49], das für Richter grundlegend für die künstlerische Produktion war.

Elementare Formen

Richters Weg zur künstlerischen Abstraktion von diesen führte über die psychologische Verarbeitung der modernen Welt. Dabei ging es jedoch keinesfalls um die Befindlichkeiten und Empfindsamkeiten des Künstlersubjekts, sondern um psychotechnisch analysierbare und mechanisierbare Empfindungen der modernen Seele. Der Sinn für die neuen Bewegungsformen der Moderne war kontrollier- und trainierbar. „Empfinden ist ein ebenso präzise organisierter und mechanisch exakter Prozeß wie Denken"[50], stellte Richter in einer kurzen Notiz in der Zeitschrift *G* fest. Diese Überzeugung ging nicht zuletzt wohl auch auf die naturwissenschaftliche Erforschung des Empfindens und der Sinneswahrnehmung zurück.[51] Er sprach von der „schlecht trainierten Seele"[52], die noch nicht zum Organ einer neuen Wahrnehmung der modernen Welt geworden war.

Ähnlich wie die Wahrnehmung des Großstädters durch die Verkehrsströme verändert wurde, unterzog auch der Film die Kunst jener Zeit einer Neuordnung: „Das betraf sowohl ihre Gegenstände und Materialien, ihre Verbreitung und Rezeption als auch die Wechselwirkung unter den verschiedenen Gattungen und technischen Medien."[53] Nicht nur deshalb galt der Film als Inbegriff modernen Lebens. Dabei wurde der Verkehr freilich nicht direkt in Bilder übersetzt, sondern die Kunst nahm den Umweg eines Abstraktionsprozesses, der den Wahrnehmungsprozess zergliederte, um nicht aus der individuellen Seele des Künstlers, sondern in einem universellen Formenvokabular einen formalen Bewegungsprozess zu gestalten.

Richter ging es um die Überführung der Mobilität in eine Kunst der Bewegung, die sich einer reinen Formensprache bediente. Die Elemente dieser ästhetischen Sprache der Bewegung wurden mittels eines grundlegenden „Prinzips der Anschauung" hergeleitet, der „Polarität", die er ganz im Sinn der Weimarer Avantgarden „als generelles Lebensprinzip"

49 Vgl. Hans Richter: Film (1922). In: Freunde der deutschen Kinemathek e.V. (Hg.): Hans Richter. Film ist Rhythmus. Berlin 2003, S. 20-22, hier: S. 20.

50 Hans Richter: Die schlecht trainierte Seele. In: G. Zeitschrift für elementare Gestaltung III (1924). Reprint herausgegeben von Marion von Hofacker, München 1986, S. 44-47, hier: S. 44.

51 Vgl. etwa Ernst Mach: Beiträge zur Analyse der Empfindungen. Jena 1886.

52 Richter: Die schlecht trainierte Seele; Vgl. hierzu den Beitrag „Seelentraining" in diesem Band.

53 Anne Hoormann: Lichtspiele. Zur Medienreflexion der Avantgarde in der Weimarer Republik. München / Paderborn 2003, S. 13.

verstand.[54] Helmut Lethen hat dieses „Polaritätsdenken“[55] der Zwischenkriegszeit in einem Schema veranschaulicht, das sich neben anderen über die in diesem Zusammenhang wirksamen Gegensätze konstituiert: Verwurzelung vs. Mobilität, Authentizität vs. Künstlichkeit, natürlicher Zyklus vs. mechanische Zeit.[56] Dem entsprachen die „Kontrast-Beziehungen“, die Richter anwandte, um seine ästhetische Formensprache der Bewegung zu gewinnen. So ergab sich ein „Alphabet“ elementarer Prinzipien der Anschauung, namentlich waren das: „Proportion, Rhythmus, Zahl, Intensität, Lage, Klang, Zeitmaß usw.“[57] Daraus ergab sich ein Netzwerk der „reinen Beziehungen der Formen untereinander“[58]. Die Bewegung der Formen zeigte sich „in einem einheitlichen durch das ganze Bild gehenden Rhythmus“[59]. Richter entwickelte dabei die Technik von Rollen- und Bewegungsbild von Viking Eggeling weiter.

Die Protagonisten der abstrakten Filmkunst bildeten in ihrem Selbstverständnis eine gesellschaftliche und kulturelle Avantgarde[60], die sich nicht der Masse oder dem Publikum zuwandte, sondern den neuen Möglichkeiten moderner Kulturtechnik, die es ästhetisch auszuprobieren galt. Sie wähnte sich an der kulturellen Front einer modernen Bewegung, die sich von Überkommenem abwandte, um die Zukunft im bewegten Bild herzustellen. Dabei ging es zunächst um die Dynamik der Bewegtbilder selbst. „Der Film braucht kein Publikum. – Der Film *braucht Künstler!*“ (Abb. 2), hieß es in einer Einschaltung der Zeitschrift *G*, die sich mit den Mitteln der Reklame an die Kulturproduzenten wandte und sich keineswegs

54 Hans Richter: Prinzipielles zur Bewegungskunst. In: Freunde der deutschen Kinemathek e.V. (Hg.): Hans Richter. Film ist Rhythmus. Berlin 2003, S. 18-20, hier: S. 18; Vgl. hierzu auch den Beitrag „Bewegungskunst“ in diesem Band.

55 Diese Wendung geht laut Helmut Lethen auf Lessing zurück. Vgl. Helmut Lethen: Drei Männer im Schutt. Eine denkwürdige Konstellation nach dem II. Weltkrieg. Drei Kinder der Satisfaktionsgesellschaft. In: Wolfgang H. Zangemeister / Will Müller-Jensen / Jürgen Zippel (Hg.): Gottfried Benns Absolute Prosa und seine Deutung des „Phaenotyps dieser Stunde“. Würzburg 1999, S. 47-61, hier: S. 49.

56 Helmut Lethen: Der Habitus der Sachlichkeit in der Weimarer Republik. In: Bernhard Weyergraf (Hg.): Literatur der Weimarer Republik 1918-1933. München 1995, S. 371-445, hier: S. 406f; ähnlich auch das Schema kultureller Codes in Gumbrecht: 1926.

57 Richter: Prinzipielles zur Bewegungskunst, S. 19.

58 Ebd., S. 18.

59 Ebd.

60 Die künstlerische Avantgarde befand sich in gewisser Nähe zur angewandten Forschung (Militär, Reklameforschung, Logistik) und erinnerte damit, wohl unwillentlich, früherer Bedeutungen von avant garde, etwa im Sinn einer militärischen Vorhut. Dazu Winfried Wehle: Avantgarde. Ein historisch-systematisches Paradigma ‚moderner‘ Literatur und Kunst. In: Rainer Warning / Winfried Wehle (Hg.): Lyrik und Malerei der Avantgarde. München 1982, S. 9-41.

vor dem Publikumsgeschmack verneigte. Nur so konnte Filmkunst etabliert werden: durch unbedingten Gestaltungswillen, der sich auf das, was noch nicht eingelöst war, richtete. Überkommene künstlerische Techniken und Ausdrucksformen galt es hinter sich zu lassen. Oder in Richters Worten: „Es gibt noch keinen Film, nur eine perverse Abart photographierter Literatur."[61]

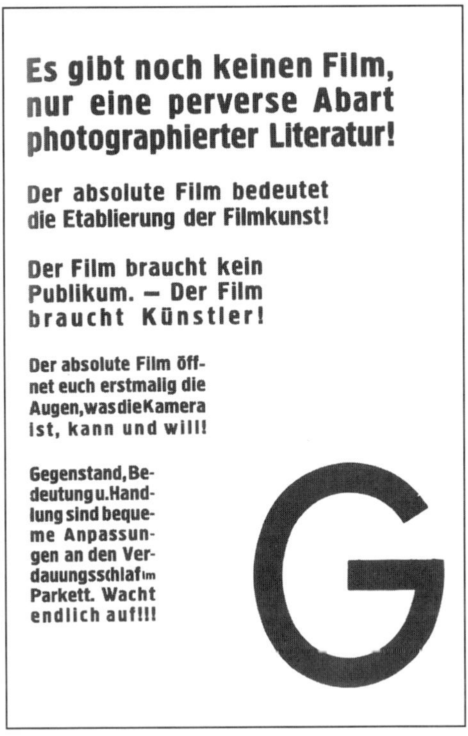

Abb. 2.

Bewegung als Vollendung des Bildes

In *Rhythmus 21* nutzte Richter die Möglichkeit, Bewegung „völlig künstlich zu erzeugen: durch Aneinanderreihen künstlicher, passend zusammengesetzter Einzelbilder, z.B. von Zeichnungen."[62] Die Animation des Films geschah teilweise auf einem Tisch, teils in einer Druckmaschine, deren Mög-

61 Hans Richter: Es gibt noch keinen Film. In: G. Zeitschrift für elementare Gestaltung V-VI (April 1926). Reprint herausgegeben von Marion von Hofacker, München 1986, S. 107.; vgl. auch Abb. 2.

62 Richter: Filmgegner, S. 8-9.

lichkeiten von „stop motion and forward and backward printing"[63] er nutzte. Auf diese Weise stellte Richter Filme her, die jenseits der Unterscheidung von abstrakt oder gegenständlich einen ‚Bewegungsvorgang' zeigen sollten, dessen Rhythmus sich aus dem Wechsel von Kontrast (hell vs. dunkel), Lage (horizontal vs. vertikal), Form (groß vs. klein), und Geschwindigkeit (schnell vs. langsam) ergaben und eine ‚sinnliche Gestalt' bildeten, die den Wahrnehmungsweisen des ‚Verkehrssinns' strukturell homolog waren. Was er damit schuf, waren Bewegtbilder, die in künstlerischer Formensprache, die Elementarbewegungen der Moderne zeigten.[64] Die Dynamik des Films ergab sich aus der Spannkraft der Bildkompositionen. Richter wählte eine unkonventionelle Strategie: „rather than attempting to visually orchestrate formal patterns, he focused instead on the temporality of the cinematic viewing experience by emphasizing movement and the shifting relationship of form elements in time."[65]

Die frühen Filme Richters, wie *Rhythmus 21*, waren Experimente über die moderne Wahrnehmung der Welt in Bewegung. „Um den modernen Lichterscheinungen auch in der Malerei einen Ausdruck zu verleihen, suchten die Künstler nach neuen Mitteln."[66] Sie begannen sich wahrnehmungspsychologischen Fragen zu widmen. So ging es nicht zuletzt darum – wie in den Laboratorien der Psychologen – herauszufinden, mit welchen Mitteln der Film wirkte[67], um gezielt Bildfolgen zu kreieren, die dem „Empfindungsapparat" einen „optischen Rhythmus" vor Augen führen, der sich nicht zuletzt an den Maximen zeitgenössischer Kompositionstechnik orientierte.[68] Der abstrakte Film galt Richter, Eggeling oder Ruttmann als neuer Weg zwischen Musik und Malerei, deren Vollendung er bildete.[69] Richter ging es darum, wie „die Form von der Lichtbewegung absorbiert" wurde und „die Bewegung des Lichts dominiere"[70], und damit eine Dynamisierung des Bildes ermöglichte, die in der Malerei zwar vorbereitet, nicht aber ver-

63 Gideon Bachmann / Jonas Mekas: From Interviews with Hans Richter during the Last Ten Years. In: Film Culture Nr. 31 (1963/64), S. 26-35, hier: S. 29.

64 Vgl. hierzu den Beitrag „Elementares Kino" in diesem Band.

65 Richard Suchenski: Hans Richter. In: Senses of Cinema Nr. 49 (2009). http://www.sensesofcinema.com/2009/great-directors/hans-richter/#13 (2.3.2012).

66 Hoormann: Lichtspiele, S. 101.

67 Richter: Die schlecht trainierte Seele, S. 44: „Es fehlt dem Film allgemein heute noch der Ueberblick über die Mittel durch die er wirkt."

68 Ebd.

69 Vgl. Hoormann: Lichtspiele, S. 84.

70 Ebd., S. 177.

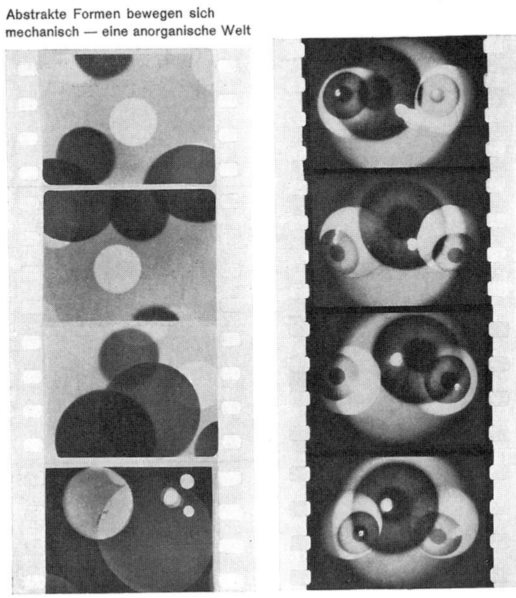

Abb. 3: Hans Richter: „Abstrakte Formen bewegen sich mechanisch – eine anorganische Welt".

wirklicht werden konnte. Der Film war „Malerei mit Zeit"[71], insofern eine Art „sichtbare Musik"[72].

Die neuen Phototechniken schufen einen noch unergründeten Möglichkeitsraum sachlicher ‚Phantasie' der Bewegung mit offenem Zukunftshorizont. Die Dynamik der Bilder ergab sich aus der Kombination von „äußerem Gegensatz" und „innerer Verwandtschaft"[73] der Elementarformen, die Richter in seinen Bewegtbildern kombinierte. Bewegung konnte in der Fläche der Filmleinwand durch die Lage der Elemente zueinander, durch veränderliche Proportionen, das Gleiten, Pulsieren, den Stillstand usw. aus den elementaren Formen hergestellt werden. Was der Zuschauer dann erlebte war Bewegung, die sich als künstlerische Handhabung von Zeit visualisierte:

71 Walter Ruttmann: Malerei mit Zeit (1919/20). In: Jeanpaul Goergen (Hg.): Walter Ruttmann. Eine Dokumentation. Berlin 1989, S. 73-74.

72 Theo van Doesburg: Abstracte Filmbeelding. In: De Stijl 4. Jg. (1921), Nr. 5, S. 71-75, hier: S. 71; vgl. auch Ders.: Film als reine Gestaltung. In: Die Form. Zeitschrift für gestaltende Arbeit 4. Jg. (1929), Nr. 10, S. 233-234.

73 Richter: Die schlecht trainierte Seele, S. 45.

> Je deutlicher auf eine mittlere Stundengeschwindigkeit von hunderttausend Bildern eingegangen wird, und je verständiger die *Zeit* (in ihren Teilen und als Einheit) gehandhabt wird und gedacht wird, um so fühlbarer erhält der Film seine Gestalt.[74]

Die abstrakten Vorgänge der Lichtbilder standen in Bewegung. Sie zeigten sich als reine Beziehungen der Formen untereinander. Die Flächenkunst der Malerei wurde in die Zeit projiziert. Daraus ergab sich ein rhythmisches Gefüge. Was man in Richters Film sieht, sind Abstraktionen der Bewegungsformen der Moderne. Er versteht darunter Bewegungen, die ihren Antrieb aus sich selbst beziehen, und sich aus dem Fortschritt speisen, der nicht zuletzt auch technisch verstanden wurde und in den Städten seine Spuren hinterließ. Trotzdem ging die Bewegungskunst Richters *nicht* einfach von der Bewegung der „äußeren mechanischen Welt"[75] aus, sondern nahm den Umweg über das Innere „einer Erkenntnis"[76] der modernen Welt. Deren Leben sollte sich nicht aus der Vergangenheit heraus erklären, sondern fand „in der Sphäre des Psychischen"[77] ihren ästhetischen Ausdruck. Die Kunst war für Richter die „Sprache der Psyche"[78] einer neuen Zeit. Eine neue Zeit im doppelten Sinn: Es war freilich die Epoche der industriellen und technischen Moderne, deren innere Dynamik und pulsierender Rhythmus in den Bewegtbildern von Hans Richters *Rhythmus 21* auf abstrakte Weise anschaulich wird. Die avantgardistische Kraft dieses Projekts besteht im gezielten Einsatz der transformatorischen Wirkung des Filmbildes auf die Psyche des modernen Subjekts. Wie „in allen Dingen der Welt", so Ernst Jünger mit Blick auf die Fotografien einer „veränderten Welt", zeigten sich auch in den Lichtbildern die „Machtverhältnisse" der Weimarer Kultur.[79] Was er über die Fotografien der Zwischenkriegszeit sagt, gilt in anderer Weise auch für die Lichtbilder der Bewegungskunst: „die Verwendung des Lichtbildes kann nur in einer, seiner eigentümlichen Gesetzmäßigkeit korrespondierenden Weise"[80] geschehen. Genau solche „eigentümlichen Gesetzmäßigkeiten" der elementaren Bewegungsformen der Moderne werden in *Rhythmus 21* in wenigen Minuten vorgeführt. Sie hinterlassen den Eindruck einer neuen, genuin modernen Zeitvorstellung,

---

74 Hans Richter: Bei 25 Meter pro Sekunde geht es nicht mehr um das schöne Bild! In: G. Zeitschrift für elementare Gestaltung V-VI (April 1926). Reprint herausgegeben von Marion von Hofacker, München 1986, S. 114.

75 Hans Richter: Film 1922. In: De Stijl 9. Jg. (1926), Nr. 6, S. 91-92, hier: S. 91.

76 Ebd.

77 Richter: Prinzipielles zur Bewegungskunst, S. 19.

78 Ebd., S. 20.

79 Ernst Jünger: Einleitung. In: Edmund Schultz (Hg.): Die veränderte Welt. Eine Bilderfibel unserer Zeit. Breslau 1933, S. 7-9, hier: S. 9.

80 Ebd.

die ihren Antrieb in der technischen Bewegung fand, doch ihre Dynamik aus sich selbst generierte.

Abbildungsverzeichnis

Abb. 1: Verkehrsszenen in Hans Richter: Filmgegner von heute – Filmfreunde von morgen. In: Jeanpaul Goergen / Angelika Hoch / Erika Gregor / Ulrich Gregor (Red.): Hans Richter. Film ist Rhythmus. Berlin 2003. S. 12.
Abb. 2: In: G. Material zur elementaren Gestaltung V-VI (April 1926). Reprint herausgegeben von Marion von Hofacker, München 1986, S. 107.
Abb. 3: Hans Richter: Filmstudie. In: Freunde der deutschen Kinemathek e.V. (Hg.): Hans Richter. Film ist Rhythmus. Berlin 2003, S. 89.

Werbe-/Industriefilm: Vereinte Empfindung im Rhythmus von *Philips Radio*

Lydia Nsiah

> Dieser Film hier gibt keine „Haltepunkte“, an denen man in Erinnerungen umkehren könnte, man ist – ausgeliefert – zum „Fühlen“ gezwungen – zum Mitgehen im Rhythmus – Atmen – Herzschlag: – . . . der durch das Auf und Ab des Vorgangs, d a s deutlich machen kann, was Fühlen und Empfinden eigentlich ist . . . ein Prozeß – B e w e g u n g.[1]
> —Hans Richter, 1924

Mal weiß, mal schwarz tasten geometrische Formen die Leinwand ab. Die Quadrate und Rechtecke werden kontinuierlich kleiner und größer, wandern von einem Eck ins andere. Lage und Proportion der Formen ändern sich durch schnelle Schnitte, womit Raum für neu hinzukommende Elemente geschaffen wird. Bis zuletzt das schwarze Quadrat im Weiß der Filmleinwand verschwindet.

Der Bildrhythmus in Hans Richters dynamischer Malerei *Rhythmus 21* basiert auf einem Gestaltungskonzept, das seine skizzierte Vorform in Partituren findet. In Rekurs auf seine filmischen Rhythmus-Studien[2] schreibt Richter in der von ihm 1923-1926 herausgegebenen Zeitschrift *G* über die „schlecht trainierte Seele“ und weist den Rhythmus von Bewegung als grundlegendes, schöpferisches Element des Films aus. „Unter Film verstehe ich optischen Rhytmus [sic], dargestellt mit den Mitteln der Phototechnik; beides als Material einer Phantasie, die aus dem Elementaren und Gesetzmäßigen unserer Sinnesfunktionen heraus schafft.“[3] Für Richter muss ein Film sowohl aus einheitlichen als auch aus verschiedenen Bewegungsabläufen bestehen, um eine Empfindung – nach ihm ein „mechanisch exakter Prozeß“[4] – im Zuseher hervorzubringen. Die Beherrschung dieses

---

1 Hans Richter: Die schlecht trainierte Seele. In: G. Zeitschrift für elementare Gestaltung III (1924). Reprint herausgegeben von Marion von Hofacker, München 1986, S. 44-47, hier: S. 45. (Hervorheb.i.Orig.)

2 Die Illustrationen zu seinem Rhythmus-Konzept im eben genannten Text stammen ziemlich sicher aus *Rhythmus 21* und *Rhythmus 23*. Auch wenn diese nicht betitelt sind, deuten die abgebildeten quadratischen und rechteckigen Formen auf diese Rhythmus-Studien hin. Vgl. Freunde der Deutschen Kinemathek e.V. (Hg.): Hans Richter. Film ist Rhythmus. Berlin 2003, S. 89.

3 Richter: Die schlecht trainierte Seele, S. 44.

4 Ebd.

‚schöpferischen' Prozesses wird durch das Wechselverhältnis von Trennung und Verbindung der innersten Verwandtschaft und des äußersten Gegensatzes von (visuellen) Bewegungen evoziert.[5] „So wie Trennung notwendig ist, um physisch wahrzunehmen, dem Wahrgenommenen Grenzen zu geben, so ist Bindung nötig, um das Wahrgenommene in Verbindung zueinander zu setzen."[6] Film bietet erstmals die Möglichkeit, einen derartigen Prozess zu steuern und einem breiteren Publikum zugänglich zu machen, um so die lebendige Kraft der Empfindung zu ‚entfetten'.[7] Die Bedeutung von Rhythmus im Film für eine wahrnehmungsfördernde Verschränkung von ‚ästhetischen' Theorien und den Lebensrealitäten einer industrialisierten Gesellschaft wurde vor allem ab den 1920er Jahren von zahlreichen Vertretern der historischen Avantgarden (Germaine Dulac, René Clair, Hans Richter, Len Lye, u.a.) sowohl in deren Filmen, als auch in Manifesten proklamiert.[8]

Nimmt man nun das Rhythmusschema Richters und vergleicht es mit Henri Lefebvres philosophischer Abhandlung *Rhythmanalysis: Space, Time and Everyday Life*[9], lassen sich erstaunliche Parallelen feststellen. Beide sehen Rhythmus als vereinende Konstante: Richter konzentriert sich dabei auf die künstlich erzeugten Rhythmen im Film, Lefebvre hingegen analysiert urbane Alltagsrhythmen. Mit den Rhythmus-Kategorien ‚Wiederholung' und ‚Differenz' (Lefebvre) bzw. ‚einheitliche' und ‚verschiedene Bewegungsabläufe' (Richter) reihen sich beide Konzepte in die Erforschung und Analyse ‚natürlicher' und ‚künstlicher' Wirkungsräume von Rhythmus für den ‚modernen' Menschen ein.

Mein Fokus richtet sich auf den Wirkungsraum von Rhythmus im Werbe- und Industriefilm.[10] Im Dazwischen von Kunst und Industrie angesiedelt, erweitert der avantgardistische Werbe-/Industriefilm mit Hilfe

---

5 Vgl. ebd.

6 Ebd., S. 45.

7 Vgl. ebd., S. 46.

8 Vgl. u.a. René Clair: Rhythmus, Rhythmus! In: G. Zeitschrift für elementare Gestaltung IV (April 1926). Reprint herausgegeben von Marion von Hofacker, München 1986, S. 115-116.

9 Henri Lefebvre: Rhythmanalysis: Space, Time and Everyday Life. London / New York 2004.

10 Die Abgrenzungen zwischen den Genres Werbefilm und Industriefilm sind z.B. in Bezug auf *Philips Radio* fließend. Einerseits wirbt der Film offensichtlich mit der Marke Philips und seinem Produkt, dem Radio. Andererseits zeigt der Film hauptsächlich industrielle Fertigungsprozesse und wurde ausschließlich in der Philips Fabrik in Eindhoven (Niederlande) gedreht. Selbst die Firma Philips vermarktete den Film nicht als Werbefilm, sondern als „künstlerischen Dokumentarfilm". Vgl. André Stufkens: Joris Ivens: Weltenfilmer. Europäische Stiftung Joris Ivens. Nimwegen 2009, S. 80.

von rhythmischen Filmtechniken seine ästhetische Wirkungskraft um eine ökonomische, die dem auftraggebenden Unternehmen zu Gute kommt. Joris Ivens' *Philips Radio*[11] von 1931 fungiert in der folgenden Rhythmusanalyse – die sich insbesondere der Kombination von differenten und sich wiederholenden Bewegungsabläufen in Bild und Ton widmet – als produktives Beispiel für die Vereinigung der filmästhetischen Verwendung und der industriellen Verwertung von Rhythmus im Film.

Nach Lefebvre misst Rhythmus die Dauer von Zeit durch die Bewegung von sich wiederholender und differenter Momente. „Everywhere where there is interaction between a place, a time and an expenditure of energy, there is rhythm."[12] Der menschliche Körper repräsentiert in diesem Feld der Interaktion den Berührungspunkt von sozialem und biologischem Rhythmus.[13] Die Kombination dieser Rhythmen funktioniert individuell. Der menschliche Rhythmus ist also janusköpfig, das heißt, er wird von der Wahrnehmung und Aufnahme sozialer, vergangener und zukünftiger Rhythmen beeinflusst. „Lefebvres Konzept folgend ist Rhythmus: „a science, a new field of knowledge [*savoir*]: the analysis of rhythms; with practical consequences"[14]. Als konstruktive Forschungskategorie hilft Rhythmus das Wissen über gesellschaftliche Zusammenhänge und Anordnungen zu erweitern. Rhythmus wird zu einem übergeordneten Wissenschaftsbegriff und agiert somit als Analyseinstrument, das die Erforschung von Interferenzen ästhetischer, alltäglicher und ökonomischer Ausformungen einer industrialisierten Gesellschaft und deren ‚praktischen Konsequenzen' zulässt. Lefebvre befasst sich neben der Korrespondenz von linearen und zyklischen Rhythmen im Alltagsleben auch mit deren manipulativen Charakter.[15] „Producers of the *commodity information* know empirically how to utilise rhythms. They have cut up time"[16]. Auch hier schreibt sich Differenz in alltägliche Monotonie ein: „The repetitive monotony of the everyday, rhythmed by the (mediatised) media need not bring about forgetting of the exceptional."[17]

---

11 Joris Ivens: Philips Radio. DVD. 36 min. Europäische Stiftung Joris Ivens. Nimwegen 2009. (Niederlande 1931).

12 Lefebvre: Rhythmanalysis, S. 15. (Hervorheb.i.Orig.).

13 Vgl. Stuart Elden: Rhythmanalysis. An Introduction. In: Henri Lefebvre: Rhythmanalysis: Space, Time and Everyday Life. London / New York 2004, S. vii-xv, hier: S. xii.

14 Lefebvre: Rhythmanalysis, S. 3.

15 Z.B. im Hinblick auf die künstliche Erzeugung von Rhythmen durch Medien, Staat und Militär. Vgl. Kap. „Dressage" und „Manipulations of Time." Ebd., S. 38-56.

16 Ebd., S. 48. (Hervorheb.i.Orig.)

17 Ebd., S. 50.

Für den avantgardistischen Werbe- und Industriefilm bedeutet dies: nur unterschiedliche, aber korrespondierende Zeichen werden – in Bewegung – ein effektives Ganzes. Rhythmus findet darin seinen Platz im Hinblick auf die In-Bewegung-Setzung von Zeichen. In diesem Zusammenhang lassen sich Einzelbilder und Töne als Zeichen verstehen, die vom filmischen Apparat bewegt werden – der Filmemacher reguliert deren Rhythmus.

Mit Lefebvres Bedeutung von Rhythmus für das alltägliche Leben werden die Kategorien Wiederholung und Differenz ausschlaggebend: „When it concerns the everyday, rites, ceremonies, fêtes, rules and laws, there is always something new and unforeseen that introduces itself into the repetitive: difference."[18] Nach Lefebvre gibt es im Alltag keine absolute Wiederholung, da diese im alltäglichen Leben automatisch einen Moment der Differenz, sei es auf Grund von Zufall oder Fehlverhalten, produziert. Die Verbindung zwischen beiden Gegensatzpaaren erzeugt einerseits Kompromisse, andererseits Interventionen. Als Beispiel für eine derartige Verbindung, die Zeit durch Rhythmus bemisst, fungiert bei Lefebvre die runde Uhr, die vom linearen Sound des ‚Tick-Tack'[19] begleitet wird. Eine dialektische Relation zwischen sich gegenseitig messender zyklischer und linearer Zeit wird kreiert.

Ebenso messen sich Bild und Ton des Werbe- und Industriefilms gegenseitig – mit Zuhilfenahme eines künstlich erzeugten Rhythmus, der Gesetzen ästhetischer Affektivität und ökonomischer Effizienz folgt. Für einen Avantgardisten wie Richter bedeutete die Einbeziehung von Gesetzmäßigkeiten in die Produktion des ‚schöpferischen' Prozesses Film die Möglichkeit, dem Menschen zu einer denkfähigen ‚Seele' zu verhelfen.[20]

Für das in Auftrag gebende Unternehmen ging es darum durch die ‚innovative Verpackung' von Werbebotschaften im avantgardistischen Werbe-/Industriefilm, Konsumenten und ihr Verhältnis zu einem bestimmten Produkt in deren Empfindungen zu steuern. Die werbepsychologische Forschung kann hier neben ästhetischer und ökonomischer Wirkungskraft als dritte Ebene für die Kreation eines effizienten Kräfteverhältnisses zwischen repetitiven und differenten Rhythmen angesehen werden. Lefebvre spürt die erwähnte Kombination von Differenz und Wiederholung in den realen Rhythmen des Alltags auf.

Richters Rhythmusschema hingegen richtet sich auf die Koexistenz von Differenz und Wiederholung in den künstlichen Rhythmen des Mediums Film. „Ziel [der Avantgarden, L.N.] ist: durch die Kraft der künstlerischen Ordnung, überzeugt von der Bedeutung des Rhythmischen (als einem unwiderstehlichen Naturprinzip) zu einer hundertprozentigen Ki-

---

18 Ebd., S. 6.

19 Vgl. ebd., S. 8.

20 Vgl. hierzu den Beitrag „Seelentraining" in diesem Band.

nosprache zu kommen."[21] Für Richter ist Rhythmus ein ,vereinendes Konzept': „Rhythm is not definite, regular succession in time or space, but the unity binding all parts into a whole."[22] Rhythmus eröffnet die Möglichkeit, ein ,Gesamtkunstwerk' zu kreieren, das in einer universellen Sprache spricht. „Richter saw film as a means of accessing laws of movement more fundamental than any single medium and, ultimately, of rendering those laws available for a broader project of *Gestaltung*."[23] In seinen frühen Filmen, so auch *Rhythmus 21*, bewegte Richter graphische, geometrische Formen mit der Möglichkeit des filmischen Apparatus und kreierte dadurch neue rhythmische Muster, in denen die Kategorien Wiederholung und Differenz, also ,einheitliche' und ,verschiedene Bewegungsabläufe' enthalten sind. Partituren fungieren hier als eine Art Basis des filmischen Rhythmus – bewegte Bilder benötigen das Maß des Taktes, um in ,visuelle Symphonien'[24] transformiert werden zu können. Schon 1894, kurz vor der ersten offiziellen Filmprojektion der Brüder Lumière, postulierte der Psychologe Thaddeus L. Bolton im *American Journal of Psychology* im Hinblick auf die Bedeutung von Rhythmus für Musik: „It is the regular monotonous recurrence of the same rhythm without sufficient variations that is displeasing and not the rhythmic flow itself."[25]

Mittels der Betrachtung von visuellen und tönenden Rhythmen als gleichwertige Elemente sowie der Rekurrierung auf Richters ,vereinendes Rhythmus-Konzept', können die fast ausschließlich musikalisch verwendeten Begriffe Takt und Metrum auch auf Film angewandt werden. Folgt man dieser These, so existieren Takt und Metrum auch in visuellen Rhythmen. Rhythmus verbindet nach Lefebvre zudem Gegensatzpaare wie mechanisch-organisch, zyklisch-linear, kontinuierlich-diskontinuierlich und different-wiederholend. Rhythmus bezieht sich also auf ein Polaritäts-Konzept, das auch Richter für seine Arbeiten beansprucht.[26] Dieses avantgardistische Konzept, das auf die Kreation von elementaren Prinzipien der Gestaltung und deren universelles Verständnis zielt, findet im experimentellen Werbe- und Industriefilm einen besonderen Ausdruck. Hier oszil-

21 Hans Richter: Film von morgen (1929). In: Freunde der deutschen Kinemathek e.V. (Hg.): Hans Richter. Film ist Rhythmus. Berlin 2003, S. 56-62, hier: S. 57.

22 Hans Richter: Rhythm (1926). In: Freunde der deutschen Kinemathek e.V. (Hg.): Hans Richter. Film ist Rhythmus. Berlin 2003, S. 38.

23 Michael Cowan: Bewegungskunst (in diesem Band). (Hervorheb.i.Orig.)

24 Vgl. u.a. Germaine Dulac: From Sentiment to Line (1927). In: Antonia Lant (Hg.): Red Velvet Seat: Women's Writings on the First Fifty Years of Cinema. London / New York 2006; Vgl. hierzu auch den Beitrag „Notation" in diesem Band.

25 Thaddeus L. Bolton: Rhythm. In: Stanley Hall (Hg.): The American Journal of Psychology 6. Jg. (1894), Nr. 2, S. 145-238, hier: S. 167.

26 Vgl. Hans Richter: Prinzipielles zur Bewegungskunst. In: De Stijl (1921), Nr. 7, S. 9-12.

liert Rhythmus zwischen ‚Form und Wirkung', also zwischen seiner ‚Produktion und Wahrnehmung'.[27] Dieser prozessuale Zustand von Rhythmus verleiht Werbe- und Industriefilmen, die auf die psychologische Wirkungsmacht der filmischen Gestaltung setzen, eine affektive Qualität. Betrachtet man die zeitgenössischen Debatten über Werbung und seine Wirkung auf Konsumenten, so lässt sich erschließen, dass die Bedeutung von Rhythmus spätestens von den frühen 1920ern an diskutiert wird. Fritz Pauli, ein deutscher Werbeexperte mit guten Verbindungen zu Unternehmen und Werbeforschern, publizierte 1926 sein Buch *Rhythmus und Resonanz als ökonomisches Prinzip in der Reklame.*[28] Für ihn muss Rhythmus harmonisch aufgebaut sein – ohne jegliche Interventionen. Eine gute Werbung sollte also den Regeln von harmonisch konstruierten Rhythmen folgen. Zur Veranschaulichung seiner These gibt Pauli an, man müsse beispielsweise bei der Gestaltung von Leuchtschildern bzw. Verkehrsreklame eine strikte Silbentrennung der dargestellten Wörter verfolgen. Bei der Produktion eines Werbe-Trickfilms sollen hingegen die repetitiv angeordneten Einzelbilder einem sich – während der gesamten Länge des Films – nicht verändernden Takt untergeordnet werden.

Für Pauli repräsentiert Wiederholung das Grundelement für die psychologische Werbewirksamkeit. Betrachtet man die die unten abgebildete Werbefilm-Graphik Paulis genauer, handelt es sich zwar um eine „einheitliche Gestaltung von innerer Bewegung"[29], diese repräsentiert jedoch auf Grund der eingearbeiteten Differenzen (Zuwachs von Formen) keine absolute Wiederholung. Kader um Kader kommen rechteckige Formen hinzu, wodurch ein eingängiger, kontinuierlich wachsender Bildrhythmus produziert wird. Mit Blick auf die Einzelkader wird also schnell klar, dass Rhythmus in seinen Einheiten per se differente Momente enthalten muss, um ein ‚harmonisches' Gesamtbild beim Betrachter zu evozieren. Obwohl Paulis Einzelbilder an Richters Filmpartituren erinnern, exkludiert Pauli die zweite effektive Ebene der Rhythmus-Gestaltung, nämlich die „Verschiedenheit der Ausdrucksmittel"[30], nach Richter abhängig von Lage, Proportion und Lichtsphäre der verwendeten Form. Von einer Unterstützung oder auch nur Erwähnung avantgardistischer Gestaltungskonzepte kann bei Pauli demnach keine Rede sein: „Die Kunst hört eben dort auf, wo die Gesetzmäßigkeit beginnt."[31] Ähnlich sieht es der deutsche Psychologe Fritz

27 Vgl. Christa Brüstle u.a.: Zur Einleitung: Rhythmus im Prozess. In: Dies. (Hg.): Aus dem Takt. Rhythmus in Kunst, Kultur und Natur. Bielefeld 2005, S. 9-27, hier: S. 12.

28 Fritz Pauli: Rhythmus und Resonanz als ökonomisches Prinzip in der Reklame. Berlin 1926.

29 Richter: Die schlecht trainierte Seele, S. 48.

30 Ebd., S. 47.

31 Ebd., S. 29.

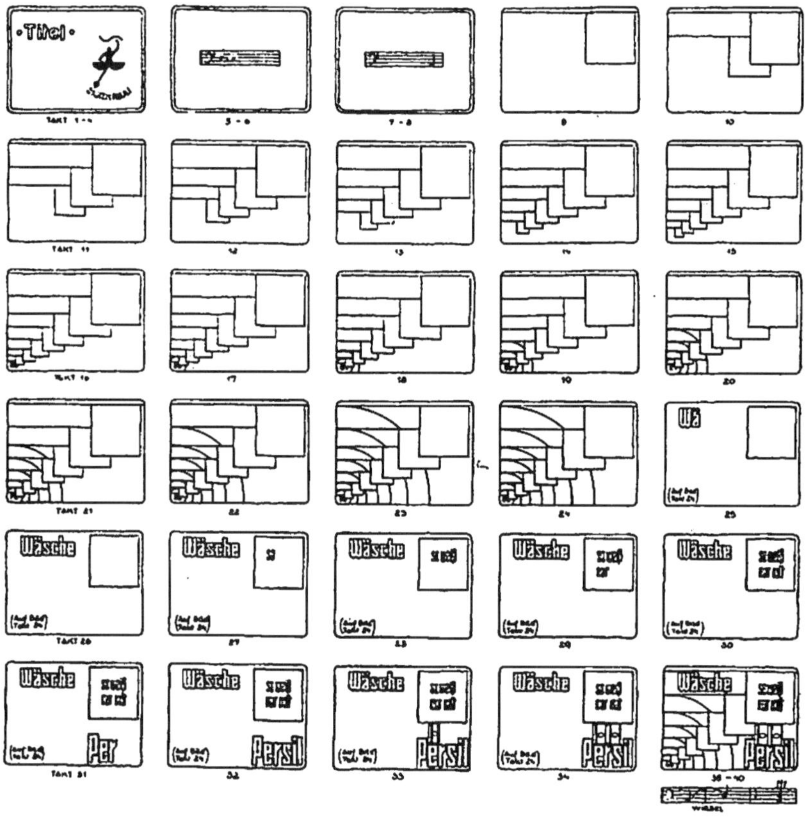

Abb. 1: Skizze zu einem Werbefilm für Persil.

Giese, der in seinem Artikel „Psychoanalytische Psychotechnik“[32] in der von Sigmund Freud herausgegebenen Zeitschrift *Imago* über die praktische Anwendung von psychoanalytischen Erkenntnissen für das Wirtschaftsleben schreibt. Jedoch lässt er den (intendierten) Zufall als werbewirksame Komponente in der folgenden Formulierung nicht außer Acht: „Der optischmotorische Rhythmus feiert den Reklamehöhepunkt im Trickfilm, welcher in ganz beliebiger Sukzession Reklameinhalte vorführt, und zwar im Sinne genetischer Folge.“[33] Er schreibt weiter: „Er [der Psychologe] wird dann wahrscheinlich gewisse Typen finden und seine akustisch-optisch-motorische Reklamerhythmik zuschneiden können auf die Gesetz-

32 Fritz Giese: Psychoanalytische Psychotechnik. In: Sigmund Freud (Hg): Imago. Zeitschrift für Anwendung der Psychoanalyse auf die Geisteswissenschaften 10. Jg., Nr. 1. Leipzig / Wien / Zürich 1924.

33 Ebd., S. 11.

mäßigkeit der unterbewußten Rhythmik."[34] Pauli und Giese streichen klar die Wichtigkeit von Rhythmus im Werbefilm für eine psychologische Werbewirksamkeit heraus. Als Positionen aus der Psychologie und Werbeexpertise der 1920er Jahre rekurrieren sie jedoch vordergründig nur auf einen Pol des erwähnten ‚vereinenden Rhythmus-Konzepts' – auf das Kontinuierliche, das sich Wiederholende und das Lineare. Avantgardistische Werbe- und Industriefilme scheinen diesen Instruktionen keineswegs zu folgen. Auch mit (erweitertem) Blick auf die experimentelle Psychologie gab es die Tendenz Differenzen in die Forschung mit einzubeziehen. „Yet it slowly became evident that such one-sidedness would make any practical application impossible."[35]

„Nur Bewegung zu sehen", schreibt Richter, „organisierte Bewegung – weckt auf, weckt Opposition, weckt Reflexe (?) aber – vielleicht – auch Genuß."[36] Joris Ivens *Philips Radio* stellt ein gutes Beispiel für ein Rhythmus-Konzept dar, das Polarität – also das Kräfteverhältnis zwischen Wiederholung und Differenz – im Werbe- und Industriefilm inkludiert. Ivens arbeitet in *Philips Radio* insbesondere mit der Montage von Bild und Ton, indem er reale Aufnahmen mit der von Lou Lichtveld eigens komponierten Soundebene kombiniert. Als einer der ersten Tonwerbe-/Industriefilme besticht *Philips Radio* durch seine visuell starke, an den Stummfilm angelehnte Sprache und die Neukomposition des Produktionsprozesses. Ausschließlich in der Philips Fabrik in Eindhoven (Niederlande) gedreht, zeichnet sich der Film durch seine avantgardistische Tonästhetik aus. In Lou Lichtvelds Kompositionen werden Originaltöne aus der Fabrik mit Musik und Körpergeräuschen (Atmen, Husten) sowie kurzen Einspielungen von gesprochenem Wort kombiniert. Die Möglichkeit mit Ton zu arbeiten bedeutete für die Filmavantgardisten jener Zeit (z.B. Hans Richter, Joris Ivens, Oskar Fischinger) neue Dimensionen des Films erschließen zu können. Das im kommerziellen Film präsente sprechende Wort war damit nicht gemeint: „Ich sehe allerdings im Gegensatz zu den bisher geäußerten Ansichten im Ton nicht das Mittel einer naturalistischen Illustration des Filmbildes, sondern *seine freie künstlerische Ergänzung*."[37]

Als „Industrielle Symphonie" – wie der Untertitel des Films lautet – konzipiert, hat *Philips Radio* einen symphonischen Charakter, der durch die rhythmische Montage von Bild und Ton repräsentiert wird. Ivens und Lichtveld arbeiteten, wie auch Richter, mit Partituren als Basis für die

34 Ebd., S. 12.

35 Hugo Münsterberg: Psychology and Industrial Efficiency. Boston / New York 1998 (erstmals 1913), S. 9.

36 Richter: Die schlecht trainierte Seele, S. 44.

37 Hans Richter: Neue Mittel der Filmgestaltung (1929). In: Freunde der deutschen Kinemathek e.V. (Hg.): Hans Richter. Film ist Rhythmus. Berlin 2003, S. 47-50, hier: S. 45. (Hervorheb.i.Orig.)

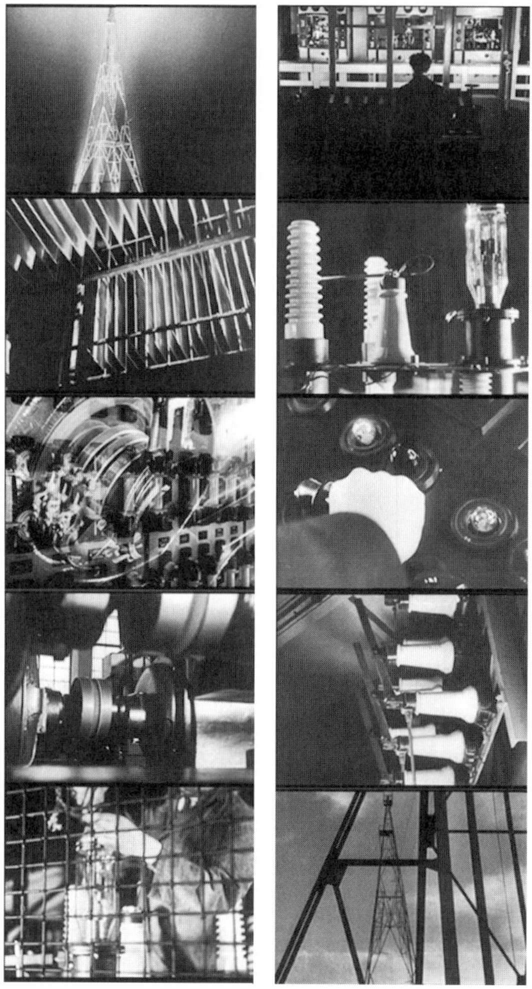

Abb. 2: Diskontinuität in *Philips Radio.*

Kombination von visuellen und tönenden Rhythmen. Obgleich die visuelle Sprache des Films sehr stark an den Stummfilm, vor allem durch die Verwendung von Zwischentiteln, erinnert, hebt Ivens die Arbeit mit Ton im Film auf eine Ebene und kreiert so eine aufschlussreiche zeitgenössische Auseinandersetzung mit dieser neuen technischen Möglichkeit des Films.

Der konzeptuelle Aufbau des Films besticht vor allem durch Diskontinuität: Ivens verschiebt gewisse Produktionsschritte, merkbar etwa an den Zwischentiteln, die nicht immer das beschreiben, was man sieht. Dieser fragmentierte, diskontinuierliche Stil fungiert als starkes Prinzip in Ivens' Film und wird von Lichtvelds Stimmungsmusik unterstützt[38]: Lichtveld erzeugt durch den regelmäßigen Wechsel der Klänge kurze Tonfragmente. In der ersten Einstellung sehen wir klingende Schallwellen, gleich danach ertönt die Ankündigung „Es folgt: der Philips-Film." Wir werden direkt in die Philips Fabrik ‚geführt' und empfinden bei der Betrachtung der schnell geschnittenen Aufnahmen von rotierenden Maschinen nahezu ein Schwindelgefühl. In der folgenden halben Stunde werden einheitliche und verschiedene Bewegungsabläufe visuell und tönend rhythmisiert. Einstellungen messen sich gegenseitig, indem sie in schnellen Schnitten einander beschleunigen und verlangsamen. Bild und Ton fordern dabei einander heraus. Diskontinuierlich angeordnete Fragmente gestalten in Kombination mit den visuellen Großaufnahmen der Produktionsprozesse aus dem Film ein konstruktives Ganzes. Innerhalb einer Szene von 30 Sekunden werden im Schnelldurchlauf Fabriksaufnahmen aneinander geschnitten und mit Lichtvelds Musik und Geräuschkulisse rhythmisch kombiniert. Vergleicht man diese Kaderanordnung mit Paulis Schema, wird klar, dass es sich hier um eine Bildrhythmik handelt, die der Differenz innerer Bewegung verschrieben ist. Zusätzlich wird bei fast jeder Einstellung eine differente, melodische Stimmung suggeriert. Die unterschiedlichen Einstellungen, gepaart mit verschiedenen Tonfragmenten, unterstützen eine diskontinuierliche, ‚innere' Bewegung im Filmbild (und erzeugen so eine gewisse Unruhe), die jedoch in einer kontinuierlich bewegten Einstellung mündet. Ton- und Bildebene werden in dieser, die Szene abschließenden, Einstellung gleichgeschaltet. Wir sehen einen Mann von der Seite, der das fertig produzierte Philips Radio anschaltet. Von den zuvor vorherrschenden abgehackten, maschinellen Klängen werden wir in die melodische, harmonische Ruhe der Musik aus dem Radio überführt. Die visuellen und tönenden Rhythmen des Films arbeiten somit beide mit dem Prinzip der Polarität von Differenz und Wiederholung. Gleichzeitig irritieren die fast futuristischen Aufnahmen und Toneffekte den Rezipienten. Mit seiner Gestaltung des Filmrhythmus in *Philips Radio* versucht Ivens, die „unbewusste Rhythmik"[39] des Publikums anzusprechen.

38 Vgl. Stufkens: Joris Ivens.

39 Giese: Psychoanalytische Psychotechnik, S. 12.

> Der Zuschauer muss die Begriffe in Zusammenhang mit dem Namen des Produkts im Unterbewusstsein behalten, sodass er sich, wenn drei Tage später über Radios gesprochen wird, vor allem an die großen Prinzipien und an diesen einen Namen erinnert.[40]

Eine „Industrielle Symphonie“ im wahrsten Sinne des Wortes: die Philips Glasbläser werden als Musiker stilisiert; der Rhythmus der einzelnen Arbeitsschritte tut sein Übriges. Nachdem das letzte Glied des Philips Radio, der Lautsprecher, an der Reihe ist, mündet der Film in einem dynamischen Finale. Der Prozess der Verpackung (dabei ist kurz die Marke Philips zu sehen) und des Transports werden mit Kamerafahrten und abwechslungsreicher Geräuschkulisse zu einer Karussellfahrt, die schließlich in einer an Oskar Fischingers Werbefilm für die Agentur Tolirag (*Kreise – Alle Kreise erfasst Tolirag*, 1933) erinnernden Rhythmisierung der besagten Philips Lautsprecher endet. In Überblendungen der runden Form des Lautsprechers hüpft dieser auf und ab, vermehrt sich und wird zu einer einzelnen großen Form, die zuletzt das ganze Filmbild ausfüllt. „Philips“ hat das letzte Wort.

Indem er die impliziten Prinzipien von Rhythmus, also die Polarität von Wiederholung und Differenz adaptiert, schafft Ivens eine rhythmische Stimmungsvision. Lichtveld und Ivens führen uns nicht nur die Möglichkeiten der Erzeugung von Rhythmus im Film vor Augen, ebenso erwecken sie in einer kurzen Szene unseren eigenen biologischen Rhythmus: sie lassen uns in absichtlich versetzter Bild- und Tonfolge zusammen mit einem Philips Arbeiter atmen.[41] Ivens verwendet in seinem 36-minütigen Film für die Firma Philips also unterbrechende Elemente, indem er Bild und Ton miteinander korrelieren lässt. Damit schafft er eine innovative, filmische Realisierung der avantgardistischen Vision einer universellen Sprache. Implantiert in das Feld von Werbung und ökonomischer Effizienz fordert er so den Zuseher in dessen Wahrnehmung heraus. Ökonomie und Kunst werden durch das Experimentieren mit Partituren von Bild und Ton zusammengefügt und erwecken somit die Aufmerksamkeit und den Geschmack des Konsumenten. Derart werden visuelle und tönende Rhythmen intermodular kombiniert und kreieren einen synergetischen Effekt sowie eine gegenseitige Intensivierung. Das Publikum ‚empfindet‘ somit gleichermaßen die Werbebotschaft wie die ‚schöpferische‘ Qualität des Films.

Abbildungsverzeichnis

Abb. 1: Fritz Pauli: Rhythmus und Resonanz als ökonomisches Prinzip in der Reklame. Berlin 1926. S. 27.
Abb. 2: Joris Ivens: Philips Radio. DVD. 36 min. Nimwegen: Europäische Stiftung Joris Ivens 2009. (Niederlande 1931). 18:02 - 18:19 min.

---

40 Zitiert nach Stufkens: Joris Ivens, S. 74.

41 Vgl. hierzu auch den Beitrag „Körper“ in diesem Band.

Wirbel

Robert Matthias Erdbeer

> Reality is the Waterloo, Will o' the wisp, or siren of artistic genius.[1]
> —Wyndham Lewis, 1914

> The vortex is the point of maximum energy.[2]
> —Ezra Pound, 1914

Ab 1:52 wird Hans Richters *Rhythmus 21* spürbar hektischer. Die Pulsation der auf- und abgeblendeten Quadrate, Rechtecke und Stäbe, ihr ‚organisches' Erscheinungsbild, gerät in Aufregung und suggeriert auf diese Weise einen Miniplot, der, wie im Röntgenfilm,[3] den Quasi-Organismus von außen erregt. Hier wird im raschen Wechselspiel ‚elementar gestaltet', sprich: ergänzt und verschoben, ersetzt und entfernt. Der ‚Bluthochdruck' der Form, der dann im ‚Blutkreislauf' der Rechteckformationen aufgefangen wird (2:39-2:46, Abb. 1-3), markiert Bedeutsamkeit und mündet in den Überblendungswirbel einer schnellen Schluss-Sequenz (2:47-2:49, Abb. 4-8). Was geht hier vor? Wird man zum Zeugen eines geometrischen Orgasmus? Des quadratischen Infarkts? Befördert diese umgekehrte Quadratur der Kreise – die Verzirkelung, Verwandlung und Verwirbelung der Rechtecke – nicht eine allegorische Lektüre, die dem scheinbar willkürlichen Formenspiel ein höheres Geheimnis oder Narrativ entringt? Sind Adjektion, Transmutation, Immutation und Detraktion nicht immer schon bedeutungsschwangere Verfahren der Rhetorik und Stilistik aller Künste? Überhaupt das Geometrische: War es nicht immer schon ein esoterisches Projekt?

I. Parawissenschaft und Parakunst

Die Esoterikfähigkeit moderner Kunst, so meine These, liegt gerade darin, dass sie aktuelle (Medien-)Techniken und wissenschaftliche Diskurse, Alltagswelt und Popularkultur subtil vernetzen kann. Sie antwortet damit auf ein Begehren, das vom Aufklärungskalkül der Wissenspopularisierung nicht befriedigt wird, das in der Unverständlichkeitskaskade aus Expertensprachen, High Technology, ästhetischer Erfahrung und prekärem Selbst ein höheres Kalkül vermutet,

1 Wyndham Lewis: Relativism and Picasso's Latest Work. In: Ders. (Hg.): BLAST. Review of the Great English Vortex. Bd. 1. London u.a. 1914, S. 139f., hier: S. 139.

2 Ezra Pound: Vortex. In: Wyndham Lewis (Hg.): BLAST. Review of the Great English Vortex. Bd. 1. London u.a. 1914, S.153f., hier S. 153.

3 Vgl. den Beitrag „Körper" in diesem Band.

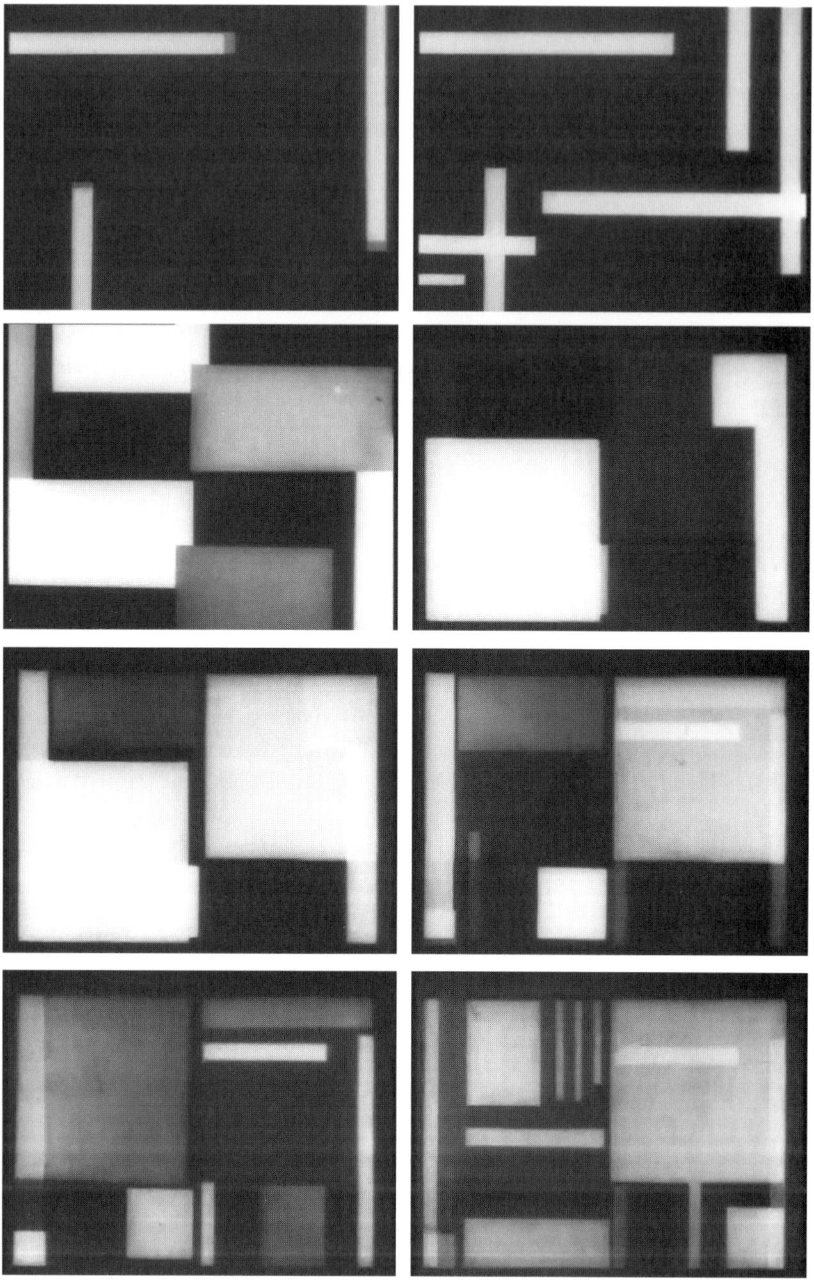

Abb.1-3 und 4-8: Zwei Serien – Verzirkelung, Verwandlung und Verwirbelung in *Rhythmus 21.*

das allein mit künstlerischen Mitteln zu beschreiben (oder zu erleben) ist. Moderne Kunst, die dieses leisten, also auf der Basis wissenschaftlicher und medialer Subdiskurse *meta*wissenschaftlich tätig werden will, ist ‚Parakunst'. Zu diesem Zweck bedarf sie nicht nur der ästhetischen Finesse, sie bedarf auch eines rituellen Handlungsrahmens – und der Rückbindung an den exakten Wissenschaftsdiskurs. Wie diese Ritualisierung als okkulte Einweihung betrieben und in eine neue Subjektivität verwandelt werden kann, beschreibt im vorliegenden Sammelband der Beitrag Benedikt Hjartarsons. In meinem Beitrag geht es um den szientifischen Ereignishorizont, in dem sich Richters *Rhythmus 21* bewegt.

Bereits die Suggestion von Organizität und wuchernder Vitaldynamik auf der einen, Konstruktion, Gestaltautonomie und Mechanismus auf der andern Seite, macht den Film zum Grenzprojekt moderner Kunst. Er illustriert den Wechsel vom Abstrakten (also dem, was von natürlichen Objekten ‚abgezogen' wurde, aber noch mimetisch rückgebunden bleibt) zum radikal Konkreten, also zu den Basiselementen visueller (literarischer, architektonischer) Zeichen, Verfahren und Codes.[4] Die Austreibung des Narrativen (und Ambigen) aus den Kunstobjekten, die mit dieser Konkretion verbunden ist, bewirkt die Migration bedeutungsstiftender Erzählungen ins Feld der Rezeption: des Kunsterlebens und der Kunstkritik. Sie lässt sich daher auch als Arbeitsteilung deuten: Das ästhetische Objekt wird vom *container* zum *incentive* der Erzählungen und Wahrheitsspiele, die der Leser, Hörer und Betrachter mit ihm ausführt – und vor allem auch: ausführen soll. Dies allerdings ist keine Einladung zur Deutungswillkür; das gereinigte Objekt erscheint vielmehr als Zeichen und Symbol im Sinne eines Gegenwissens, das vom kongenialen Geist erschaut, erlebt, empfunden, oder auch korrekt beschrieben und gedeutet werden soll. ‚Elementar' ist diese Kunst-Gestaltung[5] nicht nur durch den Deutungs- und Bedeutsamkeitsexport, der die Semantik säubert, das Zusammenfallen von Autonomie und Funktionalität verheißt und durch Verzicht auf explizite Poetologien seine esoterischen Prämissen camoufliert.[6] Elementar ist sie zugleich auf diskursive Weise, nämlich dort, wo ihre Konkretionen nicht-ästhetische Diskurse filtern, transformieren und für künstlerische Letztbegründungen verfügbar machen. Damit wird moderne Kunst für allegorisch-esoterische Lektüren frei, die diese diskursive Basis

4 Dies lässt sich idealtypisch an Mondrians Entwicklung der konkreten Malerei beobachten, die noch objektbezogen, also als ‚abstrakte' beginnt. Im Bauhaus-Kontext wird die objektive Reinigung als Funktionalismus gefeiert.

5 Vgl hierzu den Beitrag „Architektur" in diesem Band.

6 Im Bauhaus-Kontext wird die Kontamination von Form und Konstruktion strategisch naturalisiert und spiegelt die Einheit von „Wesen" und „Zweck": „Die konstruktive Funktion ist als Architektur erfaßt. Aus dem konstruktiven Gedanken der formale Aufbau entwickelt. Konstruktion und Form sind eins geworden, klar, logisch, einfach, unzweideutig, gesetzmäßig." Ludwig Hilbersheimer: Konstruktion und Form. In: G. Zeitschrift für elementare Gestaltung III (1924). Reprint herausgegeben von Marion von Hofacker, München 1986, S. 24-26, hier: S. 26.

(das Arkanum, die ‚primäre Wirklichkeit' des Kunstobjekts) rekonstruieren sollen – idealerweise ebenfalls im Modus einer esoterischen, arkanen Kunst.

Carl Einstein persifliert bekanntlich solche metaphysischen, erkenntnistheoretischen (und lebenspraktischen) Verheißungen mit Blick auf ihre Hauptvertreter, die er ‚Dilettanten des Wunders' nennt. Zugleich bestätigt er auf diese Weise eine Grundbedingung des ‚abstrakten' (eigentlich: ‚konkreten') Expressionismus: Im Diskurs der Avantgarde bedeutet jedes seiner Elemente mehr als nur es selbst. Elementare Kunst, so kann man schließen, ist heteronome Kunst, ist ‚Parakunst' insofern, als sie auf Diskursen fußt und Zielen folgt, die nicht-ästhetisch sind. Hier trifft sie sich mit ihrem wissenschaftskompensatorischen Pendant, der Parawissenschaft. Denn Parawissenschaft ist ein Erkenntnisspiel mit Zielen und Verfahren, die sich im Vergleich zum strengen Wissenschaftsdiskurs als außer-, gegen- oder metawissenschaftlich definieren und zugleich als Wissenschaftskritik verstehen: als Vertreter non-konformer Forschung, als Erlebnis einer höheren Erkenntnis, als Subjekterweiterung und Resonanz des Körpers, als Erzählung und Sorge um sich. Exakte Wissenschaft ist somit ebenso Voraussetzung für Parawissenschaft wie autonome Kunst für Parakunst. Zusammen bilden Parawissenschaft und Parakunst, so meine These, den Ereignishorizont der ‚esoterischen Moderne' – als verwandte Erben jenes metaphysischen Begehrens, das man einst als ‚Religion' bezeichnet hat. Versteht man *Rhythmus 21* als Projekt der Parakunst im Sinne dieser Überlegungen, so muss man fragen, welches (para-)wissenschaftliche Arkanum mit ihm aufgerufen wird. Es könnte der Diskurs des Wirbels sein.

II. Im Strudel der Physik

Dies führt zum Wirbeltanz der hektischen Formen zurück. Im diskursiven Spektrum lässt sich dem organischen Modell der Pulsation ein atomares an die Seite stellen, das um 1920 im exakten Wissenschaftsdiskurs bereits historisch, eben deshalb aber für den esoterischen Diskurs von Interesse ist: die Wirbel- oder Vortex-Theorie. Im Jahre 1858 hatte Hermann von Helmholtz auf der Basis einer „merkwürdigen Analogie der Wirbelbewegungen des Wassers mit den electromagnetischen Wirkungen electrischer Ströme" ein dynamisches Modell begründet, das konstant bewegte, von der ruhenden Umgebungsmasse isolierte Materien beschreibt.[7] Drei Punkte des Modells erweisen sich dabei als esoterikaffin:

---

7 Hermann von Helmholtz: Über Integrale der hydrodynamischen Gleichungen, welche den Wirbelbewegungen entsprechen. In: Journal für die reine und angewandte Mathematik 55 (1858), S. 25-55, hier: S. 27. Als „Wirbelbewegungen" definiert der Physiker „Bewegungen, denen ein [von der Umgebungsmasse abhängiges] Geschwindigkeitspotential nicht zukommt", denn: „Die Existenz eines Geschwindigkeitspotentials schließt die Existenz von Rotationsbewegungen der Wassertheilchen aus". Ebd., S. 33.

> Die Untersuchung ergiebt nun, daß wenn für alle Kräfte, welche auf die Flüssigkeit wirken, ein Kräftepotential existirt
> 1) kein Wassertheilichen in Rotation kommt, welches nicht von Anfang an in Rotation begriffen ist.
> 2) Die Wassertheilchen, welche zu irgend einer Zeit derselben Wirbellinie angehören, auch indem sie sich fortbewegen, immer zu derselben Wirbellinie gehörig bleiben.
> 3) Daß das Product aus dem Querschnitte der Rotationsgeschwindigkeit eines unendlich dünnen Wirbelfadens [...] constant ist [...]. Die Wirbelfäden müssen deshalb innerhalb der Flüssigkeit in sich zurücklaufen, oder können nur an ihren Grenzen endigen.[8]

Aus letzterem, so Helmholtz, folge, „daß ein Wirbelfaden nirgends innerhalb der Flüssigkeit aufhören"[9] kann. Die esoterische Umschreibung deduziert aus diesen physikalischen Prozessen drei zentrale Eigenschaften, die auch und vor allem die *materia prima* begründen: Anfangslosigkeit, Konstanz und Unzerstörbarkeit.

Die Aura dieser Urvermögen wirkte rasch auf den exakten Wissenschaftsdiskurs zurück. Sir William Thomson, der bekanntlich als Lord Kelvin in die Wissenschaftsgeschichte eingegangen ist, ernannte Helmholtz' Wirbel zu Arkana einer neuen Äthertheorie. In seiner 1867 publizierten Schrift „On Vortex Atoms" rief er mit Bezug auf Helmholtz' Hydrotheorie begeistert aus, „that this discovery inevitably suggests the idea that Helmholtz's rings are the only true atoms".[10] Denn – hier zeigt sich schon die Anschlussfähigkeit der szientifischen Debatte an die ältere Naturphilosophie *und* an den expressionsästhetischen Diskurs der neuen Esoterik: „any portion of a perfect liquid which has ‚wirbel-bewegung' has one recommendation of Lucretius' atoms – infinitely perennial specific quality. To generate or to destroy ‚wirbel-bewegung' in a perfect fluid can only be an act of creative power."[11] Damit aber ist zugleich das Stichwort einer expressionspoetischen Bewegung aufgerufen, die im frühen 20. Jahrhundert auf die Wirbeltheorie zurückgegriffen hat: der *Vorticism*, der den ‚wahren Vortex' aus der Unbeweglichkeit der zeitgenössischen Ästhetik herauswirbeln will.

Die junge Avantgardebewegung, die im Vorkriegsengland zwischen 1912 und 1915 recht erfolgreich war, schließt somit über einen wissenschaftlichen Diskurs des 19. Jahrhunderts ans Naturverständnis der *philosophia naturalis* an. Kann der Atomenwirbel doch als Urdynamik nicht nur

8 Ebd., S. 26.

9 Ebd., S. 36.

10 Sir William Thomson Lord Kelvin: On Vortex Atoms. In: Proceedings of the Royal Society of Edinburgh 6 (1867), S. 94-105, hier: S. 94.

11 Ebd.

der Naturentwicklung, sondern auch der kreativen Kunstprozesse, ja des Lebens überhaupt betrachtet werden – als Verfahren einer lebensphilosophischen Dynamik, welche für den physikalisch-mathematischen Diskurs dasselbe leistet wie einst Haeckels ‚Cytopsyche' für den biologisch-esoterischen (als ‚Zellseele') und Schulers ‚Chemotaxe' für den chemisch-esoterischen Diskurs der Zeit (als ‚Telesma'). Durch die Verdichtung der Verwirbelung im (Ur-)Atom als kleinster Einheit[12] glückt hier nämlich nichts geringeres als die Vereinigung des Mikrokosmos mit dem Makrokosmos (in Gestalt des Äthers). Somit unterstützt die Wirbelkompression zum einen Kelvins Forderung nach der ‚multiplen Kontinuität' der Welt-Materie,[13] die bereits der Fechnerschen Psychophysik und ihrer esoterischen Erweiterung als Ziel zugrunde lag.[14] Sie induziert jedoch, zum anderen, im ruhigen Umfeld Ströme, die der Lebenskraft zu explosionsartigem Durchbruch – einem „*BLAST*" – verhelfen. Dieser Umstand, so das Argument der gleichnamigen Vortizismus-Zeitschrift, sei „the reason why a movement towards art and imagination could burst up here [im langweiligen England, M.E.], from this lump of compressed life, with more force than anywhere else".[15]

Der Wirbel als Diskursprodukt aus Wissenschaft und Parawissenschaft, Naturphilosophie und Esoterik wird auf diese Weise anschlussfähig für ein Avantgardebegehren, das im Rückgriff auf die Wissenschaft vom Vortex eine höhere Vitalitäts-, Erlebens- und Bewusstseinsform erstrebt. Sie macht sich Luft im Sinne einer Kompressionsdynamik, die das Sinnkontinuum aus Kunst und Leben dadurch sichert, dass sie dessen Lebensstrom ventilartig befreit (und dadurch sichtbar macht, vgl. Abb. 9). Wie Richters *Rhythmus 21* zielt sie dabei nicht auf einen Wirbel, der im Kunstwerk selbst Bedeutung stiftet, sondern der im Rahmen der viralen Vortextheorie auf den Betrachter oder Leser übertragen wird:

> At any period an artist should have been able to remain in his studio, imagining form, and provided he could transmit the substance and

12 Vgl. ebd., S. 95: „The possibility of founding a theory of elastic solids and liquids on the dynamics of more closely-packed vortex atoms may be reasonably anticipated."

13 Ebd., S. 96. Kelvin spricht von „multiple continuity".

14 Vgl. Gustav Theodor Fechner: Elemente der Psychophysik. 2 Bde. Leipzig 1860. Fechner proklamiert hier einen psychophysischen Parallelismus, der die Kontinuation von Leib und Seele mathematisch fassen und – im Zend-Avesta aus dem Jahre 1851 – auch im Jenseits garantieren will. Hier kehrt bereits das (damals pseudowissenschaftliche) Atom in den Diskurs zurück – in der Atomenlehre aus dem Jahre 1855 –, um als Träger dieses psychophysischen Kontinuums zu dienen. Vgl. Gustav Theodor Fechner: Über die physikalische und philosophische Atomenlehre. Hg. von Ecke Bonk. Wien / New York 1995.

15 Wyndham Lewis (Hg.): BLAST. Review of the Great English Vortex. Bd. 1. London u.a. 1914, S. 32.

> logic of his inventions to another man, could have, without putting brush to canvas, be[en] the best artist of his day.[16]

Das Beste, was er dabei produzieren könne, seien wirkungsmächtige „MACHINES OF LIFE“, die Wyndham Lewis selbst im Vorgriff auf die Filme Richters als „a sort of LIVING plastic geometry“ beschreibt.[17] Der Künstler öffnet hier – als Magier wie als Bio-Techniker – das Tor zum Wirbel, dessen ‚logische Substanz‘ in ihm (und seinen Rezipienten) an Gestalt gewinnt. In diesem Sinne fördert *BLAST* die Kunst des Individuums. Es geht um „THE VORTEX IN HIM“.[18]

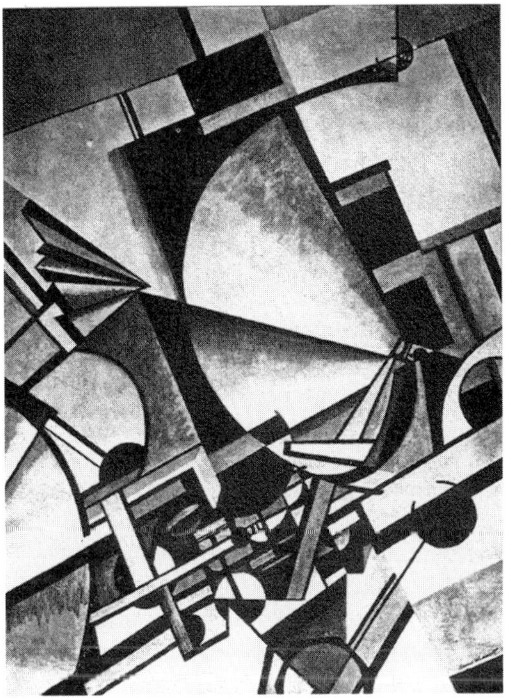

Abb. 9: Edward Wadsworth: *A Short Flight*.

16 Wyndham Lewis: Futurism, Magic and Life. In: Ders. (Hg.): BLAST. Review of the Great English Vortex. Bd. 1. London u.a. 1914, S. 132-135, hier: S. 135.

17 Lewis: Relativism and Picasso's Latest Work, S. 140.

18 Long Live the Vortex! In: Wyndham Lewis (Hg.): BLAST. Review of the Great English Vortex. Bd. 1. London u.a. 1914, S. 7-8, hier: S. 8; Vgl. dazu auch Wyndham Lewis: Life is the important thing! In: Ders. (Hg.): BLAST. Review of the Great English Vortex. Bd. 1. London u.a. 1914, S. 129-131, hier: S. 130: „It is true, ‚Life is there all the time.‘ But he [the average man] cannot get at it except through himself.“

III. Der Wirbel als Gestalt

Der Vortex ist kein Freibrief für Beliebigkeit. Im Gegenteil. Sein Telos heißt Gestalt. Sein Anwalt ist Friseur:

> BLESS the HAIRDRESSER. He attacks Mother Nature for a small fee. [...] He makes systematic mercenary war on the WILDNESS. He trims aimless and retrograde growths into CLEAN ARCHED SHAPES and ANGULAR PLOTS.[19]

Die Überführung der natürlichen Vitaldynamik in artistisch-geometrische Gestalt ist ein Projekt des Systematikers. Der Wirbel wird im Kunstwerk zugerichtet, doch auf eine Weise, die die atomare, komprimierte, mathematisch abbildbare Vortex-Ordnung hinter dem vermeinten Chaos der Natur zum Vorschein bringt. Der heikle Grundgedanke – „Chaos invading Concept and bursting it like nitrogen"[20] – wird also durch den Umstand aufgefangen, dass das Chaos selbst bereits Konzeptcharakter hat. Der Wirbel nämlich ist, wie Helmholtz eindrucksvoll belegt, viral und autonom, komplex und einfach, strukturiert und strukturierend zugleich.[21] Die Vortexkunst ist ein Geniestreich, weil sie die exakte Mimesis des strengen mathematischen Modells im Zuge einer eigenen, gewissermaßen ‚traditionsfreien' Modellbildung *reinszenieren* kann. Zu diesem Zweck benötigt sie geeignete Umgebungen sozialer, medialer und verfahrenstechnischer Natur.

Ein Kahlschlag ist hier freilich nicht von Nöten; die Umgebung selbst ist längst schon – mit Deleuze gesprochen – ‚glatt' und ‚ungekerbt'. Gerade weil die Kunst des Vortex „not a question of the characterless material climate around us"[22] ist, kann sie sich die Moderne als Natur erschließen und verfährt dabei im besten Sinne ‚primitiv': „The artist of the modern movement is a savage [...]: this enormous, jangling, journalistic, fairy desert of modern life serves him as Nature did more technically primitive man."[23] Auf diese Weise wird der Künstler zum Friseur der fehlgeleiteten Moderne, die es jetzt an ihren Wurzeln, besser: Wirbeln, zu frisieren gilt. Der vortizistische Friseur ist freilich kein Vertreter einer realistisch-bürgerlichen Mime-

---

19 Manifesto I. In: Wyndham Lewis (Hg.): BLAST. Review of the Great English Vortex. Bd. 1. London u.a. 1914, S. 9-28, hier: S. 25.

20 Manifesto II. In: Wyndham Lewis (Hg.): BLAST. Review of the Great English Vortex. Bd. 1. London u.a. 1914, S. 30-43, hier: S. 38.

21 Schon Helmholtz selbst beschreibt das Wirbelphänomen mit geometrischen Begriffen, wenn von „Wirbelflächen", „Wirbellinien", von „geradlinigen oder kreisförmigen Wirbelfäden" oder gar vom „rechtwinkligen Parallelepipedon" die Rede ist. Helmholtz: Über Wirbelbewegungen, S. 26f., 29.

22 Manifesto II, S. 36.

23 Ebd., S. 33; vgl. hierzu auch den Beitrag „Primitivismus" in diesem Band.

sis, die Lewis als „relaxed initiative"[24] verwirft. Sein Werk ist ‚radikal' und bietet eine Form der „native art", die aus der Urstruktur der endlosen Verwirbelung sich selbst als Individuum formiert – als Vortexform des Neuen Menschen: „Beyond Action and Reaction we would establish ourselves".[25] Im Umkehrschluss erscheint die Vortexkunst als „organism of this new Order and Will of Man"[26]. Wie sieht sie aus? Nach Wyndham Lewis muss sie allererst neurotisch sein:

> In a painting certain forms MUST be SO; in the same meticulous, profound manner that your pen or a book must lie on the table at a certain angle, your clothes at night be arranged in a set personal symetry [sic], certain birds be avoided, a set of railings tapped with your hand as you pass, without missing one.[27]

Die Kreativneurose, die hier Rhythmen, Rechtecke und Symmetrien schafft, betont nichts anderes als die exakte Grundstruktur des Vortex, die in *Rhythmus 21* als dynamisches Verfahren sichtbar wird.

In *BLAST* ist auch der (para-)wissenschaftliche Thesaurus aufgerufen, der den vortizistischen Prozess als *transmutatio*-Verfahren einer neugeschaffenen Chemie beschreibt: „The chemistry of the Present is different to that of the Past. With this different chemistry we produce a New Living Abstraction."[28] Diese quasialchemistische, vitale Abstraktion ist Konkretion im Sinne eines Dynamismus, der die Avantgarden spaltet; ihr Produkt, der Wirbel, bildet nichts mehr ab. Nach Lewis ist die Aufgabe des Vortizismus eben dieses: „to avoid representation" dort, wo die abstrakte Kunst noch immer gegenstandsverhaftet bleibe: „objects in your most abstract picture always have their twins in the material world".[29] Verworfen wird aus diesem Grunde auch „the naturalistic method of ‚cubing' on a posed model"[30], wie sie für Picasso typisch sei. Hier freilich gilt erneut die Ausgangsformel: „Intrinsic beauty is in the Interpreter and Seer, not in the

24 Wyndham Lewis: A Review of Contemporary Art. In: BLAST. Review of the Great English Vortex, Bd. 2, London u.a. 1915, S. 38-47, hier: S. 41.

25 Manifesto II, S. 30, 37. Hier zeigt sich überdies die Nähe zum Konzept der russischen Biokosmisten, wo das vortizistische self fashioning auch im „correcting [of] the grotesque of our physique" bestehen soll. In: Manifesto I, S. 25. ‚Unser Körper muss unser Werk sein', hat man das damals genannt.

26 Manifesto II, S. 39.

27 Wyndham Lewis: Fêng Shui and Contemporary Form. In: Ders. (Hg.): BLAST. Review of the Great English Vortex. Bd. 1. London u.a. 1914, S. 138.

28 Wyndham Lewis: Our Vortex. In: Ders. (Hg.): BLAST. Review of the Great English Vortex. Bd. 1. London u.a. 1914, S. 147-149, hier: S. 147.

29 Lewis: A Review of Contemporary Art, S. 43.

30 Ebd., S. 44.

object or content“[31], eine Formel, die das Dogma vom bewussten Repräsentationsverzicht mit Blick auf den Betrachter wieder lockert. Dazu liefert Lewis eine aufschlussreiche Anekdote aus dem Alltag eines Vortizisten:

> A Vorticist, lately, painted a picture in which a crowd of squarish shapes, at once suggesting windows, occurred. A sympathiser with the movement asked him, horror-struck, „are not those windows?“ „Why not?“ the Vorticist replied. „A window is for you actually A WINDOW: for me it is a space, bounded by a square or oblong frame, by four bands or four lines, merely.“[32]

„The artist“, folgert Lewis, sei „in certain cases [...] less scandalized at the comprehensible than is the public“, eine Einsicht, die nichts anderes als den im Rezeptionsdiskurs bestehenden Bedarf nach esoterischer Geheimnishaftigkeit umschreibt. Aus Sicht des Produzenten wird dann – paradoxerweise – das Mimetische und Leichtverständliche zum Künstlerisch-Arkanen, das mit Umsicht zu betreiben sei: „To paint a recognisable human being should be the rarest privilege, bestowed as a sort of ‚Freedom of Art‘.“[33]

Zu diesem Zweck imaginiert der Vortizist nichts weniger als ein geheimes Gremium, dem sich der Mimesis-Vertreter stellen müsse: „Only after passing a most severe and esoteric Board and getting a CERTIFICATE, should a man be allowed to represent in his work Human Beings, Animals, or Trees.“[34] Der Esoteriker des Vortizismus wiederum entdeckt das Wesen seiner Kunst im Material, „the poetry, that is to say, that is inherent in matter“, oder, anders ausgedrückt: ihr „spiritual weight“.[35] Hier, auf der basalen Ebene des Materials, ist dann auch jenes wahrhaft „unavoidable representative element“ zu finden, das natürliche und konkretistische Verfahren, Welt und Künste, aber auch den künstlerischen mit dem mathematisch-physikalischen Vortizismus verknüpft: „the logic and mathematics at the bottom of both are the same“[36]. Der Vortizismus steht damit im Paradigma des im Wiener Kreis entwickelten Isomorphiegedankens einer einheitlichen logischen Struktur von Sprache, Text und Welt. Nur wer sie – praktisch ohne sie zu suchen – findet, trifft am Ende die dem Kunst-Natur-Verhältnis inhärente Emotion. Es ist die Fähigkeit zur „ACCIDENTAL RIGHTNESS“[37], die den Vortizisten zum perfekten Arrangeur der Formen macht. Auf die-

31 Long Live the Vortex!, S. 7; Vgl. auch Lewis: A Review of Contemporary Art, S. 45: „Nature itself is of no importance.“

32 Lewis: A Review of Contemporary Art, S. 44.

33 Ebd.

34 Ebd., S. 47.

35 Ebd., S. 45.

36 Ebd., S. 55.

37 Ebd., S. 46.

se Weise mündet Lewis' *Vorticism* letztlich in den klassischen Geniekult, demzufolge die Natur dem Künstler (und damit sich selbst) die Regel gibt. Die Mimesis, die hier entsteht, ist Poiesis; ihr Vortex ist authentisch, selbstidentisch, logisch, zirkulär und dauerhaft. Ihr Resultat ist eine radikale Naturalisierung alles dessen, was der Vortizismus stiftet: „the best paintings being in the same category as flowers, insects and animals."[38] Der Vortex ist Natur.

IV. ‚Vortexturen'

Die Texturen, die der Vortex schafft – man könnte sie auch *Vortex*turen nennen – sind die ‚Vor-Texturen' aller Kreativität. Aus ihrer atomaren Feinstruktur und Energetik wirbeln die Texturen aller Künste: Bilder, Melodien, Texte und das Medium des Films hervor. Dass diese Energetik auch zur Statik, ja zum Stupor eines idiosynkratischen Verstummens führen kann, wird in der Vortexlehre ausdrücklich als Tugend ausgeflaggt:

> The Vorticist is at his maximum point of energy when stillest.
> The Vorticist is not the Slave of Commotion, but its Master. [...]
> Our Vortex desires the immobile rhythm of its swiftness.[39]

Damit freilich kommt ein Zug der Wirbeltheorie zum Vorschein, der den ursprünglichen Kontinuitätsgedanken der Materie, den Zusammenhang der Dinge, auch als Produktionsverhalten modelliert: *Kontemplation*. Die Aufhebung der biologischen und maschinellen Eile (einschließlich des explosiven *blast*) im Rhythmisch-Immobilen garantiert vor allem eines: Ewigkeit. Dem atomaren Wirbel, der, weil unzerstörbar, unvergänglich ist, entspricht im produktionsästhetischen Diskurs „THE PRIMARY PIGMENT". „The vorticist", so Ezra Pound in *BLAST*, „relies on this alone; on the primary pigment of his art, nothing else."[40] In Anlehnung an Theorien von Kandinsky, Einstein, Goll und anderen Vertretern der ‚primären Wirklichkeit' entwickelt Pound ein überschaubares Tableau der Künste, das – als vortizistischer *Laokoon* – der jeweiligen Kunst ihr (freilich nicht ganz unerwartetes) Primärpigment verleiht:

> EVERY CONCEPT, EVERY EMOTION PRESENTS ITSELF TO THE VIVID CONSCIOUSNESS IN SOME PRIMARY FORM. IT BELONGS TO THE ART OF THIS FORM. IF SOUND, TO MUSIC; IF FORMED WORDS, TO LITERATURE; THE IMAGE, TO POETRY; FORM, TO DESIGN; COLOUR IN POSITION, TO PAINTING; FORM OR DESIGN IN THREE

38 Ebd.

39 Lewis: Our Vortex, S. 148f.

40 Pound: Vortex, S.153.

> PLANES, TO SCULPTURE; MOVEMENT TO THE DANCE OR TO THE RHYTHM OF MUSIC OR OF VERSES.[41]

Lessing selber hätte es nicht besser ausgedrückt.

Henri Gaudier-Brzeska schließlich, Vortizist der ersten Stunde, unterwirft die Vortexturen einer epischen Verzeitlichung, indem er der Kulturgeschichte selber vortizistische, d.h. dynamische Gestalt verleiht. Am Ursprung aller Künste nämlich steht, wie zu erwarten war, der Vortex, der bereits die Höhlenmalerei als „PALEOLITHIC VORTEX“[42] bestimmt. Die Theorie erhält hier ihre transhistorische ‚große Erzählung‘, die auch den Gestaltwandel der Vortexenergie beschreibt. So kann der Mensch im Land des „HAMITE VORTEX“, in Ägypten, seine esoterischen „far reaching speculations“ in die neue Formsynthese überführen:

> Honour to the divinity! Religion pushed him [man, M.E.] to the use of the VERTICAL which inspires awe. His gods were self made, he built them in his image, and RETAINED AS MUCH OF THE SPHERE AS COULD ROUND THE SHARPNESS OF THE PARALLELOGRAM.[43]

Der Abriß mündet in die Aggregatzustände des modernen Vortex der Jahrhundertwende und – als Höhepunkt – des Vortizismus selbst:

> VORTEX OF A VORTEX!!
> VORTEX IS THE POINT ONE AND INDIVISIBLE!
> VORTEX IS ENERGY! and it gave forth SOLID EXCREMENTS in the quattro é cinquo cento, LIQUID until the seventeenth century, GASES whistle till now. THIS is the history of form value in the West until the FALL OF IMPRESSIONISM.[44]

Medial betrachtet ist der höchste Aggregatzustand der Vortex-Energie der Vortex-Film. Zwar hat es diesen nie gegeben; in den frühen experimentellen Filmen zeichnet sich indessen eine vortizistische Dynamik ab, die in Marcel Duchamps *Anémic cinéma* von 1926 klar zum Ausdruck kommt (Abb. 10). Noch 1930 inszeniert Jean Cocteau in seinem Film *Le sang d'un poète* die surreale Macht des Wirbels (Abb. 11), und dies mit der vortizismusfreundlichen Prämisse, der Poet erschaffe hier „a realistic documentary of unreal events“ (Zwischentitel). Reminiszenzen an die Kraft des Vortex schließlich finden sich um 1930 bis in den Revuefilm, der den Menschen selbst zum Vortex der Performance macht (Abb. 12): Erfüllt wird hierin eine alte Forderung der Vortizisten (wenn auch nicht – wie zu befürchten ist – in ihrem Sinne): „WE ONLY

41 Ebd., S. 154.

42 Henri Gaudier-Brzeska: Vortex. In: Wyndham Lewy (Hg.): BLAST. Review of the Great English Vortex. Bd. 1. London u.a. 1914, S. 155-158, hier S. 155.

43 Ebd.

44 Ebd., S. 156.

WANT THE WORLD TO LIVE, and to feel its crude energy flowing through us."[45] Diese hochbedeutsame Ästhetisierung, die als Energetik aus der Tiefe längst vergangener (und widerlegter) wissenschaftlicher Diskurse kommt, als parawissenschaftliches Relikt vom Vortizismus aufgegriffen, esoterisch aufgeladen und poetisch umgewandelt wird, um schließlich populärästhetisch als Revue zu enden – dieser wirbelhafte Rhythmus der Verschiebungen, Ersetzungen und Überformungen hat seinen ersten Filmprotagonisten in Hans Richter. *Rhythmus 21* ist aus diesem Grunde nicht nur ein Exempel der Verzirkelung, Verwandlung und Verwirbelung avantgardistischer Gestaltkultur. Er steht zugleich am Schnittpunkt einer apokryphen esoterischen Diskursgeschichte, die den Wirbel zur dynamischen Zentralfigur erhoben hat.

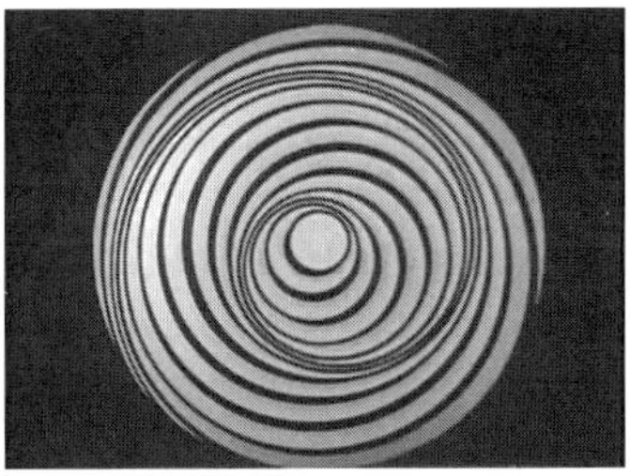

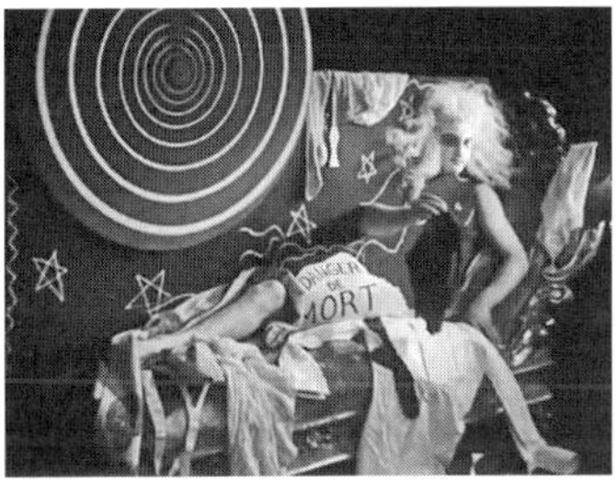

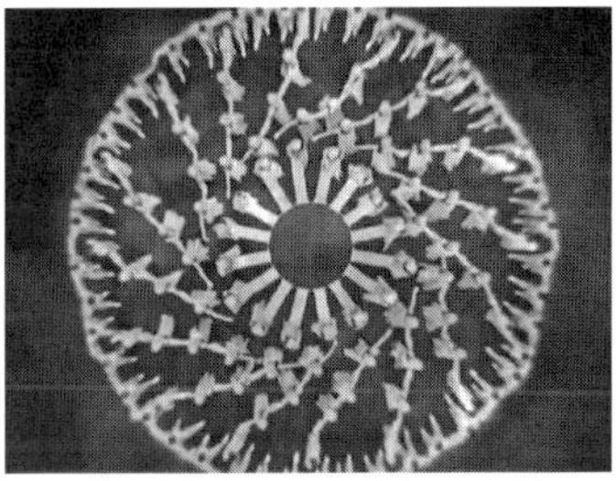

Abb. 10-12: Die Zukunft des Vortext – Wirbel, Wirbel mit Figur und Wirbel aus Figuren

Abbildungsverzeichnis

Abb. 1-8: Hans Richter: Rhythmus 21. DVD. 3 min. London: BFI 2001. (Deutschland 1921).
Abb. 9: Edward Wadsworth: A Short Flight. In: Wyndham Lewis (Hg.): BLAST. Review of the Great English Vortex. Bd. 1. London u.a. 1914.
Abb. 10: Marcel Duchamps: Anémic Cinéma. Frankreich 1926.
Abb. 11: Jean Cocteau: Le sang d'un poète. Frankreich 1930.
Abb. 12: Busby Berkeley: Dames. USA 1934. (Tänzerinnen [Aufsicht]).

45 Long Live the Vortex!, S. 7.

Auswahlbibliographie zu *Rhythmus 21*

a) Texte von Hans Richter

Bücher

Filmgegner von heute – Filmfreunde von morgen. Berlin 1929. Reprint: Zürich 1968.

Film: jesteren, heden, morgen. Pamphlet für die niederländische Filmliga, Sondernummer der Zeitschrift *Filmliga*. Amsterdam 1935.

Kampf um den Film. Verfasst 1934-39. Erstveröffentlichung: München 1976.

Begegnungen von Dada bis heute. Briefe, Dokumente, Erinnerungen. Köln 1973.

Aufsätze

Universelle Sprache. Pamphlet. Gemeinsam mit Viking Eggeling. Forst in der Lausitz 1920. Verschollen.

Prinzipielles zur Bewegungskunst. In: De Stijl 4. Jg. (1921), Nr. 7. Reprint herausgegeben von Ad Petersen, Amsterdam 1968, S. 109-112.

Erklärung vor dem Kongress der Internationale Fortschrittlicher Künstler Düsseldorf vom 30.5.1922. Unterzeichnet von Hans Richter. In: De Stijl 5. Jg. (1922), Nr. 4, S. 59-65. Reprint herausgegeben von Ad Petersen, Amsterdam 1968, S. 203-204.

Film. In: De Stijl 5. Jg. (1922), Nr. 6. Reprint herausgegeben von Ad Petersen, Amsterdam 1968, S. 91-92.

Rhythm. In: Little Review (Winter 1926), S. 21.

Neue Mittel der Filmgestaltung. In: Die Form 4. Jg. (1929), Nr. 3, S. 53-56.

Film von Morgen. In: Das Werk 6. Jg. (1929), Nr. 9, S. 278-284.

Richtigstellung. In: Lichtbildbühne (2.4.1930).

Bemerkungen zu meinen Arbeiten. In: Hamburger Filmgespräche, Bd. 3, Hamburg 1967, S. 13-21.

Beiträge aus *G – Zeitschrift für elementare Gestaltung*

G. Zeitschrift für elementare Gestaltung. (Hg.): Hans Richter. Berlin 1923-26, insg. 5 Hefte (Nr. I-V/VI). Reprint herausgegeben von Marion von Hofacker, München 1986.

Material zur elementaren Gestaltung. Reprint: Nr. I, S. 1-2; Nr. 3, S. 1-3.

Die Eroberung der Maschinen. Reprint: Nr. III, S. 24.

Die schlecht trainierte Seele. Reprint: Nr. III, S. 34-37.

De Stijl. Reprint: Nr. III, S. 60.

Der Querschnitt. Reprint: Nr. III, S. 61.

Die Kunst von heute: Ausstellung abstrakter Kunst, Paris, Dezember 1925. Reprint: Nr. IV, S. 11-14.

Teil einer Partitur zu dem Film Rhythmus 25. Reprint: Nr. V, S. 11.

Die eigentliche Sphäre des Films. Reprint: Nr. V, S. 18.

b) Sekundärliteratur

Arnheim, Rudolf: Über Bewegungskunst. In: Sozialistische Monatshefte 32. Jg. (1926), Nr. 5, S. 312-315.

Bagier, Guido: Der kommende Film. Stuttgart 1928.

Behne, Adolf: Der Film als Kunstwerk. In: Sozialistische Monatshefte 27. Jg. (1921), Nr. 20, S. 1116-1118.

Cook, Adolf: Visual Music in Film, 1921-1924: Richter, Eggeling, Ruttman. In: Charlotte de Mille (Hg.): Music and Modernism, 1849–1950. Newcastle 2011, S. 206–228.

Dencker, Klaus Peter: Optische Poesie. Von den prähistorischen Schriftzeichen bis zu den digitalen Experimenten der Gegenwart. Bielefeld 2011.

Doesburg, Theo van: Abstracte Filmbeelding. In: De Stijl 4. Jg. (1921), Nr. 5. Reprint herausgegeben von Ad Petersen, Amsterdam 1968, S. 71-75.

Elder, R. Bruce: Hans Richter and Viking Eggeling: The Dream of Universal Language and the Birth of the Absolute Film. In: Alexander Graf / Dietrich Scheunemann (Hg.): Avant-Garde Film. Amsterdam 2007, S. 3-53.

Elder, R. Bruce: Harmony and Dissent: Film and Avant-garde Art Movements in the Early Twentieth-Century. Waterloo, ON 2008.

Emons, Hans: Das mißverstandene Modell. Zur Rolle der Musik im abstrakten Film der Zwanziger Jahre. In: Klaus-Ernst Behne (Hg.): Film – Musik – Video oder Die Konkurrenz von Auge und Ohr. Regensburg 1987, S. 51-63.

Foster, Stephen C. (Hg.): Hans Richter: Activism, Modernism, and the Avant-Garde. Cambridge 1998.

Freunde der deutschen Kinemathek e.V. (Hg.): Hans Richter: Film ist Rhythmus. Berlin 2003.

Gärtner, Ulrike / Kai Uwe Hemken / Kai Uwe Schierz (Hg.): KunstLicht-Spiele. Lichtästhetik der klassischen Avantgarde. Bielefeld 2009.

Gehr, Herbert / Marion von Hofacker (Hg.): Hans Richter: Malerei und Film. Frankfurt a.M. 1989.

Gray, Cleve (Hg.): Hans Richter by Hans Richter. Pioneer of Dada and the Experimental Film. London 1971.

Hagener, Malte: Moving Forward, Looking Back: The European Avant-Garde and the Invention of Film Culture, 1919–1939. Amsterdam 2007.

Hein, Birgit: Künstlerische Avantgarde und der Film. Zur Geschichte des Experimentalfilms. In: Helmut Korte / Johannes Zahlten (Hg.): Kunst und Künstler im Film. Hameln 1990, S. 51-62.

Hilberseimer, Ludwig: Kunst: Bildende Kunst. In: Sozialistische Monatshefte 27. Jg. (1921), Nr. 9, S. 465–469.

Hofacker, Marion von (Hg.): Reprint: G. Zeitschrift für elementare Gestaltung. Hans Richter (Hg.), Berlin 1923-26, insg. 5 Hefte (Nr. I-V/VI). München 1986.

Hoormann, Anne: Lichtspiele: Zur Medienreflexion der Avantgarde in der Weimarer Republik. München 2003.

Hoßmann, Gisela: Hans Richter 1888-1976. Das bildnerische Werk. Köln 1985.

Kurtz, Rudolf: Expressionismus und Film. Berlin 1926. Reprint: Zürich 2007.

Lawder, Standish D.: The Cubist Cinema. New York 1975.

Levinson, Jerrold: Nonexistent Artforms and the Case of Visual Music. In: Ders.: Contemplating Art: Essays in Aesthetics. Oxford 2006, S. 129-142.

Macrae, David: Painterly Concepts and Filmic Objects: The Interaction of Expression and Re-Production in Early Avant-Garde Film. In: Dietrich Scheunemann (Hg.): European Avant-Garde: New Perspectives. Amsterdam 2000, S. 137-154.

Maur, Karin von der (Hg.): Vom Klang der Bilder. Die Musik in der Kunst des 20. Jahrhunderts. Stuttgart 1985.

Mertins, Detlef / Michael W. Jennings (Hg.): G: An Avant-Garde Journal of Art, Architecture, Design, and Film. Englischsprachige Übersetzung von G. Zeitschrift für elementare Gestaltung. Los Angeles 2010.

Schmitz, Norbert M.: Der Film der klassischen Avantgarde, oder Die gescheiterte Autonomie des Kinos. In: Heinz Arnold (Hg.): Aufbruch ins 20. Jahrhundert: über Avantgarden. München 2001, S. 138-154.

Starr, Cecile: Hans Richter. In: Robert Russett / Cecile Starr (Hg.): Experimental Animation. New York 1976, S. 49-56.

Teige, Karl: Zur Ästhetik des Filmes. In: Das Kunstblatt 9. Jg. (1925), S. 332–339.

Turvey, Malcolm: Dada Between Heaven and Hell: Abstraction and Universal Language in the Rhythm Films of Hans Richter. In: October 105. Jg. (2003), S. 13-36.

Turvey, Malcolm: The Filming of Modern Life: European Avant-Garde Film of the 1920s. Cambridge 2011.

Väliaho, Pasi: Mapping the Moving Image: Gesture, Thought and Cinema Circa 1900. Amsterdam 2010.

Volkmann, Barbara / Rose-France Raddatz (Hg.): Hans Richter 1888–1976: Dadaist, Filmpionier, Maler, Theoretiker. Berlin 1982.

Westerdale, Joel: The Musical Promise of Abstract Film. In: Christian Rogowski (Hg.): The Many Faces of Weimar Cinema: Rediscovering Germany's Filmic Legacy. Rochester 2010, S. 153-166.

Wilmesmeier, Holger: Deutsche Avantgarde und Film. Die Filmmatinee "Der absolute Film" (3. und 10. Mai 1925). Münster 1994.

Wolfradt, Willi: Grosse Berliner Kunstausstellung. November Gruppe. In: Der Cicerone 5 (1923), S. 522-523.

Zurhake, Monika: Filmische Realitätsaneignung. Ein Beitrag zur Filmtheorie, mit Analysen von Filmen Viking Eggelings und Hans Richters. Heidelberg 1982.

Anhang I:
Prinzipielles zur Bewegungskunst
(Hans Richter)

PRINZIPIELLES ZUR BEWEGUNGS-KUNST

VON HANS RICHTER

Erklärung. — Die abgebildeten Zeichnungeu stellen Hauptmomente von Vorgängen dar, die in Bewegung gedacht sind. Die Arbeiten werden im Film ihre Verwirklichung finden. Der Vorgang selbst: gestaltende Evolutionen und Revolutionen in der Sphäre des rein künstlerischen (abstrakte Formen); analog etwa den unserem Ohr geläufigen Geschehnissen der Musik. Wie dort tritt die Handlung (in ganz geistiger Bedeutung) mit dem reinen Material auf, und findet in diesem reinen Material Spannung und Auflösung in einem Sinn, der, weil alle materiellen Vergleiche und Erinnerungen wegfallen, elementar-magisch ist.

I. Genealogie (überhistorisch). a) Cézanne-Derain-Picasso versuchten durch wissenschaftlich-intuitive Methode eine Zerlegung von Naturobjekten vorzunehmen, die dahin führte, gewisse elementare Beziehungen der Form objektiv zu fixieren (und sie in einem einheitlich durch das ganze Bild gehenden Rhythmus anzuwenden).

b) Während bei diesen Malern alle Erfahrungen am Naturobjekt gemacht und auf dieses wieder angewandt wurden, geht ein neuer Weg nicht vom Naturobjekt aus, sondern von den reinen Beziehungen der Formen untereinander. — — — Damit entsteht die Möglichkeit, die Malerei nicht nur als Flächenkunst zu betrachten, sondern auch in die Zeit zu projizieren.

c) Daß Cézanne, Dérain und Picasso nicht zum Resultat der realen Bewegung als Moment auch der bildenden Kunst gekommen sind, liegt daran, daß Dérain und auch Cézanne trotz des polaren Konstruktionsgedankens, auf dem jedes ihrer Werke beruht, die Naturwahrscheinlichkeit betonen und sich (obgleich in dieser Betonung synthetisch) an etwas binden, was eine ganz reine Erkenntnis der Formbeziehungen (die zur Bewegung führen sollen) verunmöglicht. — Picasso dagegen löst das Naturobjekt zugunsten der Untersuchung reiner

Formbeziehungen auf und erzielt damit neue Freiheiten wieder aber nicht von solcher Konsequenz und rhythmischen Einheitlichkeit (Synthetik) wie Cézanne und Dérain.

d) Aus solchen Gründen konnten diese Maler das Zeitproblem nicht erkennen, — Erst durch die synthetische Lösung von Formbeziehungen, die ohne Naturanlehnung vielmehr auf einem polar-rhythmischen Anschauungsprinzip (mit allen Unterabteilungen der Rhythmik) beruhen, erkannte Viking Eggeling die Möglichkeit, rhythmische Vorgänge auch auf die Zeit auszudehnen und erschloß damit das Gebiet einer neuen Kunst.

II. Generalbaß. Die „Sprache" (Form-Sprache), die da „gesprochen" wird, beruht auf einem „Alphabet", entstanden aus einem elementaren Prinzip der Anschauung: Polarität.

Polarität als generelles Lebensprinzip = Kompositionsmethode jeder formalen Äußerung. Proportion, Rhythmus, Zahl, Intensität, Lage, Klang, Zeitmaß usw. Empirisch als Kontrast-Beziehung der großen und kleinen Gegensätze; spirituell als Analogie-Beziehung der Dinge, die sich in einer anderen Sphäre wieder voneinander unterscheiden. Schöpferischer Wechsel und logisches Gleich und Ungleich im Gedanken des betreffenden Werks.

Der große Wille und das sichtbare Ziel dieser Arbeiten ist nicht in ihnen begrenzt.

Die ästhetischen Prinzipien des Alphabets zeigen den Weg zum Gesamtkunstwerk, und zwar deswegen, weil diese Prinzipien, deren man sich undogmatisch, synthetisch bedient, nicht nur für die Malerei maßgebend sind, sondern in gleichem Maße für Musik, Sprache, Tanz, Architektur, Schauspiel. Der Gedanke einer Kultur als die Totalität aller schöpferischen Kräfte von einer gemeinsamen Wurzel aus zu einer unendlichen, vielfältigen Form (nicht Addition, sondern Synthese).

III. Definition von „Kunst". a) Transzendentale Definition: Kunst = menschlicher Schöpfungswille. Als solcher Organ des Individuums sich in einen trans-

zendentalen Welt Sinn zu geben. (Über-individuelle = transzendentale Bestrebung.) Kunst, dient der Verwirklichung einer höheren Einheit: der Idee des Menschen in der Menschheit: der Vollendung des Individuums in einer höheren Organisationsform. Das „Ganze“, die Menschheits, = Synthese des Einzelnen (konstruktives Prinzip).
Der Wille, dieses Ziel zu erstreben, ist eine ethische Forderung. Ethik beruht auf der Erkenntnis, daß wir einer vollkommeneren Existenz fähig sind, und enthält das Postulat solcher Erkenntnis nach zu handeln; — Forderung einer totalen Ethik (zum Unterschied von religiöser oder philosophischer Ethik) „auf Totalität hin“ zu handeln.
Das schöpferische Verhältnis zwischen dem Individuum und der dieses umfassenden Einheit, ist die Synthese; logisches Verhältnis, schöpferischer-nichtmathematischer Art. Eindeutigkeit des Vielfältigen, sinnvolle Beziehung der Kontraste in Analogien (polare Synthese).
Wenn an der Idee von einem totalen „Sein“ die menschlichen Schöpfungskräfte (sofern sie zur Synthese fähig sind) bedeutenden Sinn bekommen, so bildet die „Synthese“ das Merkmal transzendentaler Bestimmung.
Folge solcher Erkenntnis = Zucht dieser Kraft, die zur Einheit sämtlicher schöpferischen Äußerungen des Menschen führt — Kultur.
b) Praktische Definition: Äußerste Ökonomie der Mittel. Nur eine wirkliche Disziplin der Elemente und elementarste Anwendung derselben ermöglichen es, darauf weiterzubauen. — Immer wieder zu betonen: Kunst ist nicht subjektive Explosion eines Individuums, sondern organische Sprache der Menschen von allerernsteter Bedeutung, und muß deshalb in seinen Grundlagen so irrtumsfrei und so lapidar sein, daß es als solche: als Sprache der Menschheit, wirklich benutzt werden kann. Es ist ein Irrtum, zu glauben, daß der Sinn der Kunst in der einzelnen Leistung beruhe, vielmehr stellt die Kunst selbst dem Individuum die allgemeine Aufgabe, den Teil seiner Arbeit, der dem Willen zugänglich ist, für den Bau und die Bereicherung gerade dieses Ge-

dankens zu verwenden. Solche gleichsam wissenschaftliche Problemstellung ist weniger eine Hemmung des Intuitiven (auf dem künstlerisches Schaffen letzthin beruht), als vielmehr dessen elementares Mittel. Der Impuls ist zwar die Voraussetzung der Schöpfung, aber die Macht über die Elemente ist Bedingung, eine solche zu vollenden.

c) Kritisches Verhältnis. Da die Sprache der Psyche = (die Kunst) von einschneidenderer, weil nicht so gehemmter Wirkung für den Menschen ist, wie die Welt der Begriffe, gegen die uns das (mißbrauchte) Wort fast abgestumpft hat, so ist eine sachliche Art der Untersuchung und Unterscheidung — nicht sentimentaler Art all der Grundlagen der Kunstsprache von entscheidender Bedeutung für die kritische Beurteilung.

Anhang. Es ist zweifellos, daß das Kino als neues Arbeitsfeld der bildenden Künstler von Produktionen der bildenden Kunst schnell und stark beansprucht werden wird. Um so wesentlicher ist es darauf hinzuweisen, daß das einfache Nacheinander von Formen an und für sich sinnlos ist, und daß Sinn erst durch die Kunst (obige Definition) geschaffen werden kann. Für diese neue Kunst ist es absolut erforderlich, eindeutige Elemente zu haben. Ohne diese kann zwar ein (noch so verführerisches) Spiel entstehen, aber niemals eine Sprache.

ONTVANGEN BOEKEN EN TIJDSCHRIFTEN

Lumière (2e jrg. no. 10), — Bouwk. Weekblad (42 jrg. no. 27, 28, 29, 30 en 31). — Bouwwereld (no. 26-27-28-29 en 30). — Klei (Jubileum nummer 13e jrg. no. 13 en 14). — L'Art Libre (3e jrg. no. 7). — Der Sturm (12e jrg. heft 7) — Melos (2e jrg. no. 9). — L'Esprit Nouveau (no. 9). — La Revue de l'Epoque (3e jrg. no. 19). — Ultra (1e jrg. no. 13, 14 en 15). — De Ploeg (3e jrg. no. 26, 27, 28, 29 en 30). — De Gulden Winckel (20e jrg. no. 7). — La Vie des Lettres (7e jrg. no. 4 en 5). — La Cité (Revue mensuelle Belge. Architecture-Urbanisme-Art-public 2e jrg. no. 4 en 6). — Libertaire (1e jrg. no. 2). — Les Marges (21e jrg. no. 85). — Menschen (Clarté II 5e jrg.). — Les Humbles (sixième série no. 6). — Le Pilhaou-Tibaou (supplément illustré de „391"). — Sélection (no. 10).

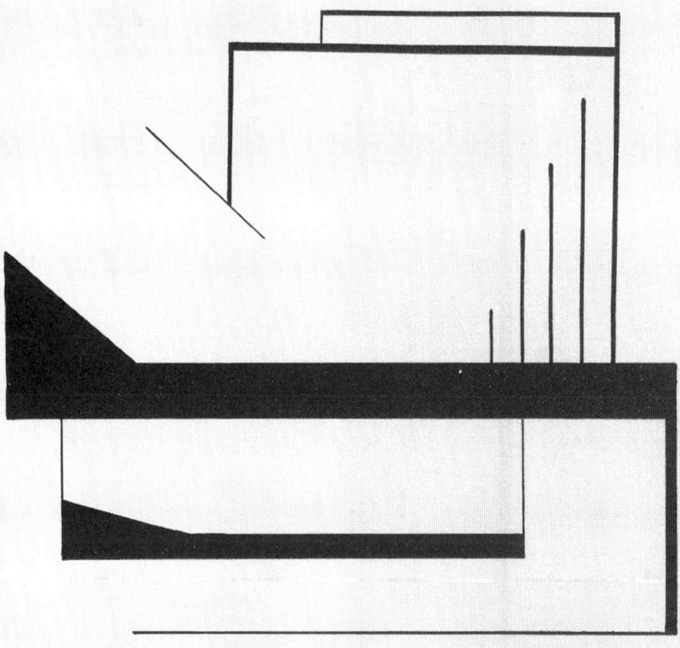

VIKING EGGELING FRAGMENT AUS DEM HORIZONTAL-VERTIKALORCHESTER 83

IV 7 1921

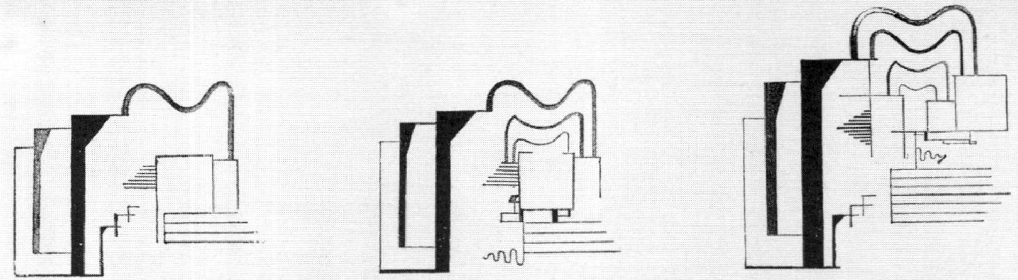

VIKING EGGELING

DREI MOMENTE DES HORIZONTAL-VERTIKALORCHESTERS

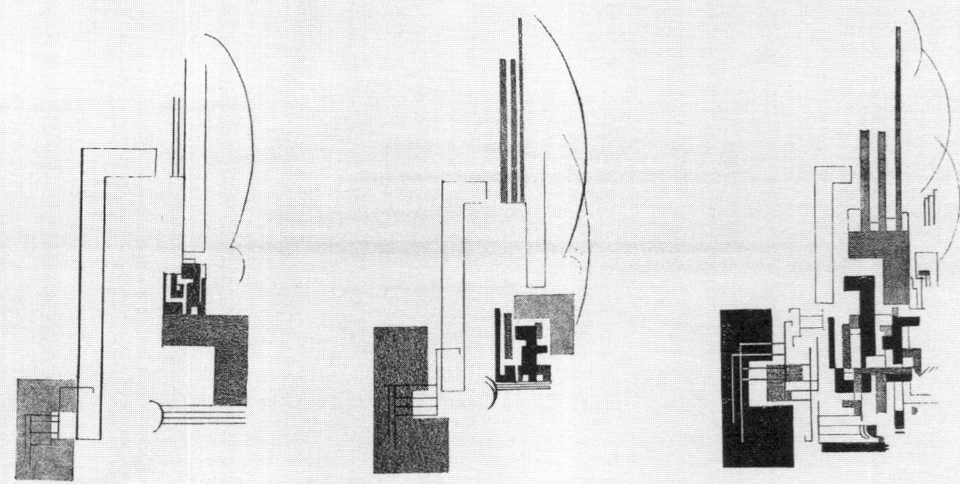

HANS RICHTER

DREI MOMENTE DER KOMPOSITION „SCHWER-LEICHT" (PRÄLUDIUM)

IV 7 1921

85

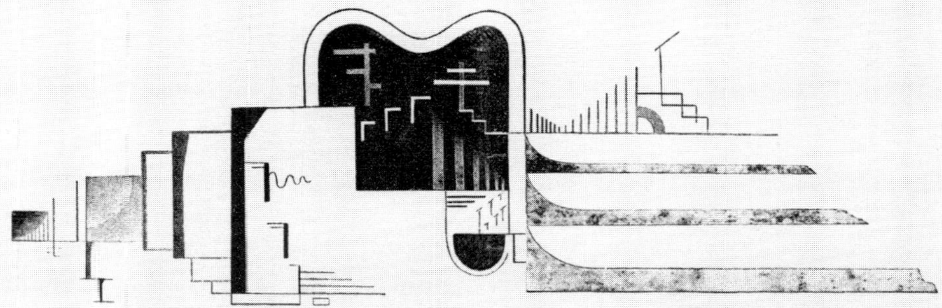

VIKING EGGELING HAUPTPARTIE DES HORIZONTAL-VERTIKALORCHESTERS

IV 7 1921 89

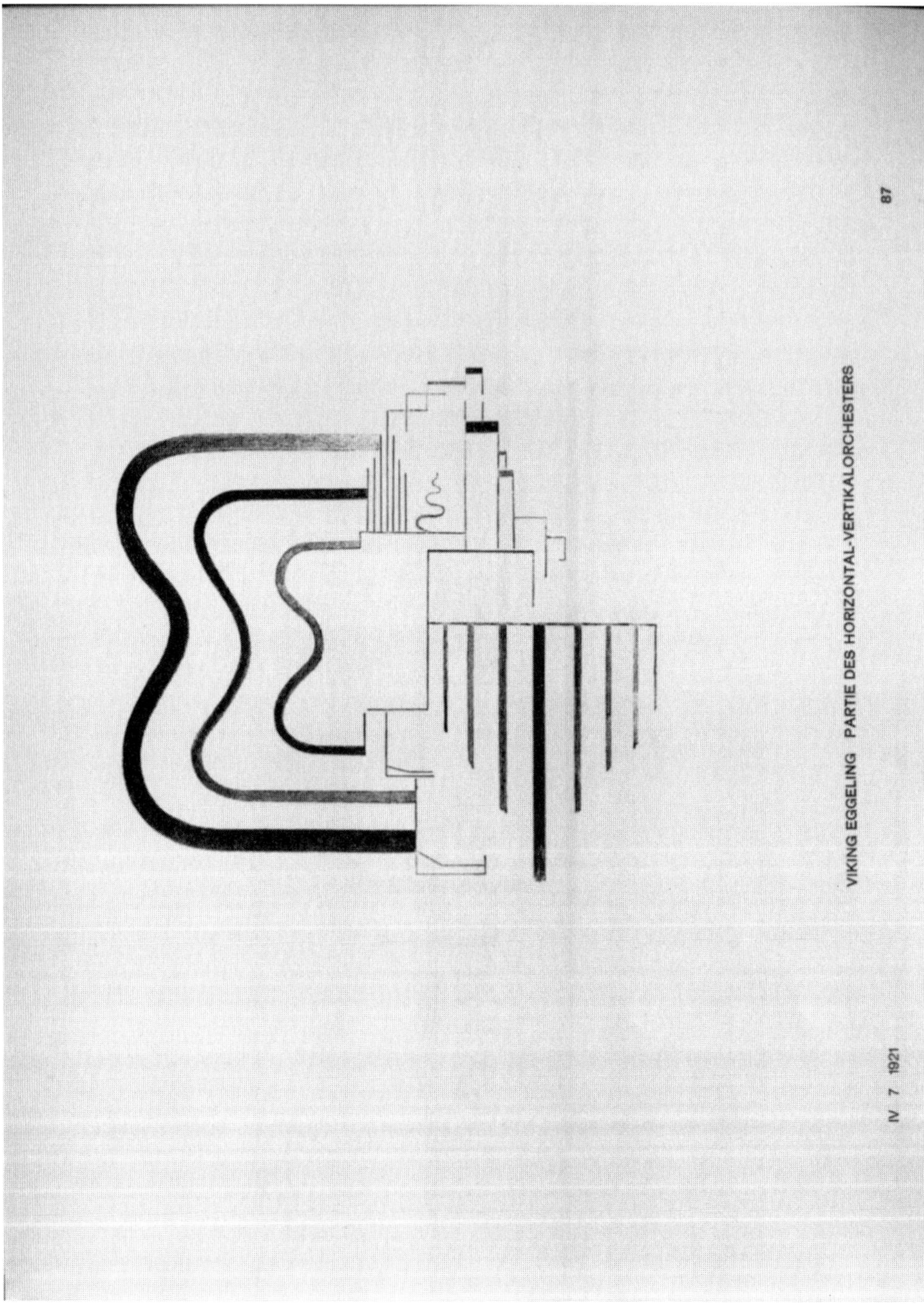

Anhang I: Hans Richter: Prinzipielles zur Bewegungskunst.
In: De Stijl 4. Jg. (1921), Nr. 7. Reprint herausgegeben von Ad Petersen, Amsterdam 1968, S. 109-112.

Anhang II: Die schlecht trainierte Seele (Hans Richter)

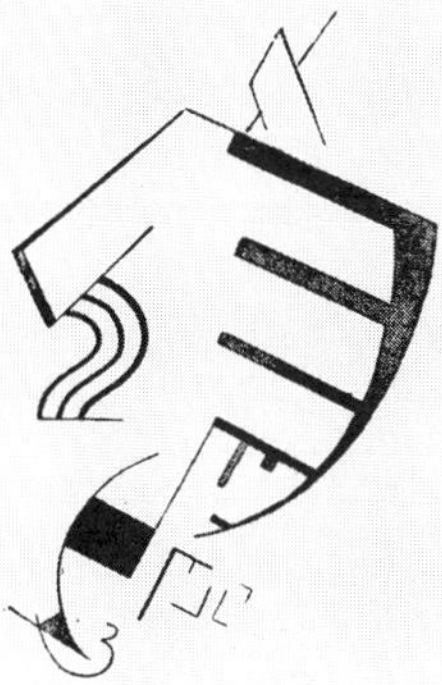

Die Elemente des Bildes untersuchend fand **VIKING EGGELING** in der Synthese der Anziehungs- und Abstossungskraft, dem Verhalten von Kontrasten und Analogien das grundlegende Prinzip der Gestaltung. Die Möglichkeit, diese am statischen Bild gewonnenen Erfahrungen auch nacheinander, d. h. rhytmisch abzuwandeln, auch in der Zeit zu verwenden, führte ihn 1919 dazu die ersten Entwürfe für einen **FILM** (s. Abb.) zu machen, der auf solchen, in der bildenden Kunst gewonnenen Resultaten beruhte und das erste Werk gesetzmäßigen Aufbaus der modernenKunst, insbesondere dieZeit betreffend, darstellte.

Die Tat E'S, einen schöpferischen Gesichtspunkt für die Gestaltung gefunden zu haben, geht über jede Spezialität (auch die des Films) hinaus und verankert die Erfahrungen der Sinne im Gebiet tiefsten Wissens.
H R

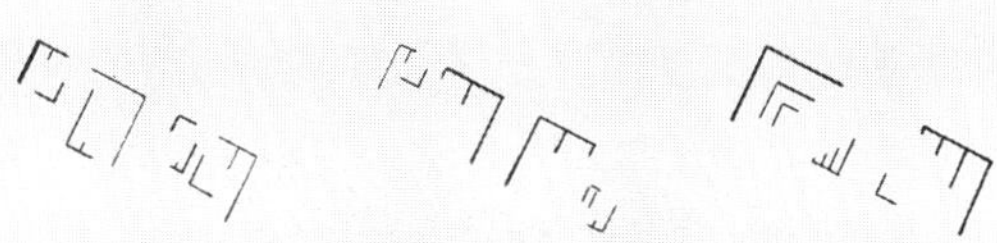

Die schlecht trainierte Seele

Empfindungen, heißt es, kommen einem im Schlaf, brüten sich selbst aus, sind einfach da! Das stimmt nicht. Empfinden ist ein ebenso präzise organisierter und mechanisch exakter Prozeß wie Denken; aber das Bewußtsein dieses Prozesses oder noch mehr die IDENTITÄT mit ihm ging verloren, fehlt; deswegen wurde „Fühlen" = „Sich hingeben" — ein Gebiet getrennt von der Einsicht und Aktivität des heutigen Menschen.

* * *

Von allen Gebieten, die sich um unser Empfindungsvermögen bemühen, wird dieser Mangel am deutlichsten im Film, der keine traditionelle Vorurteile hat und deswegen den Zustand einer sentimentalen Passivität in monumentalsten Proportionen ausbreiten kann.

Das heutige Kino zeigt weder die eigentlichen Möglichkeiten der PHOTOGRAPHIE noch die der BEWEGUNG. Es fehlt dem Film allgemein heute noch der Ueberblick über die Mittel, durch die er wirkt, es fehlt ihm Verständnis dafür, daß schöpferische Gestaltung, Beherrschung des Materials ist, in Übereinstimmung mit den Funktionen unseres Empfindungsapparates (daß darin Aufgaben liegen —) und — es fehlt ihm die Kenntnis dieser Funktion. — Die heutigen Spielfilme sind auf grobe Effekte aus, im Sinne des Theaters. — Unter Film verstehe ich optischen Rhythmus, dargestellt mit den Mitteln der Phototechnik; beides als Material einer Phantasie, die aus dem Elementaren und Gesetzmäßigen unserer Sinnesfunktionen heraus schafft. — In das Gebiet dieser Frage gehört der abgebildete Film.

* * *

Nicht bei Ansichtskartenansichten ausruhen können, — erwartete Liebesscenenhaltung mit wohlverdientem Endeffekt, nicht vorfinden, — anstelle von bekanntem Arrangement der Beine, Arme, Köpfe, in Prunksalons und Fürstenhöfen . . . . . . nur Bewegung zu sehen, organisierte Bewegung — weckt auf, weckt Opposition, weckt Reflexe (?) aber — vielleicht — auch Genuß.

44 •

Dieser Film hier gibt keine „Haltepunkte", an denen man in Erinnerungen umkehren könnte, man ist — ausgeliefert – zum „Fühlen" gezwungen – zum Mitgehen im Rhytmus – Atmen – Herzschlag; – . . . der durch das Auf und Ab des Vorgangs, das deutlich machen kann, was Fühlen und Empfinden eigentlich ist . . . ein Prozeß – Bewegung.

Diese „Bewegung" hat ihre organischen Voraussetzungen, ist nicht gebunden an das Erinnerungsvermögen (Sonnenuntergänge, Beerdigung –) nicht an das „Ideal" (Held, keusche Jungfrau, smarter Geschäftsmann) nicht an Gefühle des Mitleids (Streichholzmädchen, ehemals berühmter, jetzt armer Geiger, betrogene Liebe –) überhaupt nicht an einen „Inhalt", sondern folgt unabhängig von diesem bestimmten, dieser „Be wegung", eigentümlichen mechanischen Gesetzen.

Die lebendige Kraft, die wir in dieser „Bewegung" besitzen, an und für sich ein wunderbares Phänomen, kann ebenso gut lahmliegen wie zum Bestandteil menschlicher Macht werden, – aber man müßte im Stande sein, diesen Prozeß zu beherrschen, um das Gebiet der Empfindungen ebenso unserem Urteil zugänglich zu machen, wie die anderen menschlichen Willensgebiete, aus deren Entwicklung die „Seele" bisher ausgeschaltet blieb.

Die allgemeinen Grenzen des Prozesses, die Art seines Entstehens, charakterisieren im wesentlichen folgende 3 Hauptmomente, deren Kenntnis ich Viking Eggeling verdanke auf dessen grundlegenden Forschungen meine Arbeit beruht.

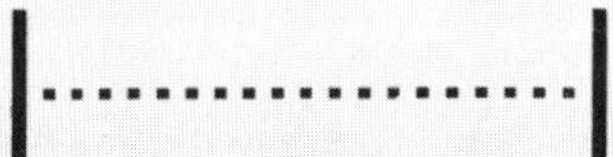

ÄUSSERSTER GEGENSATZ:

1. Um wahrzunehmen, müssen (ganz gleich, ob es sich um optische, akustische etc. Eindrücke handelt oder um reine Phantasie-Vorstellungen) Unterscheidungsmerkmale, Gegensätze verstanden sein, geschaffen werden. Was nicht unterschieden ist (keine Grenze hat) ist nicht wahrnehmbar. Die äußersten Pole bezeichnen die äußerste Wahrnehmbarkeit.

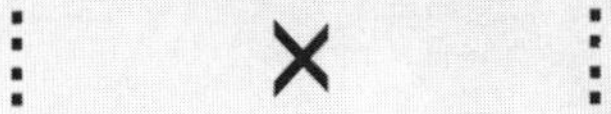

INNERSTE VERWANDSCHAFT:

2. Um zu einer Vorstellung dieser wahrgenommenen Unterschiede zu kommen, d. h. um die Menge der Verschiedenheiten als Teile eines Ganzen sehen zu können – müssen Ähnlichkeiten, Verwandtschaften bestehen. So wie Trennung notwendig ist, um physisch wahrzunehmen, dem Wahrgenommenen Grenzen zu geben, so ist Bindung nötig, um das Wahrgenommene in Verbindung zueinander zu setzen.

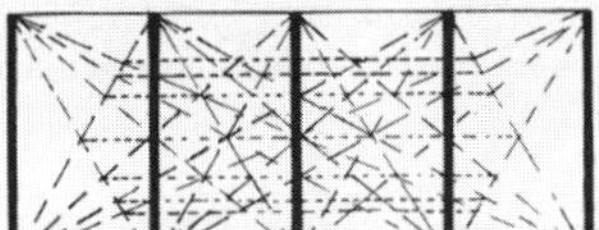

FUNKTION AUS BEIDEN:

3. Durch das zusammenhängende Funktionieren beider, durch das Wechselwirken von Trennen und Verbinden entsteht Empfinden.

• 45

Dieser Prozeß ist schöpferischer Art.

* * *

Der Film macht es möglich, diesen an sich elementaren Vorgang auf die mannigfaltigste Weise zu gestalten. – Ob das in Form von „abstrakten" Lichtspielen, Abenteurerfilmen, oder durch heute noch unbekannte Mittel geschieht, ist nebensächlich gegenüber der Tatsache, – daß UNSERE VORSTELLUNGEN EINER FUNKTIONELLEN GESETZMÄSSIGKEIT UNTERLIEGEN, von der die Einheitlichkeit und Stärke unserer Empfindungen abhängt. – In dieser Hinsicht (von Einheitlichkeit und Stärke) wären aber doch noch weitgehende Anforderungen zu stellen! – Was heute als „Empfinden" blüht, ist ein passives Ausgeliefertsein an Unkontrollierbares . . . . . (von Helden, keuscher Jungfrau und smarten Geschäftsmann, s. oben) von konfektionierten Gefühlen vergangener und nie dagewesener Jahrhunderte, aus denen sich unsere Seele als ein tolles Wesen zusammensetzt, das uns tyrannisiert und das Weltbild hin und herzerrt.

Die lebendige Kraft die wir im Empfinden besitzen, ist verfettet, der Atmungsprozeß gehemmt, die Seele ohne eine Kultur ihrer Mittel, weniger eine M a c h t als eine S c h w ä c h e.

Aber für den heutigen Europäer sind das im allgemeinen „formale" Spezialfragen.

Das eben ist ein Irrtum.

Die Kultur solcher „Gesetzmäßigkeiten" gibt keineswegs nur die Möglichkeit, neuartige oder „bessere" Kunsthandelsprodukte zu starten, sondern gehört zu den elementaren Erziehungsfragen unserer Psyche, die auf diese Weise mit einer gewissen „Denkfähigkeit" ausgestattet wird – einer solchen die zwar in ihrem Bau vorgesehen ist aber brach liegt. Diese Denkfähigkeit gibt der Seele Machtmittel: Urteilskraft und Aktivität, d. h. Eigenschaften, die dem ganzen Menschen in seinem Handeln zu gute kommen und für seine allgemeine Orientierung unentbehrlich sind. Hans Richter.

B. Beispiele für die Verschiedenartigkeit der Ausdrucksmittel – selbst bei Beibehaltung des „formalen" Elements.

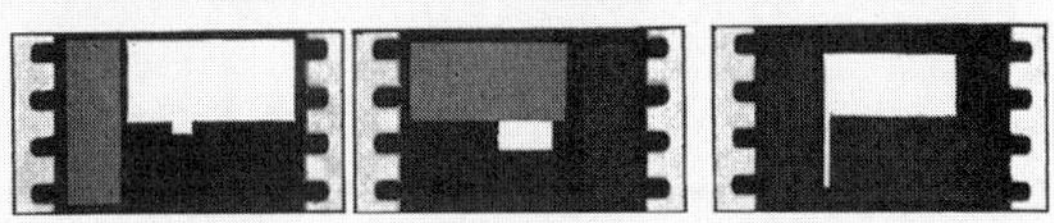

a) **Lage** Bewegungsart { in Fläche : Raum / als Schlag : Gleiten }

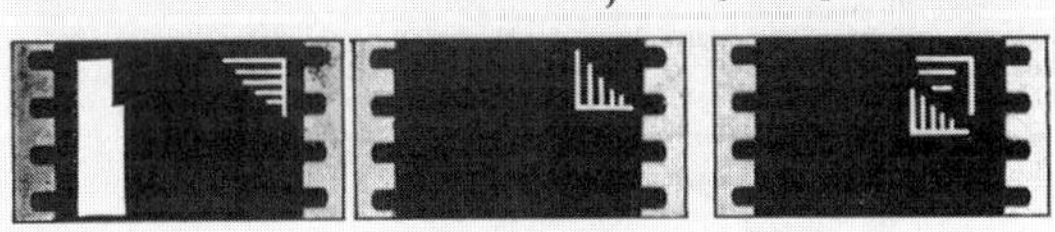

b) **Proportion** Bewegungsart = Stillstand : Spiel / Lage etc.

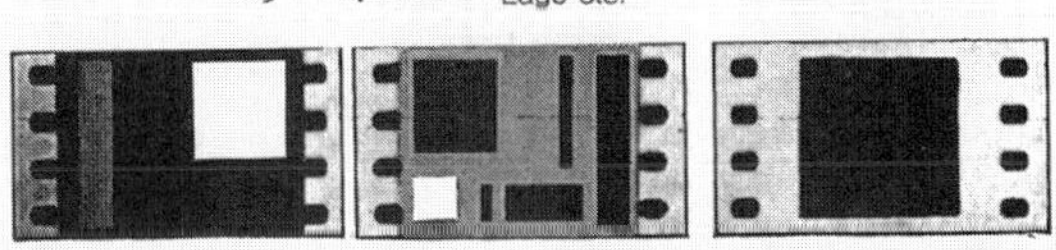

c) **Lichtsphäre** Zahl / Proportion etc.

A. Beispiel für einheitliche Gestaltung von Bewegung.

Fortlaurender Rhytmus, gegengespielt von schlagartiger Begleitung (rechts, links, mittel) – Ruckartiger – Abschluß.

Die Massen wachsen an, lösen sich auf, vereinigen sich maximal – Im Wechsel von hell : dunkel, horizontal : vertikal, groß : klein, schnell : langsam etc. – untereinander durch verwandte Eigenschaften wieder verbunden.

Die einzelhafte „sinnliche Gestalt", die „Form" – ob abstrakt oder gegenständlidh ist vermieden. Dieser Film ist auf den Bewegungsvorgang konzentriert.

– und □ ($^1/_1$, $^1/_2$ und $^1/_3$) dienen als einfachstes, ökonomischstes Gestaltungsmittel um die – Bewegung räumlich zu begrenzen; im Bau des □ sind die wesentlichen Elemente der Orientierung – horizontal : vertikal – als Dominante gegeben. Die Form ist also nicht willkürlich gewählt. – Improvisation ist ausgeschaltet. Sowohl der Bau des Rhytmus als auch die formalen Verhältnisse im einzelnen sind gebildet innerhalb einer bewußten Ordnung.

H R

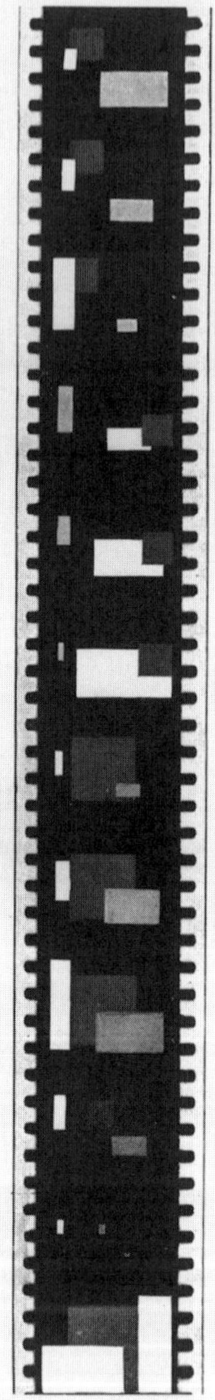

Hans Richter: Die schlecht trainierte Seele.
In: G. Zeitschrift für elementare Gestaltung III (1924).
Reprint herausgegeben von Marion von Hofacker, München 1986, S. 44-47.

Autorenverzeichnis

Christoph Bareither, ist Doktorand im Fach Empirische Kulturwissenschaft an der Universität Tübingen. Veröffentlichungen im Bereich Film-, Literatur- und Kulturwissenschaft. Zuletzt: Fritz Lang: „M – Eine Stadt sucht einen Mörder". Texte und Kontexte. (Hg., Würzburg 2011).

Kurt Beals, ist Doktorand im Fach Germanistik an der University of California, Berkeley, wo er zum Thema Medienpoetik im 20. Jahrhundert promoviert. Veröffentlichungen auch als Übersetzer von experimenteller Lyrik.

Erik Born, ist Doktorand in den Fächern Germanistik und Mediävistik an der University of California, Berkeley. Forschungsinteressen sind u.a. Medienarchäologie und die Geschichte der Mystik.

Michael Cowan, ist Associate Professor für World Cinemas und German Studies an der McGill University in Montreal. Zahlreiche Publikationen in den Bereichen der Film-, Literatur-, Kultur- und Körpergeschichte. Zuletzt: Technology's Pulse: Essays on Rhythm in German Modernism (2012) und Cult of the Will: Nervousness and German Modernity (2008).

Paul Dobryden, ist Doktorand im Fach Germanistik an der University of California, Berkeley, wo er eine Dissertation zu filmischen Dispositiven der 20er Jahre schreibt. Aufsätze zum deutschen Film in The New History of German Cinema (im Druck) sowie in der Zeitschrift Film & History (2010).

Robert Matthias Erdbeer, Dr. phil., lehrt Neuere deutsche Literatur an der Westfälischen Wilhelms-Universität in Münster. Er war Research Fellow am Internationalen Forschungszentrum Kulturwissenschaften (Wien) und am Center for Advanced Studies (Sofia). Publikationen: Die Signatur des Kosmos. Epistemische Poetik und die Genealogie der Esoterischen Moderne (Berlin/New York 2010); zahlreiche Aufsätze zur Literatur- und Wissensgeschichte, zuletzt: Paläopoiesis/Paleofiction. Kognitionspoetik und ‚Erlebenswissenschaft' bei Laßwitz und Hörbiger. In: Renko Geffarth u.a. (Hg.): Aufklärung und Esoterik. Wege in die Moderne. (Berlin/New York; im Druck).

Karin Fest, studierte Film- und Medienwissenschaften, Cultural Studies und Französisch in Wien und Paris; Seit 2009 wissenschaftliche Mitarbeiterin am Ludwig Boltzmann Institut für Geschichte und Gesellschaft in den Projekten „Film.Stadt.Wien", „Like Seen on the Screen" und „Archäologie des Amateurfilms“; Forschungsschwerpunkte sind Film and Media Studies, Visual Culture und Moderne, Filmvermittlung.

Benedikt Hjartarson, ist Außerordentlicher Professor für vergleichende Literaturwissenschaft und Kulturwissenschaft an der Universität Island. Mitglied des Lenkungsausschusses von EAM (Europäisches Netzwerk für Studien zu Avantgarde und Moderne) seit 2007 und Vorstandsmitglied des Nordischen Netzwerks für Avantgardestudien 2003-2009. Autor zahlreicher Aufsätze über die europäische Avantgarde, die auf Isländisch, Deutsch, Dänisch, Englisch und Schwedisch erschienen sind.

Rob McFarland, Associate Professor, lehrt Kunst-und Architekturgeschichte, Deutsche Literatur und Film an der Brigham Young University; Co-Direktor von: Sophie: A Digital Library of Works by German-Speaking Women (sophie.byu.edu); zahlreiche Aufsätze in den Themenfeldern Architektur, Literatur, und Urban Studies.

Klaus Müller-Richter, lehrt Neuere Deutsche Literatur, Film und Philosophie an der Universität Tübingen. Zahlreiche kulturwissenschaftliche Aufsätze und Monografien zur Literatur und zum Film der Moderne sowie zur Poetik der Metapher; zuletzt: Imaginäre Topografien (Hg., Bielefeld 2007); Metapher und Geschichte (Wien 2007).

Birgit Nemec, ist Forschungsstipendiatin und Lehrende an der Medizinischen Universität Wien und Fellow im Doktoratskolleg *Naturwissenschaften im Kontext* der Universität Wien; derzeit: Visiting Scholar am Department for History and Philosophy of Science in Cambridge. Zu ihren Forschungsschwerpunkten zählen Memory Politik im Stadtraum sowie visuelle und materielle Kulturen der Anatomie im 20. Jahrhundert.

Lydia Nsiah, bildende Künstlerin und Medientheoretikerin, arbeitet an ihrer Dissertation im Rahmen des von der ÖAW geförderten DocTeam-Projekts „Sponsored Films und die Kultur der Modernisierung“ am Ludwig Boltzmann Institut für Geschichte und Gesellschaft und der Akademie der bildenden Künste; Schwerpunkte: Avantgarde und Werbung, Wahrnehmungstheorie, übergreifende Medienphilosophie, audiovisuelle Künste; zuletzt: Hybrid Fotofilm, Dem Sehen Zeit und Raum geben (Wien, turia + kant, 2011).

Katrin Pilz, studierte Geschichte und Kulturwissenschaften in Wien und Rom, frühere Arbeiten zur Sozialgeschichte der Radiologie und Forschungsschwerpunkte zu visuelle Kulturen der Medizingeschichte. Zur Zeit arbeitet sie an der Université Libre de Bruxelles und der Universität Wien an ihrem Ph.D. Projekt zur historischen und kulturellen Untersuchung wissenschaftlicher Filme.

Mark Purves, Assistant Professor, lehrt Russische Literatur des 19. Jhds. an der Brigham Young University; Aufsätze zur Kunstgeschichte der Sowietunion, sowohl zur Literatur von Tschechow, Tolstoi, uva.

Holger Wilmesmeier, Dr. phil., ist freier Illustrator, Kunstpädagoge, Kunsthistoriker und Rundfunk-Autor (SWR2), zahlreiche Aufsätze, Vorträge und Rundfunk-Beiträge zur Kultur- und Kunstgeschichte (Film, Comics, Kabarett), u.a.: „Hans Richter". In: Neue Deutsche Biographie (München/ Berlin 2003); „Die Binär-Gesellschaft". Essay in: Telepolis (Heise-Verlag, August 2006); „Der Leonardo-Mann. Von der Proportionsstudie zur Wellness-Ikone". Vortrag (Wella-Museum, Darmstadt 2009/Dante Alighieri Gesellschaft, Darmstadt 2010); „08.06.1794: Robes-pierre eröffnet die Feier des ‚Höchsten Wesens'", SWR2 Zeitwort (2012).

Mario Wimmer, Historiker, lehrt Geschichte und Wissenschaftsgeschichte an der ETH Zürich, Veröffentlichungen zur Sozial- und Kulturgeschichte des Wissens seit 1800, zur Historiographiegeschichte und zur Nachgeschichte des Nationalsozialismus; zuletzt: Archivkörper. Eine Geschichte historischer Einbildungskraft (Konstanz 2012).

Ingo Zechner, lebt als Historiker und Philosoph in Wien; Projekte (Israelitische Kultusgemeinde Wien, Ludwig Boltzmann Institut für Geschichte und Gesellschaft, Österreichisches Filmmuseum), Lehrveranstaltungen (Universität Wien), Vorträge und Publikationen zu Philosophie, Film, Literatur, Musik, Holocaust-Studien, NS-Vermögensentzug und Restitution. Homepage: www.ingozechner.net.